LIVING TOGETHER

The transition to majority rule wasn't easy. But it has produced a fascinating "rainbow nation" characterised by diverse origins and, at its best, a united purpose

SO-AGG-400

It has become one of the most difficult questions to answer. Indeed, sensible people have simply stopped asking it: who or what is the typical South African? Other countries might have a stock of comfortable national stereotypes to fall back on, but in South Africa cultural clichés change from suburb to suburb, never mind city to city.

Historically, the stock image of Africa started with the stereotypical "noble savage": people and cultures both primitive and vibrant, still magically in touch with the ways of the natural world. And let's not forget that crucial sense of rhythm, honed after generations of dancing around ceremonial fires.

South Africa has an extra element. The white settlers, the people responsible for inventing apartheid, live here too: burly, bearded, khaki-clad folk who clutch rifles to keep marauding lions, rhinos and the occasional restless native at bay. It's the image most people had of the Afrikaner, and it's the way many people imagine all white South Africans to be.

But these stereotypes have little basis in reality. South Africa is an extraordinary tapestry of race and culture. And despite the problems of the past, it's a society that's beginning to find great strength in diversity.

A complex culture

Diversity is at the heart of South Africa's young democracy. No fewer than 19 different parties participated in the first democratic election in 1994, collectively representing practically every

LEFT AND RIGHT: educational opportunities for girls have considerably improved in South Africa, but many women still face a struggle for equality.

aspect of the country's political, religious and social spectrum. Following that election, linguistic diversity was recognised when the ANC accorded official status to 11 languages: English, Afrikaans, Zulu, Xhosa, Sotho, Venda, Tswana, Tsonga, Pedi, Shangaan and Ndebele.

Switch on the television in South Africa today and you'll find news broadcasts coming at you in each of the four main language groups – English, Nguni (Zulu and Xhosa), Afrikaans and Sotho – while radio tells it like it is in all 11 languages. Switch over to a local football match and you'll get your commentary broken up into 15-minute slots, alternating between Zulu and Xhosa, English and Sotho.

The one thing first-time visitors shouldn't pack is the preconception of a nation divided into two basic groups of black and white. Nothing is simple in South Africa; it's a far more interesting place than that.

Melting-pot – or divided society?

South Africa's 49 million inhabitants are comprised of four main elements. Indigenous Africans form the overwhelming majority, but 9 percent of South Africans are of European descent, while another 9 percent consists of people of mixed origin (known as coloureds), and one in 40 South Africans claims Indian/Asian descent.

The key division within black South African society is between the Sotho (South Sotho, Bapedi, Tswana), and the Nguni (Zulu, Xhosa and Swazi). Originally, academics split nations between these two groups on the basis of language, location and population patterns – early Nguni settlements tended to be dispersed, whereas the Sotho lived in concentrated towns. Additionally, societies such as the Shangaan-Tsonga belong to neither group. Nor do the people of Venda, whose 30 independent chiefdoms include the Lemba, who claim to be a lost tribe of Israel.

The main cultural divide among white South Africans is along linguistic lines. There are the

SURVIVING AGAINST THE ODDS

The last surviving San and Khoikhoi communities fell into the coloured category, although their numbers are now so small that they can no longer be said to represent distinct social groupings. A few small bands of San still roam the arid Kalahari desert, pursuing their traditional nomadic hunter-gatherer lifestyle.

Of the Khoikhoi, several communities of Griqua (one of the main clans) have settled around Kimberley in the Northern Cape province; while the last surviving Nama, another key group in this category, live in an area situated near Steinkopf on the north-west coast.

English-speakers, many of whom descend from the 4,000 British who settled in the Eastern Cape in 1820, and there are the Afrikaners, whose mother tongue Afrikaans is considered to be the world's most modern language, having evolved from the archaic Dutch spoken by early Cape settlers and spiced with various European, African and Oriental influences.

Other, smaller groups abound. South Africa's Jewish community (about 70,000 strong) has made an indelible impression on cultural and economic life, with the likes of Barney Barnato and Alfred Beit having played an important role in the establishment of the mining industries. A sizeable group of Jewish refugees from the Baltic settled in the country after World War I and

INSIGHT GUIDES
SOUTH AFRICA

APA PUBLICATIONS L
Part of the Langenscheidt Publishing Group

✳ INSIGHT GUIDE
SOUTH AFRICA

Editorial

Series Manager
Rachel Lawrence
Publishing Manager
Rachel Fox
Art Director
Steven Lawrence
Picture Editor
Tom Smyth

Distribution

UK & Ireland
GeoCenter International Ltd
Meridian House, Churchill Way West
Basingstoke, Hampshire RG21 6YR
sales@geocenter.co.uk

United States
Ingram Publisher Services
1 Ingram Boulevard, PO Box 3006,
La Vergne, TN 37086-1986
customer.service@ingrampublisher
services.com

Australia
Universal Publishers
PO Box 307
St Leonards NSW 1590
sales@universalpublishers.com.au

Worldwide
**Apa Publications GmbH & Co.
Verlag KG (Singapore branch)**
7030 Ang Mo Kio Avenue 5
08-65 Northstar @ AMK
Singapore 569880
apasin@singnet.com.sg

Printing

CTPS-China

©2011 Apa Publications UK Ltd
All Rights Reserved

First Edition 1992
Fifth Edition 2011

ABOUT THIS BOOK

The first Insight Guide pioneered the use of creative full-colour photography in travel guides in 1970. Since then, we have expanded our range to cater for our readers' need not only for reliable information about their chosen destination but also for a real understanding of the culture and workings of that destination. Now, when the internet can supply inex-haustible (but not always reliable) facts, our books marry text and pic-tures to provide those much more elusive qualities: knowledge and discernment. To achieve this, they rely on the authority of locally based writers and photographers.

How to use this book
The book is carefully struc-tured both to convey an understanding of South Africa

and to guide readers through its sights and activities:
◆ To understand South Africa today, you need to know about its past. The **Features** section, indicated by a pink bar at the top of each page, covers the country's History and People, with chapters on South Afri-can culture and the arts. These lively, authoritative essays are writ-ten by specialists.
◆ In addition to this unique history, South Africa is a destination for nature lovers. Our **gazeteer** pro-vides you with an on-the-spot refer-ence source to help you identify animals on safari.
◆ The main **Places** sec-tion, indicated by a blue bar, provides a full run-down of all the attractions worth seeing. The principal places of interest are coordinated by number with full-colour maps.

LEFT: Cape Malay minstrels, Hout Bay.

written guidebooks to destinations all over Africa, including *Insight Guide*s to *Tanzania and Zanzibar, Namibia,* and *Gambia and Senegal*. He is also a regular contributor to specialist travel and wildlife magazines.

The history and features chapters were updated by **David Smith**, Africa correspondent of *The Guardian* newspaper in the UK and its website. He is based in Johannesburg and has written widely on South African arts and culture, history, politics, sport and travel and is regularly interviewed by the BBC, CNN and South Africa's eNews, as well as numerous radio stations.

The Story of South African Music and the photo feature on *Iconic Music* were written by **Iain Harris,** a music writer based in Cape Town who also runs a travel company offering music-related travel opportunities in Africa.

The current edition builds on the work of contributors to previous editions, including **David Bristow**, **Vincent Carruthers**, **Rodney Davenport**, **Stephen Gray**, **Bridget Hilton-Barber**, **Ian MacDonald**, **Sabine Marschall**, **Jeff Peires**, **Gary Rathbone**, **Christopher Till** and **Wendy Toerien**.

Many of the images in this book were taken by **Ariadne Van Zandbergen** a specialist in African wildlife and travel photography and a regular contributor to Insight Guides. Her work also features in many travel and environmental magazines.

This edition was copy-edited by **Paula Soper**, proofread by **Catherine Jackson** and indexed by **Helen Peters**.

◆ The **Travel Tips** listings section, with a yellow bar, provides a convenient point of reference for information on travel, hotels, restaurants, sports and festivals. Information may be located quickly by using the index printed on the back cover flap – and the flaps also serve as bookmarks.

◆ Photographs are chosen not only to illustrate geography and attractions but also to convey the moods of the country and the activities of the people.

The contributors

This fully revised and updated edition was commissioned by series editor **Rachel Lawrence**. The principal updater was **Philip Briggs**, a South African travel writer specialising in Africa. He first backpacked between Nairobi and Cape Town in 1986 and has been travelling the highways and byways of Africa ever since. He has

The main places of interest in the Places section are coordinated by number with a full-colour map (eg ❶), and a symbol at the top of every right-hand page tells you where to find the map.

Contents

LEFT: Cape Point.

Maps

Inside front cover:
South Africa.
Inside back cover:
Cape Town.

Travel Tips

THE BEST OF SOUTH AFRICA: TOP ATTRACTIONS

From watching the most savage of beasts to sampling the subtle bouquet of a shiraz wine, the experiences available in South Africa are as vast as the country's never-ending landscape

△ **Cape Town** The Mother City is simply the most rewarding and enjoyable city in sub-Saharan Africa, with a spectacular setting matched by its lively nightlife, restaurant scene and great shopping. *See page 149*

▽ **Cradle of Humankind** This Unesco World Heritage Site west of Johannesburg hosts the inspiring Maropeng Visitors Centre and Sterkfontein Caves, where a near-complete 3.5 million-year-old skeleton is the oldest hominid fossil in the region. *See page 267*

△ **Sun City/Pilanesberg Game Reserve** The over-the-top Sun City complex borders the altogether more authentic Pilanesberg, home to the Big Five and unusually well-suited to budget DIY visits. *See page 265*

△ **uKhahlamba-Drakensberg Park** This composite park protects southern Africa's largest and tallest mountain range. *See page 249*

◁ **Mpumalanga's Panorama Route** The escarpment rising to the west of the Kruger Park is studded with beautiful waterfalls and beauty spots. *See page 280*

▽ **Table Mountain National Park** Highlights of the park include the rotating cableway to the top of Table Mountain, Cape Point Lighthouse, and the penguins of Boulders. *See page 157*

△ **Cape Winelands** Explore historic Stellenbosch and wine estates such as Vergelegen or Boschendal to enjoy the intoxicating combination of fine food, first-class wine and superb mountain scenery. *See page 178*

▽ **Hermanus** This characterful small town east of Cape Town offers the world's finest land-based whale watching, particularly over August to October. *See page 183*

△ **Storms River Mouth** Crossed by suspension bridge, this is the scenic highlight of the lovely Garden Route National Park. *See page 198*

▽ **Kruger Park** Hosts some of the world's highest concentrations of lions, elephants, zebra, giraffe, leopards and rhinos. *See page 283*

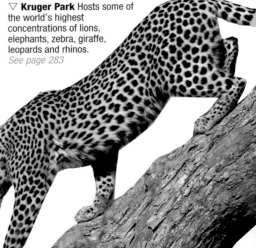

THE BEST OF SOUTH AFRICA: EDITOR'S CHOICE

Spectacular Big Five-viewing, ancient rock art paintings, magnificent spring wildflower displays and superb Cape Dutch architecture are just some of South Africa's innumerable highlights... here, at a glance, are some recommendations to help you plan your journey

SAFARIS

● **Sabi Sand and MalaMala Game Reserves** Catering to those with deep pockets, these legendary reserves offer the most reliable leopard watching in Africa. *See page 291.*

● **Hluhluwe-Imfolozi** The largest of the Zululand reserves, and the best place to spot rhinos. *See page 238.*

● **Addo Elephant National Park** Known for its elephants, this park also protects the most varied habitats of any South African reserve. *See page 204.*

● **Madikwe Game Reserve** Excellent Big Five viewing is offered in this malaria-free reserve on the Botswana border. *See page 272.*

● **Kgalagadi Transfrontier Park** Protecting the red dunes and dry watercourses of the Kalahari, this remote park offers some of the best predator viewing. *See page 309.*

SMALL FAUNA AND FLORA

● **De Hoop Reserve** De Hoop, the largest protected area of fynbos in the Cape, harbours bontebok and Cape mountain zebra, and offers good marine wildlife viewing too. *See page 184.*

● **Namaqualand** The arid plains along the West Coast support an extraordinary diversity of succulents that burst into magnificent flower in the spring. *See page 313.*

● **Barberspan Bird Sanctuary** Regarded to be South Africa's most important avian wetland habitat, it is home to flamingos, ibises and waders. *See page 308.*

● **Ndumo Reserve** Any of Zululand's reserves offers good birdwatching, but Ndumo is the pick, both for tropical water birds and for species otherwise restricted to Mozambique. *See page 241.*

● **Bird Island Nature Reserve** Over 100,000 Cape gannets breed on this small island in Lambert's Bay, reached on foot via a causeway. *See page 174.*

● **iSimangaliso Wetland Park** Snorkel or dive on reefs, watch hippos and crocs lurking in the waters of St Lucia Estuary, climb the world's tallest forested dunes, or just revel in the extraordinarily diverse birdlife found at this Unesco World Heritage Site. *See page 237.*

ABOVE: Namaqualand. **LEFT:** Madikwe Game Reserve.

HISTORY AND CULTURE

• **Drakensberg rock art** Arguably the world's best open-air gallery, the caves and shelters contain thousands of ancient rock paintings. *See page 250.*

• **Robben Island** Now a Unesco World Heritage Site, this small island is where Nelson Mandela and other ANC members were imprisoned. Tours are conducted by former prisoners. *See page 157.*

• **Grahamstown Arts Festival** The university town of Grahamstown comes into its own in June, when it hosts a nine-day arts and fringe festival that attracts hundreds of theatrical, musical and other acts. *See page 209.*

• **Lesotho** The remote mountains of the "Kingdom in the Sky", best explored on horseback, offer a great opportunity to experience contemporary rural African culture in the company of the welcoming Basotho people. *See page 325.*

• **Mapungubwe National Park** Guided tours to the hilltop royal city that stood at the centre of a vast trade empire in medieval times, with the bonus of plentiful elephants and other wildlife along the Limpopo River. *See page 292.*

ADVENTURE ACTIVITIES

• **Imfolozi Trail** A great overnight hike through the Hluhluwe-Imfolozi Game Reserve. *See page 238.*

• **Caged Shark Dive, Mossel Bay** Just a few steel bars protect viewers from the rapacious "great white". *See page 190.*

• **White water rafting** The best white water rafting south of the Zambezi is on the Great Usutu River, southern Swaziland. *See page 323.*

• **Bloukrans Bridge Bungy Jump** Reputedly the highest bungy jump in the world plummets 215 metres (700ft). *See page 198.*

• **Otter Trail** South Africa's most popular hiking trail follows the stunning Tsitsikama coastline over five days. *See page 199.*

ABOVE: the captivating Two Ocean's Aquarium.

TOP FAMILY ATTRACTIONS

• **Lion Park** Dense with lions and other game, Johannesburg's safari-style drive-through zoo is the ideal alternative to visiting a game reserve (where wildlife must actively be sought) for youngsters with low boredom thresholds. *See page 268.*

• **Gold Reef City** Initially a replica of goldrush-era Johannesburg built to celebrate the city's centenary, this is now more popular for its selection of thrilling and, in some cases, heartstopping adventure rides. *See page 267.*

• **Two Oceans Aquarium, Cape Town** From seahorses and squids to dolphins and penguins, this excellent aquarium will appeal to children of all ages, as will its equally worthwhile counterparts in Durban, East London and Port Elizabeth. Feeding time for the seals, sharks and other marine predators draws a crowd. *See page 157.*

• **Monkeyland, Plettenberg Bay** Guided walks through the large forested enclosure, which contain monkeys and lemurs from around the world. *See page 197.*

• **uShaka Marine World, Durban** Offering exciting splashy water rides, this is the centrepiece of Durban's child-friendly waterfront, which also boasts a snake park and aquarium. *See page 222.*

• **Ostrich Farms** Several farms around Oudtshoorn let you ride, eat and buy the hollowed eggs of the world's largest – and most bird-brained – feathered creature. *See page 192.*

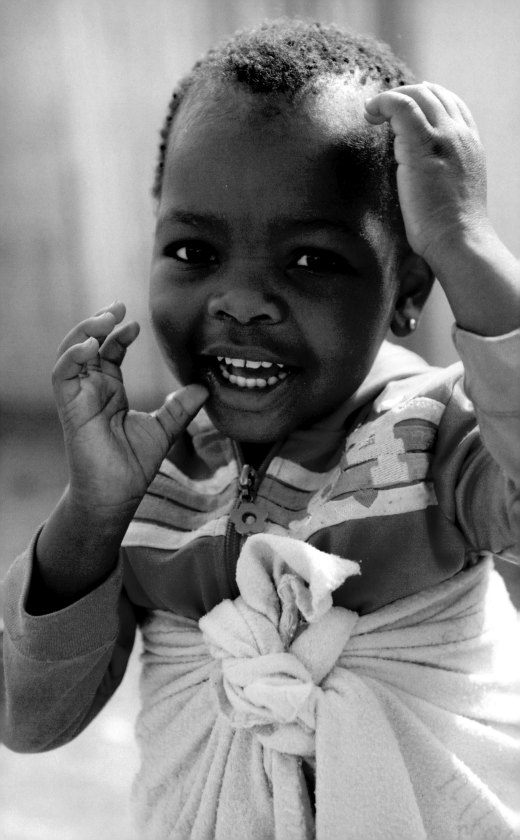

THE SHAPE OF GOOD HOPE

South Africa is a land of exceptional natural beauty
and cultural variety. Now, it also offers visitors
the chance to witness a nation reborn

Ranked third in the world in terms of biodiversity, South Africa supports all the iconic big game for which Africa is renowned, but it is also home to some ten percent of the world's known plant species, and more endemic birds than anywhere else on the continent.

Culturally, South Africa is equally diverse: a unique and engaging blend of European, Asian and indigenous influences, with modern cities such as Johannesburg and Cape Town juxtaposed against such antiquities as the prehistoric rock art of the uKhahlamba-Drakensberg–the world's greatest open-air art gallery–and a plethora of hominid fossils unearthed in the dank limestone caves of the Cradle of Humankind, stretching back 3.5 million years.

Game parks and beaches

South Africa's Kruger National Park epitomises the African safari with vast stretches of savannah, studded with flat-topped acacias, teeming with immense herds of elephant, buffalo, lion and leopard. It protects an astonishing 147 mammal species, including almost one-third of the world's surviving rhinos.

For a more intimate safari experience, there is Sabi Sand, MalaMala and the other exclusive private reserves that border the Kruger, while elsewhere you have the relatively compact likes of Madikwe and Pilanesberg Game Reserves, which offer similarly scintillating game viewing in an area totally free of malaria.

In contrast to the sweltering subtropical bush are unspoilt, sun-drenched, palm-lined beaches, windswept islands, and craggy peninsulas overlooking wide bays frequented by dolphins and whales.

For more incredible diversity there are the remote red dunefields of the vast Kgalagadi Transfrontier Park, the misty forests of the southeastern coastal belt, the sedate old-world architecture and prolific winelands around Stellenbosch and Franschhoek, the breathtaking magnificence of Table Mountain, the peerless spring wildflower displays of Namaqualand, and the towering rock amphitheatres and grassy slopes of the

PRECEDING PAGES: Cape Town's colourful Bo-Kaap district; white rhino, Madikwe Game Reserve; sunset at Sea Point. **LEFT:** young girl, Imizamo Yethu township.
ABOVE LEFT: beach huts, Muizenberg. **ABOVE RIGHT:** eland, De Hoop Nature Reserve.

ukhahlamba-Drakensberg Mountains, which even, incredibly, support a low-key seasonal ski resort at Rhodes.

Cultural variety

Evidence of prehistoric human occupation of South Africa includes the abandoned medieval gold-trading emporium at Mapungubwe Hill, as well as the world's finest assemblage of rock paintings and engravings, ranging from 20,000 to a few hundred years old.

There are still many rural areas where traditional African cultures survive remarkably intact, albeit often in easy collusion with modern technologies such as mobile phones and satellite television. Yet at the same time the country's largest cities – Johannesburg, Cape Town and Durban – form urban melting pots for a 21st century fusion culture far more exciting than the sum of its once fractious parts.

What of the future?

Critics of the present ANC leadership argue that cronyism and corruption have prevented it from sustaining the progressive momentum generated by Nelson Mandela, the country's first democratically elected president, who retired in 1999. Whether that's true or not, there is no denying that the country is still plagued by economic and educational disparities.

South Africa comes across as a forward-looking country, and rightly so. It has advanced a long way in the past 20 years. Lest you doubt it, pay a visit to Johannesburg's Apartheid Museum, and ponder on the poignant profundity of its slogan: "Today, apartheid is exactly where it belongs: in a museum". Better still, take a boat trip from Cape Town to Robben Island (now a Unesco World Heritage Site), where Nelson Mandela was incarcerated for 18 years. The tourist guides are all former political prisoners.

Talking to these activist-turned-guides, you might see their changed circumstances as emblematic of the gulf between past and present.

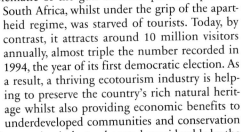

South Africa, whilst under the grip of the apartheid regime, was starved of tourists. Today, by contrast, it attracts around 10 million visitors annually, almost triple the number recorded in 1994, the year of its first democratic election. As a result, a thriving ecotourism industry is helping to preserve the country's rich natural heritage whilst also providing economic benefits to underdeveloped communities and conservation agencies. Indeed, this fast-growing industry–boosted considerably by the high profile enjoyed by South Africa during the 2010 FIFA World Cup– now generates about ten percent of the national GDP, and provides direct employment to more than 500,000 people, many from previously disadvantaged backgrounds. ❏

Top: hand-carved masks for sale at Green Point Flea Market, Cape Town.
Above Left and Above Right: street performers on the V&A Waterfront, Cape Town.
Right: Cape Mountain zebra, Mountain Zebra National Park.

> *The term "coloureds" refers to those of mixed descent, most of whom speak Afrikaans as a first language, but also includes a number of other sub-groups such as the 200,000-strong Malay community in Cape Town's Bo-Kaap district.*

became involved in trading and manufacturing, laying the foundations for one of the most prosperous sectors of the local economy.

More recently, the 1960s saw an influx of Lebanese, Italian and Greek Cypriot settlers, as well as Portuguese from Madeira, Mozambique

Shaped by conflict

A series of wars – including the frontier wars of the Eastern Cape, the Zulu Wars and the Boer Wars – established the basis of the relationship between South Africa's different communities, both black and white. This bleak history, along with the 1913 Land Act and the brutal legacy of apartheid, largely defined South African society as it is today.

Most of South Africa's socio-linguistic groupings are traditionally associated with a specific location, a situation that was exploited by the engineers of apartheid, who attempted to confine 42 percent of the population to the 13

and Angola. The Soviet invasions of Hungary (1956) and Czechoslovakia (1968) also brought with them new immigrants. All these people played an important role in the economy by supplying new skills and helping to create job opportunities.

South Africa's Asian communities number around 1 million collectively and are largely descended from indentured labourers who were brought over from India to work on the sugar farms of KwaZulu-Natal in the 1860s, and from China to work in the Witwatersrand mines in 1904.

FAR LEFT: Cape Malay woman. **LEFT:** car park attendants. **ABOVE:** University of Cape Town students.

percent of the land designated as nominally self-governing homelands.

Today, most Zulus still inhabit the province of KwaZulu-Natal, while the Eastern Cape and parts of the Western Cape remain Xhosa territory, and the Northern Cape, North West province and Free State are inhabited by the Sotho and Tswana. Different parts of Mpumalanga and Limpopo provinces are variously home to the Venda, Pedi, Shangaan and Ndebele peoples.

Regional bias can be noted among the non-indigenous communities. The Western Cape, Northern Cape, North West, Free State, Limpopo and Mpumalanga are all strongly Afrikaans, with the first two also forming important strongholds for the coloured community. Kwa-

Zulus

Today, Zulus regard themselves as South African citizens rather than members of a tribe

South Africa's largest black nation has been subjected to some particularly crude stereotyping in the past, from the caricature of the cattle-herding peasant to that of the bloodthirsty tribalist, sporting leopardskin and brandishing a shield and spear.

Based on fragments of apartheid propaganda, bolstered by the "tribal" souvenirs mass-produced for the tourist market, such images have little bearing on reality. Most Zulus today view themselves as citizens of South Africa, rather than identifying themselves first and foremost as members of a tribe. In any case, as more and more people opt for an urban lifestyle, the old customs and traditions are fast being displaced by "Western" ways.

What is certainly true is that the Zulus were once a mighty military power. The late 18th and early 19th centuries were characterised by almost constant Zulu warfare – against neighbouring clans, against the Afrikaner Voortrekkers, and against various British regiments (KwaZulu-Natal's historic "Battlefields Route" bears fascinating and sometimes chilling testament to these torrid times). Legendary leaders such as Shaka Zulu are still a source of fireside tales and a symbol of both resistance and national pride.

This legacy has been shrewdly exploited by the right-wing Inkatha Freedom Party under the charismatic Mangosuthu Buthelezi, former Minister of Home Affairs. Although he began his political career as an ANC member, he has fallen in and out of bed with the organisation over the years; during the 1980s, the IFP also accepted secret military and financial aid from the apartheid security forces.

With a membership drawn from the most deprived rural areas of KwaZulu-Natal, where the cult of the warrior is still prevalent, the rabidly nationalist IFP was caught up in a series of bloody clashes with the Xhosa-dominated UDF which persisted throughout the 1980s and 90s. Although some analysts sought to crudely characterise this "black-on-black" violence as the latest stage in an ancient tribal feud, in fact hostilities first arose out of disputes relating to local government issues. Both black political movements were struggling for control of the townships, each attempting to build up its constituency in anticipation of an eventual redistribution of political power. In the process, thousands lost their lives.

Custom and culture

As for urban Zulus, not all have traded in their cultural roots for a briefcase or a factory job. Millions remain faithful to at least some semblance of custom and culture, consulting *nyangas* (traditional healers) and paying *lobola* (the traditional "brideprice" paid by a bridegroom to his father-in-law).

Today, with the issue of ethnicity less of a hot potato, something of an indigenous cultural renaissance is underway. There is official support for traditional black culture, from music and theatre to traditional healing. "Cultural villages" have been set up to promote indigenous crafts and customs – at Simunye Pioneer Settlement in KwaZulu-Natal, for example, visitors can spend time listening to tales of battles with the British from a Zulu perspective, filled with "unofficial" oral history. Some Zulu writers, such as Fred Khumalo, author of *Zulu Boy Gone Crazy*, feel able to take a playful approach to their identity. And black schoolchildren can now take pride in their tribal heritage without being patronised or politically branded for it. ❑

LEFT: a Zulu woman celebrates National Heritage Day in Durban's Moses Mabhida Stadium.

Zulu-Natal has a distinctly English flavour, and is home to the majority of the country's Indian population, while the Eastern Cape is split quite evenly between English- and Afrikaans-speaking whites.

So how does this social jigsaw fit together? Well, it's a relatively new experience for most as apartheid tried to confine everyone to discrete ethnic boxes. But the Afrikaner nationalists who devised it failed to grasp how this diverse conglomeration of people at the southern end of the continent could live together. The advent of democracy has heralded a new openness to cultural mixing – indeed, events such as the 2010

unofficially, though according to the 2001 census, Zulu is the mother tongue of 23.8 percent of the population, followed by Xhosa (17.6 percent) and Afrikaans (13.3 percent).

The major cities have attracted people from all over the country since the turn of the 21st century, thanks to mines and industries, and each have their own distinctive styles of communication. The townships of Gauteng gave rise to the colourful mixed street-slang known as Tsotsi-taal (gangster, or bad-boy language), which combines elements of Afrikaans and African languages with expressive American gangster slang, and typifies the style of the edgy modern youth.

FIFA World Cup suggested South Africa is not merely accepting its multicultural identity, but actually starting to embrace and thrive on it.

Land of many tongues

Language is the first clue you get that the differences between people here are not simply a matter of skin colour – the Xhosa language is as different from Venda as German is from Spanish, while English has as much in common with Afrikaans as Italian does with French.

In practice, however, English is increasingly the main lingua franca, both officially and

ABOVE AND RIGHT: South African society is more diverse than many visitors realise.

Today it's a pervasive part of everyday township lingo, full of coded names and expressions: the ever-present minibus taxis are called "Zola Budds" (because they're always crashing into each other, as athlete Zola Budd did, colliding with Mary Decker at the Los Angeles Olympics). The small, 200ml bottles of spirits commonly sold at shows and sporting events and in shebeens are called "cellulars", because they fit into your pocket like a cellphone.

Culture clashes

Apartheid did not magically disappear in 1994. Deep economic, geographical and cultural divisions are sometimes still evident in South Africa. Go to a rugby stadium and the vast majority of spectators are likely to be white; go to football and they are likely to be black. But the picture is increasingly nuanced. A theatre in Sandton, Johannesburg, might well have an overwhelmingly white audience, but at the renowned Market Theatre in another part of town, black audience members are often in the majority.

Racial prejudice still exists, too, though less overtly than when it was legitimised by apartheid. White extremists continue to describe black people as lazy and backward, while ANC youth leaders have been known to use racially charged rhetoric. There appears, however, to

sangomas (healers) – the opposing viewpoints in the Afro/Eurocentric debate become partners in the cause of victory.

Not all traditional beliefs make the modern South Africa feel comfortable. Polygamy and teenage circumcision are still practised in some cultural groups and women face a struggle for full equality. Gay and lesbian people, while having the right to marry under the constitution, often face homophobia including the so-called "corrective rape" of lesbians. But in cities such as Cape Town and Johannesburg there is a thriving gay scene in bars, clubs and an annual Gay Pride march.

be a strong middle ground of politicians, civil society and media who are quick to condemn such outbursts, and a silent majority of South Africans who are content to get on with their daily lives. For this society is already a fascinating blend of African tradition and Western influence. In the suburbs, a white householder calls in a traditional healer to prepare charms to protect his home after the sophisticated alarm system has failed to do the job. Across town, a black mother-to-be puts her faith in a Jewish, London-trained, gynaecologist rather than the rural midwife her mother went to. And at the local stadium, black and white fans urge on a player kitted out by Adidas and anointed with a secret *muti* (traditional medicine) by the team

Religion

Almost four in five South Africans follow Christianity, with Hindus, Muslims, Jews and Buddhists also major groups. A minority of the population regard themselves as traditionalists with no specific religious affiliation.

Despite crossing racial boundaries, Christianity was a tool of divisiveness during the apartheid era. The Dutch Reformed Church (DRC) lay at the heart of the apartheid mindset, citing biblical writ to justify government policy – though it also produced some powerful critics from within its own ranks. In 1986, the DRC publicly rescinded apartheid and apologised to black South Africans.

By contrast, Anglican church leaders played

> Islam arrived in South Africa in 1658, but repressive conditions meant the first mosque (in the Bo-Kaap) was only erected in 1798.

a leading role in the anti-apartheid movement, most famously Nobel Peace Prize-winner Desmond Tutu, the first black archbishop of Cape Town and head of the Anglican Church in southern Africa. The Catholic Church was also critical of apartheid. Its cross was first raised in South Africa by Bartolomeu Dias at Santa Cruz in 1488 and again by Vasco da Gama in Mossel

grouping is the Zion Christian Church, which was founded in 1914 and has its own settlement at Zion City Moria, near Polokwane in Limpopo province.

Healing and religion are closely interrelated. As Christians, however, AIC members make it clear that they do not pray to ancestors for intervention; on the other hand, like followers of indigenous religions, they don't put much store in conventional medicine. Rather, they believe in the power of faith-healers (*umthandazi*) and prayers for the sick. The biggest churches not only have a number of faith-healers with immense reputations and constantly

Bay in 1498, and today it has 2.5 million adherents in the country. The Methodists, Baptists, the Salvation Army and the Greek Orthodox Church are also well established.

The biggest grouping of Christian churches is the African independent churches (AICs), of which there are more than 4,000 with a combined membership of at least 10 million people. Most are Apostolic or Zionist churches which broke away from the mainstream denominations in the 1880s and still operate independently of them today. The largest AIC

FAR LEFT AND LEFT: *kappies* like these are worn to church. **ABOVE:** some 20 percent of Indians and Cape Malays follow the Islamic faith.

overcrowded consulting rooms, but also have their own range of herbal treatments, coffee, tea and strict rules for healthy living. Although professed Christians, faith-healers do not always undergo training.

Closing the poverty gap

Apartheid separated communities, social services, business activity and political life along ethnic lines. Bringing together these disparate threads has been, and remains, a social and economic project comparable to the challenge that faces much of eastern Europe. South Africa has the advantage of comparatively established market networks and economic infrastructure. It has the disadvantage of extreme inequality

Traditional Religion

Healers – *inyangas* or *sangomas* – are gaining respectability as an alternative to conventional Western medicine

A minority of black South Africans still follow traditional religions, most strongly in rural areas, but there are also many believers who are urbanised and "Westernised".

Traditional African religion is based on a holistic

conception of the universe. Religious practices are supposed to preserve and reinforce harmony within the web of an individual's relationship to himself and his family, to his society and environment, to the realm of spirits, both good and evil – and ultimately to God. Keeping damaging influences at bay and healing damaged relationships is therefore extremely important.

Traditional beliefs and ceremonies are informed by the animistic conviction that natural elements and objects such as rivers, trees and wind possess a soul. But the central tenet is a belief in a Supreme Being, who can only be reached by people on earth through the medium of their ancestors. Because the ancestors are already with the Godhead, they are venerated as the "living dead", and may pass on their descendants' requests regarding such important matters as rain, health and fertility.

But first the ancestors have to receive a sign. Traditionally, an animal would be slaughtered which was then divided communally and consumed – with the dead ancestors duly receiving their portion. The head of each household functioned as family priest; in matters concerning the whole community, the chief took the role. He killed the cow or goat with a spear reserved for the purpose, and conveyed the requests of the living to the ancestors.

Diviners and mediums have always played – and still play – an important role in traditional religion. According to popular belief, people are most vulnerable to illness, often caused by sorcery, when their ancestors are "facing away". Healers – *inyangas* or *sangomas* – give instruction in the rituals which will placate the ancestors and ensure good health.

Treatments

An estimated 300,000 traditional healers minister to the physical and spiritual needs of South Africa's black community. These include herbalists or *inyangas* (usually male), and diviners or *sangomas* (usually female), who specialise in divining the illness and its causes by spiritual communication with the patient's ancestors. Both kinds of healer have a comprehensive knowledge of herbal remedies and of the medicinal properties of many plant species used to make up pharmaceuticals today.

The most common treatments administered by traditional healers are poultices, lotions, ointments, hot and cold infusions, and powders rubbed into parts of the body where incisions have been made. Healers also prescribe blood-letting, enemas and emetics to flush out impurities from the system. Plants are the basis of most traditional remedies, but some also use animal and bird parts.

Today, traditional healing is enjoying a growing respectability in healthcare circles. Many conventional medical practitioners recognise the wisdom of the traditional healer's holistic approach, which incorporates psychological, social, cultural and spiritual facets in the healing process. It is also recognised that, thanks to a critical shortage of qualified doctors, a high proportion of the rural population currently depends on herbal remedies. Some South African universities have therefore introduced traditional healing as a medical-school subject, to train students in the importance of using natural resources in primary health care. ❏

LEFT: an *inyanga* prepares a herbal remedy.

in wealth, considerable backlogs in education and housing, rapid urbanisation, the lingering effects of the social disruption caused by the migrant labour system, a high rate of HIV infection, and a lack of jobs that leaves more than half the population below the poverty line.

The ANC has strived to juggle the dual – and sometimes conflicting – goals of free market economic growth and interventionist wealth redistribution. The flagship Reconstruction and Development Programme set out ambitious targets for creating jobs, building houses, extending electricity and telecommunications lines, redistributing land and improving basic

> Today, traditional medicine in South Africa works hand in hand with modern science to tackle problems such as tuberculosis.

ity and 62 per cent to running water; by 2009, this had climbed to 80 percent and 88 percent respectively. More than 3 million government subsidised houses have been built since the ANC came to power. A huge investment in combating HIV/Aids has turned South Africa from international disgrace in the Mbeki years to a widely respected global leader. But a tide

ABOVE: church service in Imizamo Yethu township.

education, health and welfare services. But this policy depends on opening up income-generating opportunities rather than re-engineering a failed interventionist blueprint. A programme of Black Economic Empowerment has made some inroads but has been criticised for enriching only a small black elite – allegedly those linked to the ANC.

On the social front, the most striking successes of the ANC have been improved electrification and water supplies to low-income communities, and extensions to the network of primary health clinics. In 1996, just 58 per cent of the population had access to electric-

of sometimes violent service delivery protests across the country suggests a growing sense of frustration at the pace of change.

Reform

Land reform has been a slow process. The government has assured local and international communities that it will not tolerate a "land grab" process widely blamed for crippling Zimbabwe. But the process is long and drawn out and, so far, against a target of 30 percent commercial farmland redistribution by 2014, only 6 percent has been achieved.

The expansion of educational opportunities under the ANC tells a mixed story. South Africa has near-universal enrolment for 10 years or more of schooling, and participation in higher education now exceeds one million, although nearly half of undergraduate students either drop out or fail.

But this rapid growth has resulted in a sharp increase of governmental education spending – some 18 percent of the national budget in 2006/07 – and has contributed to strains in management capacity and some glaring qualitative deficiencies. Science and mathematics teaching in particular is woefully inadequate, while some schools still lack basic tools such as desks and chairs, making education a subject of intense national debate.

Economic development

Historically, South Africa's fortunes have risen and fallen with those of gold, diamonds and other minerals – the mining of which accounted for 70 percent of export earnings as recently as 1990. The government's economic strategy today centres on supplementing an unhealthy dependence on extracting raw materials from the earth with the greater expansion of manufacturing sectors.

Since 1994, manufacturing growth has been steady, and annual investment in plants has grown by 30 percent. Strong export growth in recent years has been spread across a wide

SHIFTS IN POLICY

ANC policy since 1996 has moved away from its former commitment to nationalisation. The government now tends to play down its socialist past and play up the fact that it is committed to a moderate, growth-driven economic programme which will provide for the privatisation of many state assets, as well as a reduction in the size of the civil service.

The so-called "route of Africa" – the typical snap replacement of a right-wing settler regime by a left-wing liberation movement which soon displays feet of clay – seems to have been short-circuited in the case of South Africa.

range of products, thanks to a more competitive exchange rate, favourable regional and global market trends, and export incentives.

Another welcome economic stimulant has been South Africa's rapid transition from tourist pariah to one of the world's travel hotspots, making it one of the top destinations to visit. Tourism is now the world's fastest-growing industry, and it is estimated that one new job is created for every eight tourists who visit South Africa annually.

The rapid growth in this sector, which received an unprecedented boost from the 2010 FIFA World Cup, is a potential economic goldmine in which South Africans from all backgrounds are claiming a stake.

Career prospects

But arguably the biggest obstacle to economic development is unemployment. The official rate shows that one in four South Africans is without a job, and some analysts believe the true figure is closer to one in three, including millions of frustrated young black men who have little prospect of finding work.

The ANC government has had to balance the need for reform with that of stabilising an economy that was already ailing badly in 1994 and might easily have collapsed after the election due to lack of faith.

It has thus committed itself to a fairly conservative regime of tight public expenditure control and falling budget deficits. Inevitably, this strategy came in for heavy criticism from the ANC's allies in the South African Communist Party and trade unions, but it has also reaped benefits in terms of increased international investment, a remarkable turnaround in the performance of the formerly beleaguered rand, and the slow but sure reversal of the negative balance of debt inherited from the apartheid government.

Such was the progress that, in 2010, South Africa was invited to join the "BRIC" grouping of major emerging economies: Brazil, Russia, India and China.

Undeniably, South Africa has come a long way since 1994. Transformation ideals have given way to the more tedious projects of building institutions and reconciling public spending goals to the available means. Black business interests are rapidly making more money than their unreconstructed competitors. Career prospects are now more prominent than political struggles in the minds of ambitious students. Furthermore, whatever contradictions might blight its economy, South Africa's GDP far exceeds any other in sub-Saharan Africa, and the country is also rapidly realising its potential as a continental economic powerhouse. South Africa's past still casts shadows over the country's prospects, but its policy debates are firmly focused on the challenges of the future.

Coming together

On 3 February 1997, exactly seven years after President De Klerk announced his plan to scrap

apartheid, South Africa adopted a constitution that is widely regarded to be among the most liberal in the world. A major democratic milestone, this new constitution recognised that all South Africans are entitled to a common citizenship in a sovereign and democratic state in which there is equality between men and women of all races, where all can exercise their fundamental rights and freedoms. The constitution also contained a bill of rights which guaranteed freedom of movement; freedom of opinion, religion and belief; and equality and equal protection before the law.

How did things change so quickly? Well,

there is the Mandela factor, the fact that this most remarkable political transformation was overseen by a statesman whose gift for reconciliation gained him tremendous respect across all race barriers.

Furthermore, it appears, with hindsight, that most white supporters of apartheid were motivated not by malice towards its victims, but by the fear of an uncertain future as a minority group under black rule. Once that future arrived in all its non-racial benignity, there was little to fear any more, nowhere to go but forward, and the vast majority of South Africans – black or white, male or female, straight or gay – embraced their new democratic identity with remarkable enthusiasm. ❏

LEFT: townships exist on the edges of most towns and cities. **RIGHT:** Cape Town bartender.

DECISIVE DATES

c. 8000 BC
San hunter-gatherers inhabit the south-western regions of southern Africa.

From AD 200
The semi-nomadic Khoikhoi begin farming the land.

From 1100
Other African peoples migrate into the southern African region from the north.

1488
Portuguese navigator, Bartolomeu Dias, lands at Mossel Bay.

1497
Vasco da Gama, discovers a sea route to India via the Cape.

1652
Jan van Riebeeck sets up a supply station for the Dutch East India Company.

1667
The first Malays arrive at the Cape as slaves.

1688–1700
Huguenot refugees settle in the Cape.

1779
First skirmishes between the settlers and the Xhosas, followed by eight frontier wars.

1795
The British annex the Cape.

1803
The Cape Colony reverts to Dutch rule.

1806
Britain reoccupies the Cape, the start of 155 years of British rule.

1814
The Cape is formally ceded to Britain by the Dutch government.

1818
Shaka becomes king of the Zulus.

1820
British settlers arrive in the Eastern Cape.

1820–28
Shaka extends his territory, leaving large areas devastated and depopulated in his wake.

1834
Slavery is abolished.

1836–54
The Great Trek. Over 16,000 Voortrekkers travel northwards from the Cape in order to escape British domination.

1838
Voortrekkers under Andries Pretorius defeat the Zulu under Dingane at Blood River in Natal.

1845
Natal becomes a British colony.

1848
British sovereignty is proclaimed between the Vaal and the Orange rivers.

1852
Boers found the Zuid-Afrikaansche Republiek.

1854
The Boer Independent Republic of the Orange Free State founded.

1867
Diamonds discovered at Kimberley.

1877
Britain annexes the South African Republic.

1879
The British defeat the Zulus at Ulundi.

1880–81
The Transvaal declares itself a republic. First Anglo-Boer War.

1883
Boer leader Paul Kruger becomes the first president of the Transvaal.

1886
Gold mining begins in the Transvaal and the mining town of Johannesburg is founded.

1899–1902
The second Anglo-Boer War.

1910
The Union of South Africa is proclaimed.

1912
A Black civil rights movement, the South African Native National Congress is formed, known after 1923 as the African National Congress (ANC).

1913
The Native Land Act is passed, limiting land ownership for blacks.

1925
Afrikaans replaces Dutch as the official "second language" after English.

1948
National Party wins general election. Acts enforcing apartheid follow.

1950–53
Apartheid is entrenched still further via such legislation as the Group Areas Act.

1952
The ANC launches the Defiance Campaign.

1960
69 black demonstrators killed at Sharpeville. The government bans the ANC.

1961
South Africa declared a republic and leaves the Commonwealth. The ANC launches its armed struggle.

1964
ANC leader Mandela is sentenced to life imprisonment.

1966
Apartheid's chief architect, Hendrik Verwoerd, is assassinated in Parliament.

LEFT: Stone Age tools found at Thulamela.
RIGHT: controversial president Jacob Zuma.

1967
The first human heart transplant is performed by Christiaan Barnard in Cape Town.

1975
The Zulu cultural movement *Inkatha* is revived by Chief Mangosuthu Buthelezi in Natal.

1976
600 killed in student uprising clashes in Soweto.

1984
Anglican Archbishop Desmond Tutu is awarded the Nobel Peace Prize.

1989
F.W. de Klerk succeeds P.W. Botha as President.

1990
Mandela released after 27 years in prison.

1991
All apartheid laws are repealed. Declaration of Intent signed at the Convention for a Democratic South Africa (CODESA).

1993
President de Klerk and Nelson Mandela receive the Nobel Peace Prize.

1994
The first democratic election is held and Mandela becomes president.

1995
A Truth and Reconciliation Commission appointed under Archbishop Desmond Tutu.

1996
NP withdraws from coalition. Parliament adopts a new constitution which is implemented a year later.

1998
The Truth and Reconciliation Commission ends describing apartheid as a crime against humanity.

1999
ANC wins general elections, Thabo Mbeki takes over.

2004
In South Africa's third democratic election, Mbeki and the ANC win a 70 percent majority.

2006
Former Deputy President Jacob Zuma is aquitted of rape and corruption charges.

2008
Mbeki resigns over allegations that he interfered in the corruption case against Zuma.

2009
The ANC wins its fourth election with Zuma succeeding Motlanthe. The economy enters recession for the first time in 17 years.

2010
South Africa hosts the FIFA World Cup, the first time it has been staged in Africa.

BEGINNINGS AND COLONISATION

Africa is the cradle of humankind. Indigenous cultures
thrived for millennia. Then the Europeans arrived, opening
a new chapter of conflict and conquest

The earliest known varieties of humankind emerged in Africa. Physical anthropologists call them hominids, meaning that they were more than apes but less than humans. More than 300 hominid remains, some dating back about 3.5 million years, have been found at the Sterkfontein Caves and other sites in the Cradle of Humankind, a Unesco World Heritage Site in Gauteng.

But not all hominids were the same. The *Australopithecus* (an "upright-walking small-brained creature") co-existed in South Africa with the more sophisticated *Homo Habilis* for more than a million years before finally biting the dust.

The Cradle of Humankind is a Unesco World Heritage Site spanning 47,000 hectares and 12 major fossil sites. It produced "Mrs Ples", a 2.5 million-year-old skull from an intermediate species between ape and human.

Remains of our own direct ancestor, *Homo sapiens sapiens*, have also been found widely distributed throughout South Africa. African variants of *Homo sapiens sapiens* display genetic markers which are called Negroid by comparison with the Mongoloid and Caucasoid variants found elsewhere. This implies that black people have been living in South Africa for at least 100,000 years. Within the Negroid genetic constellation, however, different groups developed in relative isolation from each other. One notable sub-group must have lived in relative isolation in the southwestern corner of the continent for about 40,000 years. These are the Khoisan peoples, who once inhabited substantial parts of South Africa, Namibia and Botswana.

Hunter-gatherers

The Khoisan were shorter and lighter skinned than most other Africans, their languages contained clicks and other unusual consonants, and they knew nothing of agriculture or iron-working. They were mostly hunter-gatherers, and they lived in very small nomadic bands following the migration patterns of wild game.

LEFT: a ceramic head, dated to AD 500, found on an Early Iron Age site near Lydenburg, Mpumalanga.
RIGHT: San hunters armed for an expedition from a painting by Samuel Daniell, about 1830.

The Khoisan peoples concentrated mainly in what are today the Western Cape and Northern Cape provinces. Most of South Africa was occupied by other African peoples who were darker skinned and more technologically sophisticated. They spoke languages which clearly indicate their cultural links with the rest of Sub-Saharan Africa.

Internationally, these languages are known as Bantu languages, a perfectly respectable term outside South Africa. But in South Africa the word "Bantu" was so abused by the apartheid governments that it is not socially acceptable in any context.

Today, most black South Africans speak either the Sotho-Tswana languages, which are found mainly on the interior plateau, or the Nguni languages (Zulu, Xhosa, Swazi) which are found mainly along the coast.

Cultural differences

In Limpopo province one also finds Venda, which is a relative of Shona in Zimbabwe, and Tsonga, which is related to the languages of southern Mozambique. Social scientists attribute the many cultural differences between the Sotho-Tswana and the Nguni to the different natural environments in which they lived.

ENTER THE "MEN OF MEN"

About 3,000 years ago, a group of Khoisan living in northern Botswana were initiated into cattle-keeping by other Africans. Being herders (travelling with domesticated herds of cattle), not hunters, they began to call themselves *Khoikhoi* ("men of men"), to distinguish themselves from the remaining hunter-gatherers, now called the San. The Dutch nicknamed them Hottentots and Bushmen, terms now regarded as insulting. Similarly, the word *Bantu*, a linguistic term embracing South Africa's extant indigenous languages, has been rendered dubious at home as a result of its misappropriation by the apartheid government.

Water is relatively scarce in the interior, hence the Sotho-Tswana tended to live in bigger settlements and to build in stone. The coastal lands, however, are punctuated by many rivers running from the mountains to the sea. This permitted the Nguni to live in more dispersed settlements, and to change their dwellings more frequently.

Marriage practices are another example of the way in which environment influenced traditional customs. Among the Sotho-Tswana, cattle were relatively scarce, so it made good sense to marry one's cousins and keep the cattle in the family. Among the Nguni, homesteads were more dispersed, and it made more sense to forge alliances by marrying into other families and exchanging cattle with them.

The course of South African history changed irrevocably in 1652 with the arrival of Dutch traders in Cape Town. They imprisoned the leaders of the Khoikhoi on Robben Island – later the site of Nelson Mandela's incarceration.

These examples show that South Africa's indigenous black cultures were well adapted to their local circumstances. The strong emphasis placed on custom and tradition was a natural recourse of people who lacked the means to record their political and legal codes on paper,

opened a refreshment station at Cape Town. The first commandant, Jan van Riebeeck, was unable to maintain good relations with the neighbouring Khoikhoi, and he took two decisions of great importance to the future of South Africa: he established a class of permanent white settlers, and he imported slave labour.

The slaves at the Cape soon came to outnumber the white population. They came mostly from the Dutch East Indies (modern Indonesia), and they intermarried with Khoisan, other African tribes and renegade whites to form a new community, known today as coloured people. There were no slave plantations at the Cape,

but it did not prevent innovation or change. Far from being culturally monolithic and mutually incompatible, these cultures were a great deal more flexible than the architects of racial apartheid cared to admit. But their development, and very existence, was to face a unexpected challenge from overseas.

Colonisation of the Cape

European colonisation of South Africa began in 1652 when the Dutch East India Company

LEFT: Zulu Kraal near Umlazi, Natal, by G.F. Angas.
ABOVE: Ndebele warriors attacking, by C.D. Bell. The Ndebele troops carried large, oval, Nguni-type shields and short stabbing spears.

and very few big farms. Most of the slaves lost their indigenous cultures and adopted the language and religion of their masters.

However, a minority of slaves, mostly political exiles and skilled artisans who had bought their freedom, adhered to their Islamic heritages. This "Cape Malay" community still predominates in parts of Cape Town such as the Bo-Kaap, which has a distinctive style of architecture.

The first white settlers farmed wheat and wine on relatively small holdings near Cape Town. But as soon as settlement expanded beyond the mountains into the drier grazing lands of the interior, it accelerated at a frightening speed. The settlers referred to themselves as "Boers" (farmers) or "Afrikaners" (Africans) to distinguish themselves from the Netherlands officials. They took whatever land they pleased, killing the Khoisan and raising the children as servants. There was very little control by the feeble Dutch East India Company, and Boer interests were well served by their local *Heemraaden* (magistrates' council).

Meanwhile, the colony continued to expand. In 1688, the first of 220 French Protestants, known as Huguenots, arrived at the Cape. They were fleeing religious persecution because Louis XIV of France had revoked the Edict of Nantes, the last guarantee of immunity for Calvinists living in France.

The impact of this small group was more significant than might be imagined: for one thing, it increased the colony's European population by about 15 percent. The Huguenots also brought with them valuable know-how, including the ability to cultivate wine. The names of some of the wine farms (La Motte, Cabrière, Mont Rochelle) in the vicinity of Franschhoek ("French Corner") still recall the places of origin of these settlers.

Britain takes control

The British presence at the Cape was initially strategic. During the War of American Independence, an increasing number of French vessels visited the Cape on their way to India. This development greatly disturbed the British government, then on the brink of hostilities with Napoleon. When the Dutch East India Company was finally liquidated in 1795, British forces took control of the Cape as allies of the Prince of Orange, and, although briefly returning it to the Netherlands in 1803–1806, they eventually decided to keep it.

The British were dramatically more powerful than their feeble Dutch predecessors. One of the first loose ends they decided to tie up was the Eastern Frontier. Several Xhosa chieftains, headed by a rebellious ex-Regent named Ndlambe, had penetrated deep into colonial territory, defying all the attempts of the Dutch authorities to dislodge them. Colonel John Graham was instructed to inspire "a proper degree of terror" in "these savages", and to chase them over the colonial boundary. He did just that, also founding, in 1812, the town which still bears his name today.

To accelerate the region's integration into the British colonial system, the government in London decided to sponsor emigration programmes to the Cape. In 1819, some 4,000 people – mostly artisans and ex-soldiers – were granted land in the area known as the Zuurveld, bordering on the Great Fish River. Between 1820 and 1824, the settlers were shipped out from the mother country, issued with basic rations, tents and farming tools and quickly dispatched to their new frontier "farms".

The settlers were, on the whole, a literate and articulate group who were to make a lasting impression on the development of education, the press and the legal system in South Africa. However, frontier life was harsh and uncom-

A TOUGHER ENEMY

The Xhosa proved a tougher enemy than the Khoisan, being better led, better armed and more numerous. Nor did they die from European diseases in the same way.

In North America and Australia, for example, whites not only defeated the native inhabitants but came to outnumber them because the diseases that they unwittingly imported proved to be deadly to the indigenous population. Diseases, such as measles and tuberculosis, which they had never previously encountered. However, this did not happen to black South Africans, who are still by far the largest racial group in the country.

promising. Few of the settlers were experienced farmers, and many drifted towards towns such as Bathurst and Grahamstown. Those who remained on the land had to contend with a fickle climate, regular crop failures and constant raids on their stock by marauding Xhosas.

Despite petitioning the government in the Cape to provide them with adequate protection, the settlers' pleas were to no avail. Instead, the government decreed they should use their own horses and equipment while engaged in punitive expeditions. What's more, farmers were still expected to pay their normal taxes, which only added to their grievances.

The Boers shared with the new immigrants a common resentment against the administration in Cape Town. Beforehand, as already noted, they had done more or less whatever they wanted and taken more or less whatever they could, particularly land and labour. But from 1822 onwards, a British Commission of Inquiry initiated a series of reforms designed to destroy the Boer's preferred way of life. These included more effective taxation, land allocation and more determined magisterial authority. Ordinance 50 of 1828 abolished forced labour and proclaimed authority before the law regardless of colour, paving the way for the abolition of slavery in 1834.

The Boers could read the writing on the wall, and they turned their eyes to the lands beyond the Orange River which were still outside the British sphere of control. Already, small bands of coloured people known as Griquas, who had left the colony to escape racial discrimination, had set up de facto states beyond the River Orange. They dominated the surrounding black nations by virtue of their access to horses and guns. From about 1834, Boer leaders such as Piet Uys and Louis Trichardt started to send out exploratory parties to reconnoitre new territories. By 1836 the mass migration of Boers, known to history as the Great Trek, was under way.

A time of troubles

Meanwhile, a very different kind of revolution was taking place north of the Thukela River in the present province of KwaZulu-Natal. It cul-

minated in the reign of Shaka Zulu (1818–28), but it did not begin with him. The critical element in the rise of the Zulu kingdom was the militarisation of youth associations called in Zulu *amabutho*, and usually translated as "regiments". Some historians argue that this militarisation was due to the presence of Portuguese slave traders at nearby Delagoa Bay (now Maputo). But this argument falls down because the slave trade only began in the 1820s, at least 25 years after the events which led up to the formation of the Zulu state.

The 1790s saw a series of increasingly ferocious wars fought between increasingly fero-

cious chiefs, concluding with the establishment of the Shakan despotism in 1818. Shaka did not originate the regimental system, but he elaborated it to its highest point of perfection, and he erected military headquarters throughout his kingdom, in which the various regiments were housed.

The nature of these establishments has been greatly misunderstood by romantic and reactionary writers alike, more especially the fact that Zulu warriors were not allowed to marry until their regiment was dissolved by the king. Male regiments were, in fact, twinned with female regiments and their deprivation was social rather than sexual in nature. Although the Zulu warriors were physically mature men,

LEFT: a typical Boer frontier family with Khoisan servants in attendance. **RIGHT:** a private from the Dutch East India Company.

they were not regarded as independent adults but as the children of the king and had to be available at all times to do his bidding.

Shaka thus obtained a degree of despotic control over his people which was unprecedented in southern African history. Legends of his cruelty abound, and although these must be treated with caution, it does seem that he became increasingly erratic as time went on. It is quite certain that his nearest and dearest conspired against him. Shaka was assassinated in 1828 by his half-brother Dingane, with the active assistance of another half-brother, his father's sister and his personal manservant.

By this time, the Shakan method had become well understood, and it was copied by a number of mini-Shakas who carved out their own despotism in diverse parts of southern Africa, including Mozambique, Swaziland, Zimbabwe, Zambia, Malawi and Tanzania. On the other hand, wiser and more tolerant chiefs built up their power by offering succour and defence to homeless refugees. Moshoeshoe, the founder of Lesotho, is the most famous example of this kind of chief. This period of South African history is sometimes called the *Mfecane*, after a word meaning "crushing", but this term has lately fallen out of favour.

Piet Retief, leader of the Boer trekkers, or "Voortrekkers", attempted to negotiate with Dingane to obtain land in Natal south of the Thukela River. But Dingane distrusted the Boers and ordered the murder of Retief and his negotiating party. The Boers rallied their forces under Andries Pretorius, who gave his name to South Africa's administrative capital. They defeated the Zulus in 1838 at the Battle of Blood River.

Later, in the 1930s, Afrikaner historians and politicians turned the events of 1838 into a nationalist and racist myth. Retief's murder became an act of primitive savagery, and Pretorius's "miraculous" victory over the Zulus a sign that the Voortrekkers and their descendants were God's people who alone had the right to rule South Africa.

The birth of the Boer republics

After their victory, the Boers in Natal set up a new republic which proved short-lived. The British were not yet ready to surrender their imperial hegemony over southern Africa, and so they annexed Natal in 1845. The Boers, however, refused to accept this. They headed across the Drakensberg into the far interior, where they founded two republics, the Orange Free State and the South African Republic (later known as the Transvaal).

Shaka, warrior king of the Zulus, built a vast empire and wielded brutal control over his people unprecedented in southern Africa. He was assassinated in 1828 and usurped by his half-brother Dingane.

The independence of these republics was soon challenged by the British. Claiming that their jurisdiction extended to the 26th south parallel, in 1848 a British invasion force annexed the entire territory between the Orange and the Vaal rivers. Eventually, however, a change of government in London contributed to the British recognising Boer independence north of the Vaal in 1852, and south of the river in 1854. The move effectively awarded sovereignty to the Boer republics.

The character of these republics may be inferred from Article 9 of the Constitution of the South African Republic (1858). This stated unequivocally that "the people are not prepared to allow any equality of the non-white with the white inhabitants, either in Church or State".

Other laws of the South African Republic also show very clearly the goals which the Boers set themselves when they embarked on the Great Trek. Every Boer who had participated in the Trek was entitled by right to two farms, which he demarcated himself. Black chiefdoms defeated by the Boers were obliged to supply them with tribute labour. The old tradition of child labour in the form of indentures (called the *inboekstelsel* because the names of the children were recorded in a book) was continued.

And if that was not enough, in 1870 the SAR legislature passed a law called the *kaffer wet*, whereby each farmer was entitled to labour service from five black families living on his farm. This was the origin of the system of labour tenancy which still poses difficulties for the South African government today.

The frontier wars

Back in the Cape, Britain was still continuing what is now known as the Hundred Years War against the Xhosa people on its eastern frontier. Both the Xhosa and the settlers were stock farmers, dependent on sufficient grazing. After a series of devastating droughts, the white farmers started trekking eastwards, encroaching on tribal land. Subsequently, they were subjected to stock raids of increasing intensity.

The settlers, blaming the British administration for the lack of adequate protection, took matters into their own hands. Between 1819 and 1853 four frontier wars erupted in the border area, claiming thousands of lives and debilitating traditional Xhosa society for generations.

From 1856 to 1857, the extraordinary incident known as the Xhosa Cattle-Killing occurred. A young girl, Nongqawuse, prophesied that if the people killed all their cattle and destroyed all their crops, the dead would rise, new cattle would rise, and nobody would ever again lead a troubled life. Hard-pressed by the rapid disintegration of their traditional culture under severe pressure from the settlers (claimants of their ancestral lands) and the missionaries (breakers of their traditional customs), the Xhosa resorted to desperate measures. The

failure of the prophecies was manipulated by a particularly ruthless governor named Sir George Grey to ensure that Xhosa power was finally destroyed.

The manifest failure of Xhosa traditionalism following the cattle-killing set the scene for increased co-operation between settler traders and progressive Xhosa farmers. British missionaries were very active in the Eastern Cape and they encouraged the growth of an African peasant class. Here, British commercial interests led to the liberalisation of the laws of the Cape Colony. In the British colony of Natal, however, the situation was very different, and policy was far

from liberal. Here, the British established sugar plantations which were voracious of land and labour. Segregation and "native reserves" were consequently established in the colony before they were even thought of in the Boer republics. Because labour was so scarce, the British added another twist to South Africa's social fabric by introducing indentured Indian labour.

As recently as 1867, South Africa was not the unified political entity we know today. There were four white-ruled colonies and innumerable black kingdoms and chiefdoms. Britain was the dominant imperial power, but even she had more pressing concerns elsewhere.

Then diamonds were discovered and everything changed. ❏

LEFT: Table Bay in 1683, by Aernaut Smit, with the ship *Africa* in the foreground. The castle is depicted with the original entrance facing the beach.
RIGHT: the Boer leader, Andries Pretorius.

WEALTH AND WELFARE

The discovery of diamonds and gold created wealth,
cities and jobs, and also sparked war

South Africa, prior to the mid-19th century, was a rather thinly populated land with limited economic resources and a small export trade in items such as wool, ivory and hides. Before 1848 there were few roads, before 1860 no substantial banks, and until 1880 almost no railway lines. Such towns as existed were either seats of magistracy like Graaff-Reinet, or meeting places for the quarterly *nachtmaal* of the Dutch Reformed Church.

Diamond rush

All this changed after 1867, when the first diamond was found north of the Orange River. Speculators from the Cape and Natal, a few Afrikaner farmers, and local Griqua and Tlhaping tribesmen sought to benefit from the river diggings on the Vaal and the dry diggings that soon turned into the vast prospectors' camp of Kimberley. The region became a bone of conten-

> By the end of the 19th century nearly all the land in southern Africa was owned by whites, either through surveyed titles, or through government control.

tion among the British, Free State and Transvaal governments because of its strategic position. That problem was resolved, amid much controversy, by an arbitration court which ordered the proclamation of the diamond fields as the crown colony of Griqualand West.

Successful diamond mining depended on the ability of the claim-holders to control marketing, and this necessity led between 1870 and 1888 to a step-by-step amalgamation of individ-

ual claims, which was made more urgent as the mines went deeper and the work became more expensive. Cecil John Rhodes' De Beers Company eventually emerged as the pre-eminent mining house, a position it still holds.

The Kimberley mines drew in the skills of well-paid immigrants and the manual labour of low-paid Africans. The latter were recruited on contract by labour touts in collusion with chiefs, who in turn required payment of their subjects in firearms as well as other goods. The black miners were in due course housed in compounds under strict control, and subjected to close body searches to prevent diamond smuggling. The white diggers won exemption from these searches. Thus there developed a pattern of labour differentiation and control which would set a precedent for much of the industrial life of South Africa in later years.

With the birth of Kimberley, industrial South Africa came into being. It provided an urban market for foodstuffs, at first supplied largely by African farmers. Kimberley's needs also set in motion the railway age.

Gold fever

Gold, like diamonds, had been discovered in 1867, at Tati on the Transvaal border of Bechuanaland, and subsequently in various parts of the eastern Transvaal from 1874. But it was

only with the location of the main reef on the Witwatersrand in 1886 that South African gold mining began in earnest.

The Chamber of Mines, established in 1887, went some way to regulate the competition, above all by ensuring that labour was made extremely cheap, and housed in compounds as a control device. But by 1890 the Chamber found itself in opposition to Paul Kruger's government for both political and economic reasons.

The republicans resented the intrusion of foreigners (uitlanders), especially when they demanded political rights, which they were reluctant to grant. It sought to profit from

LEFT: a miner's life. **ABOVE:** diamonds are forever.

gold mining but drove up production costs by, among other means, the inefficient taxing of explosives. By 1895 it was becoming clear to governments in Europe that the Transvaal had become a focal point of power, just at a moment when the international partition of Africa was gradually moving towards a climax.

The imperial factor

The European occupation of southern Africa was a double process. On the one hand, there was the physical appropriation of the greater part of the land by white colonists as they carved out farms and worked the mineral deposits they had

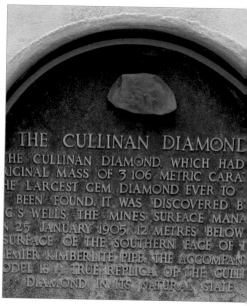

acquired through victory in frontier wars. On the other, there was a contest between Great Britain as the paramount power in the region and the Boer republics for the political control of territory.

The first phase of the Anglo-Boer conflict over territory, which developed after the recognition of republican sovereignty by Britain, was a dispute between Britain and the Free State over the control of Basutoland (current-day Lesotho) and the diamond fields. Both territories passed under British control and both were later transferred to the Cape Colony, but Basutoland was made a British protectorate in 1884, as were Bechuanaland (Botswana) in 1885 and Swaziland in 1902.

From 1868 it became a stated objective of British policy to amalgamate the South African territories politically for reasons of defence and economy. In 1875 Disraeli's Colonial Secretary, Lord Carnarvon, sought to do this, but he forced the pace, and failed to win the backing of the Cape government. In 1877 he did, however, succeed in annexing the Transvaal in an adroit move designed to put pressure on the Free State. The annexation proved a fiasco, partly because of poor administration, partly because the Afrikaner leadership under Paul Kruger organised a successful rebellion in 1880–81 and persuaded Gladstone that it would be wise to withdraw. Conventions signed in 1881 and 1884 restored the Transvaal's independence on terms which

gave Britain, at best, an ambiguous right to intervene in its affairs.

Deep-level mining on the Rand produced only narrow profit margins, partly due to Kruger's fiscal policy, and this created at least a temptation to overthrow his government.

Cecil Rhodes, prime minister of the Cape from 1890 to 1896, had already unsuccessfully attempted to incorporate the Transvaal in a South African railway and customs union, and then to encircle the republic by purchasing Lourenço Marques (Maputo) from the Portuguese. In 1895 he plotted a rebellion on the Rand to be assisted by an invasion by his British South Africa Company forces from across the border. But the Jameson Raid, planned with

the knowledge of the British Government, also failed, and seriously undermined Kruger's willingness to trust the British. Rhodes was therefore discredited and resigned.

The Anglo–Boer War

In a sustained diplomatic face-off in 1899, the British drove Kruger to the brink of war by insisting on the full recognition of *uitlander* rights. Kruger yielded ground to the point at which his pride could yield no more, and anticipated a British ultimatum by invading the coastal colonies in October.

The Anglo–Boer War of 1899–1902 at first went well for the Boers, who scored major victories. Only when the main British forces arrived were they able to invade the allied republics, occupying Bloemfontein and Pretoria by June 1900. However, the war dragged on for two more years. Boer guerrilla forces raided across the plateau. The British commander, Kitchener, responded by moving Boer women and children into concentration camps. These were a disaster, their poor sanitation causing the deaths from disease of close on 28,000 Boers. Finally, and bitterly, the Boers surrendered in 1902. Their two republics, and the gold fields, became part of the British Empire.

The conflict had a profound effect on the moulding of South African political attitudes. Most Boers believed that they were the victims of a monstrous British injustice; that the British had set out to destroy them as a people. Latter-day Afrikaner nationalism was born out of a determination to put right these wrongs by making sure that South Africa became an Afrikaner country, not a British one.

However, the myth that it was a "white man's war" which didn't affect black people has little historical evidence to support it: black people were recruited as labourers and scouts by both sides in the conflict, though the Boers were more reluctant than the British to issue them with arms. Black people also suffered directly and in large numbers during the sieges and from the destruction of farms, as well as from the concentration camps, where more than 14,000 died. But their hardships went relatively unnoticed in the published accounts and, when the war was over and the peace treaty signed, they had little to expect for their sufferings. ❑

LEFT: for three years, the Boers kept the British at bay.

Kruger and Rhodes

If ever there was a *bête noire* almost custom-made for the champion of the Boers, it was the diamond magnate obsessed with expanding the British empire

With his baggy black suit, straggly beard and enormous pipe, Paul Kruger was caricatured by the world press as a typical "backveld" Boer, but critics who underrated his undoubted political skills did so at their peril.

Born in 1825 in the Cape Colony to a Boer family of German origin, Kruger had no formal education. His first "profession" was that of lion hunter, but he quickly rose within Voortrekker ranks by showing his mettle on command, as the Boers battled to wrest land from black chiefdoms north of the Cape. By the age of 36 he had been appointed to the rank of commandant-general. In 1877, when Britain annexed the Transvaal Republic, Kruger emerged as the Boer's national champion, and was twice sent to London to try to persuade the British to abandon their policy. Finally, in 1883, he was elected president of the Transvaal, now known as the South African Republic – an office he was to hold for four terms.

He was a Calvinist to the core, with an unshakeable belief that his "volk" were God's chosen people who alone had the right to rule South Africa.

Provoked into declaring war on Britain in 1899, it was Kruger's misfortune to lead his beloved republic to defeat. When the war started to go badly he went into voluntary exile, following events closely to the final defeat of the Boer forces in 1902. Refusing to submit to British rule, he remained in exile, dying in Clarens, Switzerland in 1904. His remains were brought home for burial at Heroes' Acre in Pretoria.

Diamond magnate

Cecil John Rhodes, Kruger's lifetime rival was born in Hertfordshire, England in 1853. The son of a vicar, Rhodes was first sent out to Natal to recuperate from tuberculosis. The sickly youngster soon found his way to the new diamond fields at Kimberley, where he conceived an ambitious plan to gain total control of the entire diamond industry. By 1889, Rhodes and his mining company, De Beers Consolidated, had achieved his goal.

Obsessed with furthering the cause of British imperial expansion, Rhodes combined his commercial genius with an equally ruthless career in politics. Made prime minister of the British Cape Colony in 1890, he used intrigue and war to grab the lands of the Matabele and Shona north of the Limpopo, and establish under royal charter his personal states of Northern and Southern Rhodesia (now Zambia and Zimbabwe). This effectively blocked Kruger's South African Republic from expanding north of the Limpopo.

But a scheme to topple Kruger and seize the republic's goldfields for the British led to Rhodes' downfall. The Jameson Raid of 1895, in which Rhodes tried to organise a committee of leading *uitlanders* (dissatisfied immigrants) to overthrow the Transvaal government with the help of a column of British police, failed dismally – Kruger's government got wind of the plot before it took place. This fiasco not only marked the end of Rhodes's political career, it also helped to alienate British and Afrikaners across the whole of South Africa.

Rhodes died in his Muizenberg cottage (now a museum) in 1902, his dreams of a British "Road to the North" unrealised. Paradoxically, the glittering financial empire he built continues to be a mainstay of South Africa's economy. ❑

RIGHT: Paul Kruger, the "Wounded Lion".

UNION AND RESISTANCE

By the early 20th century, a white minority dominated
South Africa – despite the fact that black people far
outnumbered them

The Peace of Vereeniging registered the victory of the British Empire over the Boers shortly after white domination of South Africa was finally achieved. The 20th century would witness a speedy Afrikaner return to power, and then – after 90 years of assertive white dominance – the start of an impressive black resurgence.

Britain annexed the former Boer republics in 1902, but made it possible for them to regain autonomy. This was largely the achievement of generals Louis Botha and Jan Smuts, who saw the need for conciliation among whites, but left the problem of dealing with black people to the "stronger shoulders" of the future. The British government thought that extending the vote to the black population would jeopardise their aim of conciliating white minority.

Meanwhile, black political organisations watched resentfully as Britain first allowed the Transvaal and Orange River Colony to acquire white-controlled constitutions in 1907–8, and then agreed after the national convention of 1908–9 to a constitution for a united South Africa, which did substantially the same thing.

The Union of South Africa

Britain aimed to restore the South African economy by bringing the mines back into production and resettling the uprooted on the land, thereby coaxing the Afrikaner back into the imperial fold. Black labour might be essential for this task, but not black voters. Recon-

struction therefore took place, conciliation among whites began to work, and the Union of South Africa took its seat with the other white dominions in the British Commonwealth of Nations. As a member of that imperial system, South Africa took part in two world wars and played a leading role in the evolution of dominion autonomy between 1917 and 1934.

The Union of South Africa in 1910 was an embryonic industrial state, with mineral exports far exceeding agricultural, and with a developing manufacturing industry producing mainly for the local market. These years also witnessed a parallel townward movement by both Afrikaners and black South Africans.

LEFT: the proudly named "Union Express", symbol of a newly united country, carried passengers from Cape Town to Johannesburg. **RIGHT:** mineral wealth fuelled the colonial economy.

Resurgence of Afrikaner power

Afrikaner republicanism was reborn soon after union on a platform of opposition to the imperial connection and a demand for the effective recognition of Afrikaans language rights. The former found expression in the rebellion of 1914, triggered by the government's decision to invade German South West Africa, while the founding of the secretive Broederbond in 1918 led to a spread of Afrikaner cultural and economic organisations.

Both found a political mouthpiece in the National Party governments of General Barry Hertzog between 1924 and 1939: first in alliance

with the white Labour Party and after 1932 in alliance with General Smuts (until their fused United Party was split asunder when Hertzog tried to keep South Africa neutral in World War II).

Hertzog's strident nationalism was toned down once he had seen that South Africa could remain within the British Commonwealth without the rights of the Afrikaner necessarily being threatened. But this wasn't the view of a new "purified" National Party, which grew after 1934 under the leadership of Dr D.F. Malan.

Malan's party, the voice no longer just of the poor whites but also of a new brand of Afrikaner entrepreneur seeking economic power, won the 1948 election and remained in power without a break until the first democratic elections for all

> *Long before racial apartheid was formalised, black people were effectively debarred by law from political and trade union activities, and controlled in their movements by pass laws.*

South Africans in April 1994. Afrikaner voters, some of whom had been attracted to Leninism in their poverty of the 1920s, had entrenched themselves not only on the land but also in the civil service and the professions, and more recently in business too. English speakers, by contrast, remained politically marginal, though their business dominance remained strong.

Roots of black opposition

But the main catalyst for change, which gradually came to monopolise the attention of the white political establishment, was the numerical growth and urban drift of black South Africans. The controlling of black people's movements ensured that many could not move from white-owned farms to towns. The majority, who remained in the tribal reserves, were also prohibited from acquiring land outside the reserves by the Land Acts of 1913 and 1936. Thus tied down, black South Africans found it hard to organise themselves effectively to promote political or economic change.

During World War II, it seemed that segregationist policies might be reduced under pressures generated by the Atlantic Charter. The wartime government of General Smuts tried to ameliorate the conditions of urban black residents, ceased briefly to enforce the pass laws, began to build black secondary schools, made a start with black pensions and disability benefits, and professed its rejection of the principle of segregation.

But in the run-up to the general elections of 1943 and 1948, the Smuts government could not contain the rising propaganda of the National Party. Smuts's failure to initiate a change of direction led to a major confrontation with the African Mineworkers' Union in 1946, in which lives were lost. This broke black trust in Smuts. His government's attempts at policy changes, on the eve of the 1948 election, were neither sweeping enough to attract black backing nor cautious enough to prevent the white electorate from casting their votes decisively for Malan.❑

LEFT: Afrikaner general Smuts.

Gandhi

Ejection from a South African train roused Gandhi's spirit of protest and led to the philosophy of passive resistance

The development of the sugar cane industry in the 1860s in what is now KwaZulu-Natal meant that large numbers of indentured Indian labourers were imported by the British colonial authorities to work in the plantations. Many settled in South Africa after finishing their contracts, establishing small businesses. Thus trade connections with India grew, and Durban, in turn, developed into South Africa's most distinctively multi-cultural city.

In 1893 a 24-year-old advocate named Mohandas Karamchand Gandhi came to South Africa to act in a lawsuit between two Indian trading firms. Having landed at Durban, he caught a train to Pretoria in connection with the suit. He had a first-class ticket, but during the journey a white passenger objected to his presence in the compartment, and he was ordered to move to a third-class coach. Ignorant of South African racial prejudice, he refused – and was promptly ejected from the train. He spent the night at Pietermaritzburg station. The incident made such an impression on Gandhi that in later life he declared it had been the single most important factor in rousing his spirit of protest and determining his political career.

Gandhi's subsequent involvement in the Indian community's struggle for civil rights kept him in South Africa for 21 years. It was here that he first developed the philosophy of *satyagraha* which made him world famous.

Passive protest

Satyagraha means "keep to the truth". Gandhi considered truth a central life principle – one which meant, in practice, resisting injustice not with force, but with the superior powers of love and spiritual conviction. Hence his conception of passive resistance as a form of political protest.

The community of Indian entrepreneurs in Natal was a flourishing one, but deeply resented by white traders who disliked undercutting. Attempts to

establish Indian businesses in the Transvaal were met with restrictions on residential and trading rights; Natal also imposed a £3 tax on Indians who wished to stay in the colony after the expiry of their indentures. The young Gandhi quickly became one of the Indian community's most articulate and influential leaders, founding the Natal Indian Congress in 1894.

But it was in protests against the Immigration Act of 1913, restricting Indian settlement in the Transvaal, that his passive resistance campaign reached its climax. Strikes were organised in the coal mines of northern Natal, which soon spread to sugar and other plantations. Finally, on 1 November, more

than 2,000 *satyagrahis* started a march to the Transvaal with the intention of breaking the law and being arrested and imprisoned. Gandhi himself was sentenced to 9 months' imprisonment.

The net result of all the upheaval, the Indians' Relief Act of 1914, addressed some of the community's chief grievances, such as the hated £3 tax. However, Indians were still denied any sort of official political representation.

Nonetheless, Gandhi considered his work in South Africa completed and returned to India, where he immediately threw himself into the struggle against British rule. His ideal was finally realised in August 1947, when India became independent. Tragically, only a few months later in January 1948, he was assassinated by a Hindu fanatic. ❑

RIGHT: the philosopher-politician Mahatma Gandhi.

THE RISE AND FALL OF APARTHEID

The 1950s saw segregationist policies entrenched into a system that would stain the subcontinent for nearly half a century

The National Party headed by Dr Daniel François Malan, a preacher and journalist before becoming a politician, won the 1948 general election by a narrow margin. The bulk of support came from recently urbanised whites who feared the challenge of blacks in the marketplace, especially as the African National Congress (ANC), in association with the African Mineworkers' Union, showed signs of growth during the 1940s.

The new government's response was to bring out a legislative programme designed to entrench white (and by implication Afrikaner) dominance. The principles of apartheid (separateness) dominated the government's legislative programme from the start. It enacted a Population Registration Act to slot everybody into an appropriate race group, as well as to outlaw interracial matrimony or sexual relations, and a Group Areas Act to divide every town in South Africa into defined sectors where only

members of particular groups could own or occupy property. This required the physical removal of many coloured and Asian households, but few white citizens. Most resented of all were the "pass laws" which restricted the movements of black people. The legislation was buttressed by laws designed to undercut political resistance, beginning with the Suppression of Communism Act. It was followed by measures that would restrict individuals and organisations, while denying them right of appeal.

Growing black resistance

After Dr Hendrik Frensch Verwoerd – a chief promoter of apartheid legislation – became prime minister in 1958, the policy was devel-

PASSIVE RESISTANCE

A campaign against the pass laws (which were designed to segregate the population, and which restricted the movements of black people throughout white areas) during the war eventually led to the launching of the Defiance Campaign in 1952, a well-orchestrated, large-scale passive resistance tactic by African, Asian and coloured movements to offset the tercentenary celebrations of white settlement in the Cape. Its forceful suppression led to the public adoption of a freedom charter at Klipfontein, near Johannesburg, in 1955 – a broad social democratic affirmation designed to achieve widespread public support.

oped to promote territorial partition so that the African reserves could be turned into "independent homelands" whose citizens could on that pretext be deprived of access to political rights in the South African heartland. Verwoerd tried to establish border industries to enable black people living in the homelands to find employment in "white" South Africa with minimal daily travel; but he would not allow white capital to finance such development. His successor, Balthazar Johannes Vorster, a lawyer and staunch supporter of traditional Boer principles, removed this restriction; but by 1970 it was clear that job creation in the homelands fell

had its agenda cut out. Two years earlier the Union of South Africa had been forged out of the ashes of the Boer–British struggle, but had ignored the position of the vast majority of the country's citizens.

Protests

The ANC spent its first years protesting the historical errors committed at the Union. But its critics accused it of being an organisation of elderly men fighting to preserve their hard-won, middle-class privileges. Impatient activists joined the fledgling labour movements that advocated more radical action. In 1943 the ANC

far short of providing a living for the number of Africans required by government policy to live there.

Such policies strengthened support for the ANC. The oldest existing political party in the country, it had formed for six decades the vanguard of black political aspirations. It was in January 1912 that representatives of the country's major African organisations met in Bloemfontein to form the South African Native National Congress. The movement, which was soon renamed the African National Congress,

Youth League was formed by a group of young men whose political legacy is still felt: the brilliant Anton Lembede, Oliver Tambo, Walter Sisulu and an enigmatic young lawyer, Nelson Mandela. They were soon strong enough to stage an internal coup and to get their candidate, Dr James Moroka, elected president. This marked the beginning of a new strategy of direct, non-violent confrontation.

Documents confiscated by the police when they broke up the Klipfontein gathering (*see box opposite*) formed the basis for the first of a number of "treason trials" which marked the next 35 years. The defendants were all found innocent in 1961, but in the meantime divisions opened up within the ANC. A group

LEFT: grand vizier of apartheid, Dr Hendrik Verwoerd.
ABOVE: Sharpeville, 1961. Police bullets killed 69 protestors, hitting many in the back.

of "Africanists" led by Robert Sobukwe was disturbed by communist influences on ANC policy, arguing that if a racist government was in power the assertion of African nationalism was the real note to strike. Driven out of the ANC in 1958, they broke away to form the Pan-Africanist Congress (PAC).

When the government launched its campaign for a republic in 1960, the ANC and PAC were at daggers drawn, yet both were angling for mass support by promoting anti-pass demonstrations linked to wage demands. Some 30,000 Africans marched on the Houses of Parliament in Cape Town. Police bullets killed 69 protesters

at Sharpeville, near Vereeniging on the South Rand, on 21 March, and the government, clearly frightened, banned both the PAC and the ANC, driving them underground. The world condemned the Sharpeville shootings, and South Africa's ostracism in world affairs began.

White responses

In a whites-only referendum, Dr Verwoerd obtained a narrow victory to proclaim a republic and his government subsequently decided to leave the British Commonwealth. Sharpeville had shown the inadequacy of passive resistance and drove the African resistance movements into violent opposition.

The ANC and the PAC set up bases in exile in

> *In 1962, the police captured the underground leaders of the ANC, headed by Nelson Mandela, outside Johannesburg. After an eight-month trial they received life sentences in the notorious Robben Island prison.*

Lusaka, Dar-es-Salaam and London, but found it hard to make much impact locally or internationally. For almost 10 years the South African government managed to keep a lid on black political activity. Activists were rounded up and held under detention without trial.

In September 1966, Hendrik Verwoerd was stabbed to death in the House of Assembly by a parliamentary messenger. His successor, B.J. Vorster, was better at silencing opposition than developing strategies for change. But when capital started to flow back into South Africa, he tried to revive the socio-economic aspects of apartheid. Investment corporations were set up to develop the homelands. The expansion of black businesses, black housing, black schools and black immigration into the white area was made harder.

By 1970 the number of jobs created in the homelands was seen to be nowhere near that required if Africans were to be able to "flow back" from the white areas. The government decided to press ahead with homeland "independence", starting with the Transkei in 1976. The aim was to create alternative allegiances, thus depriving all citizens in "independent" homelands of their South African citizenship even if they still lived in the republic.

The tide turns

On 16 June 1976, Soweto, the large African residential location outside Johannesburg, erupted after a government decision to enforce the use of Afrikaans as a language medium in schools, though the grievances were far wider and included objections to homeland independence. Much of the drive came from a new Black Consciousness movement led by Steve Biko, an activist from the Eastern Cape.

Over a period of 18 months the burning of public buildings, schools, liquor outlets and cars had most of the African townships in flames and the conflagration soon also spread into coloured and Indian residential areas. On 18 August 1977, Biko was arrested by the security police. Twenty-six days later he died from head injuries sustained during interrogation.

Black consciousness was too well-rooted to be effectively extinguished; it re-emerged in other forms, linking Africanist aspirations to a socialist ideal. Many young activists fled the country, joining the waiting structures of the ANC in exile. This influx of new blood rejuvenated and strengthened the movement considerably. Led by Oliver Tambo, the ANC redoubled its onslaught against the government on two fronts: the military, where they achieved moderate successes with sabotage attacks on strategic installations; and international isolation, where

creation of the giant Congress of South African Trade Unions (COSATU). Church leaders emerged as vocal spokesmen for black aspirations, with men like Archbishop Desmond Tutu and Dr Allan Boesak. Tutu became the second South African to win the Nobel prize for peace (the first, in 1960, was Albert Luthuli, a Natal teacher who had become leader of the ANC in the 1950s).

World opinion

In the 1960s and 1970s, Vorster's government had offended world opinion by refusing to support sanctions against the white rul-

they continuously pushed for strong punitive measures – economic sanctions, arms embargoes and cultural and sporting boycotts.

Internally, black opposition re-emerged in 1985 with the formation of the United Democratic Front (UDF), a loose federation of anti-apartheid movements, linked ideologically to the ANC. A new generation of black leadership – "the '76 generation" – came to the fore. When they were restricted, trade unions became a focal point of political activity, leading to the

LEFT: Hector Pietersen, the first victim of the riot police at Soweto, 16 June 1976.
ABOVE: a groundswell of public violence was a hallmark of the apartheid years.

ers of Rhodesia, and by holding out against the transfer of power in South West Africa (present-day Namibia), in a dispute with the United Nations which had started soon after World War II. Talk of international sanctions, beginning with an arms embargo in 1963, was spreading to include economic and cultural boycotts. Almost the whole world condemned the republic's policies.

Vorster's government fell after disclosures of serious financial mismanagement in the running of its propaganda activities. The scandal divided the ruling National Party and propelled the defence minister, Pieter Willem Botha, to the premiership. Botha restored effective control over government. He also tried to rebuild

Truth and Reconciliation

Some victims of apartheid demanded vengeance, but the South Africa of Mandela and Tutu went another way

The line between victims and criminals was sometimes a thin one in South Africa. It seemed scarcely possible that the scars left by 40 violent years of apartheid could be healed, yet the government attempted to do just that.

The Truth and Reconciliation Commission (TRC) was established in 1995. It was based on an acknowledgement that there had been violence and human rights abuses on all sides. Dr Dullah Omar, the former Minister of Justice, asserted: "A commission is a necessary exercise to enable South Africans to come to terms with their past on a morally accepted basis and to advance the cause of reconciliation."

Under the chairmanship of Nobel Peace Prize-winner Archbishop Desmond Tutu, the TRC aimed to investigate gross human rights violations committed by all parties between 1 March 1960 and 10 May 1994. It also aimed to recommend reparation for victims. The regular televised sittings of the TRC included shocking disclosures of atrocities committed by senior officials in the National Party, the police and the Defence Force, as well as members of the Inkatha Freedom Party, the ANC and PAC and other organisations involved in the anti-apartheid struggle. Extraordinarily, the TRC was not geared towards punishing offenders. Instead, they were to be granted amnesty and indemnity if their crimes could be proved to have been "politically motivated" – while victims were given the chance to speak out about the injustices done to them and so perhaps liberate themselves to some extent from the burden of their memories.

Justice and forgiveness

Tutu's insistence that the TRC's emphasis was less on "settling things legally" and more on allowing all South Africans to come to terms with the past in a cathartic spirit of reconciliation angered some of the families of apartheid victims, who indicated that they would instead prefer to see justice done. Yet Tutu was adamant in his espousal of a Christian philosophy of forgiveness. "South Africa cannot step confidently into the future unless and until it has made an honest effort to come to terms with its past. And the TRC is that effort," noted the *Star* newspaper.

Human rights activist Alex Boraine structured the TRC after several years of research. He studied 15 similar bodies worldwide, in countries such as Guatemala, El Salvador, Chile and Argentina, and reached a somewhat depressing conclusion. In most cases, the key perpetrators of human rights abuses – high-ranking military officials – had simply ignored the whole process. "Each commission was supposed to help the victims of an unjust regime start a healing process, but in the end, they all gave up trying. Each has left behind an underclass of victims who have never had any reparation for what they went through," he noted.

South Africa's TRC, which published its 3,500-page report in October 1998, may have got closer to a solution, although the legacy of apartheid is still felt in race and class inequalities.

One poignant legacy of the TRC continues. It recommended the setting up of a missing person's task team to search for the people who disappeared during the apartheid years – in some cases, their families did not not even know whether they were dead. In 2010, the task team found the bodies of six people hanged by the state for the stoning of a police vehicle in 1962. The healing goes on. ❑

LEFT: TRC hearings took place all over the country.

the economy, which went into deep recession from 1982 as a result of a sustained drought and a dramatic fall in the gold price, aggravated by a move among the world's banks to impose a stranglehold on South Africa's borrowing.

Far from trying to abolish apartheid, Botha attempted in 1983 to make it irremovable. He secured white electoral support for a new constitution, which not only made him an executive president (as distinct from the largely formal office created in 1961) but also created ethnically distinct Houses of Parliament for whites, coloured people and Indians, with no representation for black Africans.

Furthermore, the homeland structures, Verwoerd's brainchild, were beginning to collapse as "independent" states – in some instances through the exposure of corruption, in others through the overthrow of ruling dynasties – ground to a standstill. In Natal, even though KwaZulu's Inkatha movement had opposed independence, something like open warfare developed between Inkatha and ANC supporters as each side attempted to build up its constituency in anticipation of an eventual redistribution of political power.

Paralysed by a manifest inability to keep his policies on course and in the face of a growing

This led to renewed violence in the new coloured and Indian constituencies when a general election was held in 1983. By then, the ability of black organisations to conduct effective resistance had markedly increased as industrial workers and resistance leaders in the townships began to act together.

The ANC, for its part, was now concentrating on building up its links with the international community, setting up missions in many parts of the world where the South African government was not represented, and even acquiring diplomatic recognition in some.

ABOVE: ANC supporters campaign for non-racial, democratic elections.

threat from a new Afrikaner right wing, P.W. Botha was forced out of office by a ministerial rebellion in September 1989. The future direction of the National Party was thus thrown into confusion on the eve of a general election which had been forced upon it by a deadlock with the Coloured House of Representatives arising out of the terms of the 1983 constitution.

Apartheid in reverse

Botha's mantle fell on the shoulders of the Transvaal leader of the National Party, Frederik Willem de Klerk, who won the 1989 white general election by an outright majority over opponents of both left and right after seeking a mandate for unspecified reform. Educated and confident, de Klerk was an example of a new generation of Afrikaners who came of age after the introduction of apartheid and began to question the very basis of the system they inherited.

Because he was known to be a supporter of narrow, white "group interests", many doubted his will to go for real change. But South Africa could no longer afford to maintain apartheid in an increasingly hostile world, with a weakened economy, and with a ruinously expensive war which had broken out on the South West African border against members of the South West African People's Organisation (SWAPO).

Opening the parliamentary session of 1990, de Klerk undertook to remove apartheid, promising sweeping reforms. He planned to move cautiously, consulting the ANC leadership step by step. On 11 February 1990 he unconditionally released Nelson Mandela, the last of the imprisoned ANC leaders, after he had served 27 years in jail. It was a momentous decision because it signalled to a world which had long regarded Mandela's imprisonment as a symbol of apartheid's evil that a milestone had been passed. Six weeks later de Klerk removed another source of international protest: he attended the independence celebrations as

"BLACK-ON-BLACK" VIOLENCE

During the 1980s and early '90s, parts of KwaZulu-Natal and Gauteng turned into battlegrounds as something like open warfare raged between members of the Zulu Inkatha movement (later, the Inkatha Freedom Party and the voice of Zulu nationalism) and the Xhosa-dominated UDF (sympathisers of the then-banned ANC).

Mostly, UDF-backed "civic" movements were fighting to discredit Inkatha councillors who had been elected under the unpopular local government legislation of 1983. Thankfully, this form of civil unrest has now declined almost to the point of non-existence.

South West Africa became Namibia, ending a deadlock that had lasted more than 40 years.

De Klerk found a willing negotiating partner in the pragmatic Mandela. Opening the South African Parliament in February 1990, he said the government wished to negotiate a new constitution with equal political rights for all. The ban on political opponents was lifted and the leaders of the liberation movements released from jail or allowed to return from exile.

The odd couple

Hopes for the country's future centred to a degree around de Klerk and Mandela – a fact the outside world recognised by awarding them jointly the 1993 Nobel Peace Prize.

After prolonged multi-party negotiations, South Africa's first democratic elections took place in April 1994. They were described by one official as "unmitigated chaos": many ballot papers went missing, while allegations of fraud and malpractice were rife. Yet millions of people who had never seen a ballot paper before queued for hours under a hot sun to cast their vote. Old women, some aged more than 100, were pushed in their wheelchairs to the booths. White women lined up alongside their maids. Archbishop Desmond Tutu danced a jig for the cameras after voting in Cape Town. A Johannesburg radio station played Louis Armstrong's

being accorded a state visit to Britain in 1996. At home, however, there were accusations of ANC corruption and authoritarianism, while the big question was how long the black majority would wait for the president to make good his promises to improve their economic wellbeing.

Transition

"The wheels of government grind slowly," was all Mandela would say. But at least they *were* grinding, and the transition to black majority rule – an event which only a few years before had seemed utterly improbable – had been achieved without the predicted bloodbath.

What a Wonderful World. After 342 years and 23 days, white rule had come to an end.

Despite the allegations of chicanery, the election was declared free and fair, and the ANC emerged with 62 percent of the vote. On 10 May 1994, Nelson Mandela, former prisoner 466/64, became president. F.W. de Klerk, meanwhile, became one of two vice-presidents.

The "marriage" between Mandela and de Klerk lasted until 1996, when de Klerk took the National Party out of government and into opposition. Mandela remained an international hero,

LEFT: a first-time voter proudly displays proof of her newly won democratic rights. **ABOVE:** the unlikely architects of a revolution: Mandela and de Klerk.

South Africans, white and black, had accomplished the miracle themselves, without the intervention of international tribunals or peacekeeping forces. Hope, although still fragile, had begun to bloom again.

But in 1999, the MP Patricia de Lille presented a dossier to parliament containing numerous allegations of bribery relating to a 60 billion rand arms deal. It was the prelude to a decade in which corruption and cronyism would haunt South African politics.

The ANC had been re-elected that year but Mandela retired to make way for his deputy, Mbeki. His presidency earned praise for sound macroeconomic management but criticism for its preoccupation with racial politics and its

Mandela

South Africa's first black president, and a giant of 20th century politics, Mandela dedicated his life to the fight against racial oppression

Born the son of a chief in 1918 in rural Qunu, Transkei (now the Eastern Cape), a member of the Thembu royal household, Nelson Rolihlahla Mandela first became involved in politics as a student at the University of Fort Hare. It was here

that he met Oliver Tambo, later to become the African National Congress's first president-in-exile.

After being expelled from Fort Hare for their role in student strikes, both young men moved to Johannesburg. Here, Mandela met Walter Sisulu, and the three – Tambo, Sisulu and Mandela – became key movers in ANC politics, helping to found the ANC Youth League in 1944. The League was extremely influential in pushing the ANC towards adopting a more radical stance on protest action, and, in particular, founding the 1952 Defiance Campaign, based largely on Gandhian principles of nonviolence. Mandela established (with Tambo) Johannesburg's first black law firm in 1952, and in 1958 he married Winnie Madikizela, a social worker.

When the ANC was banned in 1960, the organi-sation decided that the time for peaceful protest was over. Mandela went underground to form *Umkhonto we Sizwe* (the Spear of the People, commonly known as MK), and to organise a campaign of sabotage. Tambo left the country to re-establish the ANC in exile.

Mandela survived "underground" for 17 months, training as a guerrilla fighter in Algeria and visiting Britain and many African states in search of support for MK. He became famous for staying a step ahead of the police but his luck ran out in 1962 when he was caught in a police trap. His links with MK as yet unknown, he was charged with "leaving the country without permission" and given a five-year jail sentence. Then, in 1963, the police raided MK's Rivonia headquarters and discovered evidence of Mandela's role in the organisation. He and eight others were found guilty of plotting to overthrow the state and sentenced to life imprisonment. Mandela was sent to Robben Island.

Human rights

For the next 26 years, the ANC's leaders in exile struggled to keep the organisation active and united. They were helped in no small measure by Mandela's fame as an internationally respected leader and symbol for human rights, which grew the longer he remained in prison. After his release in 1990, Mandela went on to play a central role during the four long, troubled years of multi-party negotiations, which finally culminated in South Africa's first democratic elections in April 1994. On 10 May of that year he was inaugurated as South Africa's first black president, a position he held until his retirement at the next election in 1999.

In 1996, Mandela divorced his wife, Winnie, a loyal ANC member whose reputation had become increasingly tarnished by scandal, including a conviction for kidnapping. Two years later he married Graca Machel, widow of the former Mozambican president, and set about building himself a retirement home back in Qunu. In 2009, the UN general assembly declared his birthday, 18 July, "Nelson Mandela International Day".

Despite the problems his government had trying to implement an ambitious programme of reform, Mandela remained enormously popular throughout his term of office. He had come to be seen as the living embodiment of new, longed-for standards and values in post-apartheid South Africa, and his departure marked the passing of an era. ❏

LEFT: statue of Nelson Mandela in Johannesburg.

"quiet diplomacy" towards neighbouring Zimbabwe's autocratic president Robert Mugabe.

Mbeki was also accused of a tepid response to South Africa's biggest health crisis after he defied scientific opinion to question the link between HIV and Aids. His health minister, Manto Tshabalala-Msimang, notoriously suggested beetroot, lemon juice and garlic as potential Aids remedies. The government's inaction was blamed by a Harvard University study for resulting in 300,000 preventable deaths.

In April 2004, South Africa celebrated a decade of democratic rule as the ANC remained in power with a 70 percent majority. But in 2005, Mbeki fired his deputy president, Jacob Zuma, provoking an unexpected backlash within the ANC that would ultimately prove his undoing.

When, in 2008, a court ruled there was reason to believe that corruption charges against Zuma were politically motivated, Mbeki was blamed and his enemies seized their chance, forcing him to resign. Kgaleme Motlanthe became caretaker president before Zuma led the ANC to another victory in the 2009 election.

Unlike the intellectual Mbeki, Zuma was a self-taught populist who served time on Robben Island. He was also South Africa's first Zulu president and a polygamist who, by the end of 2010, had three wives after marrying a total of five times. Having previously been charged with and acquitted of rape, he became embroiled in a further scandal when it emerged he had fathered a child out of wedlock – believed to be his 20th overall.

World Cup

But it was Zuma who inherited the historic mantle of the 2010 FIFA World Cup, the first time sport's biggest showpiece had been hosted in Africa. Sceptics had questioned whether South Africa could complete stadiums on schedule, provide sufficient accommodation and transport and keep foreign visitors safe in a country plagued by violent crime.

The month-long football tournament was widely judged an extraordinary success. South Africans walked tall amid a surge of euphoria, racial unity and patriotic pride. Danny Jordaan, the chief World Cup organiser, said of the 11 June kick-off: "It was a day as big as when South

RIGHT: Cape Town stadium, one of several venues built for the 2010 FIFA World Cup.

For the 2010 FIFA World Cup, thousands took to the streets, singing and dancing and blowing the vuvuzela, a long, noisy plastic horn that became a worldwide phenomenon.

Africans cast their vote in the first democratic election." More than three million spectators attended the matches live and anecdotal evidence suggested that crime actually went down.

The event was credited with challenging centuries old perceptions of Africa as a "dark continent" of war, famine and chaos, but came

at a price: 38 billion rand, according to government figures. It also raised the bar of expectations for South Africans, and the honeymoon ended swiftly with a damanging public sector strike over wages.

In August 2010, Jackie Selebi, the former national police chief, was sentenced to 15 years in prison for taking bribes. It was a symbol of the culture of corruption, self-enrichment and ostentatious displays of wealth that, according to numerous media reports, continued to blight what had become the most unequal society in the world. The World Cup had shown South Africans what they were capable of; it also challenged them to turn the momentum into something that will endure. ❑

THE PERFORMING ARTS

Despite drastic cuts in subsidies to performing arts bodies,
a cultural renaissance is getting underway

The growth of indigenous theatre in South Africa has been inextricably linked to the country's harsh political realities. The 1980s, in particular, produced a wealth of "protest plays" focusing on the damaging social and psychological effects of apartheid. Unfortunately protest art loses its momentum once its cause is won.

Complexes such as the Market Theatre in Johannesburg, which became renowned as "the theatre of the struggle", built their reputations as avant-garde centres staging original works which reflected the lives and aspirations of all South Africans. It was a laborious process, often hampered by state censorship, but produced some memorable theatre that was exported to international stages.

Theatrical works

Actors and playwrights who succeeded abroad include Athol Fugard (*A Lesson from Aloes*) and the hugely successful partnership of John Kani and Winston Ntshona (collaborators with Fugard on *Sizwe Banzi Is Dead* and *The Island*) who were both honoured with American theatre's highest accolade, the Tony Award. An expatriate actor, Zakes Mokae, later won the award for his performance in Fugard's *Master Harold and the Boys*.

Often dubbed "the father of black theatre", Gibson Kente provided through his "theatre of the townships" numerous opportunities for aspiring writers and actors to become major stars. This provided the impetus for talented writers such as Mbongeni Ngema, Barney

PRECEDING PAGES: live music. **LEFT:** classical ballet.
RIGHT: modern drama.

NEW BOUNDARIES, FRESH TALENT

Local opera has seen a remarkable infusion of fresh talent since the early 1990s. Composer Bongani Ndodana-Breen's work is especially notable for the way it fuses divergent Western and African traditions – his 1998 opera-oratorio *Uhambo* (based on the epic poem by Guy Butler) deploys an *imbongi*, or praise singer, alongside a chamber orchestra and soloists. Also notable is Cape Town's Michael Williams, whose opera productions draw on a mix of Xhosa, Kenyan and North American Indian folklore. Roelof Temmingh's chamber operas also continue to win prizes both at home and abroad.

Simon and Percy Mtwa to take their trail-blazing production, *Woza Albert*, onto the international stage.

Works of the playwright Mbongeni Ngema have also been performed across the world. Ngema's *Asinamali* wound up on Broadway in 1987 and won a Tony nomination for best director. In 1988, he took his hit musical, *Sarafina*, (depicting students involved in the Soweto riots opposing apartheid) to New York's Lincoln Center Theatre and then to Broadway, where it played to capacity audiences for 11 months. *Sarafina* has also been made into a film starring Whoopie Goldberg.

The arts and the ANC

The end of apartheid has brought enormous changes to the performing arts. The ANC's developmental programme is focussed on housing, education, land redistribution, health and the general upliftment of the disadvantaged. Arts and culture funding continues but is not a major priority.

Opera, theatre and ballet are officially supported in the sense that venues such as Cape Town's Artscape Theatre Centre and Pretoria's State Theatre receive state subsidies. The South African Ballet Theatre, which runs educational outreach programmes in townships such as

SOUTH AFRICA ON SCREEN

Cinemas in South Africa are dominated by Hollywood imports, but recent years have brought a wave of indigenous films that have challenged, surprised and, on occasion, taken the world by storm.

Tsotsi (2005), winner of an Oscar for best foreign language film, is based on Athol Fugard's novel. It superbly humanises those on both sides of South Africa's fence: the middle-class suburbanites and the township gangsters.

The HIV/Aids epidemic has provided a natural subject for film makers, with the most notable being *Yesterday* (2004). Its portrayal of the horrific consequences of the disease is probably a more powerful advertisement for safe sex than any number of government health commercials.

In a sign of how far the country has come, *White Wedding* (2009) is a romantic comedy that encompasses South Africans of all types and encouraged them to laugh at themselves. But arguably the most breathtaking contribution has been *District 9* (2009), a science fiction thriller.

But the most successful South African film of all time has to be Leon Schuster's *Mr Bones* (2001, 2008) movies, slapstick comedies which have reached beyond an Afrikaner audience to tickle black, coloured and Indian cinemagoers. South Africa's film industry is not yet on a scale to match those of America, India or Nigeria, but the opening in 2010 of the Cape Town Film Studios, the first custom built Hollywood-style complex in Africa, bodes well for the future.

Soweto and Alexandra but faces continued difficulties to secure funding.

The breakdown of racial segregation is particularly evident in contemporary dance. The Moving into Dance Mophatong Performance Company was founded in 1978 to use dance as a form of cultural resistance to apartheid. It mounts exciting performances, indoors or outdoors, that often combine African dance, music and ritual with modern European forms. Among the brightest talents in South African dance today is Dada Masilo, who has choreographed and performed radical, sexy re-interpretations of *Carmen*, *Romeo and Juliet* and *Swan Lake*.

A stage beyond

With the struggle over, the Market Theatre has re-invented itself as a house largely for new writing by and about South Africans: township memoirs, stand-up comedy, political satires, physical performance and music. A production regularly staged there is *Nothing but the Truth*, written by and starring John Kani, which wrestles with the legacy of apartheid and the Truth and Reconciliation Commission.

A new generation of black playwrights is exploring identity politics, for example the dislocation between growing up in a township but aspiring to wear designer labels and live in a middle class suburb. One of the most exciting talents is Paul Grootboom, whose plays *Cards* and *Foreplay* deal explicity with issues such as prostitution and HIV/Aids.

Fugard, now based in California, has maintained a consistent output. His play *Valley Song* explores issues of individual, rather than simply political, discontent. Recent works such as *Victory* have been less critically successful but his 2010 play, *The Train Driver* (directed by Fugard himself), premiered at a new theatre bearing his name in Cape Town's historic District Six before transferring to London.

The Fugard Theatre was briefly home to the all-black company Isango Portobello, which grew from a township to perform award-winning interpretations of Mozart's *The Magic Flute* (*Impempe Yomlingo*) and *The Mysteries* (*Yiimi-*

mangaliso) in London's West End. The musical *Africa Umoja*, telling the story of the nation through song and dance, has also enjoyed successful international tours.

Celebrating a new tradition

Another more positive sign is the flourishing festival scene. Mother of all gatherings is the National Arts Festival – South Africa's equivalent of the Edinburgh Festival – which completely swamps the small Eastern Cape town of Grahamstown every June and July.

Apart from a packed programme from dance, theatre, music and opera to fine art, film, caba-

ret and jazz, it has craft fairs, flea markets, buskers galore and, of course, a Fringe.

Grahamstown may dominate, but an increasing number of smaller celebrations are now appearing on the festival calendar throughout the year. One of the best-known is the Klein Karoo Nasionale Kunstefees, begun in 1994 and based in Oudtshoorn, with open-air events from music and dance to drama and poetry.

Then there's the North West Cultural Calabash, a youth-based celebration of traditional African culture based in the peaceful village of Taung. Every September, visitors come to see the displays of traditional dancing (Tswana, Tsonga and Zulu-style) and to soak up the rural atmosphere. ❏

LEFT: a scene from the Oscar-winning film *Tsotsi*, a moving study of hope and redemption. **RIGHT:** the National Arts Festival is the biggest celebration of African arts on the continent.

A STORY OF SOUTH AFRICAN MUSIC

South African music has travelled the world, and along its journey has absorbed just about every form of music it has encountered, and created something unique

South Africa is distinguished by one of the richest musical histories and most complex profusion of styles on the continent, with a diversity ranging from Zulu *maskanda*, gospel, township *kwaito*, to African jazz and "bubblegum" pop. Centuries-old traditions have mixed with new genres to evolve into South Africa's unique soundtrack.

In the beginning

The nomadic Khoisan, the earliest human inhabitants of South Africa (*see page 35*) embraced music as part of their daily life. They created a variety of instruments from their natural environment; wind instruments from animal horns, flutes from reeds, stringed instruments using muscle sinew, and the *goma* (drum) from ox skins and aloe trunks. This was South Africa's first music. Women played the *goma* to summon the spirit world and men danced for the pleasure of the gods.

Rhythm and dance allowed them to reach a trance-like state to communicate with the spirits of their ancestors.

When the Portuguese explorer, Vasco da Gama landed at the Cape in 1497, a local Khoisan band treated the expedition to a performance on reed flutes.

Early influences

While most South African styles evolved against a backdrop of urban migration, the arrival of

Western colonisers (including the British, French, Portuguese and Dutch) and Christian missionaries in the 1800s also had a profound influence on musical styles. They brought with them classical music, but most influential was church hymn music, folk music and sailor's songs, most evident in the Cape Malay tradition of the Cape. Western instruments, such as the piano, concertinas, military drum and guitar were introduced and integrated into indigenous musical styles.

Many of these styles have found their way into more contemporary traditional music, such as *mbaqanga* and *marabi*, both urban township pop music styles (*see overleaf*).

LEFT: performer at the annual Cape Town Festival.
RIGHT: music is an intrisic part of ethnic identities.

Goema – the music of Cape Town

One of the styles that most obviously synthesises all of these influences is *goema*, a fusion of traditional South African music and Cape Town's carnival sound.

The carnival's roots go back to the 18th and 19th centuries and was the music of the slaves who adhered to their Islamic heritage. The Cape Malay community still predominates today in parts of Cape Town such as Bo-Kaap, and its music has marked Eastern characteristics.

The primary instruments are banjo, mandolin, double bass and tambourine, while the *goma* drum sets the carnival's addictive rhythm. The

colourful street parade is held every year and is a celebration of freedom. It's a mix of Brazilian Carnival and New Orlean's Mardi Gras and is a spectacular sight; the performers paint their faces and are clad in flamboyant, shiny suits and carry parasols; a tradition reminiscent of the travelling minstrel troupes of the early 1820s.

This festive spirit infuses Freshlyground, the biggest pop band of recent years. The seven-piece band hail from South Africa, Mozambique and Zimbabwe and draw on an array of diverse musical influences to create an infectious fusion of Afro-pop, rock and jazz, producing many dance-floor hits.

Most recently, symphonic innovations from Mac McKenzie (a Cape Town music legend),

> *Find great live music at the Bassline in Johannesburg, the BAT Centre in Durban, and the Assembly and Zula Bar in Cape Town. For multi-city music events, visit www.jhblive.com.*

with his Goema Symphony, have put *goema* into a whole new sphere. Traditional Khoisan bows, African mbira and marimba and Cape Malay banjo are part of the instrumentation.

Jazz

In the early 20th century, the movement of black labourers caused by the gold rush created rapid urbanisation. The expanding ghettoes of Johannesburg were to spawn this culture's most distinctive musical sound: *marabi*, which was played on pedal organs and keyboards in the illicit township *shebeens* (unlicensed bars) to get people dancing. The style, similar to American Dixieland and ragtime, quickly evolved and later, idioms from American swing were blended in by popular bandleaders. One of the developments of *marabi* was *kwela*, a jive street-dance played with a penny whistle. *Kwela* and *marabi* became the backbone of Johannesburg's jazz.

The rehearsal rooms at Dorkay House, on Eloff Street, became downtown Johannesburg's jazz haven, providing a platform for established players and a training ground for new ones. It was an island in the midst of cultural oppression and the incubator of brilliant artists such as Miriam Makeba and Abdullah Ibrahim *(see page 70)*, and the space where the jazz opera *King Kong* was created *(see below)*.

AN AFRICAN JAZZ OPERA

In 1959, South African township music first exploded onto the international stage with the hit musical *King Kong*. With a score by Sowetan pianist-composer Todd Matshikiza, it told the meteoric rise and fall of South African heavyweight boxing champion, Ezekiel Dhlamini, "King Kong". This slice of township life played to sell-out audiences, not only in South Africa, but in London and New York. It made stars locally and abroad of trumpeter **Hugh Masekela** *(see page 70)*, pianist **Abdullah Ibrahim**, saxophonist **Kippie Moeketsi** and singer **Miriam Makeba**. Large numbers of the cast used the show's London run as an opportunity to flee apartheid and go into exile.

Pop

A fusion of disco, house music, hip hop and R&B, *kwaito* emerged in the 1990s as the most definitive South African pop genre – a remix of the country's history in a global context. South Africa's greatest and most controversial pop star, Brenda Fassie mashed up "bubblegum" (the early 1980s synthesiser pop of South Africa), with elements of *kwaito* and even gospel to create her very own distinct style. In the late 1990s, Moses Molelekwa turned jazz on its head and before he died at age 28 he was on the verge of creating a whole new South African musical language. He introduced *kwaito*, the post-1994

Gospel

The biggest star of the 1990s gospel scene was Rebecca Malope, from Johannesburg. She has sold millions of records, is a major TV star, and has a huge following in other parts of Africa. Joyous Celebration is a massive touring gospel extravaganza that has generated more than 10 albums, and made stars out of performers like Jabu Hlongane.

Full circle

The story of South African music is one of the subversion and assimilation of different genres. Chris McGregor and The Brotherhood of Breath

pop uprising of South African youth music, as an element of his compositions, and dared to tread where established artists were too nostalgic to go. Boomshaka, the earliest *kwaito* stars, had rousing R&B and gospel tendencies, while more recently, Brothers of Peace have incorporated jazz into their rap-*kwaito* fusion.

Kwaito's dance beat has roots in many styles including *mbaqanga*, a Zulu pop-style originating in the townships, and taken to the world stage by Mahlatini and the Mahotella Queens. *Maskanda* also features in the mix, a rural folk music made hip by the late Busi Mhlongo.

became exiles in Europe and fundamentally shifted European jazz through their innovations in avant-garde jazz. Traditional South African music turned pop on its head with the collaboration of Ladysmith Black Mambazo and Paul Simon on his *Graceland* album. In the YouTube and Facebook era, the rap-rave group Die Antwoord took foul-mouthed-prison-slang-Afrikaans-Xhosa electronica global, and it lead them to a deal with American major label Interscope.

The varied strands of South African music have combined to create a new music alive with the traditions of the past. It's come almost full circle, with the earliest music travelling the world and returning millenia later to be reinfused with a uniquely South African signature. ❑

LEFT: jazz musician, Cape Town. **ABOVE:** top jazz venue, the Green Dolphin.

ICONIC MUSIC

South Africa's diverse music scene has produced many innovative artists who have made their name on the international stage

The grandfather of world music, **Hugh Masekela** (*right*) is as iconic a South African musician as you can get. He's been the drugged out bad boy of jazz and the South African Minister of Arts and Culture. His single *Grazing in the Grass* was one of the biggest hits of 1960s America, selling millions of copies. He co-produced the legendary Rumble in the Jungle concert in Kinshasa for the boxing bout between George Foreman and Muhamed Ali.

South Africa's greatest star ever, **Miriam Makeba**, or Mama Africa, opened the door for South African music internationally, recording with artists like Harry Belafonte (with whom she won a Grammy), Paul Simon, Dizzy Gillespie and Nina Simone. She was as well known for her political activism as her music: she twice lobbied the United Nations for support against apartheid South Africa, and across Africa she was revered by liberation governments for her role as an ambassador of human rights.

Before his conversion to Islam, **Abdullah Ibrahim** was known as Dollar Brand because as a youngster he would buy a records from the passing sailors in Cape Town, for a dollar a time. His wife Sathima Benjamin introduced him to Duke Ellington when they were in exile in Switzerland, kick-starting an international career that would eventually make him one of the world's most revered jazz musicians. His song *Manenberg* became an anti-apartheid anthem in the mid 1970s and he has become known in recent times for his work with European orchestras. One of the few artists of his era still composing original works, he remains one of the most prolific, with some 160 albums released.

RIGHT: also known as *Le Zulu Blanc*, Johnny Clegg has long been the great cross-over South African artist; songs like *Impi* are sung with anthemic reverence by black and white fans alike. Across a s career and those of his two bands, first Juluka and then Savuka, Clegg has released some 20 albums and continues to tour today.

BELOW: multicultural Afro pop band Freshlyground collaborated with superstar Shakira on the official 2010 FIFA World Cup anthem and w an MTV Europe award for Best African Act – a South African first.

LEFT: "Madonna of the townships" Brenda Fassie was a hitmaker across Africa. At her death in 2004 she was the best-selling South African artist of all time.

COLLECTORS ALBUMS

• *Manenberg* by Abdullah Ibrahim (The Sun Records, South Africa). A classic South African album, Manenberg quickly became an anthem in 1970s apartheid South Africa.
• *Miriam Makeba* by Miriam Makeba (RCA Victor, USA) *(above)*. Featuring the international hit *The Click Song* (*Qongqothwane* in Xhosa), this was Makeba's debut solo album, produced by Harry Belafonte, and one of the first world music albums.
• *King Kwela* by Spokes Mashiyane (Celluloid, France). A reissue of Mashiyane's classic 1958 album, featuring up-tempo rhythmic jives.
• *The Lion Roars* by Mahlathini and the Mahotella Queens (Shanachie, USA). Culled from the glory days of the 1960s and 1970s and featuring *mbaqanga* king Simon Nkabinde.
• *Verse One* by the Jazz Epistles (Celluloid, France), featuring Dollar Brand, Hugh Masekela, Kippie Moeketsi and Jonas Gwangwa.

BELOW: Die Antwoord ("the answer") was the first South African act to go big via YouTube, and with incredible speed. Their debut single *Enter the Ninja* is one of the most viewed clips on the website. It was not, however, overnight success. Band leader Waddy Tudor Jones had been reinventing himself for more than a decade before *Die Antwoord* went global.

LEFT: Ladysmith Black Mambazo have recorded with Stevie Wonder, Paul Simon, Ben Harper and Josh Groban, amongst others, and featured on *The Lion King* soundtrack. After 45 years, and more than 50 album and DVD releases, they are still touring furiously.

THE CHANGING FACE OF ART

Its landscapes have fired imaginations for millennia. Now South Africa's vexed history and unique cultural mix are proving fertile ground for a new generation

The art of southern Africa dates back to pre-history and, it has been argued, represents the human race's longest artistic tradition. San rock art developed from this time right up to the second half of the 19th century. The paintings and engravings of the San people are found mainly in the Drakensberg and its extension from the Eastern Cape to Lesotho and Swaziland, as well as in the mountains of Limpopo province and sites on the inland plateau along the Vaal and Orange rivers. The sensitive depictions of animals and human figures painted and engraved in rock shelters are thought to be shamanistic and a link between the real world and the spirit world. There are over 15,000 documented sites in South Africa.

Western influences

The influence of Western painters and art arrived alongside early explorers. The names of 19th century chroniclers including Thomas Baines (1820–75), Fredrick I'Ons (1802–87) and Thomas Bowler (1812–69) are all synonymous with early South African painting.

Europe's influence remained strong as the Dutch tradition of landscape painting predominated, thanks to settlers such as Frans Oerder (1867–1944) and Pieter Wenning (1873–1921). They also helped establish South African-born painters J.E.A. Volschenk (1853–1936) and Hugo Naude (1869–1941), as well as artists who reflected the British and French Impressionist landscape tradition, such as Robert Gwelo Goodman (1871–1938).

Anton van Wouw (1862–1945) is commonly

regarded as the father of modern Western sculpture in South Africa. A Dutchman who arrived in 1890, van Wouw's work followed a descriptive realist tradition.

Moses Kottler (1896–1977) and Lippy Lipshitz (1903–80) followed a carving tradition, as did later artists such as Elsa Dziomba (1902–70) and Lucas Sithole (1931–94).

The influence of Expressionism reached the country in the 1920s when Irma Stern (1904–66) and Maggie Laubscher (1886–1973) returned from studies in Germany. The 1930s saw the New Group set out to explore progressive ideals. Gregoire Boonzaier (1909–2005), Terence Mac-Caw (1913–76) and Walter Battiss (1906–82) led

LEFT: mosaic in the Guga S'Thebe cultural centre.
RIGHT: landscape painter.

the break away from what they perceived to be amateurism in South African art.

Among the most prominent black artists of the early 1940s were Gerard Sekoto (1913–93), who left to live in Paris in 1947; Ernest Mancoba (1904–2002); and George Pemba (1912–2001).

Township art

Post-war developments saw a move towards abstract art theories current in Europe and the United States, but also present was a growing body of black urban artists.

Their subject matter of crowded townships and distorted expressive human figures became

known as "township art".

Mslaba Dumile (1939–91) is the best-known exponent of this genre, with Ephraim Ngatane (1938–71) another outstanding talent. Black sculptors such as Sydney Kumalo (1935–90) and Michael Zondi (1926–2008) became, together with Dumile, South Africa's first international black artists.

A further attempt to combine a European approach and African symbolism took place during the 1960s with artists such as Edoardo Villa (b. 1920), Giuseppe Cattaneo (b. 1929) and Cecil Skotnes (1926–2009) featuring prominently. The 1970s saw the rise of protest art. Despite the country's enforced cultural isolation, black artists such as Leonard Matsoso (b.

> *Among the most original black artists was Jackson Hlungwani, who liked to sit under an avocado tree in a remote village carving wood sculptures that drew on religious cosmology and are now in collections around the world.*

1949) and Ezrom Legae (1938–99) still achieved international recognition.

A new generation of artists – including William Kentridge (b. 1955), Penny Siopis (b. 1953) and Keith Dietrich (b. 1950) – came to prominence in the mid-1980s and have used a figurative style in their interpretation of contemporary events. The phenomenon of formally untrained rural artists finding their way into the mainstream of South African art can be traced to the 1985 BMW exhibition, *Tributaries*. Black sculptors from the Venda area in Limpopo province were introduced to the urban art world. Among the most original is Jackson Hlungwani (1923–2010).

People's art

The 1980s witnessed the emergence of a spontaneous public art known as "people's parks". Here, symbols of work such as tools were juxtaposed in sculptures with common junk, maps of Africa and home-made wooden weapons.

The post-apartheid era has seen the introduction – for the first time in South Africa's history – of a ministry with an arts and culture portfolio. The country now boasts 5,500 full or part-time artists, and in 2009, Riason Naidoo became the first non-white individual to be appointed director of the National Gallery.

Cape Town and Johannesburg in particular are now home to a variety of galleries including the latter's experimental Arts on Main, forming part of urban regeneration efforts in the previously unfashionable downtown. Exciting talents to watch include Lerato Shadi, a visual performance artist, and Mary Sibande, whose striking work has been displayed on giant billboards that turned Johannesburg city centre into a public gallery.

With more local artists being represented overseas in exhibitions focussing specifically on South African art, the place of the country's artists on the international art scene finally seems assured. ❑

LEFT: township art.

The First Artists

The paintings and engravings of the San hold deep spiritual and religious meaning

South Africa is home to the largest collection of Stone Age art in the world. Scattered throughout the interior of the country are more than 150,000 rock paintings and engravings created by the San hunter-gatherers, who first made their mark in southern Africa about 40,000 years ago.

This art has an occult significence, representing the San's strong identification with the animals they hunted. Some of the finest paintings depict eland hunts. The eland, largest of the African antelopes, was regarded as having supernatural powers and was the San's special link with the Godhead.

Another common theme is trance dancing, performed by the clan's shaman in order to activate a supernatural potency which would transform him and allow him to enter the spirit world.

Spirit world

Shamans entering the spirit world experienced a variety of physical and visual hallucinations, a state depicted in their art by such metaphors as "being underwater". "Death" is another, because there were certain similarities between a shaman entering a trance and, for example, a dying eland – both bled at the nose, frothed at the mouth, stumbled about and eventually collapsed unconscious.

Once in the spirit world, it was the shaman's task to cure the sick, resolve social conflict and control the movement of herds of game, including the mysterious "rain animal". Such "work" guaranteed the continued existence of San society.

The paintings and engravings depicting trance dances and the symbols of supernatural power were a means by which the shamans tried to communicate what they had undergone to their peers.

Historical events and observations of the newcomers who encroached on the San's living space were also recorded. Nguni warriors and cattle, Khoikhoian fat-tailed sheep, European settlers on horseback with rifles, ships and uniformed soldiers were all captured in surprising detail.

RIGHT: remote caves record the beginnings of the world's artistic heritage.

Sadly, the San way of life did not survive the arrival of the white man. When the hunter-gatherers who had lived in perfect ecological harmony with their environment for so many thousands of years saw the vast herds of game cut down by the settlers' guns, they launched fierce retaliatory raids. But their bows and arrows were no match for guns. The San were hunted from their lands like vermin; and today a few scattered artefacts and the rock-art sites are virtually all that remain of their culture.

Carbon-dating has shown the rock-art sites range in age from about 20,000 years to about 100 years old. However, many prime works are at remote sites which are difficult to access.

Some of the most vivid and detailed paintings are in the uKhahlamba-Drakensberg mountain range. The Giant's Castle Game Reserve has a good site near the guest chalets, and another at the Sunday's Falls Christmas Cave in the Game Pass Valley, near the south end of the reserve. The Cavern and The Stream shelter in the Cathedral Peak area are also well-known and accessible.

In the Cape, the area around Queenstown has some excellent sites, as does Barkly East. There is a 105ft (32-metre) long gallery of paintings on the Denorbin farm, between Elliot and Barkly East, which may be viewed. Driekopseiland, which lies on the banks of the Riet River near Kimberley, is one of the largest and best-known sites with over 3,500 engraved images. ❏

CARVING OUT A UNIQUE EXPRESSION

From contemporary Western to distinctly African trends, from watercolours to wooden masks, artists draw on an eclectic range of styles and forms

During the 1980s, the fight against apartheid reached its peak. For many artists, playwrights, writers and musicians the act of creation became a political one. This cultural struggle was symbolised by images of defiance, painted on walls, recited from stages and printed on T-shirts and badges. Art became a weapon of the struggle to make people aware of the realities of South African society under apartheid.

A New Medium

What made this aspect of the cultural struggle so successful was its accessibility to a broader public, a public not used to seeing art unless it was hung upon gallery walls or displayed in highbrow journals. Coffee mugs, table placemats, badges and walls – even freight containers like the one pictured above – had become the new medium for the anti-apartheid message. A host of collectives (of which the best-known were Cape Town's Community Arts Project and Johannesburg's Thupelo Arts Project) were set up to provide the necessary skills. Along with the ELC Art and Craft Centre in Rorke's Drift, KwaZulu-Natal – founded in 1962 to provide training in artistic ceramics, textiles and weaving – these have become the cornerstone of a thriving independent crafts industry. From the voluble market traders of Rosebank, Johannesburg, to the beaders and potters of remote rural villages, South Africans are defining an identity distinctly their own.

ABOVE: tightly woven baskets, a Zulu speciality.

BELOW: an artisan at work at Ethno Bongo (Hout Bay), known for exotic fashion jewellery and hand made accessories.

BELOW: townships tours throw up many surprises including this mosaic at the Guga S'Thebe cultural centre in Langa, Cape Town.

LEFT: one for the mantelpiece? Unusual contemporary, African-inspired design at Tribal Trends on Long Street in the heart of Cape Town's tourist district.

ART COLLECTIONS AND GALLERIES

Innocence, by George Velaphi Mzimba. This Soweto-born artist made his mark in the 1980s with exhibitions in South Africa, Northern Ireland, Canada and the USA. His work is currently available through the Everard Read Gallery in Rosebank, Johannesburg (tel: 011-788 4805; www.everard-read.co.za), one of the best commercial galleries in the country.

Other places to seek out the best in black art are:
• Gallery MOMO, 52 7th Avenue, Parktown North, Johannesburg (tel: 011-327 3247; www.gallerymomo.com), is a contemporary gallery representing local and international artists. A 2010 group exhibition featured Theresa-Anne Mackintosh, Rodney Place, Lyndi Sales, Mary Sibande and Ransome Stanley.
• The De Beers Centenary Art Gallery, in the Centre for Cultural Studies at Fort Hare University (tel: 040-602 2277; www.ufh.ac.za) in Alice, Eastern Cape, spans works by pioneer painters such as George Pemba to more modern artists such as Sydney Khumalo. A collection with a strong emphasis on social realism.
• The South African National Gallery, in Company's Garden, Cape Town (tel: 021-467 4660; www.iziko.org.za/sang) has, since 1990, focused on contemporary South African art including beadwork and sculpture, as well as repatriating artefacts removed in past centuries.

ABOVE: *Made in South Africa* by Gauteng artist David Koloane.

LEFT: *The Shepherd* by Ezrom Legae, 1995.

ABOVE: the Iziko South African National Gallery in Cape Town.

LEFT: Andy Warhol couldn't have done it better. Nelson Mandela's mass-produced image is everywhere when shoppers seek curios at the Victoria and Alfred Waterfront in Cape Town.

LITERATURE

Freed from the constraints of the apartheid years, fiction writers are engaged in a search for compelling new themes

The first European literature to deal with the South African experience was Portuguese. A significant part of Portugal's national epic, Luís de Camões' *The Lusiads* of 1572, deals with the early navigators' records of rounding the formidable Cape of Storms. Here the African landmass is portrayed as a hostile and dark giant, threatening to all but the most heroic Christian adventurers. He is given a mythological name, Adamastor, and a part of his body is Table Mountain that guards the entry to the land.

After the settlement of the Dutch there in 1652, the written records of the Cape are mostly in diary form. During the 18th century, this small enclave had a considerable reputation in Europe as a botanical paradise, and several travellers' records portray its slave-holding milieu. Inland over the frontier was an explorer's playground, of which a boastful adventurer like François le Vaillant could in 1795 publish his highly exaggerated accounts. Nevertheless, the travelogue of the Enlightenment included detailed records of the life and customs of indigenous peoples, together with colourful accounts of hunting big game.

British tradition

From the 1820s, with the British colonisation of southern Africa, a systematic literature began with the introduction of the press. On the Eastern frontier, the first Xhosa-language newspaper began in the 1840s, more or less at the time the emancipation of slaves became general. Missionary endeavour on many fronts, while translating the Bible, preserved the first accounts we have of the earliest oral literature in Xhosa, Zulu, Tswana and Sotho.

THE WORLD OF CAN THEMBA
edited by Essop Patel

The even older poetry and folklore of the Khoisan peoples was first taken down and translated by the German philologist Wilhelm Bleek, whose collection for the South African Library in Cape Town has not yet been exhausted by scholars. The San and Khoikhoi provide us in their mythology and history with an absorbing account of the European conqueror from their perspective.

The British frontier produced two types of writing which persist even today. Thomas Pringle (1789–1834) introduced a high-flown, romantic style of poetry, starting a tradition which stays in touch with European models, while Andrew Geddes Bain (1797–1864) began a stream of popular songs and satires which

A black writer, Sol T. Plaatjie (1876–1932), started to reformulate the Haggard-Schreiner heritage, making it sympathetic to a portrayal of black history that white writers had tended to ignore or even destroy.

The works of many South African writers have tended to dwell on the burning racial and political issues that have confronted the country. But in the writings of Sir Laurens van der Post (1906–96), such debates, if they have arisen at all, have played only a subordinate role. The essence of *The Lost World of the Kalahari* (1958), his famous book and documentary film on the San, or his gripping adventure tales, such as *Flamingo Feather, A Story like the Wind* (1972) and its sequel *A Far-Off Place* (1974), is far more the enduring culture of southern Africa's indigenous peoples and the mysteries of the vast landscape in which they live.

used the far more earthy language of the marketplace. In Bain's polyglot work we find early forms of Afrikaans, the African language that was to develop from Dutch, as well as English, French and German (the languages of the early settlers), Malay and various African languages.

Continuing the Pringle line of high culture, we have by 1883 the publication of the novel *The Story of an African Farm*. It was the first work that gave a realistic and credible portrait of the conditions of daily life on an establishment in the Karoo and of the cruel and difficult society, with its educational, commercial and religious institutions, on which it depended. The author, Olive Schreiner (1855–1920), was the daughter of a German missionary and his English wife but considered herself one of the first South Africans, owing her inspiration to the modern nation she was so influential in building.

Adventure novels

The other popular stream of writing in the late 19th century was particularly productive and successful. With the appeal of British imperialism at its height, many earlier forms became concentrated in the adventure romance. In the hands of an exponent like H. Rider Haggard (1856–1925), this new genre created one of the first modern bestsellers: *King Solomon's Mines* (1885). What is so memorable about his original adventures is the skilful way Haggard wrote them. He used an endearing, self-effacing narrator, Allan Quatermain, who was a professional hunter, settled in Durban, always willing to guide newcomers into the interior of Africa. One must remember that it had not been so long since David Livingstone had set off from the Northern Cape to find the inland Okavango Swamps of Botswana and then the great Central Lakes of Africa, nor since Burton and Speke had located the source of the Nile.

The black experience

Parts of this fiction-writing tradition are uniquely African. Magical Bessie Head (1937–86), was able to recover whole areas of the black experience from oral sources. These she converted into short stories that, while remaining African in spirit, are very familiar to white readers – *The Collector of Treasures* (1977) is a good example.

Those unfamiliar with South African writing should, however, beware of making simplistic distinctions between black and white writing. Throughout the 20th century, the great theme of South African fiction writers was precisely that relationship between races. The best example of this is Alan Paton's *Cry,*

LEFT: the work of Can Themba, the legendary chronicler of life in 1950s Soweto. **RIGHT:** H. Rider Haggard's *King Solomon's Mines* was an instant success.

the Beloved Country (1948), still the widest-read South African work of all time.

Afrikaans writing

Poetry in modern South Africa has also proved a distinguished area of its literature, particularly in Afrikaans. Indeed, it is through their poetry that many Afrikaans-language artists have shaped their tongue as a written language. Eugene N. Marais (1871–1936), a founder of lyric verse in Afrikaans, was also a respected naturalist whose classic works such as *The Soul of the Ape* (1969) helped to raise the science of zoological observation into an art form.

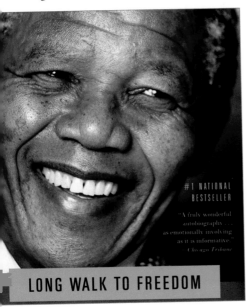

#1 NATIONAL
BESTSELLER

"A truly wonderful autobiography... as emotionally involving as it is informative."
Chicago Tribune

LONG WALK TO FREEDOM

Another Afrikaans-language poet is C. Louis Leipoldt (1880–1947). He wrote in several languages, mostly about Rhenish mission settlements which were such a feature of the Western Cape. An overt form of political expression later matured in the work of poets such as N.P. van Wyk Louw and Dirk Opperman. In the 1960s a younger generation of writers – led by Breytenbach, Brink and Etienne Leroux – emerged, and their work represented a drastic departure from the conventional Afrikaans tradition.

Modern trends

During the apartheid era, when many artists were driven into exile in Europe and the USA, autobiography became particularly rewarding among black writers. Peter Abrahams in 1954 published *Tell Freedom,* the first of many such works to recount the life histories of black people. *Down Second Avenue* (1959) by Es'kia Mphahlele is another important example of a black man's story of climbing out of a disadvantaged world of poverty and illiteracy to be educated and ultimately achieve the status of self-made writer. Nelson Mandela's *Long Walk to Freedom* (1995) is still a global bestseller.

Many contemporary novelists still concentrate on themes that explore the painfully oppressive past – for example, the bestselling *A Smell of Apples* (1993) by Mark Behr, the story of a white boy growing up in the militaristic 1960s and 1970s – but the enormous political changes that have swept South Africa since 1994 are also making their impact on the literary scene.

At the forefront of the new generation of post-apartheid writers is Zakes Mda, whose prize-winning novel about a professional mourner, *Ways of Dying* (1997) explores modern attitudes to traditional culture from a black point of view. The same theme informs Mda's more recent novels *The Heart of Redness* (2001) and *The Madonna of Excelsior* (2003), while *Black Diamond* (2009) is a witty take on South African stereotypes.

Writers are increasingly looking beyond the country's shores: Damon Galgut's novel *In a Strange Room* (2010) is based on his experiences travelling the world and was shortlisted for the UK's Man Booker Prize, while Craig Higginson's *Last Summer* (2010) is a story of thespians in Stratford-upon-Avon.

Other landmark novels include Patricia Schonstein's surreal *Time of Angels* (2003), set in present-day Cape Town, and Ivan Vladislavic's *The Restless Supermarket* (2002), which explores how the Johannesburg suburb of Hillbrow transformed from a chic café society of European immigrants to a melting pot for refugees from all over Africa.

An author cannot write about South Africa without writing about life's great themes: oppression, conquest, defeat, struggle, pride and success. So it should be no surprise that the country's modern writers come feted with honours, none more so than Nadine Gordimer and J.M. Coetzee, winners of the Nobel Prize for Literature in 1991 and 2003 respectively. ❏

LEFT: essential reading: Mandela's autobiography.

Nobel Prize Winners

While Nadine Gordimer has often explored the theme of commitment to political action, she sees herself as first and foremost a novelist

When Nadine Gordimer was awarded the Nobel Prize for Literature in 1991, approval reflected acclaim for her two life-long preoccupations: the craft of writing, and the evil of apartheid.

Born in 1923 in the small mining town of Springs, east of Johannesburg, Gordimer had an atypical childhood. Her father was a Jewish watchmaker from Lithuania; her mother English. More significantly for her development as a writer, her mother took her out of school at the age of 11 on the pretext of a heart ailment, keeping her at home until she was 16.

The young Gordimer developed a passion for reading and writing. She published her first short story at the age of 13, and her first novel, the auto-biographical *The Lying Days*, in 1953. Subsequently, as well as building up a considerable reputation as a writer of fiction, Gordimer has become known as a tireless worker for, and advocate of, free expression in South Africa.

The Nobel Prize is the most illustrious of a series of awards dating back to 1961, when Gordimer won the W.H. Smith Literary Award for her short story collection, *Friday's Footprint* (1960). Others include the Benson Medal from the Royal Society of Literature and the French international award, the Grand Aigle d'Or. Her 1974 novel, *The Conservationist*, was joint winner of the Booker Prize in the UK.

Social comment

Despite her formidable international reputation, Gordimer is somewhat underrated in her own country. Her refusal to submit her fiction to revolutionary sloganeering alienated her from many black commentators, and in the 1960s and 1970s she was also criticised for choosing not to follow other intellectuals into exile.

Post-apartheid, Gordimer continues to record and comment on the turbulent present with steely resolve. While much of her early fiction dealt with

RIGHT: Nadime Gordimer, just one of South Africa's Nobel Prize winners.

the impasse created by white supremacy, her more recent works deal with the complexities of a society in transition. Her 1994 novel, *None to Accompany Me*, explores with a ruthlessly honest eye the changes that occur within the individual.

What surprises many overseas visitors is Gordimer's relative lack of popularity among white South Africans. The chief reason for this is that readers satisfied with Wilbur Smith's bestselling blend of salacity, racial mastery and romance find Gordimer's work rather heavy going, uncomfortable, even unpalatable reading.

Still, Gordimer's writing remains accessible by comparison to the dense, ascetic prose that char-

acterises the novels of the enigmatic Afrikaans winner of the 2003 Nobel Prize for Literature. Cape Town-born J.M. Coetzee's early work, like that of Gordimer, explores the iniquities of apartheid, or a system remarkably like it. Published in 1983, the Booker-winning *Life & Times of Michael K* is arguably Coetzee's finest novel, though *Disgrace*, which secured him the Booker again in 1999 is just as compelling.

Finally, if these two fine novelists do interest you, then don't miss out on Andre Brink, a prolific and insightful Afrikaans writer who at his finest – the historical *Chain of Voices* and *Rumours of Rain*, the more contemporary *Dry White Season* and *Act of Terror* – cuts to the complex core of what makes white South Africa tick. ❑

ARCHITECTURE

The built environment reflects a rich cultural diversity – as
well as exposing the country's stark economic contrasts

South Africa's architecture reflects the country's distinctly different climatic zones, the cultural diversity of its people and, not least, the stark economic contrasts pervading every aspect of life.

The oldest surviving building in South Africa, the Castle of Good Hope in Cape Town, was built in 1666. Archaeological research in Limpopo Province and Mpumalanga, however, has uncovered several important stone ruins that predate white settlement at the Cape. Most notable is Mapungubwe Hill, which lies at the confluence of the Limpopo and Shashi rivers, and has been accorded both national park and Unesco World Heritage Site status. Constructed c. AD 950, Mapungubwe was the capital of a gold-mining civilisation that entered into regular trade with coastal Swahili ports such as Sofala, and reached its architectural apex with the construction of Great Zimbabwe (in the country of the same name) in around AD 1300.

Cape Dutch style

In response to local conditions of climate and availability of materials the 17th-century settlers of the Cape developed the Cape Dutch style, a truly vernacular architecture.

Characterised by a pitched thatched roof, a decorative gable, whitewashed walls and a symmetrical facade with shuttered rectangular windows, the early Cape Dutch houses were often built in the shape of a T; later, the larger H-plan design became more popular. A fine example is Groot Constantia near Cape Town, the homestead and wine farm built for Dutch governor

LEFT: Cape Dutch building, Stellenbosch. **RIGHT:** brilliant colour brightens a street in Khayelitsha.

Simon van der Stel in 1685. The homestead's decorative pediment was added in 1778 by German sculptor, Anton Anreith.

Other important historic buildings in Cape Town are the Tuynhuys, built in 1700, and today used as the State President's office and residence, the Old Slave Lodge (now the South African Cultural History Museum), the Old Town House on Greenmarket Square, and the South African Library.

After a hugely destructive fire in 1736, thatching was strongly discouraged in Cape Town. As a result, a new house type featuring a flat roof and – sometimes – a decorative wavy parapet became common. The oldest surviving examples are now found in the city's Malay Quarter, the Bo-Kaap. These simple one-storey buildings originally housed the fishermen, labourers and tradesmen who had come to the Cape as slaves. This district also houses the country's first official mosque, the Auwal, built in 1798. Only a few original walls survive.

As the frontiers of European settlement pressed northwards, a derivative of the Cape Dutch vernacular developed in the harsh, arid interior. The Karoo house is a flat-roofed yet pedimented building with a *stoep* (porch) and later a veranda. In the Northern Cape, early 18th-century Boer settlers responded to the scarcity of wood by building hut-like structures of corbelled stone, some of which survive in the towns of Williston and Carnarvon.

The British influence

In the 1820s, British settlers arrived in the Eastern Cape, an area previously occupied by Boer farmers. A vernacular architecture soon developed around Grahamstown, fusing the building traditions of the Cape with those of the settlers. Stone was more readily available here than in Cape Town, which led to Grahamstown's characteristic unplastered stone buildings with slate or shale roofs, some of which also have decorative open trelliswork. In Port Elizabeth, the British influence manifests itself architecturally in terraced houses with elegant Georgian and Regency verandas.

KwaZulu-Natal: an exotic blend

The cities of Durban and Pietermaritzburg also have a pronounced British architectural character, even though the province was settled before 1839 by Voortrekkers. Trees for firing kilns were plentiful in this subtropical region, facilitating the making of bricks and consequently construction with face brick. Pietermaritzburg, in particular, is famous for its Victorian salmon-coloured brick buildings with corrugated-iron roofs and pretty filigreed verandas.

In the late 19th century, the economic impact of the growing mining industry resulted in a remarkable building boom, epitomised by the monumental structure of Durban's City Hall (now accommodating the post office), built in 1884 by Philip Dudgeon in a Classical style.

Yet the city's architectural uniqueness stems from the local Asian population. Well-preserved Hindu temples are scattered throughout the Asian districts, while the city centre boasts the gigantic Grey Street mosque.

Modernism, Gauteng-style

Just as the cities of Cape Town and Durban each have their own unique architectural character, the same is true for South Africa's third major urban centre: Gauteng. At its heart lies Johannesburg, a cosmopolitan industrial centre whose growth and wealth were originally closely connected to the mining industry. Nearby is the smaller, much more provincial city of Pretoria, crowned by Herbert Baker's majestic Union Buildings (1912).

STARK STYLE

Apartheid's heyday, from the 1960s to the 1980s, saw an architectural attitude that defied South Africa's international isolation. Every major city centre proudly has a number of stark office tower blocks and public buildings, epitomised by prestigious German-American architect Helmut Jahn's tower in Johannesburg's Diagonal Street (1982), assertively competing with the architectural achievements of the rest of the world. And every town, whatever its size, has at least one Dutch Reformed church in a brutal brick and steel design, rearing a relentlessly modern spire against the bright blue sky.

Both cities have some fine examples of the architecture of the Modernist movement. A new period in South African architectural history began when the International Style first took hold at the University of the Witwatersrand in Johannesburg, under the guidance of Rex Martienssen. In Pretoria, architects like Norman Eaton made significant contributions towards the development of a regional style, adapting Modernism to local conditions.

African vernacular

In the rural areas of KwaZulu-Natal, the original Zulu beehive hut of intricately woven grass methods and decoration are still traditionally African.

The most splendid examples of African vernacular architecture are produced by the Ndebele people. These buildings have a complex system of courts and forecourts, reflecting the social hierarchy that structures both family and community.

However, the Ndebele are most famous for their ingenious way of assimilating influences from other cultures, creating a strong identity of their own in the process. This is particularly evident in the colourful decoration of their houses. ❏

has disappeared. In remote parts, a closely related type can still be found, consisting of a low wattle-and-daub cylinder with a dome-like beehive roof. Most common today, however, is the cone-on-cylinder type, often built with modern materials, or Western-influenced rectangular houses.

In rural Free State, beautifully decorated South Sotho homes are still frequent. Their rectangular shape with low mono-pitch roofs reveal Western influences, but construction

LEFT: the imposing granite structure of the Voortrekker Monument, just outside Pretoria. **ABOVE:** a covering of intricately woven thatch ensures these Zulu homes stay cool during the summer.

SUPER STADIA

The 2010 FIFA World Cup provided impetus for the construction or renovation of ten football stadia countywide, from Rustenburg and Polokwane to Durban and Port Elizabeth. Soweto's FNB Stadium, the country's largest, was upgraded with a design resembling a calabash pot, while curvaceous Cape Town Stadium was built from scratch alongside the old Green Point Stadium, and it now dominates the view over Table Bay from Signal Hill. Somewhat controversially, in a country where millions lack proper housing, the total cost of these stadia to the South African taxpayer has been estimated at 40 billion rand.

FOOD

From hearty Dutch cooking with subtle Malay influences,
to Indian curries and traditional African stews,
the national cuisine is a delicious mix

Remarkable yet true: the initial reason for European settlement in South Africa was culinary. Holland's domination of the East Indies' spice islands created heavy sea traffic past the Cape in the mid-17th century, and after three months at sea, crews would stop in Table Bay to take on fresh water from Table Mountain. This situation was formalised in 1652, when Jan van Riebeeck was charged with establishing a Dutch victualling station below Table Mountain; the vegetable garden he started still exists in the form of a park at the top of Cape Town's Adderley Street.

As the primitive settlement grew first into a seaside village, then into a town, hearty and wholesome Dutch cooking held sway. Gradually culinary ideas from the East Indies were introduced. Stews were enhanced by cloves, cinnamon, pimiento, turmeric, anise and tamarind, as were cakes and home-made sweets, confectionery and preserves.

It was not long before rice was a standard accompaniment to many dishes – a direct legacy of the Dutch/Indonesian *rijstafel* – as well as Oriental pickles and condiments. All still play a big role in the preparation of *boerekos* – traditional Afrikaner cuisine.

Influences

As well as being moulded by the passing spice trade, Cape food was influenced by East Indian slaves, political hostages and exiles, whose families transformed old Dutch recipes with the flavours of Bengal, Java, Malabar, Ceylon and Malaya. The Malay word *piesang* is Afrikaans

A popular snack throughout South Africa is biltong, *air-dried strips of salted and spiced meat reminiscent of American jerky. It is often made with beef or ostrich, but true connoisseurs favour venison, in particular kudu or springbok.*

for "banana"; small cubes of meat grilled on a short skewer are called *sosatie* (a corruption of Indonesia's *sate*).

A mouthwatering baked meat loaf, aromatic with mild curry and with a sweet/tart piquancy, is called *bobotie* after its Javanese original and can be enjoyed with a sweet-and-sour fruit con-

PRECEDING PAGES: delicious fried shrimp. **LEFT:** typical African vegetable dishes. **RIGHT:** spice market.

serve called or *blatjang*. *Bredie* is a casserole of mutton and vegetables, sometimes made with *waterblommetjie (see tint box below)*, an ingredient introduced by the local Khoi people. By contrast, *koeksisters* are advised only to those with a very sweet tooth; they are doughnut-like cakes fried in fat, then immersed in syrup.

A French influence arrived in 1688 with the Huguenots, who were fleeing the revocation of the Edict of Nantes. They settled in the beautiful Franschhoek valley, where they harvested fruit and made wine. Their technique of preserving food by long slow simmering, *confit*, means that all fruits preserved in sugar syrup,

including jam, are called *konfyt* in Afrikaans.

To the Huguenots, South Africa also owes a rich, succulent heritage of biscuits, tarts, cooking with wine, pastries and a bread roll called *mosbolletjies*, using fermenting wine as a raising agent instead of yeast.

Curry is another of South Africa's signature dishes – especially in KwaZulu-Natal, with its large Indian community. Unlike the sweet mild Malay curries associated with the Cape, the curries of KwaZulu-Natal are hotter, and usually reserved for lamb, chicken or vegetarian dishes.

Indigenous cuisine

A look at the menu at any traditional African eatery will reveal that the most popular local staple – introduced from the Americas by European settlers – is maize, known locally as *mealies*. An enormous number of dishes are made with it, the most popular being *mealie-pap* or *sadza* (a stiff porridge made from ground maize or *mealiemeal*) and hominy grits *(samp)*. Sorghum is another staple, used in dishes such as *ting* (sour porridge) and for making beer.

Beans are another key ingredient in the traditional diet, along with pumpkin, usually served stewed along with its fried flowers and seeds.

Groundnuts or peanuts are used to enhance dishes such as *morogo*, a stew made with spinach or flavoursome wild leaves. Curd or *maas* (sour milk) is another favourite dish, either on its own or with *phutu pap* (crumbly porridge).

In traditional rural communities, meat and milk are the responsibility of the menfolk. Stock is usually slaughtered on a special occasion only; game and birds are more commonly hunted and eaten instead.

Chicken, pork and mutton did not form part of the traditional diet (although that has now changed), and surprisingly fish is another recent addition. However, insects such as flying ants, along with mopani worms, are popular alternative sources of protein, roasted and eaten on their own or as a snack with porridge. Crunchy and faintly peppery, worms are much tastier than you'd think.

Delicacies from the sea

Fine-textured fish, mussels, oysters, crabs, baby squid and pilchards are all caught along the southern and eastern coastlines, but the finest seafood is to be had between November and

---

DELICIOUS DISHES

Umngqusho is said to be Nelson Mandela's favourite dish. It is made with dried maize kernels, sugar beans, butter, onions, potatoes, chillies and lemons – all simmered until the ingredients are tender. And on Western Cape menus, the dish to look out for is *waterblommetjie bredie*. The *waterblommetjie*, commonly known as Cape pond weed or Cape asparagus, is indigenous to dams and marshes here. The time to enjoy it is July and August, when the buds are plump and ready to be picked. Don't order it by using the pallid English translation ("waterlily stew") unless you wish to incur serious loss of face.

April: this is high season for the Cape's world-famous rock lobster (known locally as cray-fish), a prized delicacy so sweet and tender that vast quantities are exported to top restaurants worldwide. Similar to North Sea lobster except that it has no claws, it is served in all the traditional ways, such as thermidor, grilled or cold with mayonnaise.

Other summer delicacies are the pelagic fish, found in large shoals along the east coast of the warm Indian Ocean. Barracuda, yellow-tail, katonkel and shad are all fighting fish and therefore popular amongst anglers, but they are overshadowed by the Cape's pungently

over wood coals. In countless gardens, week-end wood fires are lit for the family *braaivleis* (Afrikaans for barbecued meat), while there is hardly a picnic spot, campsite or bungalow in the national parks that doesn't have a *braai* place. Lamb chops, curried *sosaties* and freshly picked corn on the cob are the foundations of this outdoor meal, but it can also include beef fillet, or cuts of springbok, kudu, bush-pig, eland or impala.

Then there's the coarse-minced sausage of spicy beef and pork fat called *boerewors* (*boer* means farmer, *wors* means sausage). The best specimens are usually purchased from rural

flavoured snoek. Named by the early Dutch settlers after the European freshwater pike, firm-fleshed and delicious.

Served fried, snoek is traditionally accompanied by sweet *korrelkonfyt*, a luscious jam made of honey-flavoured muscat grapes, which complements the saltiness of the snoek.

Outdoor eating

Since the first Dutch farmers cleared the Cape of lion, elephant, buffalo and buck, South Africans have relished the pleasures of meat grilled

LEFT: *biltong* – the nation's favourite snack.
ABOVE: inexpensive but sophisticated dining is one of South Africa's greatest pleasures.

butchers, who make them using the same recipes as their grandmothers. Another popular farmer's dish is *potjiekos*, a meat and vegetable stew, cooked slowly over a fire in the small black pot (*potjie*) for which it is named.

And if meat isn't your thing, South Africa's varied climatic and soil conditions are suitable to all kinds of fruit. In the Cape, there are marvellous grapes, apples and pears, while Kwa-Zulu-Natal and Mpumalanga produce tropical fruits such as paw-paws, avocados, mangos, lychees, pineapples, bananas and many others. You can get fruit fresh, as juice, or as delicious fruit rolls – fruit pulp dried in thin layers and rolled up – ideal snacks for long car trips, or as a healthy alternative to sweet desserts. ❑

CAPE WINE

Shunned by international markets during the apartheid era, Cape wine has made great steps forward in subsequent years

Wine production dates back to the very earliest days of European settlement. The first recorded vintage was produced back in 1659 by none other than Jan van Riebeeck, the founder of the Cape Colony. The baton was taken up enthusiastically by his successor Governor Simon van der Stel, who founded the Constantia Estate on the Cape Peninsula in 1685. Constantia soon became known internationally for its sweet "Vin de Constance", a favourite tipple of Jane Austen, Frederick the Great and Napoleon.

Wine production spread to the interior of the Western Cape with the arrival of the first French Huguenots in the late 17th century. Country towns founded during this period, such as Stellenbosch, Franschhoek and Paarl, remain at the heart of South Africa's wine industry to this day, and the region's historic vineyards – the likes of Boschendal, Vergelegen, Nederberg and Meerlust – are still widely regarded to produce the country's finest wines. However, the last two decades has also seen production spread further afield to areas such as the more remote Breede, Olifants and Orange River Valleys, with more than passable results.

South Africa is the world's seventh-largest wine producer (approximately 1,000 million litres annually), while export volumes increased from 120 million litres in 1998 to 410 million in 2008, with the UK being the single largest importer. Hearteningly, increased volumes have done nothing to compromise quality – on the contrary, most wine experts believe that the overall standard of South African wine is higher than ever.

ABOVE: Buitenverwachting (literal beyond expectations) is one of th most beautiful estates in the Ca noted for its fine Cape Dutch architecture and setting below Constantia Mountain.

LEFT: a Bacchic mural adorns th exterior of a wine shop in Franschhoek.

BELOW: most estates in the vicinity of Cape Town offer wine tasting – though, unless you intend to make extensive use of t spittoon, an organised tour is a safer bet than self-drive.

STYLES AND GRAPES

Until the 1970s, South Africa's winemaking tradition was strongly influenced by Germanic styles, despite Huguenot roots in the industry. As a result, South Africa was known predominantly as a producer of white wine. This has changed, however, and South African wine makers have been at pains to learn new skills and satisfy the demand for reds created by the recent growth in international markets. By 1998, some 25 percent of wine-yielding vineyards in the Cape were reds, a figure that had increased to 45 percent by 2008.

Cabernet Sauvignon is the most widely-planted red in the Cape, and it tends to produce heavy wines that form an ideal complement to steak and other red meats. Shiraz and Merlot are also gaining popularity, while Pinotage is a unique South African cultivar, developed from a cross between Pinot Noir and Cinsaut, producing a fruity, purple wine that tends to be underrated by South Africans, and thus often represents good value.

As for whites, Chenin Blanc and Columbard dominate in terms of area planted, though the latter in particular is mostly used in blends. Chardonnay is traditionally the most popular white amongst dedicated enthusiasts, and also the priciest, though its place is rapidly being supplanted by Sauvignon Blanc, a zesty complement to Cape Town's excellent seafood.

)VE: for serious ⸻ers, Le Cotte in ⸻schhoek is one of ⸻eral specialist wine ⸻ps that offer regular ⸻ing sessions ⸻lving wines ⸻duced by several ⸻erent estates.

HT: many of the ⸻t Cape wines are ⸻ured in oak barrels.

BELOW: this road sign soon becomes a familiar sight on any excursion into the Cape Winelands.

SPORT

Since the end of apartheid, sportsmen and women have made great strides in the international arena

With its rich sporting traditions and excellent facilities, South Africa is a sports fan's dream. The agreeable climate offers superb opportunities for golf, water sports, hiking and climbing – to name but a few outdoor activities – while avid spectators can catch world-class sporting action at Soweto's FNB Stadium, or Newlands in Cape Town.

Great strides

Since South Africa's readmission to the international arena, local sportsmen and women have made great achievements.

In 1995, the national rugby team was crowned world champions at Ellis Park after defeating favourites New Zealand in the Rugby World Cup final, a triumph whose impact on the process of reconciliation, barely a year after the country's first democratic election, has been immortalised in the 2009 film *Invictus*, starring Morgan Freeman as Nelson Mandela and Matt Damon as rugby caption François Pienaar. South Africa repeated the feat in France in 2007, this time defeating England in the Rugby World Cup final.

In 1996, the national football side Bafana Bafana (a Zulu phrase meaning "the boys, the boys") defied the odds to lift the African Cup of Nations trophy. South Africa also reached the first round of the 1998 and 2002 FIFA World Cup finals, and while its international ranking has slipped since then, it played credibly enough as host nation in the 2010 tournament.

KEEPING UP WITH THE GAME

If you prefer the sedentary approach to your favourite sport – taking in the action in front of the television – South African broadcast networks between them offer one of the widest ranges of televised local and international sporting action you are likely to find anywhere in the world. Live football, tennis, golf, cricket and rugby are beamed in from local venues and across the globe, so you're not likely to miss any action from back home while you're away on holiday. In the big cities, you could also head for one of the numerous sports bars, often crowded with very vocal supporters.

LEFT: Rugby World Cup winners, the Springboks, in action. **RIGHT:** Camps Bay is just one of several excellent surf spots along South Africa's coast.

The year 1996 was also when the Olympic Games were held in Atlanta. Here, swimmer Penny Heyns struck gold twice (in the 100 metres and 200 metres breaststroke), while marathon runner Josiah Thugwane stunned everyone by taking the gold medal in that most Olympian of events. In the 800 metres, track star Hezekiel Sepeng came from behind to snatch silver in breathtaking style.

Since then, South Africa has enjoyed mixed Olympic fortunes: it won five medals at Sydney in 2000 and six at Athens in 2004 (including a gold for swimmer Ryk Neethling), but its athletes returned home from Beijing 2008 with

just one medal to show for their efforts.

Then there is golfer Ernie Els, who followed in the footsteps of legendary South African golfer Gary Player by winning the US Open in 1994 – a feat he repeated in 1997. Els was still ranked among the world's top 20 golfers at the start of 2011, and was joined by three other South Africans: two-time US open winner Retief Goosen, and the emergent Tim Clark and Louis Oosthuizen, the latter a surprise winner of the British Open in 2010.

Other individual sports stars to achieve success since the moratorium on international contact came to an end are former IBF World Junior Featherweight champion Vuyani Bungu; Junior Flyweight boxer Baby Jake Matlala, who

has won both the WBO and IBF world titles in his division, and veteran tennis player Wayne Ferreira, whose appearance at Wimbledon in 2004 beat Stefan Edberg's long-standing record of 54 successive grand-slam appearances.

The challenge at home

The main challenge that faced post-apartheid South Africa was not so much world domination, as fostering the racial integration of sports that had previously been dominated by white players. Cricket is a good example, and the development programme implemented by the United Cricket Board in the 1990s has resulted in the game expanding both its player and fan base dramatically.

The country's foremost black cricketer is the recently retired fast bowler Makhaya Ntini, whose career tally of 390 test wickets, the second most ever taken by a South African, propelled him to second place in the ICC world rankings in his prime.

Consistently competitive, the national cricket side has thus far failed to win a World Cup in the abbreviated ODI and T20 formats, but under Graeme Smith, who succeeded all-rounder Shaun Pollock as captain in 2004, it spent much of the last decade ranked as the world's second-best test cricket side.

Football: the people's game

Soccer has always commanded the support of South Africa's black community, who are as loyal to their favourite teams as supporters anywhere in the world. The most important domestic tournament is the Premier Soccer League, which runs from August to May, with each of the 16 sides playing each other twice, and the lowest ranked one being relegated at the end of the season. The league tends to be dominated by Gauteng-based teams such as Mamelodi Sundowns, Kaizer Chiefs, Moroko Swallows and Orlando Pirates, which collectively won all but two of the past 14 editions, but it is also hotly contested by the likes of Cape Town's Ajax and Santos, and Durban's AmaZulu and Golden Arrows.

Once perceived to be a completely black sport, football today has an increasingly multiracial fan base, and the atmosphere at live matches – at the likes of Cape Town Stadium, Soweto's FNB Stadium and Durban's Moses Madhiba Stadium – is both vibrant and welcoming (not to say deafening, with thousands of vuvuzelas blaring approval at crucial junctures, or indeed lesser moments).

An ongoing obstacle facing the erratic national side Bafana Bafana has been its inability to consistently select key players – such as captain Aaron Makoena, his sometime stand-in Steven Pienaar, and strikers Bernard Parker and Benni McCarthy – signed to European clubs. For all that, sporadically strong showings in the African Cup of Nations and three World Cup appearances since 1998 have helped cement the game as the number-one sport among all South Africans – a status boosted immeasur-

Pietermaritzburg, provincial capital of KwaZulu-Natal. It's run "up" one year from Durban and "down" the next, from Pietermaritzburg. The Comrades made a hero of Bruce Fordyce, the accomplished ultra-distance runner who won it a record nine times between 1981 and 1990.

A long coastline and plentiful inland dams and rivers mean that South Africa is the venue for some exciting and testing canoe races, the most challenging of which is the four-day, 228km (142-mile) Berg River Marathon (www.windhoekberg.co.za) from Paarl to the coastal village of Veldrif, which includes stretches of "white water"; this is usually held in July.   ❏

ably by the communal football fever that swept the nation when it hosted the 2010 FIFA World Cup tournament.

Key events and venues

Apart from regular internationals in football, cricket, rugby and athletics, South Africa also hosts the Comrades Marathon. Held on 16 June every year, it is rated by some as one of the greatest ultra-marathons in the world – a 90km (55-mile) pilgrimage made by more than 14,000 runners every year between the coastal city of Durban and

LEFT: cricket is enjoyed at every level.
ABOVE: the Nedbank Golf Challange is held at Sun City every December.

CHALLENGING COURSES

South Africa boasts around 500 golf courses. Up there with the best is the Gary Player-designed course hacked out of the bush at Sun City. The Nedbank Golf Challenge, held here every December, invites 12 of the world's top players to compete for one of the richest prizes in international golf.

Durban Country Club has been rated among the top 100 courses in the world, while Cape Town's finest include the Rondebosch and Durbanfontein Golf Clubs. Phalaborwa's Hans Merensky Golf Club, bordering the Kruger Park, is possibly unique insofar as players are occasionally recalled to avoid a stray hippo or elephant.

MAMMALS

From the tiny shrew to the mighty African elephant, wildlife on the southern tip of the continent is simply spectacular

South Africa's richly varied mammal fauna, comprising 230 land and 43 marine species, is linked to an ecological diversity that includes no less than six major terrestrial biotic zones, ranging from desert to montane forest. For those who go on safari, however, it is the classic African woodland savannah of the northeast that holds the greatest allure, harbouring a wide range of favourites including the so-called Big Five of elephant, lion, leopard, buffalo and rhino. The Kruger National Park and bordering private reserves (now part of the Great Limpopo Transfrontier Park) is South Africa's premier game-viewing destination, but hundreds of smaller reserves countrywide protect familiar safari species alongside regional specialities.

The list that follows describes over 50 of the more conspicuous large mammal species, but do look out also for some of the smaller mammals that account for more than 60 percent of the national checklist. These include two dozen mole species, a variety of rabbits and hares, at least 75 bat species, as well as the bizarre elephant-shrew, which can be distinguished by its twitchy elongated snout. For more detailed coverage, see the field guides listed under Further Reading *(see page 372)*.

Lion *(Panthera leo)*

Tawny or fawn in colour, with manes ranging from gold to black on the male, the lion is the largest of Africa's three big cats, and also the most sociable. Prides consist of six to a dozen females and their cubs, with one or more dominant males. Most of the hunting is done by females, working as a team, usually at night, but males will usually be first to eat at a kill. Some prides specialise in hunting buffalo or giraffe, but most feed on impala, zebra or wildebeest, seizing the prey by the throat and suffocating it.

Leopard *(Panthera pardus)*

The leopard is bulkier than other spotted cats, from which it can be distinguished by its pugilistic build and elegant coat of black rosettes set against an off-white to russet background. It is a solitary animal, hunting mainly at night. A leopard will often carry a fresh kill (impala, baboons and monkeys are favoured) up a tree, safe from the reach of less dextrous carnivores.

PRECEDING PAGES: Common eland in Kwandwe Game Reserve, Eastern Cape.

Cheetah *(Acinonyx jubatus)*

Superficially similar to a leopard, the cheetah has a more greyhound-like build, with long legs, solid dark spots (as opposed to rosettes), and a small head with diagnostic black "tear-marks" below each eye. It inhabits open savannah, where it uses its impressive speed – up to 100kph/60mph over short distances – to run down medium-sized antelope such as impala or springbok. Cheetahs are usually seen singly, in pairs, or in small family groups consisting of a female and cubs. They normally hunt in the cool hours just after dawn.

Serval *(Felis serval)*

Another spotted cat, smaller than a cheetah but with a similar build, long legs and a short tail. Its black-on-gold spots give way to black streaks near the head. The serval is usually a solitary animal, but is sometimes seen in pairs or small family groups. It hunts mainly at night, and sometimes in the early morning or late afternoon, preying on small mammals, birds and reptiles. Although not uncommon, its favoured habitat of tall grass and reeds and its elusive habits mean that it is seldom seen

Caracal *(Felis caracal)*

Similar in appearance to a lynx, the caracal is a medium-sized cat, anything from pale fawn to chestnut in colour, with long, pointed, tufted ears. It is a solitary hunter, preying on mammals from mice to small antelopes, birds and reptiles. It stalks its prey as close as possible, then relies on a pounce or a short run. Its powerful hind legs enable it to leap vertically 3 metres (10ft) to swat a bird. Caracal are widespread throughout Africa's drier regions, but are mainly nocturnal and rarely seen.

African wild cat *(Felis sylvestris)*

Ancestral to the domestic cat (with which it often interbreeds near human settlements), the African wild cat is similar but less variable in appearance. Typically its dark grey-buff coat is offset by striped legs and tail, and a ginger back to the ears. A solitary nocturnal hunter, it feeds on small mammals and birds. It occurs throughout South Africa, in western areas alongside the **black-footed cat** *(Felis nigripes)*, an even smaller spotted cat endemic to Africa's arid southwest.

African wild dog *(Lycaon pictus)*

Unlikely to be mistaken for any other canid, the wil (or hunting) dog has long legs, huge ears, a whit tipped tail and a blotched black, white and tan tors No two animals have exactly the same markings. It a superb hunter – packs of 10 to 15 animals can mai tain a chase over several kilometres and overwhel much larger antelope by weight of numbers. Vulne able to diseases carried by domestic dogs, the wild do is listed as endangered, but the Kruger Park hosts on of the largest remaining wild breeding populations

Black-backed jackal *(Canis mesomelas)*

Jackals are medium-sized dogs, usually seen singly or in pairs, with an omnivorous diet of small mammals, carrion and fruit. Primarily nocturnal (but also diurnally active in protected areas), their call – a scream followed by a few short yaps – is a characteristic sound of the African night. The widespread blackbacked jackal is tawny-brown with a grizzled black back-saddle. Restricted to the extreme northeast, the **side-striped jackal** *(Canis adustus)* is smaller, paler and has an indistinct white stripe along its flank.

Bat-eared fox *(Otocyon megalotis)*

Small, grey and bushy-tailed, this fox-like insectivor is most easily identified by its black "robber mask Its enormous ears and acute directional hearing a the key to its success, allowing it to locate harveste termites nests as far as 30cm (1ft) underground. Com mon in the arid Kalahari, the bat-eared fox forms pe manent pairs, which den in burrows dug from scratc or modified from existing animal holes. It is typicall nocturnal or crepuscular, but can be conspicuous b day during the winter.

Cape fox *(Vulpes chama)*

South Africa's only true fox is a regional endemic restricted to arid and semi-arid habitats from the Western Cape to southern Angola. The smallest of South Africa's canids, the Cape fox can be distinguished from all jackals by its grizzled grey back, russet under-parts and very bushy tail, and from the bat-eared fox by its smaller ears and lack of a black mask. Its main food is invertebrates and small rodents, which it hunts by night. Although reasonably common and widespread in South Africa, it is seldom observed.

Spotted hyena *(Crocuta crocuta)*

Distinguished by its impressive bulk, sloping hind-quarters, coarse spotted coat, round face and powerful jaw, the spotted hyena, though often characterised as a pure scavenger, is also an efficient hunter. It was once thought to be hermaphroditic due to the false scrotum and penis covering the female genitalia. Clans of 10–100 individuals, led by a dominant female, are active mainly at night, when individuals maintain contact with an eerie whooping call that occasionally terminates in a demonic cackle.

Brown hyena *(Hyaena brunnea)*

This nocturnal scavenger is near-endemic to the semi-arid west of southern Africa, though its range extends into the northern Kruger Park. It is smaller, shaggier and more secretive than the spotted hyena, with a distinctive ruff-like mane of cream-coloured fur, and a similar repertoire of eerie, far-carrying whoops and chuckles. The remarkable **aardwolf** *(Protelus cristata)* is a small striped hyaenid whose distribution follows that of the few specific harvester termite genera on which it feeds exclusively.

Large-spotted genet *(Genetta tigrina)*

Similar in size and shape to a domestic cat, genets are streamlined nocturnal carnivores with short legs and an exceptionally long ringed tail. The large-spotted genet has dark blotched spots and a black tail-tip, while the **small-spotted genet** *(Genetta genetta)* has smaller spots and a white tail-tip. Both species prey on invertebrates and small mammals, and may be seen scavenging around lodges after dark. Within South Africa, the former is restricted to the eastern coastal belt while the latter ranges across the centre and west.

African civet *(Civettictis civetta)*

The size of a medium-sized dog, the civet is a stocky, powerful omnivore, its pale coat marked with dark blotches which merge into stripes nearer the head. It is a solitary hunter and may be seen at night (occasionally in the early evening) trotting with its head down in search of insects, rodents, reptiles – including venomous snakes – birds or carrion. It also eats fruit and can even digest poisonous plants. It is purely terrestrial, unlike its relative the forest-dwelling **tree civet** *(Nandinia binotata)*, which rarely comes to ground.

Ratel *(Mellivora capensis)*

A powerful, low-slung carnivore, mostly black but with a silver-grey mantle from head to tail, the ratel is the same size as a badger (its other name is honey badger after its habit of breaking into beehives to eat honeycomb and larvae). Rather secretive, it hunts mainly at night, usually unaccompanied, using its massive claws to dig out scorpions, rodents and other burrowing animals. The ratel frequently scavenges round rubbish dumps and camps in parks and reserves, and will attack humans aggressively if it feels threatened.

White-tailed mongoose *(Ichneumia albicauda)*

The largest of South Africa's 10 mongoose species, this is also very distinctive due to its unique bushy white tail. Like most African mongooses, it is solitary and hunts mainly at night. Quite common in the Kruger Park, it is often seen on night drives in neighbouring private reserves. More common in this part of the country, however, is the solitary but diurnal **slender mongoose** *(Galerella sanguinea)*, often seen darting across the road with diagnostic black tail-tip prominent.

Banded mongoose *(Mungos mungo)*

This diurnal and highly sociable predator – bands can be comprised of 50 individuals – is grey-brown with a dozen indistinct black stripes on its lower back. A true omnivore, it eats invertebrates, rodents, birds, eggs, fruit and berries. Almost as gregarious is the **dwarf mongoose** *(Helogale parvula)*, which is also one of Africa's smallest carnivores at 32cm (1ft) long including tail. Groups of 10–20 are often seen in or near the old termite mounds in which they den. Both are common in the Kruger Park.

Suricate *(Suricata suricatta)*

Also known as a meerkat, this pale grey mongoose, famed for its endearing habit of standing upright to survey the surroundings, lives colonially in old ground-squirrel burrows. Endemic to arid country from the Cape to southern Angola, it is restricted to the west of the country, where bands of up to 20 individuals are often seen on the roadside. Also common, the **yellow mongoose** *(Cynictis pencillata)* has a similar range and occasionally stands upright, but is woollier in appearance with a distinctive white-tipped tail.

Elephant *(Loxodonta africana)*

The largest land mammal, the African elephant can reach 3.4 metres (11ft) at the shoulder and weigh 6,300kg (over 6 tons). Females live in loose-knit herds, in which the oldest cow plays matriarch. Males usually leave the family at around age 12, to drift between herds, roam singly or form bachelor groups. Elephants are active 16–20 hours a day, eating, drinking, bathing or travelling in search of food – they can eat up to 150kg (330lb) of vegetation in 24 hours. *For more information, see the feature on page 115.*

Hippopotamus *(Hippopotamus amphibius)*

This huge mammal (up to 2,000kg/2 tons) is common in the waterways of the Kruger Park and Zululand, and has been reintroduced to Cape Town's Rondevlei Nature Reserve. Hippos live in groups of 10 or more, presided over by a dominant male. The thin skin lacks sweat glands and can easily dehydrate, which is why hippos stay partially or fully submerged in daylight. After dark, hippos graze terrestrially, and are often seen lumbering along well-worn trails at dusk or dawn.

Square-lipped rhino *(Ceratotherium simum)*

This bulky and peaceable grey-coated grazer is popularly called the white rhino, a name that derives from the Dutch *weit* (wide) and refers to the square lips that enable it to crop grass so efficiently. Formerly rated as Critically Endangered on the IUCN Red List, the square-lipped rhino has been the subject of one of South Africa's greatest conservation successes in recent decades, and population is now estimated at around 20,000.

Hook-lipped rhino *(Diceros bicornis)*

Also known as the black rhino, the hook-lipped rhino is no darker than its square-lipped cousin, from which it can be distinguished by a muscular hooked upper lip designed for feeding from branches and leaves. It is smaller than the white rhino with a reputation for charging at any provocation. Its horn of compressed hair is valued as an aphrodisiac which led to widespread commercial poaching throughout its range in the 1970s and 1980s. Today, the black rhino remains quite common in many South African reserves.

Giraffe *(Giraffa camelopardalis)*

The world's tallest animal, a male giraffe can grow to 5.5 metres (18ft); females are somewhat shorter. The giraffe prefers open country to woodland, although its main food is leaves, especially from the tops of acacia trees, which it grasps with its amazing 45-cm (18-in) tongue. Giraffes are non-territorial, roaming around in loose herds of up to 15, of both sexes. The subspecies found in South Africa is the **southern giraffe** *(G. c. giraffa)*, which has ragged edges to its blotchy markings.

Plains or Burchell's zebra *(Equus burchelli)*

The zebra's trademark stripes are thought to confuse predators by breaking up the animal's outline. A typical zebra herd consists of one stallion and a few mares with their foals. The plains zebra mingles happily with other herbivores, but since it can eat coarse grass unpalatable to other grazers, it's often the first species in a grazing area. Common in the Kruger Park, the southern African race is distinguished from northern forms by its pale "shadow" stripes.

Mountain zebra *(Equus zebra)*

Endemic to southern Africa, both races of mountain zebra lack shadow striping and have a chestnut-tinged snout. **Hartmann's mountain zebra** *(E. z. hartmanni)* is centred on Namibia but a small number inhabits the extreme Northern Cape. One-third of the global population of 750 **Cape Mountain zebra** *(E. z. zebra)* lives in the eponymous national park founded in the 1950s – when, with fewer than 10 individuals remaining, the fate of the closely related **quagga**, (a dark-rumped zebra hunted to extinction by European settlers) beckoned.

Buffalo *(Syncerus caffer)*

Africa's only species of wild cattle, the buffalo is very heavily built (up to 150cm/5ft at the shoulder), with relatively short stocky legs. Large ears fringed with hair hang below massive curved horns which meet in a central boss. They are gregarious, living in herds from a few dozen to several thousand in number, though it is not unusual to encounter lone bulls (which can be dangerous). They most often graze at night, and drink in the early morning and late afternoon, spending the day resting or chewing the cud.

Blue Wildebeest *(Connochaetes taurinus)*

The blue wildebeest (or brindled gnu) is an ungainly grey-brown creature with a straggly black mane and small buffalo-like horns. Herds comprise about 30 animals, but larger numbers often congregate in the grassland around the Kruger Park's Satara Camp. Endemic to South Africa, the **black wildebeest** *(Connochaetes gnou)* is smaller, blacker and has a diagnostic white tail – some 10,000 are distributed across various small reserves and private ranches centred on Free State Province.

Tsessebe *(Damaliscus lunatus)*

The southern race of the East African topi, this distinctive antelope has shoulders higher (125cm/49 inches) than its rump, a glossy tan coat with blackish upper and yellow lower legs, and stout ridged horns that curve backwards and upwards in both sexes. It is a grazer with a limited distribution in South Africa – small herds, controlled by a dominant bull, might be encountered in Ithala, Pilanesberg and the northeastern Kruger Park. The tsessebe is the world's fastest antelope, and it can outrun most predators.

Hartebeest *(Alcelaphus buselaphus)*

The hartebeest resembles the topi, but is paler, with a longer head and small curved horns whose exact shape varies greatly between a half-dozen regional races spread across Africa. The **red hartebeest** *(A. b. caama)* of southern Africa, darker and tanner than all other races, is common in the Kalahari Gemsbok and has been reintroduced into several other western reserves. The yellowish **Liechtenstein's hartebeest** *(A. (b.) lichtensteinii)* became extinct within South Africa in 1954 but was reintroduced to the Kruger Park in 1985.

Bontebok *(Damaliscus dorcas)*

This *fynbos* endemic has a similar silhouette to the topi, but is considerably smaller. Its sleek black-tan coat contrasts with bold white patches on the rump, lower-legs and snout. Both sexes have relatively long straight horns. Formerly endangered, the bontebok is now common in the likes of the eponymous national park near Swellendam and Cape of Good Hope. The similar **blesbok** *(D. d. phillipsi)* is a highveld endemic protected in several reserves and private farms in the Free State and Drakensberg regions.

Sable antelope *(Hippotragus niger)*

You could never confuse the sexes of this handsome large antelope: both have magnificent curved horns and distinctive black-and-white faces, but the male's body is jet black and the female's chestnut brown. Predominantly a grazer, the sable favours dry open woodland such as characterises the Pretoriuskop and Letaba regions of the Kruger Park, where herds of 10–30 individuals are controlled by one dominant bull. The sable has been introduced to several small South African reserves outside its historical range.

Roan antelope *(Hippotragus equinus)*

Africa's second-largest antelope (150cm/5ft at the shoulder), the roan has a stocky equine build, a short neck, and a distinct erect mane. Both sexes have backward-curving, ringed horns and black-and-white face markings. The roan is a grazer that lives in herds of 6–12, defended by an adult bull but led by a dominant female, who selects feeding areas. Within South Africa, the roan occurs naturally only in the northern Kruger Park, where it is rather scarce, but introduced herds are found in several other reserves.

Common oryx *(Oryx gazella)*

Also known as the gemsbok, this statuesque grey desert-adapted antelope has a striking black-and-white face and long, straight horns in both sexes. Three races are recognised, of which the fringe-eared and **Beisa oryx** *(Oryx beisa)* of East Africa are regarded by some authorities as specifically distinct from the southern race *(O.g. gazella)*. Predominantly a grazer, the oryx can survive for months without access to water. Small herds, led by a territorial bull, are common in the Kalahari Gemsbok and elsewhere in the Northern Cape.

Common waterbuck *(Kobus ellipsiprymnus)*

This large, robust antelope (up to 135cm/53 inches at the shoulder) has a shaggy grey-brown coat and a pronounced white ring on its rump. The male has long lyre-shaped horns, and both sexes are said to emit a smell that deters most predators. A dedicated grazer, the waterbuck is generally seen in small family groups in grassy areas near water. It is very common in the Kruger Park and some Zululand reserves, but is absent from most other parts of South Africa.

Eland *(Taurotragus oryx)*

Africa's largest antelope (up to 180cm/6ft at the shoulder), the eland has a somewhat bovine build, with a large dewlap and relatively short spiral horns, and a fawn coat with faint white vertical side stripes. Nomadic herds of 20 or more individuals are widespread in the Drakensberg and other grassland habitats countrywide, as well as in more arid regions, but they tend to be shy of humans. Active both diurnally and nocturnally, the eland is a prodigious jumper, able to clear 2 metres (6ft) from a standing position.

Greater kudu *(Tragelaphus trepsiceros)*

This elegant antelope has slender legs, big ears, a greyish coat and 6–10 white stripes on each side of the body. It's most notable for the triple-spiralled horns of the fully grown male. Small herds of females and youngsters, as well as bachelor herds, inhabit woodland or thicket habitats, where they browse on seeds, shoots and pods. The greater kudu is common in the Kruger Park, and other suitable protected areas and private ranches in the north of the country.

Bushbuck *(Tragelaphus scriptus)*

This widespread medium-sized antelope appears in various hues. The sturdy-horned males are often dark brown and the hornless females paler chestnut, but there is much variation and either sex may or may not have white spots and/or stripes. The bushbuck likes dense bush close to water, and is most active from late afternoon into early morning, but is generally shy and difficult to spot. Close-up sightings of habituated individuals can be had at the perimeter of some camps, for example Letaba in the Kruger Park.

Nyala *(Tragelaphus angasii)*

Intermediate in size between the closely related greater kudu and bushbuck, the nyala is a southern African endemic associated with thicket and riverine bush in Zululand and the northern Kruger Park. Both sexes are greyish in colour, with 10–12 vertical white side-stripes and a few spots. As with most other Tragelaphus antelope, the male is far larger and more cryptically marked than the female – and exceptionally handsome with its large spiralled horns, shaggy blue-black white-tipped mane and yellow lower legs.

Impala *(Aepyceros melampus)*

Particularly abundant in the Kruger Park, this slende
elegant, chestnut-coloured antelope is distinguishe
by unique black-and-white stripes on the rump an
tail. Males have impressive lyre-shaped horns. Impal
prefer wooded savannah, where they feed on fruit
seed pods, leaves and sometimes grass. They live i
two kinds of groups: bachelor herds (all male) an
harems of females and young. In the breeding seasor
a ram will take over a harem – and then battle wit
challenging males to preserve his breeding rights.

Springbok *(Antidorcas marsupialis)*

The springbok is the southern equivalent of the related
East African "Tommy" (Thomson's gazelle). Both species have pale brown upperparts separated from a
white belly by a broad black horizontal stripe, small
upright near-parallel horns, and – when threatened –
tend to bounce around stiff-legged, a type of behaviour
known as pronking. The migrating herds of hundreds
of thousands of springbok described by early European
settlers are a thing of the past, but small herds remains
common in the arid northwest of South Africa.

Southern reedbuck *(Redunca arundinum)*

This nondescript fawn antelope with small curve
horns (male only) is distinguished by the bare patc
found behind each ear. Pairs and family herds inhabi
moist grassland, notably in the vicinity of Lake S
Lucia. The **mountain reedbuck** *(Redunca fulvorufula*
has a black patch behind the ears, but is shaggier an
darker. It often occurs alongside the similar **grey rhe
bok** *(Palea capreolus)* – which has no bare patch bu
does have strikingly elongated, almost hare-like ears.

Oribi *(Ourebia ourebi)*

This graceful fawn-brown small antelope has a long
neck, black-tipped tail, black glandular spots below
the ear, and (male only) short straight horns. It typically lives in small groups comprised of one vigorously
territorial ram and up to three ewes. Mainly a grazer, it
is most common in the rolling grassland of the Kwa-
Zulu-Natal/Eastern Cape border. When disturbed, the
oribi emits a sharp whistle or sneeze and runs off with
stiff-legged jumps. Alternatively (and unusually for
antelopes), it might lie down to hide in long grass.

Steenbok *(Raphicerus campestris)*

Looking like a diminutive oribi, but without the black glandular spot and with shorter horns, the steenbok is South Africa's most widespread antelope, absent only from the northwest. It is common in the Kruger Park, where individuals and occasionally pairs freeze when disturbed, then suddenly bolt off. Similar, but with a darker and more grizzled coat, the **Cape grysbok** *(R. melanotus)* is endemic to the *fynbos* of the Western Cape, while **Sharpe's grysbok** *(R. sharpei)* is a tropical species whose range extends into the Kruger Park.

Klipspringer *(Oreotragus oreotragus)*

This alert-looking small antelope has a thick speckled grey coat, a unique white eye-ring punctuated by a black frontal "tear mark", and a rather stocky appearance, belying its exceptional agility in its favoured habitat of cliffs and rocky slopes. Practically always seen in pairs, the klipspringer (an Afrikaans name meaning "rock-jumper") is a widespread but habitat-specific resident – it's common in the Drakensberg, and often seen near Augrabies Falls and on the cliffs round Olifants Camp in the Kruger Park.

Grey duiker *(Sylvicapra grimmia)*

Also known as the common or bush duiker, this small antelope is typically yellowish-grey in colour, and has a distinctive tuft of black hair between its ears. Rams have short, pointed horns. It is the most widespread of all the duiker species, and the only one associated with savannah woodland rather than forest interiors. Normally seen singly or in pairs, it has a remarkably varied diet, feeding on shoots, leaves, fruits and cultivated crops, digging for tubers and roots with its front hoofs, and even taking termites and other insects.

Red duiker *(Cephalophus natalensis)*

Also known as the Natal duiker, this tiny red-brown antelope, whose short horns are separated by a dark tuft of hair, inhabits forests along and below the eastern escarpment south to Durban. Solitary and timid, the red duiker is typically glimpsed bounding across a forest path into cover, but good sightings can be had at campsites in the vicinity of St Lucia. The **blue duiker** *(C. monticola)*, the region's smallest antelope (shoulder height 30cm/1ft), is a grey-blue resident of eastern forest and coastal scrub south to Knysna.

Chacma baboon *(Papio ursinus)*

Distributed throughout South Africa, the baboon a large monkey that comes in varying shades of grey brown, but can always be recognised by its dog-like muzzle and permanently kinked tail. Baboons are diurnal and largely terrestrial, but they will climb trees to gather fruit, evade predators, or sleep. Otherwise they are found on the ground in complex social groups of up to 100, foraging, fighting, playing, grooming, nursing or courting. They feed on all kinds of plants, including crops, as well as insects, eggs and small mammals.

Vervet monkey *(Cercopithecus aethiops)*

The vervet monkey is small and slender, with a long tail, grey fur, a white belly and bare black face and hands. It is common in much of South Africa, living in troops of up to 30 individuals in savannah and woodland habitats. The vervet is agile in trees, where it forages for fruit, leaves and flowers, but it is equally at home on the ground foraging for seeds and insects. Troops are very sociable and communicate using a wide variety of calls, gestures and facial expressions.

Blue monkey *(Cecopithecus mitis)*

South Africa's one true forest primate, the blue or samango monkey is bulkier than the vervet, and its blue-grey back contrasts with pale yellow-brown under parts. Common elsewhere in Africa, the blue monkey is restricted to coastal forests within South Africa and most likely to be seen in the coastal regions of KwaZulu-Natal. Diurnal and arboreal troops of up to 30 individuals feed on leaves, fruits, seeds, gum and bark and occasionally insects and birds. A wide range of calls includes a loud, far-carrying bark to warn of danger.

Greater bushbaby *(Galago crassicaudatus)*

Also known as galagos, these small nocturnal primates belong to a family thought to be ancestral to the lemurs of Madagascar. The greater or thick-tailed bushbaby is by far the largest (80cm/2ft 6 inches overall), silver grey-brown with a darker bushy tail and large leathery ears. It is omnivorous but prefers fruit, especially figs. The smaller **lesser bushbaby** *(G. senegalensis)* has huge eyes and ears, and forages at night, usually alone, feeding on sap and insects.

Warthog *(Phacochoerus aethiopicus)*

The only African wild pig that's commonly seen by day, the warthog has a grey body sparsely covered with bristly hairs, a dark coarse mane and upward-curving tusks. It is named after the wart-like growths on its face (the male has four, the female two). Warthogs graze on a variety of grasses and, in the dry season, also root for bulbs and tubers, kneeling down and digging with their tusks. They live in family groups of females and young with one dominant male, sleeping and hiding from predators in networks of burrows.

Bushpig *(Potamochoerus porcus)*

This hairy pig varies in colour from grey to reddish brown and has a characteristic crest of hair along its spine, as well as tufted ears and a "beard". Males are larger than females (up to 170cm/5ft 6 inches long). The bushpig is probably more widespread than the warthog in South Africa, but is seldom seen because it prefers thick vegetation and is mainly active at night, snuffling around for roots, fruits and fungi. The bushpig is a favourite prey of the leopard and spotted hyena, and it is also hunted by humans for food.

Aardvark *(Orycteropus afer)*

An unmistakable creature, the aardvark is vaguely pig-like, but with a long tail, long tubular snout and huge ears. Digging is its speciality, as shown by its powerful forelegs and massive front claws, which it uses to excavate extensive burrows where it hides during the day. The aardvark is solitary and active only at night, when it may wander for several kilometres in search of termites, ants or larvae. When it finds a colony, it digs into it vigorously, lapping up insects with its long sticky tongue.

Rock hyrax *(Procavia capensis)*

Hyraxes look like large rodents, brown, round and short-legged, but are in fact distant relatives of the elephant. Rock hyraxes live in small colonies on rocky hillsides or *kopjes*, where they are often seen basking in the early morning. They feed on leaves, flowers and fruits, never moving far from the shelter of rock. They often become tame when accustomed to people, for instance around lodges. Their relative the **tree hyrax** *(Dendrohyax arboreus)* is a solitary, nocturnal forest animal with an eerie shrieking call.

Spring Hare *(Pedetes capensis)*

Despite its name, this is not a member of the rabbit family; and despite its appearance it is not related to the kangaroo. The spring hare is a true rodent, around 80cm (2ft 8 inches) long, yellowish-fawn above and paler below, with large ears and eyes, a long bushy tail and enormous hind legs. It propels itself with these in a series of leaps or hops, and uses its tiny fore-legs solely for feeding or digging. It is a solitary animal, living alone in a burrow, and largely nocturnal, feeding on roots, grass and other plants.

Porcupine *(Hystrix spp.)*

Easily recognised by its covering of long black-and-white banded quills, the porcupine grows up to a metre (3ft) in length. Two species are found in South Africa, both very similar in appearance and both sharing the same habits. They live in burrows (often several animals in the same network) in all types of habitat except thick forest, emerging only at night to forage for roots, bulbs, tubers and tree bark. A porcupine makes use of regular pathways: their quills are easily detached and often found along these trails.

Striped ground squirrel *(Xerus inauris)*

This endearing resident of plains west of the Drakensberg lives in sociable subterranean colonies of around 30 individuals. It is particularly common in the Kalahari, where semi-habituated colonies in national park's rest camps can be observed at close quarters as they scuffle around foraging and squabbling over scraps. Light grey-brown in colour with a pronounced side-stripe, and strictly terrestrial, the ground squirrel is replaced in the north and east by several more russet and arboreal species of **bush squirrel** *(Paraxerus)*.

Bats *(Order Chiroptera)*

Bats are represented by more than 1,000-plus species worldwide and at least 75 in South Africa. Most species belong to the suborder *Microchiroptera*: small, insectivorous bats that rely mainly on echolocation for navigational and hunting purposes. The larger fruit-bats – frugivores that navigate and locate food using sight and smell – are generally forest-dwellers and have a limited range in South Africa. Despite their bad reputation, bats play a vital ecological role in controlling flying insect populations.

The Elephant Clan

Strictly matriarchal and highly gregarious, the African elephant usually moves in herds of up to 30 females and youngsters

African elephants display intriguingly complex social behaviour which can be fascinating to watch. The typical elephant herd consists of a core family group, led by the oldest female, whose wisdom and memory of landmarks is vital in lean times. This family group typically includes about ten elephants, but it has strong links to bond groups of extended family, which spend up to 50 percent of their time together. The large herds formed by 5–15 bond groups are called clans, while unrelated elephants using the same area are known as a subpopulation.

Gathering of the clans

During the wet season, elephants can gather in herds of up to 500. Great excitement is displayed when two families meet. Trumpeting, growling, rumbling, defecating and urinating accompany the greeting ceremony. Trunks are entwined, with much touching and caressing as the elephants renew their acquaintance. As the water dries up and food resources shrink, the group splits up, but will stay in touch. Elephants can communicate over remarkably long distances using very low frequency infrasound, below the level of human hearing.

Research has shown that this low-frequency sound enables elephants to maintain contact over a distance of 10km (6 miles) even through heavy vegetation. The deep rumble we hear from time to time is a contact vocalisation, which only just enters the range of human hearing. Elephants use their trunk to produce the classic trumpeting sound, both in anger and exultation.

Mother love

It is particularly moving to see how gently elephants nurture their young. Calves are born at night, weighing about 100kg (220lbs), and can fit under their mother's bellies until they are six months old. A mother will use her trunk and feet to guide her baby under her tummy to shelter from the sun, or to her teats between her front legs. When on the move,

she'll hold the baby's tail, guiding it forwards, crook her trunk around its rump to help it in steep places, lift it out of a wallow and spray it to keep it cool. As the baby grows, its older sisters help to look after it, preparing themselves for motherhood.

When a baby elephant is in trouble, its core family encircles it protectively. Similar concern is also seen if an elephant is injured, its companions using their tusks to support or lift it. When an elephant dies, family members display evidence of distress and sometimes cover the body with branches.

Adolescent males, driven from the matriarchal herd when too boisterous, find companionship and safety in loosely knit and continuously changing

bachelor herds of up to 20 males, who might move together for a day, a week or a season.

When bond groups join in the rainy season, they are often joined by a breeding bull in musth, a condition recognised by a copious, pungent secretion from the temporal gland, the dribbling of urine and bouts of aggressive behaviour. Young bulls come into musth for a few days; in a prime breeding bull, it can last four to five months.

Females come into oestrus for two to six days, every three to five years. The bull chases the cow briefly, lays his trunk along her back and rears up on his hind legs. Penetration only takes 45 seconds. Immediately after mating, the cow will scream, with her family group gathering around and trumpeting loudly, as if sounding their approval. ❑

RIGHT: calves are cared for by the whole herd.

AMPHIBIANS AND REPTILES

South Africa has an incredible variety, as well as large numbers of species exclusive to the subcontinent

South Africa's ecological diversity guarantees a large number of amphibian and reptile species – most of them exclusive to the subcontinent. As most amphibians are nocturnal, it can be hard to spot any of the 130 recorded species. However, during spring and early summer, visitors are often treated to the extraordinary range of night sounds made by amphibians, from the booming croak of the African bullfrog to the snoring rasp of the guttural toads and the ringing call of the reed frogs. Then there's the Karoo toad, whose shrill, squawking cry sounds like a baby.

Frog species

Nonetheless, one of the most common indigenous frog species is rarely heard, for it lives, feeds and breeds under water. The aquatic platanna (a corruption of the Afrikaans phrase *plat-hander*, or flat-handed one) uses its agile fingers to cram food such as fish and dead animals into its mouth; it also has short claws on the inner toes of its webbed hind legs to help it dissect its prey before swallowing.

At the other extreme is the little rain frog, which can live independently of water, even for reproductive purposes. It makes its nest underground, where the larval development takes place. Eleven species of rain frog can be found in South Africa; their Afrikaans name is *blaasop*, due to their ability to inflate their bodies with air when alarmed.

Reptiles

The much-feared Nile crocodile is nowadays largely restricted to game reserves, while crocodile farming has become a popular and prosperous venture which helps to reduce the pressure

The uniquely shelled geometric tortoise, which occurs on the Cape Flats, is currently South Africa's most threatened reptile species.

on natural populations. The potential danger these reptiles pose to humans in the wild should never be underestimated – but if they are treated with respect, confrontation can be avoided.

The subcontinent has an exceptional variety of tortoises, including five marine turtles and five freshwater terrapins. The importation of the American red-eared terrapin for sale in pet shops has meant the growth of isolated colonies of discarded purchases.

Twelve species of land tortoise are found in South Africa, the highest number in any one country. The smallest species of all does not quite reach 10cm (4 inches) in length, even when fully grown.

Among the lizards, the geckos predominate. Most are nocturnal; many have adhesive pads under their toes, enabling them to hang upside-down on a ceiling or walk up a window pane. They're usually welcome house guests thanks to their voracious appetite for insects. Visitors to the Kruger Park are quite likely to spot the tropical house gecko on walls near lights after dark.

> Girdled and plated lizards are exclusively African. Most common are armadillo lizards, crag lizards and the brightly coloured flat rock lizards. If you're lucky you may see the country's largest species, the Nile monitor.

Snakes

Snakes, which are represented by around 130 species on this subcontinent, hold a morbid fascination for many people. Yet only 14 species possess a potentially fatal bite, which means that the vast majority of snakes are harmless or

Chameleon

Sixteen species of chameleon are found in South Africa, of which 14 are endemic. Not only are these extraordinary, exclusively African creatures able to change colour in response to their environment, but they also have exceptionally long, extrudable tongues with a sticky pad on the end, which they shoot out to snare their prey. Their swaying gait and crests or horns on their heads make them very distinctive. Small wonder that they are venerated as sacred by some rural communities.

LEFT: South Africa is home to several venomous snakes, but the majority of indigenous snakes are harmless. **ABOVE:** African reed frog.

not seriously dangerous. Many species, such as the dwarf adders, the harmless egg-eating snakes and also the dangerous varieties of cobras, are in fair demand with snake-keepers. However, stringent measures aimed at curbing the commercial exploitation and illegal export of this slithery souvenir are now in place.

Cases of snakebite are rare; most result from clumsy handling and walking barefoot. Adder bites (especially those of the Puff and Berg adders) can be lethal, but their venom acts slowly and allows time for treatment. Fortunately, the dangers of snakebite have been greatly reduced by the excellent quality of modern serum (*see Travel Tips, Health and Medical Care, page 369*). ❏

BIRDS IN THE BUSH

As a result of the country's location at the tip of a mighty continent, some unique forms of bird life have evolved

Visitors with an interest in bird-watching can look forward to spending hours in South Africa enjoying a rich variety of species – from the northeastern savannah where birds of prey soar effortlessly above herds of big game, through the arid interior where species have adapted to cope with semi-desert conditions, to the Western Cape, which sustains so many beautiful birds with its floral wealth.

Thanks to South Africa's position at the southern end of one of the world's largest landmasses, its bird life has evolved plenty of unique forms – some of which can now be found on other continents too. Families endemic to sub-Saharan Africa include the hamerkop, secretary bird, turacos, wood-hoopoes, sugarbirds and whydahs.

The northeastern lowveld

About 60 percent of the African continent is savannah – or "bushveld" – so it's not surprising that most indigenous species (including the birds of prey, the bustards and korhaans, kingfishers, bee-eaters, rollers, hornbills and bush shrikes) are found in this type of environment. Much of the Kruger National Park's vegetation is classic bushveld; more than 500 bird species have been recorded here, making it one of the most productive birding spots in the world.

As far as birds of prey are concerned, it is possible to see a good range of species in the course of a normal day's drive through the lowveld.

One of the most striking is the bateleur, a snake eagle with a black body, white underwings and bright red face and legs. The best-known scavengers are the vultures, which can be seen wheeling high in the sky all day long, on the lookout for dying or dead game. However, con-

trary to what most people believe, lion kills make up only a fraction of vultures' food.

Other large birds of prey include the tawny eagle, generally found on the plains, and the smaller African hawk eagle, which lives in denser woodland along the rivers.

Riverine trees often include the giant fig, which attracts fruit-eating birds like the green pigeon and various turacos, hornbills, barbets and bulbuls. Also keep a lookout here for the vivid, graceful bee-eaters, which usually perch conspicuously on top of leafless twigs of bushes or trees (or on telephone wires), and so are easy to photograph from a vehicle.

Surprisingly, most of Africa's kingfishers are woodland birds. Along the major rivers both giant and pied kingfishers are common, but in woodland areas you can see at least five species, including the woodland, grey-headed and pygmy kingfisher.

Other quintessentially African bird groups include the rollers and hornbills. All five southern African roller species – easily recognised by their brilliant blue wings – occur in the Kruger Park. Like the bee-eaters, they perch conspicuously in the open. The exceptionally beautiful lilac-breasted roller is the most characteristic bird of the Kruger Park.

Hornbills are common over most of the park, especially the yellow-billed and red-billed varie-

The highveld

The beautiful blue korhaan is one of the most distinctive birds of the open grassland, which covers much of Mpumalanga and the Free State. One of the rarer members of the bustard family in Africa, it's quite common here, and indeed – along with the bigger Kori bustard – is still sometimes hunted for its meat.

The magnificent, if somewhat ponderous, long-tailed widow, or sakabula, can often be seen sweeping across the grasslands, while the snow-white cattle egret can be seen among grazing herds, picking at grasshoppers that the cattle disturb.

ties. One to watch out for is the extraordinary southern ground hornbill, a very large, black bird with white wings and a rather grotesque red-wattled face. These tend to stick together in solemn groups of around five to 10 birds, feeding on insects, reptiles and other small animals.

Another common sight at camp sites are the metallic-blue starlings with their glossy plumage and yellow button eyes, scavenging for handouts from visitors. The distinctive sound of the red-chested cuckoo, or *Piet-my-vrou*, can also be heard throughout the spring and summer.

LEFT: the yellow-billed hornbill, found in northern KwaZulu-Natal and the Northern Province. **ABOVE:** the secretary bird kills snakes by stamping on them.

The distinctive secretary bird, which has long plumes resembling quill pens at the back of its eagle-like head, is a splendid sight to behold. You may be lucky enough to witness the dramatic spectacle of a battle between a secretary

An astonishing array of birdlife can be seen in South Africa's national parks, while the World of Birds park (see page 165), near Cape Town, is home to around 3,000 indigenous species.

bird and a snake, the bird using its long legs (it stands 1 metre/3ft high) to try and stamp the reptile to death.

Quite a few highveld birds can also be found in the mountains to the east and in the Karoo to the west. Several of the chats fall into this distributional pattern and so does the endemic ground woodpecker, a curious bird that never perches in trees, feeding off ants on the ground. It nests in an earth burrow in a vertical bank or a steep hill side.

From mountains to sea

The eastern slopes of the uKhahlamba-Drakensberg range, and the dense evergreen forests and deep valleys at its foothills, provide a dramatic backdrop for some rich bird life. The forests harbour sunbirds, flycatchers and the shy bush blackcap, a species found only in wooded valleys bordering clear mountain streams.

Orange-breasted rock-jumpers and Drakensberg siskins are endemic to the mountains of the eastern escarpment. On the grassy slopes here, you'll see grey-wing francolins, orange-breasted long-claws and cisticolas.

If there are protea bushes around, it is likely that you'll catch a glimpse of Gurney's sugarbird, whose squeaky song breaks the mountain silence. The brightly coloured forest weaver, emerald cuckoo and Knysna turaco are also found here, and in the Garden Route National Park.

FEEDING FRENZY

At Giant's Castle Game Reserve, high in the mountainous uKhahlamba-Drakensberg area, a unique "vulture restaurant" provides carrion for the endangered lammergeyer (bearded vulture) in winter. Bones are scattered on a high clifftop by the Parks Board, to protect the birds against accidental death from poisoned carcasses left out to kill jackals. Bird-watchers can photograph them from a comfortable hide fitted with one-way glass and specially cut ports for telephoto lenses – and, as there are only about 200 pairs of lammergeyer left in South Africa, this is a sight not to be missed *(see page 250)*.

South Africa's national bird, the blue crane, nests on the flatter tops of grassy spurs, laying two mottled eggs on the bare ground or rock. Overhead, the bearded vulture, black eagle and Cape vulture wheel about in search of food.

The crowned eagle in action is another extraordinary sight. After waiting in a tree to ambush an unsuspecting victim, it swoops down on its prey, carrying it off in its strong claws with the aid of its enormous wings.

The KwaZulu-Natal midlands provide some excellent birding spots. Close to Pietermaritzburg lies Game Valley, which has over 200 bird species, including water birds (kingfishers, wagtails and the hamerkop), grassland birds (long-claws, cisticolas and guinea fowl) and forest birds (trogons, robins, bush shrikes and many more). It is one of the best birding places in KwaZulu-Natal. Tracts of bushveld in the northern parts of the region are much like the Kruger Park in vegetation and avifauna. The reserves on the north coast are rich havens for waterfowl, pelicans, flamingos and the majestic African fish eagle.

In Ndumo Game Reserve, on the border of Mozambique, you can find such subtropical specialities as the purple-banded sunbird, yellow-spotted nicator and Pel's fishing owl. Here, too, are tropical water birds, including the African fin-foot and all kinds of storks, herons and bitterns. Reserves such as Hluhluwe-Imfolozi, Mkhuze and iSimangaliso also boast prolific bird life.

The arid lands

Bird-watching is relatively easy in the dry, open Karoo and the arid western parts of the country. Perhaps the most eye-catching birds here are Ludwig's bustard and the Karoo korhaan. A roadside stop will almost certainly produce some arid-zone specialities like the rufous-eared warbler, Layard's titbabbler and chat flycatcher. Travelling westward, chances improve of seeing some of the endemic larks, such as Sclater's lark (around Vanwyksvlei and Brandvlei) and the red lark (in the sand dunes near Kenhardt and Aggenys).

At the Karoo National Park near Beaufort West, you can step out of the front door of your chalet and be greeted by white-backed mousebirds, Karoo robins and the handsome bokmakierie, a member of the endemic African family of bush shrikes. The region's best-known inhabitant is the ostrich, the world's biggest bird. Males reach a height of about 2.5 metres (8ft) and weigh up to 135kg (300lbs). Although the birds are generally docile, the male – distinguished by its black plumage – can be temperamental during the mating season. Its skin may turn bright pink and it is likely to make a roaring sound – not unlike that of a lion – when approached by intruders. If all else fails, it may deliver a formidable kick with deft accuracy.

Ostriches are known for their speed and can reach up to 50km/h (30mph) – which explains why "ostrich derbies" are such popular events at farms in the Oudtshoorn area. A major part of the local economy around here is dependent

on the ostrich industry, in which every part of the bird has a use: the skin is used for leather-ware such as handbags and shoes, the feathers for dusters, and the meat for dried *biltong* – and the massive eggshells are sold as curios.

The sandy Kalahari, dotted with low shrubs and bigger acacia bushes and trees, has an abundant supply of small and large mammals, which make birds of prey a significant feature of the avifauna. Undoubtedly, the most astonishing avian spectacle here is the sight of the huge nests of the weaver bird, perched like untidy thatched roofs in the bigger camelthorn trees. These communally built structures can be up to 4 metres (12ft)

in diameter, and house up to 200 weavers. They live in these nests all year round, breeding there after suitably good rains. The dainty pygmy falcon, Africa's smallest raptor, makes its home here too. A pair of falcons may take over one or two chambers in the weaver's nest, the two species living side-by-side. The nests are dry and well-ventilated, but vulnerable to attacks by predators such as snakes and honey badgers, who frequently raid them in search of eggs and young birds.

If you position yourself near a water hole shortly after sunrise, you may see huge flocks of sandgrouse flying in to drink, sometimes in their hundreds or even thousands. Sand grouse are unique in their habit of carrying water in their belly feathers for their young to drink –

LEFT: blue cranes in a courtship dance.
RIGHT: ostriches are farmed all over the country.

the feathers are specially designed to take up large amounts of water in the manner of a sponge. The males wade into the water to soak before flying back to their thirsty chicks, which drink water from the feathers.

The *fynbos* region

Large tracts of land in the southern Cape hillsides and mountains are covered by a characteristic growth of low shrubs and bushes, known as *fynbos*. Many are pollinated by birds which come to the flowers to feed on the abundant nectar, especially of the proteas and heaths. Two of the endemic nectar-feeders are the Cape sug-

arbird and the orange-breasted sunbird. Also endemic are the protea canary, a seed-eater, and the insectivorous Victorin's warbler.

Further north, into Namaqualand (famous for its show of spring flowers), the *fynbos* assumes a more arid character. This is where one can find the cinnamon-breasted warbler and the fairy flycatcher, but bird-spotters must take a scramble into the dry, rocky hills for these special birds.

Coastal birds

The Benguela current along the southern and southwestern coastline supports a rich supply of fish, which in turn attracts large numbers of sea birds. Large flocks of cormorants can often be seen perching on rocks or flying in a charac-

teristic V-formation in search of shoals. When one is spotted, the whole flock descends upon it in a frenzy, diving into the water to gorge on their catch. Some garrulous and noisy gulls inhabit the shores, the most impressive being the kelp. These large birds often drop molluscs from great heights on to the rocks below, exposing the edible animals inside.

> *Every year, the ringed plover flies more than 10,000km (6,000 miles) from Siberia to the Western Cape.*

Large colonies of Cape gannets are found at Lambert's Bay and on small islets such as Bird Island and Malgas. This beautiful bird, with creamy plumage and distinctive black markings, can often be seen swooping down on fish in the waves below. Arctic terns or sea swallows migrate from the Arctic to the Antarctic every year, using the South African coastline as a stopover.

Bird migration

Every summer more than 100 species of bird migrate from the northern hemisphere to the South African shores. The most common migrants are waders of the sandpiper family, but they also include other birds ranging from herons to shrikes.

The journey from South Africa to Europe may take a small bird 5–7 weeks to complete. They travel at ground speeds of 40–75km/h (25–45mph) and often fly for up to 100 hours nonstop over inhospitable stretches of ocean and desert. Small birds must use flapping flight, but larger species, such as storks and eagles, can soar and glide. This is much slower, but expends less energy. Travelling these vast distances, a bird may burn up to 40 percent of its body mass.

Big soaring birds migrate by day when the heat of the sun generates thermals from the ground below, and they can utilise the rising warm air for lift. Small birds usually migrate at night at heights of up to 2,000 metres (6,500ft) above the ground. For navigation, they use the position of the sun and stars, assisted by other environmental factors such as magnetism, wind direction, smell and landmarks. This process remains one of nature's great mysteries: young birds instinctively know how to find the correct route, even in the absence of experienced adults. ❑

Insects and Arachnids

Home to 80,000 species of insect, South Africa has much to excite entomological collectors and photographers alike

The subtropical bushveld savannah in the far north of the country is home to the largest variety of insects, from the giant termite and the huge baboon spider to the beautiful emperor moths and butterflies to the barely visible lice, ticks, fleas and aphids. Here you can see an astonishing variety of vividly coloured dung beetles push their dung balls along with their hind legs, while columns of matabele ants stage raiding parties on neighbouring termite nests before they themselves are waylaid by robber flies.

Exotic fauna

The tropical region of KwaZulu-Natal's east coast harbours an endemic fauna which takes some truly exotic forms. From web-throwing spiders and multi-coloured fruit chafers to glamorous butterflies, this narrow strip of coast supports an amazing range.

Down south, the Cape's unique floral kingdom supports some equally fascinating insect life. Wingless Colophon beetles inhabit the mountain peaks – some species so rare that they are known only from the fragments of a solitary dead beetle. The protea, South Africa's national flower, plays host to a variety of beautiful chafer beetles. Forests here are home to the velvet worm, the most primitive living arthropod, which has survived almost unchanged for the past 400 million years.

Arid Namaqualand is highly regarded among entomologists for its great wealth of insects and arthropods. Especially notable is the colourful bottlebrush beetle.

Well over 100 species of mosquito are found in South Africa, including the genus Anopheles – some species of which are transmitters of malaria. They are confined to the northernmost parts of the Cape and KwaZulu-Natal as well as the lowveld.

Among the most intriguing insects in South Africa are the praying mantises. These beautiful creatures were venerated by the San-Bushmen who once inhabited much of the country.

LEFT: Cape sugarbird. **RIGHT:** Red Roman Spiders feed on termites and grow up to 7cm (3 inches) in length.

Predatory arachnids

Distinguished from insects by having eight legs rather than six, arachnids are a class of mostly terrestrial and predatory invertebrates that include spiders, scorpions and ticks. Spiders are particularly well represented in South Africa, with some 3,000 species identified to date, among them the spectacular golden orbs whose huge webs are often seen in the game reserves of the lowveld, and the scarily hairy (but essentially harmless) baboon spiders that are sometimes seen in developed residential gardens.

These large spiders are essentially harmless to people, but it's wise to give a wide berth to any

small shiny, spherical spiders you might encounter – they could be members of the genus Latrodectus – the button spider. The poisonous black variety is most commonly found in the wheatfields of the Western Cape; you should be able to recognise it by a red stripe or spot on the tip of the abdomen.

Tick-bite fever may be transmitted by the bite of the red-legged tick as well as the common dog tick. The disease is most widespread during the summer, when humans spend most time outdoors in grassy or wooded areas.

Well-known for their painful and, in some cases, strongly venomous sting, scorpions are mainly confined to drier parts of the counter and are seldom seen unless sought for – by turning over rocks or dead logs. ❏

FLOURISHING FLORA

Thanks to its ecological diversity, South Africa is graced
with some of the richest and most varied flora in the world

The flora of southern Africa is one of the richest, most beautiful and vulnerable in the world. Familiar flora includes the red-hot pokers, stelitzias (bird-of-paradise flowers), the arum lily, proteas, gladiolus, agapanthus and sweet-scented freesias. Most of these were first introduced into European botanical gardens and private collections in the 18th century. More recently, plants such as the richly coloured gazanias and the shy osteospermums, which open their petals only when the sun shines, have found favour abroad.

The Floral Kingdom

Located around Cape Town on the southwestern tip of the continent, the Cape Floral Kingdom or *fynbos* region covers about 70,000 sq km (27,000 sq miles) and is home to 8,600 kinds of flowering plants. On the Cape Peninsula alone, 2,600 indigenous species have been counted: more than in many considerably larger countries. Renowned

The Cape of Good Hope sector of Table Mountain National Park and Kirstenbosch National Botanical Gardens are excellent places to see fynbos *in its natural habitat.*

for its proteas and heathers, this is also where you'll find South Africa's most famous orchid, the red disa, known as the "Pride of Table Mountain". This area receives most of its rain in the cold seasons of the year, between April and October.

LEFT: quiver trees in the Cederburg Wilderness Area.
RIGHT: the slopes of Table Mountain are covered in *fynbos* in springtime.

The semi-deserts

North of the winter rainfall zone lies the arid area known as Namaqualand, running parallel to the Cape's west coast as far as the lower Orange River Valley. This is a dry land which receives an annual average rainfall of 50–150mm (2–6ins). The correspondingly sparse vegetation is dominated by succulents, especially shrubs with fleshy leaves.

Mesembryanthemums (*vygies* in Afrikaans), grow here in abundance. Other natives include the pebble plant (*Lithops*), plants of the similar Conophytum families, and many species of daisies, which have adapted to their parched surroundings by germinating and flowering only after good spring rains. All produce splendid blossoms of shimmering, metallic red-violet, yellow, white or copper-coloured petals, which appear in one burst in the spring.

Trees are rare in this region, but various species of tree-aloe can be found in certain parts to the north. The Karoo National Botanical Garden, at the foot of the Brandwacht Mountains near Worcester, is an excellent introduction to the local flora.

Ranking a little higher on the vegetation scale is the Great Karoo, the vast semi-desert stretching up from the Northern Cape into the Free State and beyond. The rainfall here aver

ages between 125–375mm (5–15ins) a year, and plant life is dominated by small shrubs, mainly members of the family Compositae, such as the camellia, the kapok bush and the quassia.

Great silvery plumes of feather grass and ostrich grass are a common sight here, while in the deeper valleys you will often encounter the sweet thistle, which produces a beautiful display of brightly coloured yellow blossoms in the summer months.

The savannah

Covering some 959,000 sq km (370,270 sq miles) from the Kalahari basin right across to the east coast, with a narrow strip reaching down into the Southern Cape, this is the sub-continent's largest floral region. Rainfall, which occurs primarily in summer, averages about 25 cm (10ins) a year.

This is an area of mixed vegetation, consisting mainly of grassland, with scattered trees and drought-resistant undergrowth. Although isolated trees and shrubs are the norm, there are also large patches of savannah forest – the classic bushveld. The vegetation covering much of the Kruger National Park is a good example.

Thorny acacia trees, often with a distinctive umbrella crown, are characteristic in dry parts of the region. The bizarre baobab, with its mighty trunk which often attains a diameter of several metres, can be found in the extreme north, along with the marula, the fever-tree and the ubiquitous dark-green mopani.

Eye-catching grass varieties, such as red grass, pepper grass and ostrich grass, are all common. During the dry season these grasses take on a yellow or reddish colour, which has a corresponding effect on the overall landscape. Each year, large areas are burned off; but at the beginning of the rainy season, these bleak, blackened patches are covered virtually overnight with a colourful carpet of spring flowers and fresh green shoots. The Pretoria National Botanical Garden, located in an area where savannah gives way to grassland, has examples of the plant life of both regions – as well as over half of the country's tree species.

The grassland

Covering an area of some 343,000 sq km (133,770 sq miles), the grassland area encompasses Lesotho, western Swaziland, and large parts of the Free State and Northern Province.

ROOTED IN THE CAPE

Many of Europe and America's favourite garden plants have their origins in South Africa's botanical treasure house. This is as a result of the endeavours of a number of 18th-century plant-collectors and explorers (many of them Dutch) who scoured the Cape for colourful flowers that would be suited to colder climates.

One of the best-known plants introduced in this way was the pelargonium (commonly called geranium), first brought to Europe in 1690 and then cultivated by the French for essential oils. Pelargoniums now brighten gardens and window-boxes all over the world.

Rain falls virtually only in summer; frost occurs on most nights in winter. Even so, about one-tenth of the world's 10,000 species of grass are indigenous to the area. The grasslands can be roughly divided into a western and an eastern region; of these, the western receives less than 660mm (26ins) of rainfall annually, while the eastern receives more.

The forests

Forests are in short supply in South Africa; most of the relics (victims of man's depredations) are now protected by law. Only in the Southern Cape, in the vicinity of George, will

ing from the Western Cape north into Limpopo Province, has many patches of what was once a larger forest in its deep gorges and on its more sheltered, humid slopes. Such areas are dominated by coniferous species, such as *Podocarpus*, known locally as yellowwood. These trees can grow into forest giants, reaching heights of up to 40 metres (130ft) and with massive trunks.

Species of the olive family also grow here, as does the stinkwood (*Ocotea bullata*), so-called because it has an unpleasant odour when it has been freshly cut. Stinkwood furniture is a much sought-after feature of the Knysna area.

you find extensive woodland. There are, however, small, generally isolated areas of forest in the coastal belt stretching between the sea and the mountain ranges on the continent's eastern edge, from the southwest Cape up the Garden Route and then north through KwaZulu-Natal and Mozambique.

Along KwaZulu-Natal's coastline you can still see isolated remnants of mangrove forest, growing in mud and sand. Further inland there are the remains of evergreen forests, where milkwood, ebony and wild bananas grow. The uKhahlamba-Drakensberg, extend-

The desert

The huge and desolate expanses of the Namib, a true desert, lie outside the republic's borders, stretching parallel to the coast of Namibia. In this region, almost entirely without rainfall, vegetation is scarce or entirely absent. When rain does fall, the soil comes alive with grasses whose seeds have lain dormant for years.

In places, you will see the Namib's most famous plant, the fascinating welwitschia, which resembles a giant carrot with two broad flat leathery leaves growing out of the top. It is an extremely long-lived plant, often surviving for centuries, and its appearance is all the more weird because of the way the desert wind erodes its leaves. ❑

LEFT: aloes and other succulents flourish in South Africa.
ABOVE: the protea, most famous fynbos plant of all.

THE CONSERVATION RECORD

Nature conservation is taken seriously in South Africa, with emphasis placed not only on "Big Five" reserves, but also on more fragile species and ecosystems

A recent survey of overseas visitors to South Africa revealed that nine out of 10 came primarily to experience its wildlife and unspoiled natural areas. When one realises what a wide variety of wild plants, animals and ecosystems the country has to offer, this statistic is not at all surprising. However, although wildlife is extremely significant as a cornerstone of the rapidly growing tourist industry, the importance of conserving it does not rest on this consideration alone.

Why conserve?

South Africa is listed as the world's third most biodiverse country. Covering about 2 percent of the world's land area, it is estimated it harbours some 10 percent of the world's plant species and 7 percent of its terrestrial vertebrates. Not only is it exceptionally diverse in species, but it is a rich centre of endemicity – endemics being species that occur nowhere else in the world. About 80 percent of South Africa's plant species are endemic, as are 30 percent of its reptiles, 15 percent of its mammals and 6 percent of the 600 bird species that breed there.

The plants that inhabit the southernmost tip of the continent are so different from those found anywhere else that the area has been defined as one of the six floral kingdoms of the world – the Cape Kingdom. This tiny area, only 46,000 sq km (18,000 sq miles) in extent, is thus considered equivalent, for example, to the Boreal Kingdom which includes all of Europe, North America and northern Asia, an area of more

LEFT: Addo Elephant National Park is home to over 450 elephants. **RIGHT:** tracking big game in Entabeni Game Reserve, north of Johannesburg.

GONE FOREVER

The huge herds of springbok and quagga (a now-extinct subspecies of the still-widespread plains zebra) that used to roam the Karoo plains soon disappeared before the guns of the European colonists, eager to hunt game for food and especially sport. Those dark days before the dawning of the conservation ethic (which South Africa now proudly enforces) also saw the extinction of the endemic bluebuck (a relative of the sable antelope and roan antelope) around 1800. This is the only endemic vertebrate animal known to have become extinct in South Africa.

than 53 million sq km (20 million sq miles).

This high concentration of unique wild species places South Africa on a par with the much-discussed tropical rainforest areas, such as those of the Amazon Basin, as an area of international significance for conservation.

However, nature conservation is primarily essential for this rich centre of genetic diversity, and for the maintenance of natural resources on which many of the country's people depend for their livelihood. Nature conservation is accordingly taken very seriously and South Africans have much to be proud of, at least in recent times.

Wildlife management

Africa, and thus South Africa, is famous for its amazing variety of antelopes and other grazing mammals, and for the large carnivores that prey on them. These herds of antelope used to graze from the Cape Peninsula in the south to the Limpopo Valley on the northern border.

The conservation record is not so good for native plants: at least 60 species or subspecies have become extinct since their discovery.

As the herds of wild ungulates began to be reduced by hunters in the 17th and 18th centuries, they were replaced by flocks of sheep and herds of cattle. The larger carnivores – lions,

A COMMITMENT TO CONSERVE

It has been said that the way a nation preserves its heritage is also one way to gauge the level of its civilisation. Some 72,700 sq km (28,000 sq miles) are under formal protection for nature conservation in South Africa, in more than 580 game reserves, parks and wilderness areas.

This amounts to some 5.8 percent of the total surface area – a figure which may sound quite generous, but falls somewhat short of the International Union for the Conservation of Nature's (IUCN) calculated recommendations that at least 10 percent of a country's surface area should be effectively conserved.

spotted and brown hyenas, cheetahs and African wild dogs – came increasingly into conflict with livestock farmers. These species were soon restricted to the remaining unoccupied or sparsely occupied portions of the country. Of all the larger carnivores, only the wily leopard has managed to persist in reasonable numbers outside the larger national parks and nature reserves, mainly in mountainous areas.

Today the large carnivores, the elephants, the rhinoceroses and the large herds of wild antelopes are restricted in main to the larger protected areas, particularly those in the country's northern savannahs. The greatest of these is the Kruger National Park, which since the end of 2002 has been part of the Great Limpopo

Transfrontier Park. The new park, with an area of 35,000 sq km (13,500 sq miles) links Kruger with Mozambique's Limpopo National Park and Zimbabwe's Gonarezhou National Park. The oldest park in Africa, Kruger has long been regarded as one of the world's finest examples of wildlife management.

Thanks to the range of different savannahs in the Kruger, well-prepared visitors can spend days exploring its vastness, its diversity and its unending series of wildlife interactions, without ever becoming bored. It is possible to see up to 147 indigenous mammal species, over 500 species of birds, 104 reptile species and 1,771 plant

largest national park, the 9,600-sq-km (3,700-sq-mile) Kalahari Gemsbok, with its 24,800-sq-km (9,500-sq-mile) counterpart in Botswana. The former border is along the normally dry bed of the Nossob River. The stark beauty of this semi-desert area is remarkable, with its red sand dunes dotted with low thorn trees, covered in good rainfall seasons with vast waving strands of sun-bleached grasses.

Here can be seen such dry-country specialists as the oryx (gemsbok), the red hartebeest and the springbok. Among the birds, the sociable weavers are probably the most characteristic. Their communal nests not only provide accommoda-

species here, including 357 species of trees and shrubs. From your own vehicle, from a variety of hides or on an escorted bush walk with an armed game ranger you can view some of the finest spectacles of African game available to a visitor anywhere on the continent.

Kgalagadi Transfrontier Park

Kgalagadi Transfrontier Park is the country's first foray into the peace park initiative. Situated in the Northern Cape, the park combines the areas of what was South Africa's second-

LEFT: preparing tranquilliser darts for elephants.
ABOVE: without man's help, the black rhino faces extinction in Africa.

tion for themselves but also harbour a whole community of "hangers-on", including the diminutive pygmy falcon, which appropriates and then nests in one of the many individual chambers that are built into the weavers' nests.

The tall acacia trees that grow in these riverbeds accommodate the larger birds of prey that abound in the open savannahs. There are few places in Africa where one can meet with such densities of large eagles, vultures, falcons, hawks and owls. Family parties of ostriches are frequently met with as they slowly pick their way across the dunes or run energetically along a shimmering pan. In the dry heat of midday the pace of life slows right down in these silent savannahs. At this time Kori bustards, Africa's largest flying bird species, fly in from the surrounding dune veld to stand gasping in the shade of a gnarled old camelthorn tree.

Mammalian predators are also easily located along these sparsely vegetated river beds, and this is probably one of the best places in South Africa to observe the cheetah hunting. This is also the major sanctuary for the only large carnivore which is endemic to southern Africa: the brown hyena.

Jewels of the east

In the east of the country there are many smaller savannah reserves, including Africa's oldest sur-

has built up the world population of this species to its current total of around 18,000–20,000 individuals and led to its recent reclassification from Endangered to Near-Threatened on the IUCN Red Data List. Thousands of white rhinos have been captured and safely transferred to other conservation areas in Africa; indeed, the Kruger National Park's population of more than 6,000 white rhinos is descended from individuals translocated from Imfolozi in the 1960s.

Hluhluwe-Imfolozi has also played a significant role in the conservation of the South African population of the Critically Endangered black or hook-lipped rhinoceros. Poaching

viving game reserve, Phongolo, proclaimed in 1894 just 12 years after Yellowstone National Park was established in the United States as the world's first. In 1895, nearby Hluhluwe-Imfolozi was proclaimed primarily to protect the last remaining populations of rhinoceros in Natal. These great reserves have succeeded beyond their originators' wildest expectations.

The square-lipped rhinoceros (white rhino) found its last sanctuary in the Imfolozi Reserve and this population was thought to have been reduced to fewer than 20 individuals early in the 20th century. By careful protection and through the development of methods to capture safely and transport these enormous creatures, the KZN Wildlife, which administers these reserves,

reduced the continental black rhino population from around 100,000 in the 1960s to around 4,000 today, so that the once relatively insignificant population of black rhinos held by South Africa now represents about 40 percent of the global total.

A fresh spate of commercial poaching in South Africa led to more than 300 individual rhinos (about 95 percent white) being gunned down for their horns over the course of 2010. This doesn't yet constitute a crisis of the proportions experienced in East Africa in the 1980s, since it represents an annual loss of around 1.5 percent of the national population of almost 20,000 (as compared to a birth rate of more than 6 percent).

Nevertheless, this sudden escalation of rhino poaching from near-zero levels in the mid-2000s is of great concern to conservationists.

These reserves are not only famous for their rhinoceros populations. Other mammals abound, including the most attractive of the African antelopes, the nyala, found only in the dense thickets of the southeastern lowlands. The variety of bird life is astounding, and breathtaking hours spent in the hides at waterholes in these reserves during the winter dry season will be a memory never to be forgotten. The nearby uMkhuze Game Reserve is also renowned for its hides.

Maputaland

On the northeastern coastal plain of Maputaland there are a variety of different conservation areas to visit. The centrepiece of the iSimangaliso Wetland Park, a Unesco World Heritage Site, is Lake St Lucia, which holds the country's largest populations of hippopotamus and crocodile. Waterbirds inhabit this enormous shallow lake, including large breeding colonies of white pelicans and the striking Caspian tern. If the water levels are low, vast flocks of flamingos can be seen. To the south of the estuary mouth, Maphelane Nature Reserve preserves a diverse dune forest on what are said to be the world's highest forested sand dunes.

North of the estuary mouth, iSimangaliso Wetland Park follows the coast all the way to the Mozambican border, while a proclaimed marine reserve preserves the adjacent offshore wonders. Submerged coral reefs and the associ-

There is something in the turtle's heroic exertions which drives home the message that this tenacious life force must not be summarily terminated throught mankind's exploitation or pollution.

ated myriad tropical fish species and other sea life abound in the crystal-clear waters of the warm Mozambique Current that washes these golden beaches, fringed by lush dune forests. Each summer, hundreds of loggerhead and

LEFT: an anti-poaching unit equipped with bicycles.
ABOVE: fitting a turtle with a satellite tag as part of a conservation programme.

leatherback turtles haul themselves up these beaches to bury their clutches of eggs in these protected sands. After 25 years of strict protection by Ezemvelo KZN Wildlife, which each year monitors and safeguards their breeding activity, the populations are thriving.

To witness a huge turtle heave herself out of the surf and up the beach, the moonlight glistening off her wet carapace as its ancestors must have done each year for countless millennia, and then to watch her go about this age-old ritual of reproduction, is to experience something which cannot fail to confirm the importance of maintaining the full diversity of life on earth.

The coastal lakes of Sibayi and Kosi Bay also lie within iSimangaliso Wetland Park. A short drive inland, Ndumo Game Reserve and Tembe Elephant Reserve form part of the Lubombo Transfrontier Conservation Area, together with the Maputo Special Reserve on the other side of the Mozambican border. Ndumo, the most tropical of the KwaZulu-Natal reserves, is probably the premier bird reserve in South Africa. A series of pans lined with yellow-barked fever trees are filled with an amazing variety of waterfowl, and provide sanctuary for many hippopotamuses and crocodiles.

The fig forests that fringe the rivers and pans and the thickets that cover most of this relatively small reserve (110 sq km/42 sq miles) hold a great variety of bird life. More than 400 species have been recorded from the reserve, and in the summer wet season (November to March) when migrant species are present, one may easily record upwards of 200 different species within a few days.

The high grasslands conservation areas have much else to offer. The mountainous uKhahlamba-Drakensberg Park, another Unesco World Heritage Site, running for 180km (110 miles) along KwaZulu-Natal's inland boundary with the kingdom of Lesotho, protects some of the country's most beautiful landscapes – huge, towering amphitheatres set above rolling grassy slopes, with numerous mountain streams running through forested gorges to fall tumbling over cascading waterfalls. These mountains and grasslands are home to a fabulous variety of wild flowers and several of the country's endemic bird species, such as the yellow pipit and the Drakensberg siskin. The majestic lammergeyer (bearded vulture) is still secure here, too.

The arid interior

Further west one can visit the Mountain Zebra National Park, Camdeboo National Park or Karoo National Park, as well as several provincial reserves, to obtain a glimpse of the semi-arid

TABLE MOUNTAIN NATIONAL PARK

Most of the Cape Peninsula forms part of this 2,500-hectare (6,200-acre) park, which incorporates Boulders Beach, the Cape of Good Hope and the Silvermine Nature Reserve. Species are protected from agriculture, farming and urban sprawl, fire and marauding alien vegetation. World-famous Table Mountain, which forms the backdrop to the country's mother city, Cape Town, is the park's focal point. Visitors can take relatively easy day walks some way up the mountain (the easiest route starts in Kirstenbosch Botanical Gardens), or use the cableway, which runs every 10–20 minutes, to reach the summit.

Karoo ecosystem, now mainly used for sheep farming. The Karoo is probably the most characteristic of South Africa's ecosystems. For those who enjoy wide-open spaces and stark semi-desert landscapes, a trip through the Karoo, with planned stopovers at several of the relatively small reserves, will be well worthwhile.

The majority of the Karoo's animal and plant life is unique to this area. Those visiting the region shortly after good rains can witness levels of biological activity unsurpassed in any of the other ecosystems of South Africa. The fields of brightly coloured flowers, a host of insects and flocks of nomadic birds breeding in such an area provide an absolutely unforgettable spectacle.

Whereas in most other countries it is the semi-desert ecosystems which are best conserved in national parks, the converse is used to apply to South Africa. This situation has changed since then, however, and in addition to the various parks of the Karoo, recent years have seen the gazetting of the Namaqualand National Park in the vicinity of Kamieskroon, an area renowned for its colourful spring wildflower displays,

> About 2,000 plant species are thought to be facing extinction unless trends in habitat destruction are halted.

and the Richtersveld National Park, in the arid mountainous region just south of the Orange River border with Namibia. The more established but smaller Augrabies Falls National Park, higher up the Orange River, is also worth a visit, both for its spectacular scenery and to see some of the rich semi-desert fauna and flora of the country's western arid zone.

Forests, lakes and fynbos

Further south still, is the well-watered coastal strip in the Eastern and Western Cape provinces. Here are found the country's largest evergreen forests. The Tsitsikamma sector of the Garden Route National Park allows the visitor a chance to see the region's dense temperate forests. The enormous yellowwood trees, their canopies often festooned with "old man's beard" lichens and the forest floor beneath them damp and mossy, are a far cry from the semi-desert Karoo ecosystems which are located only a few hours drive inland.

The coastal park not only has a spectacular five-day hiking trail – called the Otter Trail after the Cape clawless otters which can sometimes be seen feeding along this coastline – but also has an underwater trail for snorkellers or scuba divers. The Knysna Lagoon and the Wilderness Lakes, also both part of Garden Route National Park fall within the major temperate rainforest areas of the Southern Cape; these verdant forest landscapes only add to the beauty of the area.

The oceanic waters off South Africa harbour

a rich variety of marine mammals, including Cape fur seal, several species of dolphin *(see box page 199)* and southern right whales. The latter breed off the southern Cape Coast, usually arriving in June and leaving in December, when sites such as Hermanus and False Bay offer some of the world's finest land-based whale watching *(see feature pages 186–7).*

The future

Sitting on the top of Table Mountain and looking down on to the seemingly never-ending suburbs of Greater Cape Town, one cannot help feeling uneasy about the conservation future in South

Africa. Within a single lifetime, the Cape Flats, which lie between the Cape Peninsula and the Hottentots-Holland Mountains to the east, have been engulfed by a spreading wave of humanity. What used to be an area of exceptional wetlands and a veritable garden of wild flowers is now virtually completely covered by factory land, suburbia and small agricultural holdings.

Wattles introduced from Australia choke the native vegetation on the last remaining scraps of uncultivated land. Sadly, many of the plants and animals of this area and the adjacent Cape Peninsula are now threatened with extinction. Indeed, 39 plant species have already been lost from the Cape Peninsula; 15 of them peninsular endemics.

LEFT: semi-desert vegetation in the Karoo National Botanical Garden. **ABOVE:** expanding towns and cities present a threat to South Africa's natural landscape.

With a human population that is currently growing extremely rapidly (the population has burgeoned from approximately 18.3 million in 1960 to an estimated 50 million in 2010), all the many pressures on South Africa's natural environment are now intensifying.

It is essential that conservation agencies continue to receive all of the necessary funds to carry out their important task of protecting the natural resources of South Africa for the benefit of all its peoples, including the generations still to be born.

A visitor who, having enjoyed the wonderful country and its superb national parks, wishes

that was set to benefit. The new South African Constitution, for example, contains a clause guaranteeing the "environmental rights" of every citizen; their rights to a clean and healthy environment, and the rights of both present and future generations to a well-conserved and cared-for natural environment.

With the country's readmittance to the international community has come the ratification by South Africa of several important international conventions, most important of which (from a nature conservation perspective) is the Convention on Biological Diversity. Not only was this treaty ratified, but an extensive policy

to do something constructive to assure the future of conservation might consider taking out membership in one of the many local conservation societies which work directly with local projects. The oldest and largest of these is the Wildlife and Environment Society of South Africa, which first came into existence a century ago during the initial campaign to establish the Kruger National Park. It now has over 15,000 members, and runs a variety of high-profile conservation education programmes.

The new South Africa

When the new government came to power following the historic April 1994 democratic elections, the environment was one of the causes

development process was carried out to support its local implementation, ending in the production of a Government White Paper on the topic. Another important treaty recently ratified was the World Heritage Convention, preparing the way for Unesco to inscribe eight of South Africa's sites as World Heritage Sites between 1999 and 2007.

The time of transition also allowed several initiatives that have long been stalled to proceed: for example, in 1998, the government finally approved the creation of Table Mountain National Park, incorporating the mountain itself and the Cape Peninsula's remaining natural areas. Similarly, the long, drawn-out debate on the possibility of mining the dunes on the eastern shores of Lake St Lucia was ended when the Cabinet ruled that this mining would not be permitted. Several other national parks have been created since 1994, and the period has also seen the creation or partial development of half-a-dozen Transfrontier Parks, most importantly Kgalagadi and Greater Limpopo (the latter incorporating the Kruger).

Unfortunately, not all of the recent changes have been so positive, with many of the provincial conservation agencies losing the majority of their experienced conservation professionals as a result of an ill-conceived and poorly-executed downsizing of the civil service.

amazing number of different institutions, this campaign had mobilised more than 6,000 unemployed people, most of them women. Today, it supports more than 300 projects countrywide.

It has not only benefited streams and rivers, but also the native plants and animals that would otherwise have been replaced by rapidly spreading stands of invasive alien plants.

In many ways, the "Working for Water" programme epitomises the government's approach to conservation: doing everything it can to care for the environment, while at the same time taking into account the real needs of South Africa's predominantly poor population. ❏

Working for Water

Probably the single biggest environmental success story of the new South Africa has been the "Working for Water" programme of the National Water Conservation Campaign. Begun under the visionary guidance of the former Minister of Water Affairs and Forestry (www.dwaf.gov.za), Professor Kadar Asmal, this huge project ultimately aims to remove all alien trees from mountain catchment areas throughout the land, thus solving South Africa's single most serious nature conservation problem. Involving an

LEFT: giraffe in Kruger National Park.
ABOVE: the Working for Water programme has helped to preserve valuable water sources.

FINDING OUT MORE

The major fund-raising organisation for the environment in South Africa is the local branch of the World Wide Fund for Nature (WWF); www.wwf.org.za. Check for the latest local projects. Other very informative websites are operated by South African National Park (SANParks; www.sanparks.org), Ezemvelo KZN Wildlife; www.kznwildlife.com and Cape Nature Conservation; www.capenature.co.za. For those interested in volunteer work in the conservation, reputable organisations include Projects Abroad; www.volunteer-conservation-south-africa.org, African Conservation Experience; www.conservationafrica.net and AVIVA; www.aviva-sa.com).

PLACES

A detailed guide to the entire country,
with principal sites clearly cross-referenced
by number to the maps

Blessed with reliable sunshine, a sensational 3,000km (1,875 miles) coastline studded with dramatic cliffs and wide sandy beaches, a lofty mountainous interior crisscrossed with hiking trails, and some of the world's finest wildlife sanctuaries, South Africa is an extremely appealing destination for nature lovers and outdoor enthusiasts alike.

By African standards, this is an easy country to negotiate, well-organised and efficiently run. The road network and tourist infrastructure are excellent too, from the southern tip of the Cape to brash Johannesburg, whose gold mines have provided so much of the country's wealth. And, almost two decades on from the demise of apartheid, the country's once divisive cultural richness is now a source of inspiration for locals and outsiders alike.

Roughly five times the size of Britain and three times as large as California, South Africa is an enormous place, and it would be difficult to explore in its entirety without a few months to spare. And while the public transport system is improving, a rental car is desirable if you want

to see as much of the country as can be squeezed into the frame of a normal vacation. To help first-time visitors settle on a basic itinerary, we have therefore organised the chapters that follow along a series of standard routes – not so much a prescriptive list of stops and sights as a basis for creative improvisation and overlap.

Classic sights are undoubtedly the Kruger National Park and associated private reserves, which form one of Africa's most compelling safari destinations. There is Cape Town, one of the world's most appealing cities, set on a peninsula of almost indescribable beauty. The opportunities for heading off the beaten track are limitless, whether it's to the far reaches of Limpopo Province with its sacred lakes and rain queens, to the majestic foothills and peaks of the uKhahlamba-Drakensberg, or to the stirring expanses of the stony Karoo and sandy Kalahari. Whatever you decide, South Africa boasts a wealth of attractions suitable to all tastes and interests. ❏

PRECEDING PAGES: uKhahlamba Drakensberg Park; Graaff-Reinet; Cape Town and Table Mountain at dusk. **LEFT:** Cape of Good Hope Nature Reserve. **ABOVE LEFT:** Port Elizabeth. **ABOVE RIGHT:** elephant in Pilanesberg National Park.

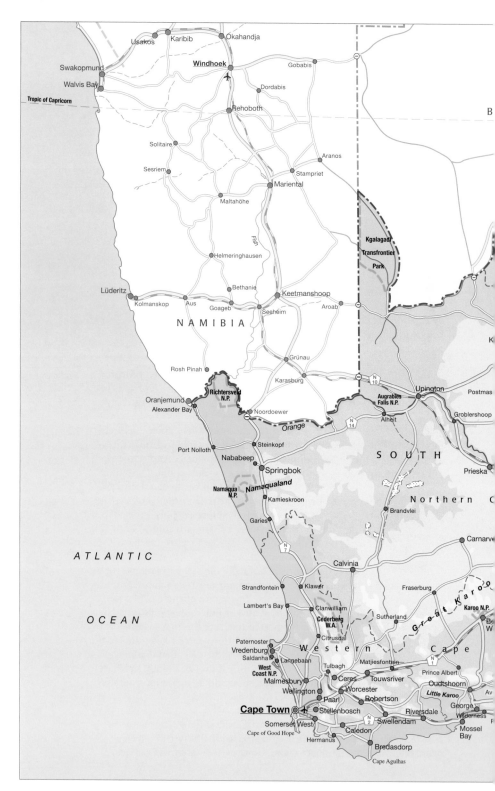

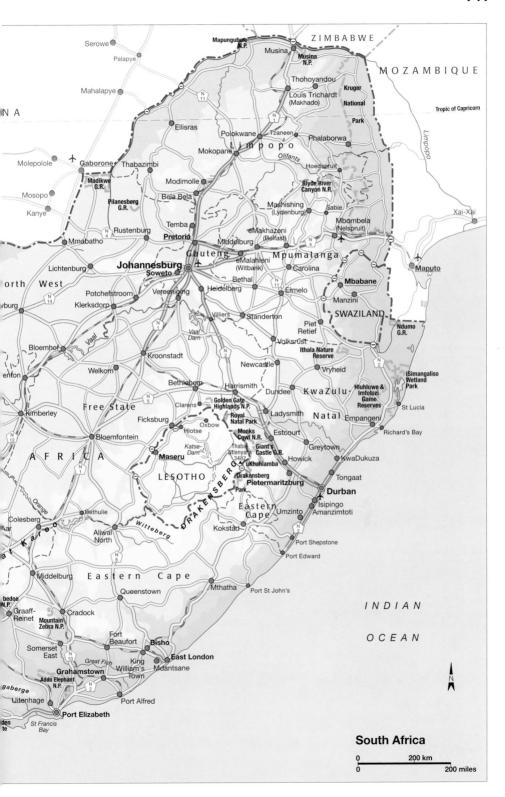

South Africa

| 0 | 200 km |
| 0 | 200 miles |

CAPE TOWN AND PENINSULA

A mountain plateau flanked by two oceans, graced with long, uncrowded beaches and some of the world's most unique vegetation

When he sailed into Table Bay aboard the Golden Hind in 1580, Sir Francis Drake famously proclaimed it to be "The fairest Cape… in the whole circumference of the earth". And that much still holds true today: South Africa's oldest and most characterful city, set at the northern tip of the breathtakingly beautiful Cape Peninsula, **Cape Town ❶** can lay justifiable claim to be one of the most beautiful and engaging cities anywhere in the world.

The Mother City

The scenery is certainly a large part of Cape Town's appeal. Sloping uphill from Table Bay, the compact city bowl has a majestic setting, with the iconic outline of Table Mountain towering a full kilometre above. The rest of the Cape Peninsula is even more beautiful, combining striking oceanic vistas, blissful beaches and sleepy old fishing villages with an interior of historic valleys planted with neat vineyards set below the 60km (36-mile) backbone of craggy mountains that run between Cape Town and Cape Point. All of this is complemented by a climate that generally wafts between pleasant and sublime, at least when the fierce but cleansing southeaster known as the Cape Doctor isn't howling.

Often referred to as the Mother City,

Cape Town is the country's oldest European-founded settlement, and the most cosmopolitan town anywhere in sub-equatorial Africa.

Historical accounts of the Cape generally begin with the arrival of Jan van Riebeeck, who founded a Dutch East India Company victualling station at the site still known as the Company's Garden in 1652. But the Cape was first known to Portuguese navigators as early as 1488, when Bartolomeu Dias pioneered a sea route round to the Indian Ocean. And of course Khoikhoi

Main attractions
COMPANY'S GARDEN
DISTRICT SIX MUSEUM
LONG STREET
BO-KAAP
V&A WATERFRONT
ROBBEN ISLAND
TABLE MOUNTAIN
KIRSTENBOSCH NATIONAL
  BOTANICAL GARDEN
GROOT CONSTANTIA
BOULDERS BEACH
CAPE POINT
CHAPMAN'S PEAK DRIVE

LEFT: Table Mountain overlooks the city.
RIGHT: Clock Tower, V&A Waterfront.

The Keiskamma Altarpiece on display at the Iziko Slave Lodge celebrates renewed hope brought by antiretroviral drugs to communities in the Eastern Cape.

herders and San hunter-gatherers inhabited this corner of Africa long before the Portuguese showed up – indeed, archaeological evidence of human activity on the peninsula dates back some 40,000 years.

Today, Cape Town sometimes comes across as a Molotov cocktail of first and third world ingredients. The city centre's graceful Victorian, Georgian and Art Deco buildings will strike a chord of familiarity to European visitors, while North Americans may feel unexpectedly at home in expansive malls such as the V&A Waterfront. Equally, there are the vast and emphatically African townships that stretch east of the city centre, Islamic Cape Malay enclaves such as the richly atmospheric Bo-Kaap, and above all perhaps there is

Long Street, the uncategorisable Afro-meets-Boho pulse of the city centre.

South African Museum

A good place to get a handle on this cultural puzzle – indeed, on the entire racial and cultural melting pot that is the Rainbow Nation – is at the central **Iziko South African Museum** (25 Queen Victoria Street; www.iziko.org.za; daily 10am–5pm; charge), which was founded in 1825 and relocated to its present site at the south end of the Company's Garden in 1897.

It houses a wide variety of cultural and natural history displays, among them a superb selection of rock-art panels relocated from their original settings during road construction, and a set of 2,500-year-old ceramic works

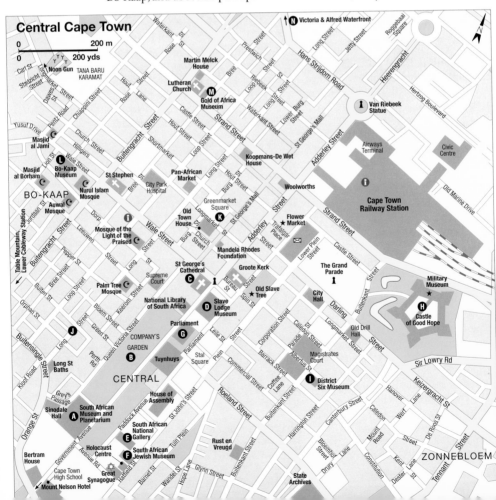

Central Cape Town

unearthed in present-day Mpumalanga. Don't miss the extraordinary Whale Well – a multisensual, multimedia display dedicated to these immense marine mammals.

The museum is one of several historic buildings abutting the 6 hectare (15 acre) **Company's Garden** Ⓑ (daily 8am–6pm; free), which were first laid out in 1652 for the Dutch East India Company, to provide a midway victualling station for its ships on the way to the East. Van Riebeeck duly planted patches of cabbages, potatoes, turnips and grains. Today the gardens form a lovely leafy retreat in the heart of the city centre: look out for a giant Outeniqua yellowwood which was planted in the 17th century, a 17-metre (56ft) tree aloe claimed to be the tallest in the country and the abundant grey squirrels introduced from America by Cecil John Rhodes.

Landmarks around the Company's Garden

At the north end of the gardens, the Anglican **St George's Cathedral** Ⓒ (www.stgeorgescathedral.com; Mon–Fri 8.30am–4.30pm) designed by Herbert Baker and built in 1901 is remembered for the political role it played in the 1980s, when it was the diocese of Anglican Archbishop Desmond Tutu, who preached anti-apartheid sermons from its pulpit. A modest but illuminating display close to the main entrance evokes the church's role in the anti-apartheid struggle. A newer addition, dating to 2004, is a courtyard labyrinth replicating the one laid in the floor of Chartres Cathedral about 1220.

Diagonally opposite the cathedral, the **Iziko Slave Lodge Museum** Ⓓ (corner Adderley and Wale streets; www.iziko.org.za; Mon–Sat 10am–5pm; charge) is housed in Cape Town's second-oldest building, constructed by the Dutch East India Company in 1679 as a dormitory for slaves shipped to Cape Town from India, Madagascar, Ceylon, Malaya and Indonesia. In the 18th century, the lodge held an average of 500 slaves in insanitary, disease-ridden rooms that lacked proper ventilation and natural light.

Now a museum dedicated to the local and global history of slavery, this

TIP

A worthwhile refuge on a rainy day, the Iziko Planetarium (tel: 021-481 3900; www.iziko.org.za; daily 10am–5pm), under the same roof as the South African Museum, hosts regular shows introducing the main features of the southern night sky.

BELOW: whale skeleton at the Iziko South African Museum; exterior of the musuem.

Jan Smuts Statue, The Company's Garden

BELOW LEFT: the Castle of Good Hope's moat with the City Hall behind; **BELOW RIGHT:** the District 6 Museum.

is an important site, mirroring the underestimated role played by slaves in the development of South Africa's languages, customs, cuisine, labour laws, religion and architecture.

On the east side of the Company's Garden, the **Iziko South African National Gallery** ● (Paddock Avenue; www.iziko.org.za; Tue–Sun 10am–5pm charge), which during the apartheid era built up an impressive collection of mainly Western art, including works by Gainsborough, Reynolds and Rodin. The current acquisitions policy is now biased towards indigenous art. Check out the gallery shop for some interesting gifts.

Nearby is the **South African Jewish Museum** ● (88 Hatfield Street; www. sajewishmuseum.co.za; Sun–Thur 10am–5pm, Fri 10am–2pm; charge), housing a rich collection of items depicting the history of the Cape Town Hebrew Congregation and other Cape congregations. The museum incorporates the beautifully restored Old Synagogue, South Africa's oldest such edifice, built in 1862, and the Great Synagogue, built in 1904.

In the same compound, the **Cape Town Holocaust Centre** (www.ct holocaust.co.za; Sun–Thur 10am–5pm, Fri 10am–1pm; free) is dedicated to the holocaust associated with World War II, but places these events in the context of racism and the struggle for freedom in South Africa.

Close by, the **Houses of Parliament** ● (Parliament Street; www.parliament. gov.za; guided tours by advance arrangement only) were built in 1864 in High Victorian style. Close by is **Tuynhuys**, the office of South Africa's State President, built in grand Colonial Regency style. At the southernmost tip of Government Avenue, in the shadow of Table Mountain, the city's best-known hotel, the pale pink **Mount Nelson**, prides itself on retaining a grand colonial atmosphere, exemplified by the sumptuous afternoon tea.

Towards the old Castle

Back on Adderley Street you'll pass the historic **Groote Kerk**, the oldest church in South Africa, containing an elaborately carved pulpit.

Turn right into Darling Street to

see the **City Hall**, whose baroque Victorian embellishments and honey-marble facade overlook the **Grand Parade**, once a military training field and now a parking lot.

On the eastern side of the Parade, the sturdy stone **Castle of Good Hope** ⓗ (Buitenkant Street; www.castleofgoodhope.co.za; daily 9am–4pm; Key Ceremony at 10am and noon Mon–Fri; Firing of Signal Cannon: 10.10am and 12.10pm Mon–Fri, 11am and noon Sat; charge) was completed in 1697, making it the oldest surviving intact structure in South Africa. With its 10-metre (30ft) thick walls and five corner bastions, each named after one of the various titles of the Prince of Orange, the castle is today a military headquarters; it also houses a military and maritime museum and collection of paintings, Cape silver and furniture and Asian porcelain.

A couple of blocks south of the castle, the superb **District Six Museum** ⓘ (25A Buitenkant Street; tel: 021-466 7200; www.districtsix.co.za; Mon 9am–1.30pm, Tue–Sat 9am–4pm; charge) was established in 1994 to commemo-rate what was originally Cape Town's sixth municipal district, established in 1867. Home to a vibrant multiracial community, District Six was rezoned as a Whites Group Area in 1966, leading to the forcible removal of its inhabitants to the Cape Flats, and the destruction of their homes. Today, the eponymous museum displays a combination of personal mementos, old photographs and evocative recordings that not only pay poignant testament to community life in the mixed-race suburb, but also illuminate the casual cruelty of the divisive policies that destroyed it.

Long Street and the northwest City Bowl

Two blocks northwest of the Company's Garden, buzzing **Long Street** ⓙ is the longest, liveliest and most famous – some would say infamous – street in Cape Town. It links mountain and sea, and you can stand with your back towards the mountain at one end and see ships berthed in the dock at the other. Long Street has always represented the cosmopolitan heart and soul of this maritime city, and today it has

The Kat building in the Castle of Good Hope houses the William Fehr collection of Africana relating to the Cape's earliest colonial period.

BELOW: nightlife on Long Street.

The Auwal Mosque, on Dorp Street, was founded in 1798.

BELOW:
Greenmarket
Square flea market.

many faces. Anything – and everything – happens here. There are delis, cafés, restaurants, all-day bars, live music venues and nightclubs; churches and mosques; clothing shops specialising in cloth from all over the continent, or African items, antiques and bric-a-brac shops, markets and pharmacies; pawn shops and porn shops; funky boutique hotels and grungy backpacker lodges, even a misplaced Turkish steam bath.

The tone of Long Street ranges from smart to seedy to downright sleazy, and these contrasts are its very essence. The buildings that line the street are similarly diverse, forming a veritable textbook of the architectural styles that have come and gone in Cape Town. The buildings span every century, from the earliest days of the colony to the present. At No. 206 is Cape Town's most exuberant high Victorian building, awash with ornate metalwork, turrets and fancy gables. At No. 185 is the **Palm Tree Mosque** (not open to non-Muslims), converted from a house on the site early in the 19th century The palm tree is still at the door in what was once the garden.

Shops, markets and stalls

At the mountain end of Long Street on the corner of Orange Street, **Long Street Baths** (tel: 021-400 3302; daily 7am–7pm; charge) have been a city institution since they opened in 1908 The complex includes a heated swimming pool, steam and dry-heat rooms and a massage parlour.

It's also a fantastic place to browse for those who like their shopping to come with character and whimsy rather than chain store predictability. whether you're poking around the myriad stalls of the multi-storey **Pan-African Market**, digging through the gem-strewn racks of the **African Music Store**, or seeking out vintage clothes or Africana books.

Two blocks east of Long Street, **Greenmarket Square** is another uncontrived highlight of the city centre, abuzz as it is with flea-market stalls manned by a pan-African assembly of French-speakers from Senegal and Mali, or Swahili speakers from Kenya and Tanzania, selling artwork and other goods from all over the continent. The square is a congregation

Cape Town's Kramats

A magic circle of kramats – the tombs of holy men who once lived and worked within Cape Town's Muslim community – graces the city, forming an important part of local Islamic lore. Muslims believe the circle provides Cape Town with a protective spiritual barrier, helping to prevent natural disasters.

Before making a pilgrimage to the Holy City of Mecca (as is required of every Muslim, if he can afford it), local believers will visit each kramat in turn. There is a shrine to Sayed Abdurahman Matura, Prince of Ternate, on Robben Island and one to Nureel Mobeen at Oudekraal near Bakoven beach. The tomb of Abdumaah Shah lies by the gate to Klein Constantia farm in the Constantia valley. Of the two shrines on the slopes of Signal Hill, one contains the remains of Tuan Guru, the Cape's first imam and founder of the country's first mosque.

One of the most spiritual and revered shrines in the country is the tomb of Sheik Yusuf, near Eerste River in the township of Macassar (take the Firgrove turning on the N2 from Cape Town to Stellenbosch). Yusuf was a 17th-century nobleman who, having rebelled against the high-handed authority of the Dutch East India Company in his native Indonesia, was exiled to the Cape for his pains. His tomb was erected as recently as 1925 by Hadji Sullaiman Shah.

point for buskers and cultural voyeurs of all sorts, and it is lined by cafés and characterful old buildings, notably the **Old Town House** (tel: 021-481 3933 www.iziko.org.za; Mon–Fri 10am–5pm, Sat 10am–4pm; free), a grand baroque building dating from 1761 that holds the Michaelis Collection of Dutch and Flemish art, including a treasured Frans Hals portrait.

The Bo-Kaap

West of the city centre, beyond Buitengracht Street, is one of Cape Town's most exotic districts – the **Bo-Kaap** (Upper Cape), or Malay Quarter. Here, winding, narrow streets are flanked by restored early 18th- and 19th-century cottages painted in pastels – originally slave quarters, stables and a military barracks. This was where many of the Muslim Batavian slaves imported by the 17th-century Dutch colonists settled, alongside powerful imams exiled from Indonesia where they had challenged Dutch colonial rule. Their descendants still live here, and they have, by and large, kept the community's Cape Malay identity intact. This

part of town is also the centre of the Cape Minstrel's Carnival, which takes place in January. Bo-Kaap has several venerable mosques, burial grounds and "kramat" shrines (see page 154), notably **Auwal Mosque** in Dorp Street, one block south of the museum, which was founded in 1798, making it the oldest such edifice in South Africa. Another point of interest is the unique Cape Malay cuisine, best sampled at Biesmiellah or the Noon Gun Tearoom (see pages 349–350).

The main tourist focal point here is the **Bo-Kaap Museum** ❶ (71 Wale Street; www.iziko.co.za; Mon–Sat 10am–5pm; charge), whose "wavy" parapet is a unique surviving feature of a type of building common to the city in the third quarter of the 18th century. All the early woodwork survives, including the original teak windows, teak shutters, the doors and decorative fanlight above the front door. Inside, it has been restored to resemble the home of a Muslim household of the 19th century. Most of the furniture is either English or Dutch, and of a type found in such a house at the time. The museum

Cape Malay flower seller in Trafalgar Place.

BELOW: vibrantly coloured buildings in Bo-Kaap.

EAT

Raise a glass to Table Mountain whilst cruising the harbour on Cape Town's only floating eatery, the Sea Horse Cruising Restaurant & Bar (tel: 021-419 3122), which departs from the V&A Waterfront for dinner at 8pm daily.

contains photographs and pictures depicting the lifestyle of the community as well as interesting relics of daily life such as a fish-seller's horn, once typical of the door-to-door fish hawkers who frequented the city's streets.

Overlooking Bo-Kaap, the **Noon Gun**, located on Signal Hill at the top of vertiginous Longmarket Street, offers magnificent views of the ocean and Table Mountain. Following a long tradition dating from colonial times, when the gun signalled the arrival of an important ship, a cannon shot is fired every day at noon. Today the cannon isn't loaded by hand, but fired automatically with an electronic signal from Cape Town Observatory.

Off Buitengracht Street, between the Bo-Kaap and the Waterfront, the **Gold of Africa Museum** Ⓜ (96 Strand Street; tel: 021-405 1540; Mon–Sat 9.30am–5pm; charge) is housed in the 18th-century Martin Melck House, a fine original townhouse dating from 1788. Operated by Anglo-Gold, the world's largest gold mining company, the museum houses a stunning collection of gold jewellery and cultural

artefacts from around the African continent. West Africa, particularly the Akan kingdoms, gets a good showing – there are examples from Mali, Senegal and Ghana – but there are items from Zimbabwe and South Africa as well, backed up by good background information on the cultural and symbolic importance of gold in African cultures.

The Waterfront

For the best part of 50 years, the oldest part of the harbour, the **Victoria & Alfred (V&A) Waterfront** Ⓝ (www.waterfront.co.za; daily) lay in a state of disrepair. Then in the 1980s it was given a thorough face-lift, emerging as a multifaceted playground crammed with shopping malls, crafts markets, cinemas, five-star hotels and a quay-to-quay choice of almost 100 pubs and restaurants, all set below the spectacular backdrop of Table Mountain. Despite being somewhat artificial, the V&A Waterfront is easily the most successful tourist development of its kind in South Africa, and many visitors to Cape Town make several visits

BELOW: Victoria & Alfred Waterfront.

here. For a seal's-eye perspective, join a boat trip around the harbour – several kiosks along the waterfront offer departures every hour or so.

A highlight of a visit to the waterfront is the **Two Oceans Aquarium** (tel: 021-418 3823; www.aquarium.co.za; daily 9.30am–6pm; charge), which brims with marine life of all shapes and dimensions, from delicate seahorses and spiky sea urchins to colourful reef fish and rapacious great white sharks. Among several innovative displays is a rocky walk-in aviary inhabited by black oystercatchers, African penguins, and rockhopper penguins.

At the southeast side of the complex, the **Clock Tower Centre** – housed in a bright red clock tower built c.1880 – offers a 360-degree view of the harbour and surrounds. Situated within the complex, **Tourism Cape Town Information Centre** (tel: 021-405 4500; daily 9am–9pm) is an excellent source of local and national tourist information, with an internet café attached, as well as an exclusive wine shop that specialises in international deliveries.

The clock tower is also home to the Nelson Mandela Gateway to **Robben Island** (tel: 021-413 4220; www.robben-island.org.za; 3–4 hour tours depart daily at 9am, 11am, 1pm and 3pm; charge). Originally a penal colony for errant slaves, Robben Island became one of the most notorious prisons in the world. Many of the top officials in South Africa's first post-apartheid government were held here at some point, including Nelson Mandela, who spent nearly 20 years in Section B.

Recently proclaimed a Unesco World Heritage Site, Robben Island and its old jail buildings now function as a museum dedicated to the struggle against apartheid, visitable only on guided tours that leave four times daily from the Nelson Mandela Gateway (see tint box below).

Table Mountain

A flat-topped block of horizontally bedded sandstone that dominates the skyline of Cape Town, **Table Mountain ②** is a lodestone to all who live there. This compass, anchor and wilderness in the heart of the Mother City is known to locals simply as "the

You're bound to spot dassies (rock hyraxes) on the top of Table Mountain. Also known as the rock rabbit, the dassie is, in fact, more closely related to the elephant.

BELOW: Robben Island ferry.

Robben Island

Notorious as the prison where Nelson Mandela served the first 18 years of the life sentence he received at the Rivonia Trail of 1963-4, this little kidney-shaped island 11km (7 miles) off the shores of Green Point was named by the Dutch for the seal (rob) colony they encountered here. It has a grim history: this was where Jan van Riebeeck kept rebellious Khoikhoi leaders captive; later, the British used it as a general dumping-ground for lepers, paupers and lunatics. A military base during World War II, it was taken over by the Department of Prisons in 1960, and quickly acquired a reputation as South Africa's most notorious penal colony.

Today, South Africa's own Alcatraz has been turned into a Unesco World Heritage Site, national monument and museum, which can be visited only on one of the four official guided tours that leave from the V&A Waterfront's Nelson Mandela Gateway daily. Up to four hours in duration, the tours include a 30 minute boat ride in either direction, a coach tour of the island (visiting the quarry where prisoners served hard labour in the hot sun), and a walking tour of the prison and Mandela's old cell, guided by a former prisoner. Dolphins often accompany the boat to the island, and once there African penguins – which recolonised the island in 1983 after an absence of 180 years – are more likely to be seen than the seals from which the name "Robben" derives.

TIP

If the Peninsula's troops of chacma baboons become dependent on tourist handouts, they can become annoyingly persistent. Please don't feed them.

BELOW: on board the cable car to the top of Table Mountain.

mountain", while the earliest inhabitants of the area, the indigenous Khoikhoi, referred to the distinctive montane ensemble that incorporates Table Mountain, Devil's Peak, Lion's Head and Signal Hill as Hoerikwaggo, literally "Mountains in the Sea".

To the top

No visit to Cape Town is complete without ascending Table Mountain to enjoy the views that stretch in all directions: over the City Bowl, Waterfront, Table Bay and Robben Island to the north, across Camps Bay and the wave-battered Atlantic seaboard to the west, across False Bay to the Hottentots Holland in the east, and over the undulating mountainous spine of the Cape Peninsula to the south.

Be aware, however, that the views – as well as the operation of the cableway to the top, and the feasibility of hiking there – are wholly dependent on the weather, so it is always advisable to visit Table Mountain early in your stay in Cape Town. The most popular and effortless way to reach the summit is with the **Table Mountain Cableway**

(Tafelberg Road; tel: 021-424 818 www.tablemountain.net tickets availabl at the base or online), which opene in 1929 and celebrated carrying its 2 millionth passenger to the top in 201(Following a major upgrade in 199 the 64-passenger cars rotate throug 360° as they ascend, so that all pas sengers get views both of the rock fac below the upper cableway, and ou across the city and coastline below. I takes between three and nine minute to get to the top, depending on th wind resistance.

Routes by foot

The other way to the top is by foo A popular route is **Platteklip Gorge** following a 3km (1.6-mile) path tha zigzags uphill from Tafelberg Road it takes fit walkers about an hour t complete in one direction, and if yo turn right at the top, a path leads to th Upper Cableway, from where you ca take the cable car back down to Tafel berg Road.

Other options include the 6km (4 mile) **Pipe Track**, which starts at Kloo Nek, continues on to Corridor Ravine and takes a total of about five hours u and down, and the **Contour Path** tha starts at the Rhodes Memorial.

The steep path up **Skeleton Gorge** starting at Kirstenbosch Botanical Gar den, was a favourite of former presiden Jan Smuts, who walked it regularly into his seventies. It leads through lush forest then climbs over steep rocky sec tions to Maclear's Beacon, erected by the astronomer Sir Thomas Maclear in 1843 at the mountain's 1,086 metre (3,560ft) summit.

However you ascend Table Moun tain, be aware that a chill wind often blows across the plateau, making a sweater or windbreaker necessary and that the fickle weather condi tions means you should also take suit able protection in case it rains. If you ascend on foot, be prepared to turn back at the first hint of the mist that frequently blankets the upper reaches of the mountain.

The relatively flat section of the mountain above the cableway is serviced by a busy restaurant and coffee shop, and crisscrossed with several walking trails through a montane *fynbos* community of 1,500 plant species, 50 of which are endemic or endangered. A highlight of the mountain in season is the flowering protea shrubs, which often attract *fynbos* endemics such as Cape sugarbird, protea canary and orange-breasted sunbirds.

As for mammals, the rock hyraxes that scramble across the rocks around the coffee shop are neither so habituated nor so visible as in the days when feeding them was permitted.

You may encounter troops of chacma baboon or even the immense eland antelope, the endemic Cape grysbok or the endearing grey mongoose. A small population of the goat-like tahr, introduced from Asia in the 19th century, was heavily culled in 2004, an ecologically sound move that nevertheless attracted strong criticism from sentimental locals; a handful of survivors and their descendants are still seen from time to time.

Eastern slopes

Table Mountain forms the centrepiece of the Table Mountain National Park (tel: 021-701 8692; www.sanparks.org), a vast but discontinuous protected area that was gazetted in 1998 to cover some 73 percent of the Cape Peninsula. The park incorporates a number of former nature reserves and other protected areas, such as Boulders Beach, the Cape of Good Hope, and the magnificent 560-hectare (1,380-acre) **Kirstenbosch National Botanical Garden ❸** (Rhodes Drive; tel: 021-799 8783; www.sanbi.org; Sept–Mar daily 8am–7pm, May–Aug daily 8am–6pm; charge) gracing the mountain's eastern slopes. The formally laid-out beds of Kirstenbosch display some of South Africa's showiest flora before blending into the natural protea *fynbos* and yellowwood forests on the mountain slopes. In total, more than 5,000 plant species are found in the gardens, along with a varied selection of birds.

Flanking Table Mountain are the imposing peaks of **Lion's Head** and **Devil's Peak**. It was on the slopes of the latter, according to legend, that a

Check the wind direction before heading out: if a southeasterly is blowing it will bring the chilly waters of the Antarctic along with it.

BELOW LEFT: view of the city from Table Mountain.
BELOW RIGHT: Kirstenbosch National Botanical Garden.

George Frederick Watt's statue Energy *at the Rhodes Memorial.*

retired soldier named Van Hunk was challenged by the devil to a pipe-smoking contest. The result of their showdown can best be judged in the summertime, when a seemingly motionless sheet of cloud (popularly known as the "tablecloth") often hovers over the mountain top.

Devil's Peak is also the site of the **Groote Schuur Estate** ❹, once owned by Cecil Rhodes. Bequeathed to the nation on his death in 1902, it now includes a number of ministerial residences as well as the campus of the University of Cape Town. The Groote Schuur Hospital and Medical School here was the scene for the world's first heart transplant, performed by Professor Christiaan Barnard in 1967. Higher on the same slopes, the

Rhodes Memorial (Residence Road; www.rhodesmemorial.co.za), designed by Herbert Baker and built in 1912, is an impressive U-shaped building fronted by Doric columns and a massive flight of 49 steps, offering wonderful views across northern Cape Town and the Cape Flats to the jagged Hottentots Holland Mountains.

The Cape's grape

Head out on the Eastern Boulevard or De Waal Drive, both of which become the M3 route.

Continue along this road, leaving the city behind you, and climb Wynberg Hill (where Jan van Riebeeck first extended his vineyards), before dropping down into leafy Constantia Valley. This is one of Cape Town's

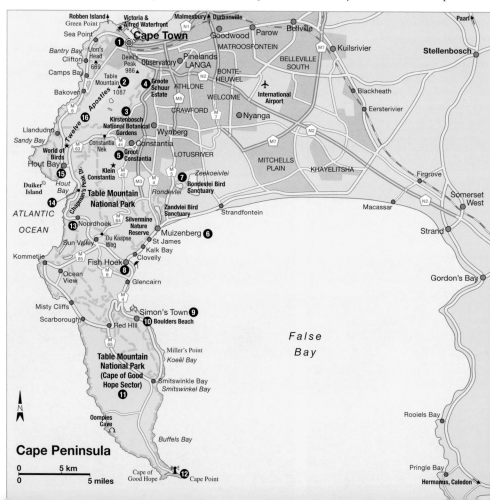

most beautiful suburbs, and certainly its most exclusive.

Here, you can visit the site first developed by early Dutch governor Simon van der Stel in 1685 as his private estate. As well as building a modest homestead here which he named **Groot Constantia** ❺ (Groot Constantia Road; www.grootconstantia. co.za; Nov–Apr daily 9am–5.30pm, May–Sept daily 9am–4.30pm), van der Stel planted vines. A century later, the farm had become world-famous for its wines (a drop of "the finest old Constantia that ever was tasted" soothes Elinor Dashwood's broken heart in Jane Austen's novel *Sense and Sensibility*), and the homestead enlarged and converted into a splendid manor house. Bought by the Cape government in 1885, Groot Constantia is now run as a model wine farm. The house and old wine cellar now house the Iziko Groot Constantia Museum (tel: 021-794 5140; www.iziko.org.za; daily 10am–5pm).

Van der Stel's original farm was later divided into a number of smaller plots. **Klein Constantia** (Klein Con-

stantia Road; tel: 021-794 5188; www. kleinconstantia.com; Mon–Fri 9am–5pm, Sat 9am–1pm), with its magnificent maturation cellars set inside a mountain, is one of the Cape's most rewarding wineries. So, too, is nearby **Buitenverwachting** (Klein Constantia Road; tel: 021-794 3522; www.buitenverwachting.co.za; Mon–Fri 9am–5pm, Sat 9am–1pm), whose name translates as "beyond expectation" – a fair description of this gracious old manor house in its lovely setting of spreading vineyards and oak-dotted hillsides. The restaurant it contains is excellent, too.

Also centred on a lovely old manor house, **Steenberg Estate** (Steenberg Road; tel: 021-713 2211; www.steenbergvineyards.co.za; Mon–Fri 9am–6pm, Sat–Sun 10am–6pm) is known for its award-winning wines, excellent restaurant and one of the best golf courses in the Cape.

Finally, there is **Constantia Uitsig** (Spaanschemat River Road; tel: 021-794 6500; www.constantia-uitsig.com), which houses two award-winning restaurants as well as a more moderately priced café that forms an ideal lunch stop.

The Lion's Head marks the start of the Atlantic Seaboard.

BELOW: Groot Constantia.

It is off Cape Point that the Flying Dutchman, a phantom ship with tattered sails and a broken mast, is doomed to sail until the end of time – a legend which inspired an opera by Wagner.

The Cape Peninsula

Cape Town stands at the northern end of the spectacular Cape Peninsula, a 60km (36-mile) long sliver of mountainous land that runs southward from the city to Cape Point, flanked by the wild open Atlantic to the west and the stiller, warmer waters of False Bay to the east. It's best to dedicate a full day to the circular road trip that follows both sides of the peninsula's coastline, allowing plenty of time to stop to swim and admire the views, to picnic or eat at a restaurant, and to take in the many historic buildings and the unique fauna and flora. Equally, you could cover different parts of the circuit on different days, for instance travelling to Cape Point for the views, or to Muizenberg for a swim, or to Scarborough for a leisurely seafood lunch.

Wherever you travel on the peninsula, a near-constant is the dramatic scenic contrast between the swelling ocean and the epic mountain chain that connects Table Mountain to Cape Point. Much of it now protected in Table Mountain National Park, the peninsula embraces such famous formations as the Twelve Apostles, Constantiaberg and Noordhoek Peak, while a network of precipitous mountain passes and coastal drives links its rocky coves, sandy beaches, residential villages and fishing communities like beads on a necklace.

To make the most of a drive round the peninsula, you should set out early – ideally, just as the sun breaches the jagged Hottentots-Holland Mountains and dapples the surface of False Bay. Travelling clockwise, the journey begins at **Muizenberg** ❻ on the east coast, about 20km (12 miles) from the city centre. This bustling seaside town was a popular resort in Victorian times; it was in a cottage here (now a small museum) that Cecil Rhodes spent his last years when his health prematurely failed him. The beachfront here has become rather tacky, but the surf is still splendid.

The nearby **Rondevlei Bird Sanctuary** ❼ (www.rondevlei.co.za; daily except Christmas Day 7.30am–5pm, until 7pm Dec–Feb; charge;) is mainly of interest to bird-watchers, with 230 species recorded including a resident popula-

BELOW: the sandy shores of Clifton.

tion of the uncommon great crested grebe, but visitors are also likely to see the hippos that were reintroduced a few years back to help thin out the aquatic vegetation.

Running south from Muizenberg down the False Bay coast, narrow Main Road follows closely alongside the railway line, passing the pretty village of **St James** (with its much photographed row of colourful beach huts), **Kalk Bay** (whose old fishing harbour is home to tame seals and an excellent fish market) and **Fish Hoek** ❽ (with what is arguably the peninsula's safest swimming beach).

Simon's Town and Boulders

From Fish Hoek, fork left on to the M4, and follow the winding road through Glencairn to the historic port settlement of **Simon's Town** ❾. Named after Simon van der Stel, who first recommended it as a safe winter anchorage, it was a Royal Navy base from the time of the second British occupation of the Cape in 1806 until it was handed over to the South African Navy in 1957. The main road, George

Street, is lined with attractive Victorian facades, while Jubilee Square's best-known landmark is the statue of Able Seaman Just Nuisance, a Great Dane who befriended and became a mascot of the Royal Navy during World War II prior to his death in 1944.

Military history buffs will enjoy the **SA Naval Museum** (West Dockyard; tel: 021-787 4686; daily 10am–4pm; charge), while local history is the main focus of the **Simon's Town Museum** (Court Road; tel: 021-786 3046; Mon–Fri 9am–4pm, Sat 10am–1pm, Sun 11am–3pm; charge), housed in a 1777 building that started life as the winter residence for the Dutch East India Company's Governor at the Cape.

At the southern end of Simon's Town, the giant granite rocks at **Boulders Beach** ❿ (Kleintuin Road; www. sanparks.org; daily 8am–6.30pm; charge) were first used as a breeding site by a few pairs of African penguin in 1985. Now incorporated into part of Table Mountain National Park, the beach hosts several thousand of these comical and fearless birds, forming one of just three breeding colonies on the African

Boulders Beach is home to colonies of African penguins.

BELOW: colourful beach huts at St James.

Unsurprisingly, township street art celebrates the country's new generation of political leaders such as Thabo Mbeki.

mainland. The main breeding colony at the north end of the enclosed beach is accessible by a network of stilted boardwalks and viewing platforms, while the secluded beach at the southerly end sometimes offers visitors the opportunity to swim alongside penguins – an unforgettable experience.

Cape of Good Hope

Leaving Simon's Town, the M4 winds up past **Miller's Point** and **Smitswinkel Bay** with wonderful views down to the sea far below. A 12km (8-mile) turn-off to the left takes you to Table Mountain National Park's 7,750-hectare (19,000-acre) **Cape of Good Hope** sector ⓫ (www.sanparks.org; Oct–Mar daily 6am–6pm, Apr–Sept daily 7am–5pm; charge).

Extraordinarily scenic, even by the Cape's high standards, the Cape of Good Hope, with its innumerable viewpoints and uninhabited beaches, warrants a full day's exploration. For those with limited time, however, the one "must do" is **Cape Point Lighthouse** ⓬, which was built in 1913–19 and affords breathtaking views over

sheer cliffs whose innate drama genuinely evokes the sense of being at the edge of the continent. The most southerly point on the peninsula, the lighthouse can be reached either via a short but very steep footpath, or a funicular (a cable-drawn railway designed for steep slopes).

Cape of Good Hope is rewarding for its fauna and flora. Protected since 1939, the vegetation is near-pristine and consists mainly of *fynbos* – the major vegetation type of the Cape Floral Kingdom, the smallest, and for its size, the richest of the world's six floral kingdoms. Scattered with attractive winter-blooming protea bushes, the reserve supports a wide selection of *fynbos* birds, while larger wildlife includes Chacma baboon, Cape mountain zebra, eland, bontebok, grey rhebok and grysbok.

Marine wildlife is also well represented, from the seals, cormorants and oystercatchers that haunt the shore to the whales and dolphins that are frequently seen out at sea.

The Atlantic Seaboard

To complete the loop around the peninsula, returning to the city along the western seaboard, turn left as you leave the reserve, then left again where the road forks, 8km (5 miles) later. This will take you past the hamlets of **Misty Cliffs** and **Scarborough**, and the fishing village of **Kommetjie**. Turn left onto the M6 at the next intersection (if you go straight on it will take you through the Fish Hoek Gap), then left again after 900 metres (½ mile) and you will reach **Noordhoek** ⓭. This is where Cape Town residents head if they want to be alone at the beach; it's 7km (4 miles) long and it is wildly scenic – breathtaking, even.

Back on the M6, the road snakes steeply upwards on a nerve-racking 9km (5-mile) journey around **Chapman's Peak Drive** ⓮ (www.chapmanspeakdrive.co.za). One of the world's most spectacular scenic drives, this route reopened as a toll road in early 2004, after

Best Beaches

Given Cape Town's seductive summer climate, visitors are often surprised by the chilly water temperatures at the many popular bathing beaches – among them Clifton, Camps Bay, Llandudno and nudist Sandy Bay – that run along the Atlantic Seaboard of the western Cape Peninsula. It has a lot to do with the whims of the southeasterly wind. When this wind pushes the warm surface water away from the western shore, the water is replaced from underneath. This phenomenon is called upwelling, bringing with it the cold Antarctic water of the Benguela Current. Which means that water temperatures can be as low as 12°C or even 10°C (54–56°F) after a strong "blow". Ironically, it is in the winter (June–Aug), when the southeaster abates, that the Atlantic beaches experience their warmest sea temperatures.

Those who enjoy swimming in the sea are generally advised to head to the warmer beaches fronting False Bay along the eastern side of the peninsula: Muizenberg, Fish Hoek or even the more remote Strand Beach near Somerset West. But locals will tell you that the real secret to choosing a beach is the wind direction: if there is a cloud-cloth on Table Mountain it means the southeaster is blowing and you should head straight for Clifton or Llandudno; but if there is a northwesterly sea fog brewing, go to Muizenberg and environs.

having been closed for several years due to rock falls. It would be something of a challenge to steer around this road's 114 curves while also admiring the view – but fortunately there are several parking spots at which you can stop and enjoy the scenery.

You should now return to Ou Kaapse Weg then follow the M3 to Constantia and past the entrance to Groot Constantia, continuing over Constantia Nek to **Hout Bay** ⑮, another fishing village turned satellite suburb. Not only is it the headquarters of the peninsula's rock-lobster fleet, but freshly caught fish of all description are sold daily off the quayside – so it's hardly surprising that the village has some fine seafood restaurants.

The main tourist focus here is the old harbour, or Mariner's Wharf (tel: 021-790 1100; www.marinerswharf.com; daily 9am–5.30pm), which has a decent selection of seafood restaurants, along with a selection of shops and craft stalls aimed at tourists.

A popular excursion from Hout Bay is to nearby **Duiker Island**, a breeding site for thousands of Cape fur seals. The old harbour is lined with kiosks offering 45–60 minute boat trips out to see the island; typically a boat leaves every 30 minutes or so in the morning, but departures are infrequent after lunch.

Meanwhile, the giant walk-in aviary at the **World of Birds** (Valley Road; tel: 021-790 2730; www.worldofbirds.org.za; daily 9am–5pm; charge) is Africa's largest bird park and offers the opportunity of nose-to-beak encounters with a wide selection of exotic and endemic species including the crowned crane, the bald ibis and the photogenic Indian blue peafowl with its beautiful iridescent feathers.

Kalk Bay Lighthouse.

Heading north

From here over Suikerbossie Hill, you'll be able to peer down into Llandudno with its perfect sickle-shaped beach and rocky points. This is near the journey's end, but some of the best is still to come. After Llandudno, the grand profiles of the **Twelve Apostles** ⑯ (Table Mountain's western buttresses) come into view, jutting out like the prows of gigantic ships at anchor along the shore. When the southeaster

BELOW LEFT: Cape Point Lighthouse.
BELOW RIGHT: diving in Hout Bay.

Khayelitsha is the second largest township in South Africa, after Soweto near Johannesburg.

BELOW LEFT: cyclist on Chapman's Pass. **BELOW RIGHT:** absailing down Table Mountain.

whips its tablecloth over the crags, the clouds look like sea swells frothing around their tightly berthed hulls.

The M6 now winds through some of the most sought-after and exclusive residential addresses in the country: Camps Bay, Clifton and Bantry Bay. The first two also have popular beaches, the sort where high society sun-lovers go more to see and be seen than to frolic in the (very cold) sea. From Bantry Bay, the road passes the busy seaside suburbs of Sea Point and Green Point before leading back to City Bowl.

Cape Town active

Cape Town's post-apartheid resurrection as an international tourist hub has been mirrored by a veritable mushrooming of worthwhile day trips and adventure activities, for which further information can be obtained from the tourist office in the Clock Tower Centre or its website (www.tourismcapetown. co.za). Offering a similar insight into contemporary black South Africa as Johannesburg's Soweto Tours, township tours to **Khayelitsha** (*see feature opposite*), **Langa** (the country's oldest

township) and **Imizamu Yethu** (ne Hout Bay) also focus on the hardshi and discriminatory laws that permeate township life during the apartheid er

For other popular and relative sedate day tours, visit the **Stellenbosc Wine Routes** and whale-watching i the seaside fishing village of **Herman** (*the Western Cape chapter, see pages 17 and 183*). More energetically, variou local tour companies offer the opport nity to abseil down a 100-metre (328f cliff on Table Mountain (the views a breathtaking); kloofing (leaping fron a cliff into the water below) on th Steenbras River Gorge near Gordon Bay; white-water rafting at various site depending on the current water leve sandboarding on the dunes to the nort of the city centre; as well as canoein paragliding, water-skiing, caving, roc climbing and game fishing.

Roughly 50 established dive sites ar dotted around the waters off the penir sula, offering access to rocky reefs, sut marine caverns and swaying forests (kelp inhabited by a varied menageri of marine creatures – including shark (*see Travel Tips page 362*).

Township Life

The majority of urban South Africans live in townships, most of which have evolved from "non-white" settlements on the periphery of "white" towns and cities

The street lamps that light the city's more affluent suburbs are still shining when Khayelitsha – Cape Town's largest township – awakes. an hour's journey by overloaded minibus taxi from the city centre and industrial areas, Khayelitsha means "new home" in Xhosa, but for the 400,000 people who live here, it could as easily mean "early start".

The dawn light reveals the extraordinary array of building materials used in Khayelitsha's homes, from broken bits of advertising hoarding to bin liners and flattened tin cans. Some parts of the township now have electricity; elsewhere the wealthier houses use car batteries or jerry-rigged illegal connections to illuminate the cramped rooms. In summer, the southeaster drives sand into every corner; in winter, there is mud everywhere.

Many of Khayelitsha's residents fled to Cape Town from apartheid-era "independent homelands" such as the Transkei and Ciskei, which were ravaged by overcrowding and soil erosion, and presented a grim shortage of job opportunities. Once in the big city, however, job prospects remained limited, wages were low, and government policies forced those categorised as non-white to make their home in Khayelitsha or one of the other undeveloped, crime-ridden townships that cover the Cape Flats, the windy flood-prone plains that lie between the wealthy Southern Suburbs and the Hottentots Holland Mountains.

Township visit

Most visitors get their first glimpse of the city's townships – among them Langa ("Sun"), Gugulethu ("Our Pride"), Nyanga ("Moon") and Hanover Park (named after District Six's main street) – as they follow the busy N2 highway from the airport to the city centre. But no trip to Cape Town is complete without paying a proper visit to a township – for reasons of safety, something best done as part of an organised tour.

ABOVE: Imizamo Yethu township supports over 35,000 people at the foot of Table Mountain above Hout Bay.

Khayelitsha features in most programmes offered by township tour operators. A visit normally begins with an overview of the township from Lookout Hill, and may also take in the Khayelitsha Craft Market, set up in 1997 as a self-help organisation, and the Abalimi Bezekhaya Peace Park and Community Garden (www.alabimi.org.za). Outside Khayelitsha, the Lwandle Migrant Labour Museum (tel: 021-845 6119; www.lwandle.com; Mon–Fri 9.30am–4pm; charge) is a former hostel that preserves the bleak living conditions of the migrant labourers it housed during the apartheid era.

Langa

Cape Town's oldest township, dating from 1927, Langa is visibly wealthier than Khayelitsha, with a higher proportion of brick houses. Its cultural heart is the vibrant Guga S'thebe Arts & Cultural Centre, which hosts everything from dance classes to craft workshops. The Langa-Sharpeville Massacre Memorial, unveiled in 2010, commemorates the 50th anniversary of the tragic 1960 incident in which 69 people were killed by police fire in a protest against the pass laws.

But visiting a township is less about ticking off the prescribed sights than it is about experiencing a living culture – you might join locals for a beer in a lively "shebeen" (bar), browse among roadside stalls, or have your hair cut at an informal beauty salon. ❑

THE WESTERN CAPE

Deserted beaches, rugged mountain ranges, colourful wildflower displays, bountiful vineyards and whale watching – all within day-tripping distance of the Mother City

The hinterland within a 200km (124-mile) radius of Cape Town is an area of outstanding natural beauty, and it wouldn't be difficult to devote a fortnight to exploring its beaches, mountains, nature reserves and vineyards – and still be left with a long list of outstanding places to visit and things to do.

The Western Cape can be broken up into three broad regions – the West Coast, the Winelands and the Overberg – each of which has a distinct character and is treated as a self-contained travel circuit in this chapter. Given sufficient time, however, it is possible to plan a loop that takes in any two of these regions, or all three – you could, for instance, follow the R27 along the West Coast as far as Saldanha, then cut east along the R45 to Paarl, Stellenbosch and Franschhoek in the Winelands, then follow the R43 through Caledon to Hermanus and the Overberg.

THE WEST COAST

The roughly 200km (124 miles) of Atlantic coastline between Cape Town and Lambert's Bay offers a tantalising smorgasbord of unspoilt beaches, sleepy fishing harbours, magnificent spring wildflower displays and superb marine bird life. So why, then, hasn't this picturesque stretch of coast ever caught on as a tourist destination? The answer, in a nutshell, is that swimming conditions here tend to be chillier and rougher than along the Indian Ocean coastline, making it a poor bet for a straightforward beach holiday. Equally, the relatively low-key nature of tourist development along the West Coast does make it that much more alluring to anybody interested in a bit of off-the-beaten-track exploration.

The main road servicing this region is the N7, which runs about 50km (30 miles) inland for most of its length,

Main attractions
BLOUBERGSTRAND
WEST COAST NATIONAL PARK
STELLENBOSCH AND ITS WINELANDS
FRANSCHHOEK AND ITS WINELANDS
HERMANUS
DE HOOP NATURE RESERVE

PRECEDING PAGES: De Hoop Nature Reserve.
LEFT: Overberg coastline. **RIGHT:** Meerlust Wine Estate, near Stellenbosch.

It takes the male crayfish between seven to 10 years to reach a size at which he may legally be caught for human consumption; it takes the female 20 years.

and forms the springboard for the little-used route between Cape Town and Johannesburg via the Northern Cape (*see page 299*). For sightseeing purposes, however, a more scenic option would be to leave Cape Town along the coastal R27, through the somewhat industrialised suburb of Milnerton, towards **Saldanha** then (assuming you have a night or two to spare) on to Lambert's Bay, before returning on the nippier N7 via **Malmesbury**.

The first of several worthwhile stops along the R27, the former fishing village of **Bloubergstrand** ❶ is now little more than a suburb of the city whose centre lies less than 15km (9 miles) further south. Its main claim to fame is as the site of that classic view of Cape Town with Table Mountain in the background (the one so beloved of postcard manufacturers). Bloubergstrand also has a long sandy beach, studded with rocky outcrops in the north, and its large breakers are very popular with surfers. Quieter Melkbosstrand, 11km (7 miles) further north, has a similar view of Cape Town.

After another 40km (24 miles), a short sideroad runs west to **Yzerfontein**, a scenic fishing village set on the remote southern border of the West Coast National Park. Some 15km (9 miles) inland of this, the presciently named small town of **Darling** ❷ leapt from obscurity in 1996 when gay icon and satirist Pieter Dirk Uys converted one of its railway buildings into a delightfully kitsch cabaret theatre and museum called **Evita se Perron** (Darling Station; www.evita.co.za; Tue–Sun 10am–4pm; charge). The theatre is named after Uys's politicised Dame Edna-esque alter ego Evita Bezuidenhout – *perron* is Afrikaans for railway platform – and his one-man show, the full schedule of which is posted on the website, forms a lively and irreverent introduction to contemporary South African politics.

West Coast National Park to Lambert's Bay

About 20km (12 miles) further north along the R27, the **West Coast National Park** ❸ (tel: 022-772 2144; www.sanparks.org; daily 9am–5pm; charge) protects a 30km (18-mile) stretch of coast dominated by the

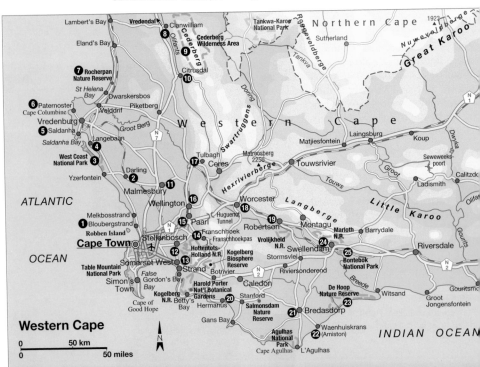

ATLANTIC OCEAN

INDIAN OCEAN

Northern Cape

Western Cape

Little Karoo

Western Cape

0 ___ 50 km
0 ___ 50 miles

Lagoon. This magnificent wetland is one of the world's most important conservation areas for migrant birds, and its islands host significant breeding colonies of Cape cormorant, Hartlaub's gull, Cape gannet and seven other species. But most people who visit this park do so to marvel at another natural phenomenon – the glorious eruption of spring wildflowers that generally takes place in August.

Open during wildflower season only, the Postberg section of the national park is a favourite stopover for botanical enthusiasts, and it also harbours large mammals such as springbok, bontebok and gemsbok. En route to Postberg, you'll pass Church Haven, a traditional Cape fishing village hugging the salt-marsh shoreline of Langebaan Lagoon. The resort village of **Langebaan 4**, on the lagoon's eastern shore, caters for a good range of water sports, including angling, yachting, water-skiing and sail boarding.

To the north, the lagoon flows into Saldanha Bay, the deepest natural harbour in South Africa. Unsurprisingly, there is a large naval presence at

Saldanha **5**, and it's also a key railway link, where enormous quantities of iron ore are deposited after being shuttled across the Kalahari from the mines at Sishen. One might wonder at the effect of all the battleship and freighter traffic on the vulnerable ecosystem of the lagoon, but the mussels that have been farmed here since 1984 remain delicious. So, too, are crayfish from **Paternoster 6**, an unspoilt fishing village some 30km (18 miles) further north – both can be sampled at local restaurants.

The rocks off Cape Columbine, which lies just 3km (2 miles) south of Paternoster, once posed a real threat to sailors; several ships came to grief here before the lighthouse was built. Today, the cape and surrounding *fynbos*-covered dunes are protected within the scenic **Cape Columbine Nature Reserve** (tel: 022-752 2718; daily; charge), which forms an excellent retreat for self-sufficient campers. The reserve is a breeding ground for gulls, cormorants and ibises among others, and is at its most attractive in springtime, when the wildflowers bloom.

Picturesque lighthouses still protect the Cape's busy shipping trade.

BELOW: walking trail through the Postberg section of the West Coast National Park.

Take One Crayfish...

Until the beginning of the 20th century, crayfish were so plentiful in Cape waters that they were viewed with disdain by the upper classes, and used instead as fodder for the inmates of the penal colony on Robben Island. Today, however, crayfish are regarded as a delicacy, commanding top billing and high prices on seafood menus in the most elegant restaurants. Indeed, so valuable has the rock lobster fishing industry become in South Africa that they are often referred to as the "red gold from the sea". The species Jasus lalandi is the one most commonly found on the West Coast, and in smaller numbers from Cape Point to East London.

To cook them yourself, bring a large saucepan of salted water to the boil. Plunge the live crayfish (one per person) firmly into the saucepan, head end first; this kills them instantly. Cover the pan and boil for about 20 minutes until the crayfish turn bright red. Now place in a pan of cold water and when cool, chop off the pincers and split each body lengthways. Remove the small sac at the back of the head (the stomach), the large intestine running from the stomach to the base of the tail, the liver and the lungs on either side of the body. Serve as simply as possible – lemon wedges, a pot of mayonnaise, brown bread and a bottle of chilled white wine are really all you need.

Found around the coastline, the indigenous Cape fur seals like Lambert's Bay, particularly.

BELOW: Cape gannets on Bird Island Nature Reserve.

Situated near the one-resort town of **Dwarskersbors** about 35km (21 miles) north of Saldanha, the **Rocherpan Nature Reserve** ❼ (tel: 0861 227 362 8873; www.capenature.co.za; Sept–Apr daily 7am–6pm, May–Aug daily 8am–5pm; charge) is home to thousands of wading birds, including seasonal concentrations of flamingos, as well as a variety of small antelope. The bird life is even more abundant around the picturesque lagoon at **Eland's Bay**. The town itself is not all that interesting, but the beach is excellent, and has become a popular weekend destination for "surfies" from Cape Town.

On the way to the small fishing town of **Lambert's Bay**, 16km (10 miles) further north (Bartolomeu Dias was the first European to arrive here in 1487), the coast grows increasingly lonely and deserted. If you don't mind the smell and the noise, walk across the stone causeway from Lambert's Bay to **Bird Island Nature Reserve** (tel: 0861 227 362 8873; www.cape nature.co.za; daily Sept–Apr 7am–7pm, May–Aug 7am–5pm; charge), with its nesting colony of around 14,000 Cape

gannets. Most of the island is closed to public access, but an observation tower provides a fine view not only of the gannets but also of the 60-odd African penguins who breed here. Cape fur seals are often present in the town's picturesque harbour.

The Cederberg

Time to head some 67km (42 miles) inland of Lambert's Bay for a change of scene. Here, just off the N7, in the heart of the irrigated Olifants River Valley, lies **Clanwilliam** ❽ – an orchard town founded at the beginning of the 18th century and still in possession of some fine historic buildings. One of them, the Old Jail (1808), now houses the municipal museum and tourist office (daily). The famous beverage known as *rooibos* (red bush) tea is grown around here.

North of Clanwilliam, the stretch of the Olifants River Valley around **Vredendal** is an emergent centre of wine production. Tastings are available at half a dozen estates, most of which traditionally specialise in cheap 'n' cheerful whites, though some 25 percent of

the local plantation now consists of red cultivars. A popular starting point is the vast Namaqua Winery (tel: 027-213 1080; www.namaquawines.co.za), an amalgamation of the long-serving Vredendal and Spruitdrift Estates whose annual output of almost ten million cases makes it the largest wine cooperative in the southern hemisphere. Tastings are available at both Spruitdrift, on the outskirts of Vredendal, though its iconic Gôiya export range – with stylised bushman painting on the label – might already be familiar to UK wine buffs.

Clanwilliam is also the springboard for excursions into the 700-sq-km (275-sq-mile) **Cederberg Wilderness Area** ❾ (tel: 027-482 2403 or 0861 227 362 8873; www.capenature.co.za; daily; charge), which protects a vast craggy mountain range whose highest peak, the 2,027 metre (6,650ft) Sneeuberg (Snow Mountain) does indeed get covered with snow each winter. Part of the Cape Floral Region Unesco World Heritage Site, the mountains are named after an indigenous cedar species *Widdringtonia cederbergensis* that still survives on the more inaccessible slopes, despite extensive deforestation. Several short walks on the lower slopes are possible to day visitors; one of the most worthwhile leads to a well-preserved rock-art panel depicting an elephant herd.

The number of overnight hiking permits for the Cederberg is strictly limited, so if you plan to hike here during the busy summer holidays, you should arrange permits (and accommodation) a few months in advance. It's definitely worth the trouble. You'll encounter bizarre sandstone formations such as the dramatic Wolfsberg Arch and the weird Maltese Cross, caves decorated with ancient rock paintings, and crystal-clear rivers to swim in. Lucky hikers might come across spoor of the mountains' secretive leopard population, but are considerably more likely to see klipspringer, baboon and rock hyrax. The Cederberg is particularly attractive and colourful during the spring wildflower season.

Back down in the Olifants River Valley, you can take a leisurely canoe trip 50km (30 miles) south to **Citrusdal** ❿, which – as its name (literally Citrus

The unique spiral horns only occur on fully grown male kudus.

BELOW: Wolfberg Arch, Cederberg Wilderness Area.

The wine cellar at Boschendal Estate, Franschhoek.

BELOW: Boschendal Estate vineyards, overlooked by the Drakenstein mountains.

Valley) suggests – exports thousands of tonnes of fruit annually. The private reserve known as **Kagga Kamma** (www.kaggakamma.co.za) can be reached from both Citrusdal and Ceres. As well as such game as kudu and springbok, you can admire some old San rock paintings, and visit a reconstructed San village, founded in 1989 with the aim of preserving the traditional lifestyle of this ancient people – or rather, with the aim of showing tourists how they live. Even though the anthropologists who set up the village have done so with the best of intentions, the place still seems very much like an open-air zoo in which the humans take the place of animals.

The drive south from Citrusdal along the N7 passes through a region that's been known as the Swartland (Black Land) since the earliest days of European settlement, most probably in reference to the *renosterbos* (rhinoceros bush) that once grew there prolifically and turns black seasonally. Today, it might more accurately be known as the *geel* (yellow) land, since it produces about 15 percent of the national wheat crop – as well as being a burgeoning centre of wine production. The Swartland Winery (tel: 022-482 1134; www.swwines.co.za; tastings and cellar tours, Mon–Fri 8am–5pm, Sat 9am–2pm), which lies some 50km (30 miles) before Cape Town on the outskirts of **Malmesbury ⓫**, is one of the country's largest cooperatives, using grapes grown on almost 100 different farms to produce a popular range of 20-plus everyday wines (the Shiraz and Columbard deserve singling out) and a more limited selection of reserve reds in good years.

THE WINELANDS

The traditional centre of Cape viniculture, and home to its highest concentration of vineyards today, is the mountainous region situated immediately east of Cape Town itself. Known as the *Boland* (Highland), this region – studded as it is with literally hundreds of wineries, and distinguished by some beautiful montane landscapes and elegant Cape Dutch architecture – begs extended exploration over a few days Indeed, it would require a full week of

dedicated effort to cover each of the dozen or so wine routes thoroughly

A more normal strategy is to pick one or two routes, depending on your main interests. If you're after classic Cape Dutch architecture and memorable mountain scenery, then concentrate on the venerable estates that grace the footslopes of the Hottentots Holland Mountains around Somerset West, Stellenbosch and Franschhoek – all of which can easily be visited as a day trip from Cape Town. On the other hand, serious wine-tasters looking to ship home a few bargains might prefer to head for the relatively remote and untouristed routes centred on Wellington, Worcester or Robertson.

Most estates open from around 9am–4pm daily for tasting and the more popular ones generally charge a nominal charge, but some have abbreviated opening hours or close altogether on Saturday or Sunday – full details are provided in free booklets at the tourist offices in Stellenbosch or Cape Town, or you can ring the estate to confirm. At tasting sessions, it is customary to deposit the tasted wine in a spittoon, but few people do so; unless a driver designates him or herself, there's a strong case for even the most independent-minded of travellers hooking up with one of the many organised wine-tasting tours that run out of Cape Town daily and generally take in up to five different estates.

Stellenbosch

An obvious first port of call in the Boland is **Stellenbosch** ⑫, which lies about 30km (18 miles) east of Cape Town as the crow flies, and is connected to it by regular passenger trains and several different road routes (the quickest being to take the N2 west past the airport then to turn north onto the R310). Founded in 1679 by the Dutch Governor Simon van der Stel, this architectural jewel is the second-oldest town in South Africa, and lies at the heart of the winelands. It's known for its university, the first Afrikaans-

language institution of higher education to have been established anywhere in the country, and for having the largest number of Cape Dutch houses of any town in the region. The most harmonious examples are to be found on Dorp, Church and Drostdy streets.

On and facing Die Braak village green, are the Rhenish Church, the VOC Kruithuis (Powder House; Sept–May Mon–Fri 9am–2pm; charge), a white-washed munitions magazine that was built in 1777 and now serves as a low-key military museum, and the **Burgerhuis Museum** (tel: 021-887 0339; Mon–Fri 8am–4.30pm, Sat 10am–1pm and 2–5pm), an H-shaped Cape Dutch building dating to 1797. Heading up Dorp Street, you pass the century-old **Oom Samie se Winkel** (Uncle Samie's Store; Mon–Fri 8.30am–5.30pm, Sat–Sun 9am–5pm; tel: 021-887 0797), an old-fashioned shop stocked with all sorts of curiosities, and the picturesque **Lutheran church**, built in 1851.

Just off Dorp Street, the **Stellenbosch Village Museum** (37 Ryneveld Street; tel: 021-887 2948 Mon–Sat 9.30am–5pm, Sun 10am–1pm and

The Cape Dutch architecture of the winelands is as rich as the grapes on offer.

BELOW: a tasting room at the Rustenberg wine estate.

Grapes need careful handling.

BELOW: Cape Dutch house, Vergelegen Wine Estate.

1.30–4pm; charge) is the town's premier museum comprising an entire block of impressive antique buildings, including the Schreuderhuis, which is the country's oldest surviving townhouse, built in 1709. Others in the row include the elegant Cape Dutch Blettermanhuis (1789), the Georgian-styled Grosvenor House (1803) and the fine mid-Victorian Murray House (1850).

Wine tasting

The most popular attraction around Stellenbosch, however, is the **Cape Winelands**, comprising hundreds of estates nestling in the surrounding valleys and foothills. Divided informally into several different "wine routes", the first of which was established in 1971, most of these estates have a public wine-tasting room open from around 9am–4pm daily, though some operate shorter hours and many close on Saturday or Sunday. Admission to some estates is free, but the more popular ones now charge a nominal tasting charge. Full details of the opening times and charges for individual estates are provided in a free booklet issued at the tourist offices in Stellenbosch and Cape Town. It is possible to explore the Winelands in a rented vehicle, but inadvisable without a spittoon-trained or teetotal designated driver. Otherwise, you could hook up with one of the many inexpensive wine-tasting tours that run out of Cape Town or Stellenbosch every day.

Those who are touring independently are faced with some tough decisions regarding which of the plethora of different estates to visit. Should you try the dry Rieslings at **Neethlingshof** (tel: 021-883 8988; www.neethlingshof.co.za), or the remarkable Pinotage produced by **Kanonkop** (tel: 021 884 4656; www.kanonkop.co.za), or the outstanding Pinot Noir and Merlot at **Meerlust** (tel: 021-843 3587; www.meerlust.com)? Much depends on your objectives and circumstances. For variety, **Simonsig** (tel: 021-888 4900; www.simonsig.co.za) produces 15 varieties of red and white wine, while the winery on the **Morgenhof Estate** (tel: 021-88 5510; www.morgenhof.com) offers just as large a selection, as well as picnic-basket lunches in summer.

If it's a genuine Cape Dutch atmosphere and mountain scenery you're after, there is no better place to start than the lovely **Rustenberg Estate** (tel: 021-809 1200; www.rustenburg.co.za) on the northeastern outskirts of Stellenbosch. However, if you're travelling with children in tow, head southwest for about 10km (6 miles) along the R310 to the **Spier Estate** (tel: 021-809 1143; www.spier.co.za), where fine wines and a quality Cape Malay restaurant are complemented by horse-riding, a small zoo and playground, a picnic site and regular steam-train connections to and from Cape Town.

Arguably the most beautiful estate in the Cape is **Vergelegen** (tel: 021-847 1334; www.vergelegen.co.za; daily 9.30am–4.30pm; charge) is consistently voted South Africa's "top winery" by readers of South Africa's *Wine* magazine.

Situated on the lowerslopes of the Helderberg above **Somerset West** ⓭, some 20km (12 miles) south of Stellenbosch, Vergelegen was granted to William van der Stel (son of Simon) in 1700 and the first vines were planted there shortly afterwards. The old manor house, now a private museum decorated in period style and set in tranquil gardens, is a fine example of Cape Dutch architecture, and its setting is equally superlative. There's a lovely coffee shop on the estate, and the wine itself – the multiple award-winning red blend in particular – is superb.

The small but picturesque **Helderberg Nature Reserve** (tel: 021-851 4060; www.helderbergnaturereserve.co.za; daily 7.30am–sunset), which stands guard over Somerset West, offers the opportunity to ramble along well-maintained footpaths across mountain sides strewn with ericas and proteas. Its best-known feature is Disa Gorge, where you can see the exquisite "flower-of-the-gods", the red disa orchid, growing on inaccessible rock faces from January to March. A remarkable variety of birds also inhabit this reserve, while seven trails range from 15 minutes to three hours in duration.

Franschhoek

From Stellenbosch, the R45 leads in a northeasterly direction for 28km (17 miles) to **Franschhoek** ⓮, or "French Corner", a reference to the Huguenots who settled here in the 18th century. The **Huguenot Memorial Museum** (www.museum.co.za; Mon–Sat 9am–5pm, Sun 2–5pm; charge) and the Huguenot Monument, completed in 1943, recall the history of these Protestant refugees, persecuted by Louis XIV because of their religious beliefs.

Blessed with perhaps the most perfect setting of any Boland town, Franschhoek is an ideal place to settle in for an alfresco lunch at one of its many superb restaurants

The wine route leading through the **Franschhoek Valley**, framed as it is by lofty mountain peaks, is spectacular too – and not only from a scenic point of view. For one thing, it includes the beautiful 300-year-old **Boschendal Estate** (tel: 021-870 4210; www.boschendalwines.com; daily 8.30am–4.30pm; free entrance, tasting charge), which is best known perhaps for its popular Blanc de Noir, an off-dry white

The Huguenot Memorial remembers the trials of the Cape's first vintners.

BELOW: La Cotte Inn wine shop, Franschhoek.

made from red grapes. Try the splendid Boschendal Brut, a champagne in all but name, or the estate's highly rated Shiraz, depending on your taste. The restaurant here is good too, or indulge in a garden "Pique Nique" before heading off to the cellars.

Famed for its superb reds, **L'Ormarins** (tel: 021-874 9000; www.rupertwines.com) also boasts a lovely Cape Dutch-style manor house, and is the site of the **Franschhoek Motor Museum** (www.fmm.co.za; Mon–Fri 10am–4pm, Sat–Sun 10am–3pm), which looks back at over 100 years of motoring history and has a collection of 300 vintage cars. **La Motte** (tel: 021-876 3119; www.la-motte.com) offers an excellent Shiraz, while **Haute Cabrière** (tel: 021-876 3688; www.hautecabriere.com) will ply you with no fewer than five different sparkling wines.

Alternatively, drop into the central **Franschhoek Vineyards Co-op Cellar** (tel: 021-870 4200; www.franschhoek-cellar.co.za; Mon–Fri 9.30am–5pm, Sat–Sun 10am–4pm) and sample dozens of wines produced by the above and other local estates.

Paarl

Some 30–45 minutes drive north of Stellenbosch or Franschhoek, and a similar distance from Cape Town along the N1, **Paarl** ⓕ (Afrikaans for Pearl) is named for the polished granite domed mountain that rises behind it. Founded in 1720, Paarl feels rather dour and unattractive by Boland standards, and the sprawling town centre can take ages to drive through. On the southern slope of Paarl Mountain, the **Afrikaans Taal (Language) Monument** is a slender granite needle, erected in 1975 to commemorate the centenary of Afrikaans being recognised as an official language.

Paarl's wine route includes some fine vineyards and several first-class restaurants. A good starting point is the central **KWV Cellars** (tel: 021-807 3007; www.kwv.co.za) or vast **Nederburg Estate** (tel: 021-862 3104; www.nederburg.co.za) on the outskirts of town. Probably the best known of all South Africa's wineries, Nederburg has received countless awards for its reserve range, while its everyday drinking wines are a ubiquitous feature on

restaurant wine lists. Other prominent local cellars include **Avondale** (tel: 021-863 1976; www.avondale.co.za), **Landskroon** (tel: 021-863 1039; www.landskroonwines.com) and **Glen Carlou** (tel: 021-875 5528; www.glencarlou.co.za), while **Rheboskloof** (www.rheboskloof.co.za, tel: 021-869 8386) has an extensive range of well-priced everyday wines, complemented by a magnificent location below Du Toitskloof Pass, 16km (10 miles) east of Paarl.

Tulbagh and Worcester

Situated on the R44 about 12km (7 miles) north of Paarl, **Wellington** ⓰ is notable for its Dutch Reformed Moederkerk built in 1838 (with an interesting spire added in 1891) and imposing Town Hall.

North of Wellington, the R301/46 passes through the wheat-golden and vine-red Land van Waveren Valley and crosses the Slanghoek Mountains over the most magnificent of all mountain passes, Bain's Kloof, until after 50km (30 miles) it emerges at the miniature historical gem and small wine-production centre of **Tulbagh** ⓱. Following a series of earthquakes that virtually demolished the town in 1968, Tulbagh's historic Church Street was rebuilt in Cape Dutch style.

The gracious **De Oude Drostdy** (tel: 023-230 0203; Mon–Sat 10am–1pm, daily 2–5pm; charge), 4km (2 miles) outside the village, was designed in 1804 by the French architect Louis Michel Thibault. Prisoners once languished in the cellar, which today serves as a storeroom for vintages from the nearby Drostdy vineyards.

Back on the N1, some 50km (30 miles) southeast of Tulbagh and 100km (60 miles) northeast of Cape Town, **Worcester** ⓲ is cupped in the lush Breede River valley at the foot of the Hex River Mountains (the highest peaks in the Western Cape and snow-dusted in winter). This small town offers a typical Boland blend of elegant Cape Dutch architecture, a beautiful setting, and vineyards on all sides.

Founded in 1820, Worcester possesses a number of neoclassical buildings, including the elegant Drostdy, probably the finest example of Cape Regency architecture in the country. So-called Worcester gables add an individual architectural accent. Many Cape Dutch gabled houses later acquired Victorian verandas with wrought-iron railings; the one at No. 132 Church Street, built in 1832, is a fine example. The town's most prominent building is the Dutch Reformed Moederkerk, built in 1824 in the neo-Gothic style.

The Worcester area has its own wine route, but while the wines are good, the estates are all relatively modern, so the architecture and landscape are less evocative than around Stellenbosch or Franschhoek. Do not leave Worcester without visiting the lovely **Karoo Desert National Botanical Garden** (tel: 023-347 0785; www.sanbi.org; daily 7am–7pm; no charge except Aug–Oct), behind the golf club north of town. Following rainy spells in spring, the landscape bursts into bloom, sprinkling the gardens with a bright carpet of flowering succulents.

The Afrikaans Taal (Language) Monument was erected in 1975 to commemorate the centenary of Afrikaans being recognised as an official language.

BELOW: Paarl vineyard.

If you want to indulge in the many free tastings at the vineyards, leave the car behind and board an organised tour.

BELOW: Harold Porter National Botanical Gardens.

Situated roughly halfway along the 100km (62-mile) road connecting Worcester to Swellendam, **Robertson** ⓳ (lies at the centre of South Africa's second-largest wine route, with almost 40 estates open to the public. Robertson is largely overlooked by tourists, partly due to its relative remoteness from Cape Town and partly because it is historically associated with dessert wines and brandies.

These days, however, the area also produces some excellent dry reds and whites. Prominent estates include **De Wetshof** for excellent Chardonnays and Cabernet Sauvignon (tel: 023-615 1853; www.dewetshof.com), **Excelsior** for good-value Cabernet Sauvignon and Merlot (tel: 023-615 1980; www.excelsior.co.za), **Graham Beck** have several good reds (tel: 023-626 1214; www.grahambeckwines.co.za), **Zandvliet** is well-known for Shiraz (tel: 023-615 1146; www.zandvliet.co.za) and attractively priced all-rounders such as **Robertson Winery** (tel: 023-626 3059; www.robertsonwinery.co.za) and **Van Loveren Estate** (tel: 023-615 1505; www.vanloveren.co.za).

THE OVERBERG

This route follows the N2 southeast from Cape Town over the Hottentots Holland Mountains and into the isolated Overberg region, whose most important tourist focus is the port of Hermanus. The most exciting route to this region is the coastal R44, which can be reached from Cape Town or the Winelands by driving to Strand then following signs pointing south to **Gordon's Bay**, an attractive resort on the shores of False Bay. Whales can often be seen frolicking offshore here during October and November. After Gordon's Bay, the R44 hugs the coastline around Koeëlbaai, with some fantastic sea views. Some 7km (4 miles) to the east, not far away from the old whaling station of Betty's Bay and dramatically situated between the Kogelberg Range and the Atlantic coast, are the **Harold Porter National Botanical Gardens** (tel: 028-272 9311; www.sanbi.org; daily 8am–6pm; charge), which are definitely worth a visit. Waterfalls and small streams splash through a *fynbos*-sprinkled landscape, inhabited by numerous colonies of baboons.

A Master Engineer

Many of the first roads in the Cape were not built, but followed the trails worn into the earth over the centuries by herds of migrating game. Sir Lowry's Pass across the Hottentots Holland Mountains, for example, was opened in 1830 and for a good deal of its length followed the track used by migrating eland. This meant that right up until the mid-19th century, Cape Town – surrounded as it is by a series of towering mountain ranges – remained virtually sealed off from the rest of the country. Villages which were only 30km (18 miles) apart, as the crow flies, took over a month to reach over the winding animal trails. In 1848, desperate for access to the interior, the Cape colonial government appointed the Scottish-born Inspector of Roads, Andrew Geddes Bain, to solve the problem.

Over the next 45 years, Bain – followed by his son, Thomas – supervised the construction of ten mountain passes into the interior, using only hand-held rock drills, picks, shovels and gunpowder. In terms of scale and logistics, these roads are extraordinary feats of engineering; many (the Swartberg Pass, the Montagu Pass, Bain's Kloof Pass, Prince Alfred's Pass) are still in daily use today. But Bain achieved something else, too; he always insisted on choosing the most beautiful routes. They make very rewarding driving.

Reached from the R44 between Betty's Bay and Hermanus, the Unesco-registered **Kogelberg Biosphere Reserve** (tel: 028-271 4792; www.kogelberg biospherereserve.co.za; summer 7.30am–7pm, winter 8am–6pm; charge) is claimed to be the world's most biodiverse habitat, with more than 1,880 plant species identified, including 77 that are unique. The reserve also harbours a wide variety of birds, a healthy baboon population, and a herd of wild horses, probably descended from beasts abandoned by soldiers of unknown affinities in the Anglo-Boer War of 1899–1902. Four hiking trails range from 6km (4 miles) to 23km (14 miles) in length, and there's canoeing on the Palmiet River.

Hermanus

Hermanus ⓴ is the largest coastal town in the Overberg. The best time to visit is spring, when the biggest visitors of all arrive in Walker Bay: the whales (*see page 186*). The municipality hires a special whale crier during September and October, who not only keeps tourists up to date on whale activity but can

even be reached by mobile phone (the Whale Hotline, tel: 083-910 1028). If you take the 11km (7-mile) cliff walk at this time of year you're almost sure to see whales; sometimes far away on the other side of the bay, sometimes only 30 metres (100ft) away and clearly visible in the crystal-clear water. An underwater microphone transmits their strange songs live back to a room in the **Old Harbour Museum** (www.old-harbourmuseum.co.za; Mon–Sat 9am–4pm, Sun 11am–4pm; charge).

Situated near Stanford some 45km (28 miles) west of Hermanus, the often overlooked **Salmonsdam Nature Reserve** (www.capenature.co.za; daily; charge) protects a mountainous area coloured by a variety of protea species and inhabited by bontebok, klipspringer and numerous birds.

From Stanford, follow the R326 and R316 for about 80km (48 miles) to sleepy **Bredasdorp** ⓴; whose **Shipwreck Museum** (Independent Street, tel: 028-424 1240; Mon–Sat 9am–5pm, Sun 10am–4pm; charge) contains an exhibition of treasures taken from ships wrecked off the stormy coast.

The distinctive white-washed cottages of Arniston have been declared a national monument.

BELOW: the Old Harbour at Hermanus.

It's another 30km (18 miles) to Cape Agulhas, the southernmost point in Africa, protected within the 210-sq-km (82-sq-mile) **Agulhas National Park** (tel: 028-435 6222; www.sanparks.org; daily; free). Formal nature trails, a museum, and interpretative and environmental centres are expected to open by 2013. Portuguese sailors gave it the name Agulhas, meaning "needles", because it is at this point that the needle of a compass points due north, with no deviation.

You can climb **Agulhas Lighthouse** (daily 9am–5pm; charge), which is the second-oldest working lighthouse in South Africa, reached via 71 steps. The magnificent beach at nearby **Struisbaai** is unforgettable, with its turquoise-blue sea and colourful fishing boats.

Just as rewarding is a detour from Bredasdorp to **Waenhuiskrans ㉒**, which is also known as **Arniston**. This fishing village with its thatched, whitewashed houses has been declared a national monument.

Running for some 50km (30 miles) along the coast east of Arniston, the **De Hoop Nature Reserve and Marine**

RIGHT: the Agulhas Lighthouse.
BELOW: mountain zebra, De Hoop Nature Reserve.

Protected Area ㉓ (tel: 028-542 1253; daily 7am–6pm; charge; www.capenature.co.za) protects what is probably the Cape's largest remaining contiguous *fynbos* habitat, together with significant populations of the endangered Cape mountain zebra and bontebok, and various other antelope and small predators. Several walking routes run through the reserve, ranging from the two-hour Klipspringer Trail to the 55km (34-mile), five-day Whale Trail. Large flocks of water birds frequent the extensive lake and wetlands formed where the mouth of the Sout ("Salt") River is blocked by dunes, while the offshore marine reserve offers great snorkelling and forms a breeding ground for an estimated 120 southern right whales between June and November.

The route rejoins the N2 some 60km (37 miles) north of Bredasdorp, near Stormsvlei. From there it's only another 12km (8 miles) to **Swellendam ㉔**, the third-oldest town in South Africa, founded in 1743. The town's Cape Dutch buildings include a fine **Drostdy** (daily; charge), built in 1746, and housing a select assortment of Cape furniture and paintings. Popular with photographers is the magnificent **Dutch Reformed Church** (Voortrek Street), a wedding-cake of a building, built in 1911, and combining neo-Gothic, neo-Renaissance and neo-baroque elements with the Cape Dutch style. The Town Hall, also on Voortrek Street, is another imposing Cape-style Victorian building.

Just 6km (4 miles) south of Swellendam is the entrance to the **Bontebok National Park ㉕** (tel: 028-514 2735; www.sanparks.org; Oct–Apr daily 7am–7pm, May–Sept daily 7am–6pm; charge), at 28 sq km (11 sq miles) the country's smallest national park. You won't see elephant, lion or rhinoceros here – just plenty of graceful little bontebok, a species of antelope hunted almost to extinction during the early part of the 20th century. Springbok and the Cape mountain zebra are also found here. ❏

The Western Cape's Coast of Whales

Whale populations are on the increase, and the Cape is one of the best places in the world to see the southern right whale in coastal waters

No fewer than 29 species of toothed whale (*Odontoceti*), including the killer whale, are found off the South African coast, along with eight species of baleen whale (suborder *Mysticeti*). But by far the most commonly spotted are the southern right whales, pods of which seek out sheltered bays along the Cape coastline every year for breeding. Between June and December, there is a good chance of seeing them all the way round the peninsula from Elands Bay on the west coast to Mossel Bay on the Garden Route. On a good day, you might see them spyhopping (standing on their tails with their heads out of water), lobtailing (slapping their flukes on the water's surface) or breaching – leaping out of the sea like a trout.

The Right Whales to Catch?

The southern right (*Balaena glacialis*) is distinguished by its V-shaped "blow" – the cloud of vapour produced when the whale exhales a large volume of air through its pair of blowholes. They are thought to live for up to 100 years; an adult can reach 16 metres (53ft) in length. They are called right whales because 18th-century whalers regarded them as the "right" whales to catch: the carcass was oil-rich, and the whalers' task of collecting their booty was made more easy by the fact that the whale floats on the water after slaughter. They were valued for their blubber, which was reduced to oil for use in margarine, soap and linoleum, and for their bones, used to make glue, gelatine and fertiliser. International legislation was introduced to protect the species in 1935, but the southern right has subsequently shown only a slight increase in numbers.

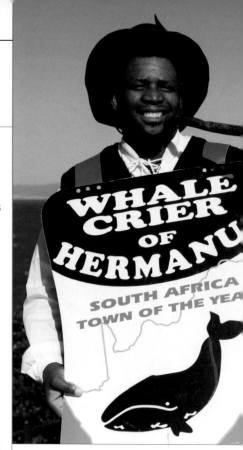

ABOVE: the village of Hermanus has the world's only official whale crier, who, during the peak whale season (Sept–Oct), parades throug the streets announcing new arrivals with a blast on his kelp horn.

BELOW: although South Africa is famed for its land-based whale watching, closer views of these giant marine mammals can be obtained on boat trips with licensed operators.

LEFT: South Africa has some of the strictest whale conservation legislation in the world, so sights like this traditional harpooner are thankfully now a thing of the past. As a result, the numbers of south right whales spotted along the Cape coast has steadily increased.

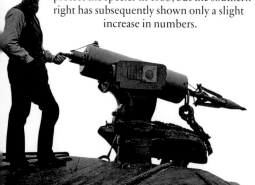

WHERE TO HEAR WHALES SING

Hermanus's Old Harbour – replaced in the 1940s after nearly a century – now houses a museum in a row of beautifully restored fishermen's cottages. As tourism has replaced fishing as the primary industry, so the museum has become a focal point for visitors to the town.

One of the museum's most interesting features is an underwater microphone, attached to a sonar buoy in Walker Bay. The eerie, sing-song sound of whales chatting to one another deep underwater is picked up and transmitted back to a public audio room in the museum. There is also a telescope for watching whales far out in the bay.

The new harbour, to the west of the old one, in Westcliff, is a bustling little fishing port, where fresh seafood – including mussels and crayfish – is sold from the docks. Boats can be hired here for deep-sea tuna and marlin expeditions.

Also in Westcliff is the start of Hermanus's famous cliff path, which follows the shore round Walker Bay to the lagoon at Grotto Beach, allowing unrivalled views of whale activity out at sea. The walk takes at least a morning; bench seats are provided along the way and many people take a picnic. There are even grander views along the Rotary Mountain Way, a scenic drive. The tasting rooms of Hamilton Russell vineyards face the Hermanus marketplace.

OVE: usually held in the last week of **tember**, at the height of the whale season, the **ular Hermanus Whale Festival attracts **ditional musicians and other local performers to normally quiet town.

HT: South Africa's commitment to marine **servation** is illustrated by the presence of **rmation boards about whales, sharks and other **erable marine creatures and habitats at **tegic points along the coast.

The Southern Right Whale - a winter visitor to our

ABOVE: with a unequalled combination of low cliff tops and clear water at the base of the cliffs, Hermanus offers some of the world's best land-based whale watching. In season, visitors are practically guaranteed a sighting.

THE GARDEN ROUTE

Wild forests and unspoilt beaches lead past hidden valleys and majestic mountains to the forested shores of Garden Route National Park

L ush and bountiful, the relatively short stretch of coastline between Mossel Bay and Tsitsikamma is popularly referred to as the Garden Route, and its timeless appeal both to foreign travellers and to South African holidaymakers is reflected in a booming guesthouse and hotel industry, not to mention the region's ever-escalating real estate prices. This, however, is a distinctly African garden – not the manicured lawns of Europe with their neat and formal layouts, but an exhilaratingly rugged coastline flanked by indigenous rainforests, blue lagoons, parallel rows of serrated mountain peaks and fields bright with *fynbos*.

Mossel Bay

Coming from Cape Town, the eastbound N2 runs inland through **Swellendam** (*see page 184*) and **Riversdale** to finally reconnect with the seaside after almost 400km (240 miles) at **Mossel Bay ❶**. Generally regarded to mark the beginning of the Garden Route, Mossel Bay also boasts the distinction of being where the Portuguese navigator Bartolomeu Dias set anchor in 1488 to become the first European to touch South African soil. The **Bartolomeu Dias Museum Complex** (www.diasmuseum.co.za; Mon–Fri 9am–4.45pm, Sat–Sun 9am–3.45pm; charge), housed inside a converted

granary, is dedicated to his memory. Displays include exhibitions of shells and shipping; best of all is the full-scale replica of Dias's surprisingly small caravel (sailing ship).

The first permanent settlement at Mossel Bay didn't begin until about 300 years later, though passing ships often stopped for water and to trade with the local tribes people. The town is still a popular holiday resort thanks to its many beaches and calm swimming pools between rocks. It has also become a sprawling industrial centre due to the

Main attractions
SEAL ISLAND
CANGO CAVES
OUDTSHOORN OSTRICH FARMS
WILDERNESS
KNYSNA
ROBBERG NATURE RESERVE
PLETTENBERG BAY
TSITSIKAMMA

LEFT: Wilderness Section.
RIGHT: ostrich farm in Oudtshoorn.

Posting a letter in Mossel Bay's unique boot-shaped postbox.

discovery of oil and natural gas reserves off its coast. Write postcards, nevertheless, because the local mail system has a long tradition: in 1500, a Portuguese sailor named Pedro d'Ataide placed a letter inside an old boot and hung it beneath a milkwood tree.

A year later, another sailor found the letter and was kind enough to forward it. The tradition continued as the tree became a message board for passing sailors. Today the tree is part of the Dias museum, and if you post your cards in the boot-shaped letterbox provided, the "oldest post office in South Africa" will process them promptly.

If Mossel Bay has sacrificed something of its former charm to industrial development, there's no doubt that it also offers some of the most alluring marine activities in the region, full details of which can be obtained from the tourist office next to the old post office. Most popular is a boat excursion to nearby **Seal Island** (tel: 044-690 3101; www.mosselbay.co.za; hourly departures 9pm–5am), where hundreds of Cape fur seals can be seen basking on the rocks and foraging in the surround-

ing waters. Somewhat more daunting (and not just financially) are the **caged shark dives** arranged by **Shark Africa** (tel: 044-691 3796; www.whitesharkafrica. com) to view predatory great white in their natural habitat. More conventional dives can be arranged out of Mossel Bay, as can kayaking expeditions. Back on terra firma – or, more accurately, suspended above it – the **Gouritz Bridge Bungee-Jump** (tel 044-697 7001; www.faceadrenalin.com daily 9am–5pm) from the N2, 35km (22 miles) back towards Swellendam is popular with adrenaline junkies.

George

Leaving Mossel Bay, the scenery grows increasingly wild as the N2 continues east towards the former lumber village of **George** ❷, founded in 1811 at the base of the Outeniqua Mountains and described a few decades later by Anthony Trollope as "the prettiest village on the face of the earth".

Situated a few kilometres inland George today is anything but a village – indeed, its population of 210,000 is twice that of any other town on the

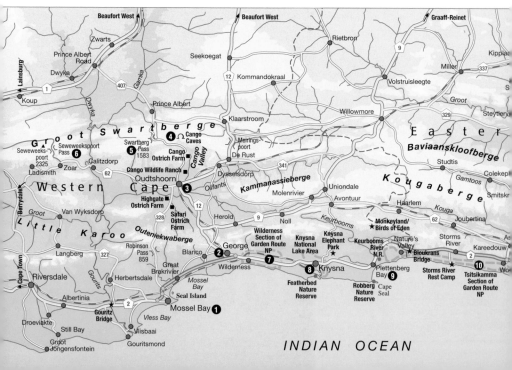

Garden Route – and few would regard it to be especially pretty. On the credit side, George does offer a good range of tourist facilities at lower prices than you'll find elsewhere in this popular area, and it's well placed as a base for numerous day trips along the Garden Route or the Little Karoo.

Within George's historic town centre stand several fine buildings. These include the **Dutch Reformed Moederkerk** with its magnificent carved stinkwood pulpit, and the elegant **Public Library** (1840) – although the latter's books have, unfortunately, all been moved to Cape Town. Outside the library is the mighty **Slave Tree**, one of the broadest oak trees in the southern hemisphere, beneath which a slave market was once held. And since we're touching on a dark chapter of South African history, the **George Museum** (Mon–Fri 9am–4pm; charge) on Courtenay Street has an exhibition devoted to the presidency of P.W. Botha, the last of the hard-line apartheid leaders, who retired to this part of the country in 1989 and lived there until his death in October 2006. It is housed in the Old Drostdy, which was built in 1811, rebuilt after fire damage in 1826, and served as a hotel from 1890 until 1972, when it was bought by the municipality and converted to a museum.

Dutch Reformed Moederkerk, George.

The Little Karoo

Situated roughly 60km (36 miles) north of George via the N12 and Outeniqua Pass, **Oudtshoorn ❸** is an increasingly popular day or overnight trip out of the Garden Route proper. It is the principal town of the Little Karoo, a somewhat arid region whose name derives from a Khoi word meaning dry. It can get blisteringly hot in summer, but Little Karoo also has an austere beauty that comes in many different guises – the serenity of far horizons, a black eagle soaring high above a silent plain, a cool breeze after a stifling day, or just a donkey cart crunching slowly along an old farm road.

Oudtshoorn was once a celebrated ostrich-feather centre: between 1880 and 1910 a number of Jewish traders from eastern Europe emigrated to South Africa, set up ostrich farms and made a small fortune exporting

BELOW: the breathtaking Swartberg Pass.

Garden Route

Graaff-Reinet
Sheldon
ansenville
Waterford
Greystone   Mentz   Klipfontein
Wolfefontein   Zuurberg National Park
a p e   Kirkwood
Glenconnor
Sunland
Bluecliff   Addo
otwinterhoekberge   Addo Elephant National Park
ieskraal   Patensie   Uitenhage   Coega
Hankey   Despatch
ntein   2   Port Elizabeth
Bethelsdorp
dorp   Jeffrey's Bay   Seaview
St Francis Bay   Cape Recife
Cape St Francis
East London

0   50 km
0   50 miles

At speeds of up to 78km/h (48mph), the ostrich can outrun most of its enemies.

BELOW LEFT:
feeding time at Cango Ostrich Farm.
BELOW RIGHT:
feather dusters for sale outside C.P. Nel Museum.

the feathers back to fashion-conscious Europe. The trade generated vast riches – 1kg (2lbs) of tail-feathers could fetch up to R200.

Ostrich boom

The **C.P. Nel Museum** (www.cpnel museum.co.za; Mon–Fri 8am–5pm, Sat 9am–1pm; charge) on Baron van Rheede Street has displays on the history of the ostrich boom. All this revenue pouring into what had hitherto been nothing more than a remote hamlet helped build a number of "feather palaces", several of which have survived the decline in the market – one such being the **Le Roux Town-house** (entrance included in museum ticket), which stands on the corner of Loop and High streets, complete with period fittings and furnishings.

Today, the ostrich industry still thrives, but the feathers are used more for dusters than for the hats and boas of high fashion. But while the feather market took a dip, the skins of this strange bird have become part and parcel of the world of high fashion. And the farms where the ostriches are bred

also form the lynchpin of an incre ingly lucrative tourist industry. W Oudtshoorn? It seems ostriches happiest in a hot, dry climate; they the type of alfalfa grown here and availability of their favourite diet supplements: sand, stones and inse

Several such farms are open to public, including the **Safari Ostr Show Farm** (www.safariostrich.co daily 8am–5pm; charge), which just outside town on the Mossel road. The homestead here boasts t from Burma, roof tiles from Belgi and marble floors. Lunch time at ostrich farm usually means an opp tunity to dine on an ostrich steak; can also try your riding skills on back of the world's largest bird watch jockeys spur on their mount a mock Ostrich Derby.

Similar entertainment is offerec other ostrich farms such as **Highg** (tel: 044-272 7115; www.highgate.co and **Cango** (tel: 044-272 4623; w cangoostrich.co.za), the latter situa 15–20km (9–12 miles) from to along the R328 towards the Car Caves (*see opposite*).

Cango caves

Situated about 2km (1½ miles) from the town centre along the R328, **Cango Wildlife Ranch** (www.cango.co.za; daily 9am–5pm; charge) was established in the 1980s as a breeding centre for endangered wildlife. One of the world's most productive breeding centres for cheetah, it has also successfully bred serval, aardwolf, African wild dog and pygmy hippo (the latter a West African rainforest species). This aside, the ranch essentially comes across as a zoo – albeit a very good one – offering the opportunity to hold hand-reared cheetahs and to see a variety of indigenous and exotic animals, including white Bengal tigers, pumas, jaguars and a colony of meerkats. A snake park, curio shop and restaurant are attached.

The fascinating **Cango Caves** ❹ (www.cango-caves.co.za; daily 9am–4pm, hourly guided tours; charge), 32km (20 miles) north of Oudtshoorn, are part of a massive system of limestone caverns that extends into the Swartberg Mountains. The caves once sheltered San bushmen whose paintings can be found on the walls. An hour-long guided tour introduces you to three of the biggest caves, after which you can either turn back or continue on a more adventurous route, which involves squeezing your way along a series of narrow, hot, damp and stifling shafts. The seat of your trousers gets just as much exercise as your shoes during this operation.

Swartberg Pass

Past the caves, the R328 continues on towards the whitewashed village of **Prince Albert** over one of the most beautiful of all South Africa's mountain passes – the **Swartberg Pass** ❺ (1,436 metres/4,700ft). Built between 1881 and 1888 and now a national monument, this gravel road climbs 1,000 metres (3,281ft) in 12km (7 miles) over the mighty Swartberg Range, with very sharp, blind hairpin bends. The views are magnificent, but this is not a drive for vertigo sufferers.

If that's not challenging enough, you could take an alternative route across the mountains via the main road (the R29) through Meiringspoort, or by the **Seweweekspoort Pass** ❻. First opened in 1857, this pass crosses the River Groot some 30 times along its 17km (11-mile) length, snaking through bare walls of vertical rock which at times stretch hundreds of metres high. Twisted bands of red sandstone and milky quartz loom above the road, their yellow-lichened crags glowing in the sun. Check the status of the road before you set out to drive through the gorge, though; it's often closed after heavy rains.

Most visitors approach Oudtshoorn via the N12 from George, either returning the way they came or using the R328 to Mossel Bay via the **Robinson Pass** (859 metres/2,818ft), or the rougher **Montagu Pass** to the east.

Coming to or from Cape Town, however, a rewarding alternative is to travel between Swellendam and Oudtshoorn using the R324 through Tradouw Pass to **Barrydale**, then to follow the R62 through the series of fertile

The Seweweekspoort Pass crosses the River Groot some 30 times.

The long beach at Wilderness is ideal for paragliding.

BELOW: making puzzles to sell at the Craft Market in Knysna.

valleys and pretty orchard villages such as **Ladismith** and **Calitzdorp**.

Wilderness

Heading east from George, the N2 passes through **Wilderness**, a bustling little resort town fringed on one side by a magnificent, 8km (5-mile) long sandy beach and on the other by the Wilderness Section of the Garden Route National Park. Shortly before the N2 enters Wilderness, it offers a superb view over a photogenic riverine gorge spanned by a disused railway bridge associated with a defunct steam train service called the Outeniqua Choo-Tjoe. Immediately after this, you can pull up at a viewpoint from where dolphins are regularly observed playing in the surf below.

The **Wilderness Section of Garden Route National Park** ➐ (tel: 044-877 0046; www.sanparks.org; daily 8am–5pm; charge) protects a series of freshwater pans – the largest being Swartvlei, Langvlei, Groenvlei and Rondevlei – connected by various tributaries of the Touws River, which empties into the ocean in the town itself.

It's a beautiful park, and the combination of open waterways, reed beds and marshes provides a rich source of food and varied habitats for a wide array of bird life, as does the surrounding bush and forest. Most attractive of all are the large wading birds that scour the shallows for food; pockets of pink flamingos, drifting across the shimmering water, straining the surface for tiny algae and crustaceans, and African spoonbills that rake the mud with their broad, wide beaks. Of the 95 water bird species recorded in South Africa, 75 have been seen bobbing about on the lakes here.

Understandably popular with birdwatchers, the Wilderness Section also offers some great rambling opportunities in the form of a network of nonstrenuous day trails, each of which is named for one of the park's six kingfisher species. A good starting point is the Half-collared Kingfisher Trail, an 8km (5-mile) circular ramble that leads through riparian woodland fringing the Touws River to an attractive waterfall that tumbles over a group of gigantic round boulders. Forest birds

Knysna's Elephants

Two hundred years ago, great herds of elephants roamed the southern Cape. Today, due to ruthless hunting, there is thought to be only one left, hidden in the secretive dark-green depths of the forests around Knysna. The lone beast – a cow – has adapted successfully to forest conditions. Although she belongs to the same species as the savannah elephants, her habits and lifestyle are now thought to be more similar to the elephants found in the equatorial forests of Central Africa.

Attempts have been made to build up the herd again, most recently in 1994, when three young elephants from the Kruger National Park were introduced into the forest. Unfortunately, the Knysna elephant fled in fear, only to be pursued by the newcomers in a chase which went on for several days and resulted in the death of one of the youngsters from pneumonia brought on by stress. The other two were eventually relocated to Shamwari Game Reserve outside Port Elizabeth after ravaging local farmland.

Although it's unlikely that you'll catch a glimpse of the lone ranger herself, the Elephant Walk from Diepwalle Forestry Station (off the R339; daily; charge) offers the chance to spot another forest giant – a 46-metre (150ft) high yellowwood known as the King Edward VII tree, which has a 9.5-metre (30ft) circumference.

such as the beautiful Knysna loerie and yellow-throated warbler are likely to be seen here, and bushbuck and duiker are present as well. A similar route can be followed on the water by renting a canoe from the main rest camp and punting gently upstream to the base of the falls.

Knysna

A short distance east of Wilderness lies the busiest resort on the Garden Route: **Knysna ❽**, founded at the beginning of the 19th century by George Rex, rumoured to be an illegitimate son of George III. Wooded hills, dotted with holiday homes, surround pretty **Knysna Lagoon**, connected to the ocean by a narrow waterway. The mouth of this canal is flanked by two huge sandstone cliffs known as **The Heads**, and it is thanks to them that Knysna never became an important harbour town: access by sea was simply too dangerous. The eastern cliff is the only one open to cars (along George Rex Drive), and the view from the top is fantastic. The western cliff can only be reached by taking a ferry excursion across the lagoon mouth to the private **Featherbed Nature Reserve** (tel: 044-382 1693/7; www.featherbed.co.za; daily excursions), home to the shy blue duiker, various birds and the endangered Knysna seahorse.

A good place for crafts, pottery and woven fabrics is **Thesen House**, a historic town house named after one of Knysna's oldest and most influential families. However, the area is chiefly known for its natural wood products, and especially hardwood furniture. The best quality products are manufactured by hand by master craftsmen, using yellowwood, dark stinkwood and ironwood judiciously culled from the surrounding forests. A popular photo opportunity – although it's rather surreal for Africa – is the **Holy Trinity Church** in the leafy settlement of Belvidere, which looks very much like an 11th-century Norman implant. By way of contrast, May is when Knysna hosts a five-day gay, lesbian, transsexual and transgender carnival called the Pink Loerie Mardi Gras (www.pinkloerie.com), the only celebration of this sort in the African continent.

Oysters served fresh from the lagoon at Knysna.

BELOW: Knysna Lagoon.

DRINK

When in Knysna, sample the frothy produce of the legendary Mitchell's Brewery on Arend Street (tel: 044-382 4685; www.mitchellsknysna brewery.com; Mon–Fri 8am–5pm, Sat 9am–1pm).

Like Mossel Bay, Knysna is a popular base for a wide range of marine and other adventure activities, including scuba diving, sailing, hiking, mountain biking, canoe trips upriver, whale and dolphin safaris and abseiling down the Knysna Heads.

The excellent **tourism office** on Main Road (tel: 044-382 5510; www. visitknysna.co.za) can provide up-to-date details of costs and booking contacts. There are also several overnight hikes through the surrounding hills, details of which can be obtained from the Department of Forestry office, also on Main Road. Don't leave Knysna without sampling the sumptuous oysters that are served fresh from the lagoon at several dockside restaurants.

Thus fortified, you'll be ready to visit **Plettenberg Bay** ❾, South Africa's most up-market seaside resort, 32km (20 miles) east of Knysna. Although the town lacks Knysna's charm, the perfectly rounded Baia Formosa (Beautiful Bay) with its golden beaches has long been a favourite with holidaymakers. Sadly, a hideous multistorey hotel, the Beacon Island, now dominates Pletten-

berg Bay's beach front from its rocky promontory.

A better option for those who like their beaches relatively unspoilt is the lengthy **Keurboomstrand**, which is ten minutes' drive to the east near the Keurbooms River mouth. During the Christmas holidays, "Plett" is extremely popular, but out of season the place is often surprisingly quiet.

Nature reserves

A bracing day hike leads through the **Robberg Nature Reserve** (tel: 044-53 2125; www.capenature.org.za; daily Feb–Nov 7am–5pm, Dec–Jan 7am–8pm; charge) some 9km (5 miles) south of Plettenberg Bay. The centrepiece of the reserve is the Robberg Peninsula whose dramatic windswept cliffs rise almost vertically from the choppy blue sea (watch out for freak waves), interspersed by several small sandy coves.

The full circle around the peninsula covers about 11 decidedly undulating kilometres (7 miles), but shorter variations are available. As the peninsula's name suggests (Robberg translates as Seal Mountain), it hosts an impre

BELOW LEFT: the Beacon Island Hotel is one of Plettenberg Bay's less attractive features. **BELOW RIGHT:** Robberg Nature Reserve.

sive colony of Cape fur seals – along with marine birds such as the African black oystercatcher. Look out, too, for the whales and dolphins that pass by seasonally.

Another scenic gem is the **Keurbooms River Nature Reserve** (tel: 044-802 5300; www.capenature.org.za; daily 8am–6pm; charge), the entrance to which lies along the N2 some 7km (4 miles) east of Plettenberg Bay's town centre, immediately before it crosses a bridge across the forest-fringed Keurbooms River. The river is hemmed in by a spectacular wooded gorge, where the Western Keurboom trees for which it is named burst into pink blossom between August and January, sheltered by giant stinkwoods and yellowwood trees. Wildlife includes vervet monkey, blue duiker, Cape clawless otter and forest and water-associated birds such as Knysna loerie, Narina trogon and African AQ. For those with the time and energy, there is no more satisfying way to explore this reserve than on the overnight canoe trail that terminates at a rustic river side hut set deep in the forested gorge.

About 10km (6 miles) west of Plettenberg Bay on the Knysna Road, the **Knysna Elephant Park** (tel: 044-532 7732; www.knysnaelephantpark.co.za; scheduled tours daily 8.30am–4.30pm; charge) does not – as might be expected – protect the few survivors of the wild herds that once roamed these coastal forests (*see box Knysna's Elephants, page 194*), but instead offers the opportunity to touch and feed a few semi-domesticated tuskers relocated from elsewhere in the country.

Knysna Elephant Park offers an opportunity to get up close to these magnificent creatures.

Monkey sanctuary

Equally contrived, but great fun all the same, is the private primate sanctuary called **Monkeyland** (tel: 044-534 8906; www.monkeyland.co.za; daily 8am–5pm; guided tours available hourly), which lies 16km (10 miles) east of Plettenberg Bay shortly before the turn-off to **Nature's Valley**. The forested sanctuary hosts about 200 monkeys belonging to a dozen species, ranging from the South American spider monkey to various Madagascan lemurs, which were rescued from domestic captivity. A visit can be combined with the neigh-

BELOW LEFT AND RIGHT: Monkeyland primate sanctuary.

Hartlaub's Turaco, just one of the species that can be seen at the Birds of Eden aviary, near Plettenburg Bay.

BELOW LEFT:
Storms River
Suspension Bridge.
BELOW RIGHT:
Tsitsikamma
Section, Garden
Route National
Park.

bouring and jointly managed **Birds of Eden** (www.birdsofeden.co.za; daily 8am–5pm), where a 1km (½-mile) walkway and suspension bridge leads through the world's largest free-flight aviary, where around 100 South African species are caged by a similar number of exotics.

Tsitsikamma

From Plettenberg Bay you can take either the N2 toll road that cuts a fairly straight path through forests and across the high coastal plain, or the byway (the R102) winding downwards past the Grootrivier and Bloukrans gorges and through sleepy Nature's Valley on the western boundary of the **Tsitsikamma Section of Garden Route National Park** ❿ (www.sanparks.org; daily 7am–7pm; charge). One of the Garden Route's best-kept secrets, Nature's Valley is a tiny forested village overlooking a wonderfully isolated beach that remains practically undeveloped for tourism – as a result, there are few more attractive places to pitch a tent than at the magical national park campsite on the edge of town.

Those who take the back road will be rewarded by the experience of sinking deep down into the forest's cool microclimate. Beneath the giant yellowwoods, the shaded floor is thick with proteas, arum lilies and watsonia; vividly coloured loerie birds dart through the dense forest canopy, while shy duiker and bushbuck hide in the undergrowth below.

Back on the N2, the single-span arch concrete bridges over the Storms, Groot and Bloukrans rivers had the distinction – when they were each newly completed – of being the biggest such structures in the world.

The **Bloukrans Bridge**, suspended 215 metres (710ft) above the river for which it is named, is also the site of the world's highest bungee jump (tel: 042-281 1458; www.faceadrenalin.com; daily 9am–5pm; charge). Either option – the N2 or the R102 – will bring you to the turn-off to **Storms River Mouth**, with its forests and unspoilt, rocky shore, its log cabins and intimidating suspension bridge at the eastern border of the beautiful Tsitsikamma Section of Garden Route National Park. Stretch-

ing for about 35km (20 miles) between Nature's Valley and Storms River, this scenic area protects a varied ecosystem of coastal lagoons, dunes, cliffs, beaches and coral reefs, complemented by an interior of steep, wooded ravines thick with ancient yellowwood trees that grow up to 50 metres (164ft) high.

Storms River

The well-run **Storms River Rest Camp**, which lies within the national park 1.5km (1 mile) west of the river mouth, has chalet accommodation and campsites, and forms a good base for swimming, snorkelling and hiking. The short walk from the rest camp to the suspension bridge across the river mouth is a must-do – look out for seals below the bridge – and if you're feeling ambitious you could ascend from there to a viewpoint high on the surrounding cliffs.

Storms River is legendary in South African hiking circles as the starting point of the **Otter Trail**, which follows the coast westward all the way to Nature's Valley, a distance of 26km (14 miles) as the gull soars and 41km (25 miles) on foot.

It is one of the country's oldest and most challenging hikes, and one of the most scenic in the world, encompassing some wild coastal scenery and crossing 11 rivers – sometimes you will need to swim rather than just wade. A good level of fitness is required as the terrain can be quite steep in places. Though not especially notable for wildlife, the Cape clawless otter is often seen along the way, as are marine, forest and fynbos birds, notably the endemic Knysna loerie and African black oystercatcher. The hike takes five days (sleeping in rest huts along the way, camping is not allowed).

Only 12 people are allowed to start daily, and because it is so popular it should be booked as far in advance as possible (tel: 012-426 5111; www.san parks.org).

For those who don't have the time to spare, no booking is required to undertake the popular day hike that effectively follows what would be the first day of the Otter Trail, running for about 4km (2½ miles) east along the rocky coast from Storms River Camp to the base of a small waterfall. ❑

TSITSIKAMMA COASTAL NATIONAL PARK

OTTER TRAIL

OTTERWANDELPAD

TSITSIKAMMASEEKUS NASIONALE PARK

This way for the Otter Trail, Tsitsikamma Section.

Dolphins

Nine of the world's 40 dolphin species have been recorded off the coast of Southern Africa. These include the endemic Heaviside's dolphin *(Cephalorhynchus heavisidi)*, which is commonly seen off the west coast, and the threatened humpbacked dolphin *(Sousa chinensis)* of the east coast.

Also present is the unmistakable orca or killer whale *(Orcinus orca)*, a ferocious pack hunter that probably ranks as the top predator in the oceanic food chain. The most conspicuous South African dolphin species is the Indo-Pacific bottle-nose *(Turslops aduncas)*, which favours shallow water - generally up to 30 metres deep - and is thus far more common close to land than it is on the open ocean. Typically moving in pods of up to 15 individuals, though groups of several hundred are occasionally recorded, the bottle-nosed dolphin is frequently seen from terrestrial vantage points all along the Garden Route (the viewpoint on

the N2 immediately west of Wilderness and Robberg Peninsula outside Plettenberg Bay are particularly good spots), frolicking and playing in the waves, or surfing in the wake of a speedboat. Bottle-noses, like most other dolphins, are believed to be highly intelligent and they communicate by means of a highly sophisticated language of clicks and whistles.

The only other dolphin species likely to be seen from the Indian Ocean coastline is the long-beaked common dolphin *(Delphinus capensis)*, a deep ocean species that frequently strays into shallower water, especially during the annual sardine run, when aggregations of more than 1,000 have been observed. The two can easily be distinguished by coloration alone: the bottle-nose is a rather uniform grey whereas the common is black with strikingly contrasting white markings on the side and belly.

MARVELS OF THE FLORAL KINGDOM

Home to more than 24,000 species – one-tenth of all known flowering plants – South Africa's flora is amongst the richest and most varied in the world

From the weird succulents of the dry Kalahari to the brilliantly coloured blossoms which transform Namaqualand's semi-desert plains in the spring, South Africa is impressively endowed with some spectacular plant life. Most enticing of all for botanists, gardeners and walkers alike is the slender strip of Cape coastline stretching inland in the west as far as Clanwilliam, around the peninsula and then east as far as Port Elizabeth. Dominated by a unique heath-like vegetation known as *fynbos* (Afrikaans for "fine bush"), this area enjoys special status as the smallest of the world's six "Floral Kingdoms", and the one with the richest species diversity.

A Threatened Kingdom

Characterised by very small or leathery leaves often protected by hairs, the three most common fynbos families are Proteaceae (including the national flower, *Protea cynaroides*, or king protea), Ericaceae and the reedy Restionaceae. *Fynbos* grows in some extremely diverse habitats – from arid salt marshes and sand dunes to mountain slopes and crags up in the cloud zone – but the best time to see it is the spring (September and October), when the veld blooms into kaleidoscopic colour. Sadly, as many as 1,326 *fynbos* species are on the endangered list, including the lovely snow protea, which only grows above the snow line in the Cederberg and defies cultivation.

LEFT: now exporte[d] over the world, the spectac[ular] Crane Flower *(Strelitzia regina[e])* indigenous to the Eastern Cape and KwaZulu-N[atal]

LEFT: the brightly coloured flowers of the water-loving red-hot poker (genus *Kniphofia*) usually bloom profusely in winter.

ABOVE: the genus *Protea*, known for its striking pink flowers, compr[ises] almost 100 species, 90 percent of which occur in the Western Cape, while others flourish in highland areas like uKhahlamba-Drakensber[g]

GREAT BOTANICAL GARDENS

Kirstenbosch *(above and left)* is South Africa's most famous garden. But eight other equally rewarding, national botanical gardens ("NBGs") are spread between the country's other major floral zones. See www.sanbi.org for further details.

• Pretoria's sprawling NBG, founded in 1946 and declared a National Monument in 1979, has examples of all major southern African vegetation types.

• In Gauteng's Walter Sisulu NBG, a dramatic waterfall provides a backdrop for more than 500 species of highveld aloes, trees and shrubs.

• The Lowveld NBG on the outskirts of Nelspruit has a spectacular series of waterfalls and river gorges, as well as the country's best outdoor collection of indigenous trees, ferns and rare cycads.

• The tranquil KwaZulu-Natal NBG in Pietermaritzburg, founded in 1872, features some superb specimens of imported trees.

• The Karoo Desert NBG near Worcester concentrates on plants from the arid semi-desert areas of the country.

• On the outskirts of Bloemfontein, the Free State NBG specialises in frost and drought-hardy plants.

• The beautiful, secluded Harold Porter NBG at Betty's Bay boasts one of the densest concentrations of *fynbos* in the country.

• The Hantam NBG outside Nieuwoudtville is especially worthwhile in Aug/Sept, since it falls into the Namaqualand springlower region.

OVE: aloes and other culents flourish in uth Africa.

HT: Outeniqua owwoods *(Podocarpus catus)* are the giants of Knynsa and tsikamma forests, ching heights of 60 tres (200ft). All owwood species are w protected by law.

RIGHT: endemic to southern Africa, the Arum lily *(Zantedeschia aethiopica)* typically occurs in moist areas. Its Afrikaans name *Varkoor* means Pig Ear, but it is also known as the Easter lily.

THE EASTERN CAPE

Sandy shores and lazy lagoons give way to high, green hills dotted with thatched huts, sweeping down to jagged cliffs – this is the traditional land of the Xhosa

An amalgamation of the eastern part of the former Cape Province and the apartheid-era homelands of the Transkei and Ciskei, the Eastern Cape is a large and ecologically diverse province whose habitats range from subtropical beaches to the arid scrub of the Karoo Nature Reserve and breezy montane grassland near the Lesotho border. The main population centre of the Xhosa people, the province has produced several prominent anti-apartheid leaders, including the former presidents Thabo Mbeki and Nelson Mandela. In 1820, Algoa Bay, the site of present-day Port Elizabeth, became the first main focal point for English settlement in the Cape, an influence that still permeates nearby towns such as Grahamstown and Port Alfred.

PORT ELIZABETH AND SURROUNDS

Coming from the west, the 160km (100-mile) trip along the N1 from Storms River to Port Elizabeth is fairly unremarkable and seldom ventures within eyeshot of the coast. That said, no self-respecting surfer would pass up on the short diversion south to the legendary **Jeffrey's Bay**, an otherwise unremarkable resort town regarded by some as possessing the world's most perfect waves. Also of interest is the **Shell Museum** (Mon–Sat 9am–4pm,

Sun 9am–1pm; donation expected), a private collection of more than 600 shells from all over the world, and the relatively unspoilt coastline protected within the more southerly **Cape St Francis Nature Reserve** (tel: 042-298 0073; daily; free), whose 120 hectares (290 acres) and 3km (2 miles) of spectacular coastline are crisscrossed by a network of walking trails from where dolphins are quite often observed.

The sixth-largest city in the country, **Port Elizabeth ❶** is an important harbour town and industrial centre, long

Main attractions
JEFFREY'S BAY
ADDO ELEPHANT NATIONAL PARK
SHAMWARI AND KWANDWE GAME RESERVES
MOUNTAIN ZEBRA NATIONAL PARK
GRAAFF-REINET
GRAHAMSTOWN
THE WILD COAST

LEFT: Valley of Desolation, Camdeboo National Park. **RIGHT:** surfers, Port Elizabeth.

Port Elizabeth began life as a military outpost to guard the first British settlers arriving in 1820. The then Cape governor, Sir Rufane Donkin, named it after his wife.

associated with the country's motor industry, the modern decline of which is mirrored by the city's general aura of having seen better days.

Together with the smaller towns of Uitenhage and Despatch, which lie immediately inland of it, Port Elizabeth now forms part of the greater Nelson Mandela Bay Municipality, but the three towns have quite separate identities, and are always referred to locally by their individual names.

Few would go out of their way to visit Port Elizabeth – or PE, as it's more often called – but those who do generally find that it lives up to its epithet of "the friendly city" and offers plenty of worthwhile sites and activities.

In the city centre, the 5km (3-mile) long **Donkin Heritage Trail** begins at the Market Place and imposing City Hall (1858), and leads to several other historic buildings including Fort Frederick (1799) and a restored and authentically furnished settler's cottage (1827) at the 7 Castle Hill Museum.

About 2km (1½ miles) south of the city centre, in the suburb of Humewood, **Kings Beach** is popular with

swimmers and surfers alike, while the nearby **Bayworld Complex** (www.bay world.co.za; daily 9am–4.30pm; seal and penguin presentations 11am and 3pm; charge) combines an excellent anthropological and natural history museum with an aquarium and snake park. Recommended for train enthusiasts is the **Apple Express** (www.apple-express.co.za; weekends, public holidays and school holidays only, see website for timetable), a recreational steam train excursion to Loerie along a track that was built in 1906 and crosses the world's highest narrow-gauge bridge.

Addo Elephant National Park

You may have failed to spot elephants in Knysna, but you'll not miss the **Addo Elephant National Park** ❷ (daily 7am–7pm; charge), which lies about 50km (30 miles) northeast of PE on the R335.

Elephants are the main attraction here, and they are easily observed at close quarters, but the park also contains substantial numbers of rhinoceros, buffalo, kudu, jackal, ground

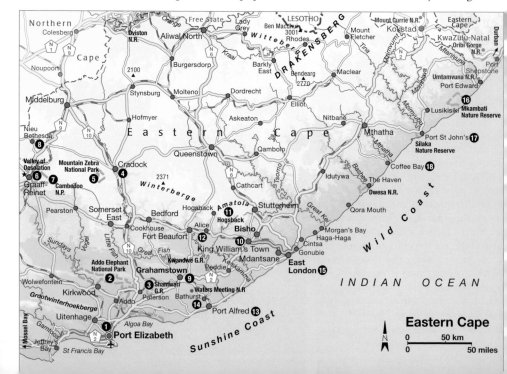

Eastern Cape

N

0   50 km

0   50 miles

squirrel and endemic birds such as the colourful bokmakierie and handsome jackal buzzard – not to mention lions, which were reintroduced in 2003.

In 1997, SANParks announced a proposal to create the Greater Addo Elephant National Park linking the arid Karoo to the Indian Ocean coastline east of Port Elizabeth. Since then, the core 200-sq-km (78-sq-mile) national park has been extended to cover around 1,700 sq km (665 sq miles) of land (with plans to expand by a further 1,000 sq km/390 sq miles) and it also incorporates a marine area of around 1,200 sq km (490 sq miles). This area includes five of South Africa's seven terrestrial biomes, an ecological diversity that exceeds any other protected area in Africa. From the visitor's perspective, however, Greater Addo remains something of a work in progress – the offshore islands with their immense bird and seal colonies are currently inaccessible to tourists, while the former **Zuurberg National Park** and **Woody Cape Nature Reserve** can only be explored on hiking trails – but this space is well worth watching.

Private reserves

Several exclusive private reserves around Addo offer a similar all-inclusive "Big Five" game-viewing package to their counterparts bordering the Kruger National Park, albeit generally in hillier terrain that supports a cover of dense woodland comprising various acacia species and the localised spekboom (literally "Bacon Tree"), a succulent whose plump leaves reputedly taste like bacon.

The best-known of these is the 200-sq-km (78-sq-mile) **Shamwari Game Reserve ❸** (tel: 041-407 1000; www. shamwari.com; access to overnight guests only), 72km (45 miles) northeast of Port Elizabeth. More than 26 species of game have been reintroduced here, including elephant, rhino, lion, leopard, buffalo, giraffe and zebra, and accommodation is spread across seven small exclusive lodges whose architecture reflects the colonial influence one might expect of an area so strongly associated with an influx of British settlers in the early 19th century.

Further inland, on the R67 about 160km (100 miles) from Port Eliza-

Port Elizabeth's Campanile commemorates the British settlers who landed here in 1820.

BELOW: statue of Queen Victoria in Port Elizabeth's Market Square.

The Elephants of Addo

In 1919, Uitenhage Town Council contracted the veteran hunter Major PJ Pretorius to undertake one of the most outrageously ambitious vermin eradication schemes of all time. Pretorius's mission was to exterminate an isolated population of elephants, already severely depleted by ivory hunters, that took refuge in the uninhabited *spekboomveld* of what is today Addo Elephant National Park.

It was no easy task, and Pretorius – nicknamed "Jungle Man" – frequently risked his life by following wounded individuals deep into the dense bush. But 14 months later, when the job was declared done, some 120 elephants had fallen to Pretorius's gun, and fewer than 20 remained. This cull is often cited as the beginning of the story of Addo Elephant National Park. Curiously, it was none other than the hunter-turned-gamekeeper Pretorius who persuaded the local authorities to set aside a sanctuary for the few remaining elephants in 1921.

Addo's elephants still made regular forays onto surrounding farmland to supplement their diet with oranges and other crops until 1954, when a steel rope fence was constructed to pen them in. By 1968, the park's elephant population had increased from a bottleneck breeding population of six to 50. Today, around 500 relaxed *pachyderms* roam the park, which ranks as one of Africa's great elephant-watching destinations.

beth, the newer and equally sumptuous **Kwandwe Game Reserve** (tel: 046-603 3400; www.kwandwereserve.com; access to overnight guests only), part of the ultra-exclusive &Beyond chain of five-star wilderness lodges, has a more overt "bush" feel to its four exclusive lodges, and it extends over 220 sq km (85 sq miles) of relatively arid terrain that offers superb game viewing, protecting a similar range of species to Shamwari.

CRADOCK AND GRAAFF-REINET

About 150km (90 miles) inland of Addo lies the town of **Cradock** ❹, founded in 1813 on the upper reaches of the Great Fish River as a frontier post to defend the region against Xhosa attacks. Like most other rural towns in South Africa, the stark monumental steeples of the Dutch Reformed church buildings are among its most notable features. Often, these were built as imitations of European churches – in Cradock, the model for the Dutch Reformed **Moederkerk**, built in 1868, was St Martin-in-the-Fields in London's Trafalgar Square.

The little town was first ma famous by the writer Olive Schrein (1855–1920), whose controversial 18 novel *The Story of an African Farm*, w a powerful attack on the arrogant ar racist attitudes of her fellow whites during the Boer War she was intern for her views. **Olive Schreiner Hou** (9 Cross Street; Mon–Fri 8am–12.45p and 2–4.30pm; charge), where s lived between 1867 and 1870, is now museum. Also of interest is a series 14 restored Victorian houses in **Mark Street** and the local history museu housed in a former parsonage th dates to 1849.

Mountain Zebra National Park

The region's main attraction, t **Mountain Zebra National Park** (www.sanparks.org; Oct–Mar 7am–7p Apr–Sept 7am–6pm; charge), lies 15k (9 miles) west of town. Some 6,600 he tares (16,300 acres) in size, the park w established in 1937 to protect the Cap mountain zebra – it was feared that might go the way of its half-horse, ha zebra cousin the quagga, which becan extinct when the last individual died i a zoo in 1883.

Through a careful programme conservation and breeding, the pa now accommodates about 300 mou tain zebras, and smaller herds hav been transferred to other parks in th province. It is also home to the endem black wildebeest and blesbok, as well springbok, kudu, cheetah, caracal, si ver fox and recently introduced her of buffalo and black rhino. A checkli of 200 bird species includes endem such as orange-breasted rockjumpe Layard's titbabbler and ground woo pecker, while the majestic black eag can sometimes be seen soaring in th sky above. Finally, don't be too su prised if you do happen to see som thing resembling a quagga here – i 1987, DNA studies on museum spec mens determined that the quagg had been a race of plains zebra, and project is currently underway to recr

ate it through selective breeding of an introduced herd of individuals with unstriped hindquarters.

Accommodation here includes the Victorian **Doornhoek Guest House**, built in 1836 and today a national monument, and a well equipped campsite. There are also hiking trails and mountain huts for keen walkers.

Graaff-Reinet

Continue another 120km (75 miles) west of Cradock, and you'll reach **Graaff-Reinet** ❻, the gem of the Karoo, enclosed by a bend in the Sundays River. Founded in 1786 (making it the fourth-oldest town in the country), it soon became a hub of political turbulence. In 1795, fed up with colonial rule and inspired by the example of the French Revolution, the inhabitants chased the government representative from town and declared an independent – albeit short-lived – republic. Despite all this, Graaff-Reinet looks today like the very model of good order, and differs markedly from the many other provincial towns which clearly grew up without any overall plan.

With the possible exception of Stellenbosch, no other town in South Africa has retained Graaff-Reinet's pervasive Cape Dutch architectural character. More than 200 of its buildings have been declared national monuments, including an entire street – **Stretch's Court** – now restored to its original 18th-century splendour.

The splendid **Dutch Reformed Church**, reputedly modelled on Salisbury Cathedral in England, and the old parsonage – built in 1811 and once occupied by one of the country's most noted churchmen, Dr Andrew Murray – have both been converted into museums. In the gardens of the parsonage, now called **Reinet House** (daily 9am–noon, Mon–Fri 2–5pm also; charge), grows the largest living grapevine in the world. With a girth of 2.4 metres (8ft) and a height of 1.5 metres (5ft), it covers an area of 124 sq metres (1,335 sq ft) – and still bears fruit.

The **Drostdy** in Church Street, completed in 1806, originally served as the seat of the local magistrate, but at the end of the 19th century it was converted into a hotel. You can no longer

War memorial, Graaff-Reinet.

BELOW: giraffe and cheetah in Shamwari Game Reserve.

The devil fire fish, an exotic import to South African shores.

BELOW: view over Graaff-Reinet.

spend the night in the Drostdy itself, but you can stay in one of the cottages behind it.

Palaeontologists consider the Karoo basin and its unbroken fossil record one of the world's great natural wonders. An extensive private collection of fossils – some exposed after an entombment of up to 230 million years – can be seen in the **Old Library** (daily 8am–12.30pm, Mon–Fri 2–5pm also; charge), situated on the corner of Church and Somerset streets. Just outside town is a statue of Andries Pretorius, the Voortrekker leader who lived in Graaff-Reinet before joining the Great Trek and leading his people to victory against the Zulus in the Battle of Blood River *(see pages 40 and 244)*.

About 14km (9 miles) west of town and definitely worth the detour is the **Valley of Desolation**, part of the 195-sq-km (75-sq-mile) **Camdeboo National Park** ❼ (formerly the Karoo Nature Reserve; tel: 049-892 3453; www. sanparks.org.za; daily sunrise–sunset; charge) and known for its bizarre rock formations of domes and pinnacles, or dolerites, with heights reaching more than 120 metres (393ft). On the outskirts of town there's a walking trail around the **Van Ryneveld Dam**, from which kudu and other typical Karoo antelope are often seen. Back in the town centre, the **Obesa Nursery** (www. obesanursery.com), named after a euphorbia species endemic to the vicinity of Graaff-Reinet, hosts a world-class succulent collection that includes several rare and endangered species.

From Graaff-Reinet, take the northbound N9 for Middelburg, then turn off after some 27km (17 miles) for the village of **Nieu-Bethesda** ❽.

In River Street here you will find the eerie, extraordinary **Owl House** (daily 9am–5pm; charge), formerly the private home of a reclusive and enigmatic artist, Helen Martins. Working chiefly at night, away from the prying eyes of the neighbours, she covered almost the whole interior of her house – walls, ceilings and some of the furniture – in crushed glass, mixed with cement. Flamboyant murals of suns, moons and stars are emblazoned on the ceilings, while enormous mirrors in all the rooms reflect the glittering whole.

Outside, in the vegetable garden, a haphazard jumble of over 300 cement sculptures (camels, peacocks, sun-worshippers and hooded shepherds) turn their faces to the east, while cement guardian owls glare balefully from the garden fence and from perches on the veranda. It's an extraordinary piece of Outsider Art, although sadly its creator didn't live to see it recognised as such – she committed suicide by drinking caustic soda in 1976.

PORT ELIZABETH TO EAST LONDON

Two roughly equidistant road routes connect Port Elizabeth to the Eastern Cape's other major city, the oceanic port of East London, which lies 250km (150 miles) to the northeast as the crow flies. The quicker of these roads is the N2 through historic Grahamstown and King William's Town, while the more scenic option is the coastal R72 via

Port Alfred – and those who want the best of both worlds can cut between Grahamstown and Port Alfred using the R67 through Bathurst.

Grahamstown

The university town of **Grahamstown** ❾, located some 130km (80 miles) east of Port Elizabeth, is certainly worth a visit. Founded in 1812 by a British soldier, Colonel John Graham, the town is steeped in British colonial history, with whitewashed Georgian and Victorian buildings in plentiful supply – **Merriman House** on Market Street, the home of a former bishop of Grahamstown (and where the ill-fated General Gordon of Khartoum spent some nights) is typical. A total of 40 churches are dotted around the town, leading to one of its nicknames: City of the Saints.

Other sightseeing includes the five museums that collectively form the **Albany Museum** (Mon–Sat 9.30am–1pm, Mon–Fri 2–5pm; charge), which is the second oldest such institution in the country. Particularly worthwhile are the **Observatory Museum**, with its bizarre camera obscura, and the **History Museum**, which focuses on local settler history and Xhosa culture, but also contains a well-preserved Egyptian mummy.

From the 1820 Settlers National Monument on Gunfire Hill, there is a magnificent view down over Grahamstown's flock of steeples. But the town is best known for the National Arts Festival (www.nafest.co.za), the largest and most diverse event of its type in South Africa, starting in early July to coincide with campus holidays.

King William's Town

After Grahamstown, **King William's Town** ❿, 110km (66 miles) further east along the N2, comes across as somewhat undistinguished. The centre of a thriving agricultural area, "King" – as it is commonly known among its residents – was founded by the London Missionary Society in 1825 and later became the capital of the colony of British Kaffraria. A stopover should include a visit to the **Amathole Museum** (Mon–Fri 9am–4.30pm, Sat 9am–1pm; charge). Here, you can view

Town Hall, Graaff-Reinet

BELOW: one of the Cape Dutch buildings that comprise the Graaff-Reinet Museum.

A demonstration at the fascinating Fossil Museum in Nieu Bethesda.

BELOW: savouring the view over the Valley of Desolation.

displays devoted to the region's British and German settlers and the culture of the Xhosa and Khoisan people.

The museum's most famous exhibit is undoubtedly Huberta the stuffed hippo. Huberta first captured the country's imagination in 1928, when she took off from Zululand on a 2,000km (1,200-mile) journey southwards. On her way, she became the most fêted hippo in history, pursued by photographers, journalists and adoring crowds alike. She popped up in cities and towns, wandering through the busy streets of Durban and gatecrashing plush parties. Tragically, three years later, she was shot by hunters while taking a dip in the Keiskamma River near King William's Town. Her remains were recovered and today take pride of place in the museum.

King William's Town lies at the junction of several roads running northward into the thickly-forested **Amatola Mountains**, a popular destination with ramblers. If you're serious about hiking, and have the time, the tough but rewarding six-day, 105km (65-mile) **Amatola Hiking Trail** begins in **Stutterheim**, on the N6 some 40km (24 miles) north of King William's Town, and terminates at the idyllic village of Hogsback. (For more information and to book accommodation in the overnight huts, contact the Keiskamma Ecotourism Network in King William's Town, tel: 043-642 2571.)

The Hogsback

The Katberg escarpment is the highest point on the Amatola Range, and in winter its peaks are often capped with snow. But it is the **Hogsback** ⑪ that makes the Amatola really memorable. Here, ferns cling to the lichened trunks of ancient yellowwoods and line the banks of rushing streams; blackberries, other wild berries and vines clamber over the forest flora.

It's a popular birding site, too, with more than 220 species recorded, including forest specialists such as the crowned eagle, black sparrowhawk, emerald cuckoo, Knysna woodpecker and Cape parrot. Blue monkey and bushbuck are the most frequently seen wild mammals. Booklets outlining marked trails through the forests are available from local hotels.

Immediately to the west of the Hogsback (about 25km/15 miles) lies **Alice** ⑫, named after the daughter of Queen Victoria. Scarcely more than a village, Alice looks distinctly down on its luck these days, although the **University of Fort Hare** on the outskirts of town is definitely worth a stop. Established in 1916 as the country's first tertiary educational institution for blacks, it counts among its alumni some of the country's most influential political and intellectual leaders, including Nelson Mandela. The main reason to visit, however, is the **De Beers Art Gallery** (Cultural Studies Centre; tel: 040-602 2269; daily in theory, but ring to confirm an appointment), which houses one of the country's best collections of contemporary art.

Back in Stutterheim, take the R61 – which branches off outside the town and leads back onto the N2 at Mthatha – for a rewarding detour towards the Lesotho border and the southern extension of the Drakensberg that's known locally as the **Witteberg** (White Mountains) because it receives snowfall with reasonable regularity.

Indeed, the remote but pretty montane settlement of **Rhodes**, which lies close to the 3,001-metre (9,990ft) **Mount Ben Macdhui**, is South Africa's one and only ski resort, albeit active only in midwinter. Many of the caves up in the mountains here are also bright with San paintings, some up to 2,000 years old; a good spot for rock art is **Maclear**, which also lies close to an amazing set of fossilised dinosaur footprints. There are numerous walks, sparkling streams and waterfalls in the **Malekgonyane Nature Reserve** on the Lesotho border, an area that's most beautiful in spring, when the montane grassland is covered in wildflowers.

Port Alfred

Back on the coast, the small settler town of **Port Alfred** ⑬ sprawls attractively either side of the Kowie River mouth almost exactly halfway between Port Elizabeth and East London. The beach here offers good swimming and surfing conditions, while other local attractions include scuba diving along a nearby reef, a superb golf course, mountain-bike trails and the wonderful overnight

Owl House souvenirs, Nieu Bethesda.

BELOW: Nieu Bethesda and one of the surreal concrete sculptures at the Owl House.

Children will enjoy the beach at East London.

canoe trail along the Kowie River. Further afield, some 53km (33 miles) back towards Port Elizabeth, the former **Woody Cape Forest Reserve** – now incorporated into the Addo Elephant National Park (*see page 204*) – is the site of a wonderful two-day hiking trail passing through an extensive dune field as well as lush coastal forest.

If you're thinking of cutting between the R72 and N2, the main settlement along the R67 is **Bathurst** , a sleepy 1820 settler village whose oh-so-English atmosphere – the only hotel is called the Pig & Whistle – is subverted somewhat by the decidedly tropical nature of the pineapples that form the main local crop. There are some great walks in the area, in particular one that leads 5km (3 miles) out of town into the **Waters Meeting Nature Reserve** and to a magnificent view over a horseshoe bend in the Kowie River.

EAST LONDON

Well-tended golf courses, hospitable people and some fine 19th-century architecture make the city of **East London** a pleasant enough place to visit. Situated at the mouth of Buffalo River, it is the only river port in the country. The two most popular bathing spots are **Orient** and **Eastern** beaches – both suitable for children – while Nahoon Beach is an excellent surfing spot with vast areas of sanded wilderness. The harbour here has a miniature version of Cape Town's V&A Waterfront – **Latimer's Landing**, complete with shops, restaurants, bars, theatres and even a weekend flea market.

Galleries and Gardens

Sadly, many of East London's fine Victorian buildings are being systematically demolished; one honourable survivor is the imposing **City Hall**, built in honour of Queen Victoria's diamond jubilee. Its whitewashed oriel windows and gables still contrast appealingly with its red-brick walls and bell tower. Equally attractive is the Edwardian **Ann Bryant Art Gallery** (www.annbryant.co.za; Mon–Fri 9am–5pm, Sat 9am–noon; free), a former private residence that today houses a collection of South African art dating from 1880 to the present.

One of the quirkiest natural history collections in South Africa is housed in the **East London Museum** (319 Oxford Street; tel: 043-743 0686; www.elmuseum.za.org; Mon–Thur 9.30am–4.30pm, Fri 9.30am–4pm, Sat 10am–1pm, Sun 10am–3pm; charge). It's strong on the local history of the Xhosa, but the real highlight is a stuffed and mounted coelacanth, an extraordinary-looking fish with fins like short, stumpy legs. It was thought to have been extinct for 80 million years. This specimen was netted in the nearby Chalumna River in 1938 – a world first.

The **Queens Park Botanic Garden and Zoo** (tel: 043-722 1171; www.el zoo.co.za; daily 9am–5pm; charge) lies on a hill between the city centre and the Buffalo River. In the middle of the beautifully laid-out garden with native plants and trees, the zoo has a

special children's section. An extension of the East London Museum accessed through Queens Park Zoo is **Gately House**, built in 1878 for Mayor John Gately, and now an interesting townhouse museum furnished with Victorian antiques.

Down on the Esplanade, the **German Settlers Memorial**, sculpted by Lippy Lipshitz, commemorates the thousands of German settlers who arrived here in the late 19th century, and whose influence is reflected in local place names such as Hamburg, Potsdam and Berlin. Also on the Esplanade, between Orient and Eastern beaches, the **East London Aquarium** (www.elaquarium.co.za; daily 9am–5pm; feeding times 10.30am and 3pm; charge) harbours more than 400 kinds of sea and freshwater creatures, including intricately patterned subtropical fish, sea anemones, squid, sharks, sea turtles, penguins and seals.

The attractive 93km (57-mile) stretch of coast between East London and the Kei River – formerly the border with the defunct Transkei homeland – is dotted with small low-key resorts but otherwise remains remarkably undeveloped by comparison to, say, the Garden Route. The most accessible resort here is **Gonubie**, whose bush-fringed beach and prolific water birds seem at odds with its location only 10km (6 miles) east of East London (but quite a bit longer by road due to the intervention of the Buffalo River). Even more remote in feel is the lovely small resort of **Cintsa**, 25km (15 miles) further east.

THE WILD COAST

The beautiful Wild Coast was once part of the Transkei, a nominally independent Xhosa homeland under apartheid. In the rural areas here, rolling grass hills are dotted with mud-and-grass huts. Women walk around with ochre-painted faces, smoking long-stemmed pipes, and old men and children urge on teams of oxen to plough the hillside fields.

As you drive through the region, you may also spot the occasional teenage boy standing by the roadside naked but for a patterned blanket, his face covered in white clay. He is an *abakwetha*, an

An abakwetha. *According to Xhosa tribal custom, teenage boys must undergo a circumcision ritual to attain manhood. During this period, the youth's face and body is daubed with clay.*

BELOW: Latimer's Landing, East London.

Xhosa woman.

initiate, and with a group of his peers he will be spending up to three weeks at a secluded bush lodge while clan elders tutor him in traditional customs (*see page 213, margin tip*).

The process culminates in a circumcision ceremony, after which the youths cleanse themselves in a river and burn all their old possessions. Then they are presented with a new set of clothes in which to return to their villages for a celebratory feast accompanied by traditional dancing. Now begins a year-long intermediary period during which the boys must keep their faces daubed with ochre clay, for according to Xhosa lore, "a boy is merely a dog", and the attainment of manhood is a serious matter. Only when that ends can they step forth into the world of men.

The Wild Coast lies between **Port Edward** in the north and **Morgan's Bay** in the south, and its wildness is apparent from the moment its deep ravines, steep cliffs and waterfalls come into view. Properly speaking, however, the coast was named after the reefs and rocks that lie some distance offshore which in the past have posed a great danger to shipping. Many of the wrecks submerged around here have still not been thoroughly explored; the vessels issue quite a challenge to divers.

Diving and dolphins

The best-known wreck is the **Grosvenor**, a fully-laden British treasure ship which came to grief on a stormy night in 1782 off the Pondoland coast. Rumours that the cargo included the glorious Peacock Throne looted from the kings of Persia have sparked off numerous attempts to recover the cargo – all of which have so far come to naught in the restless Wild Coast sea. Ironically, apart from eight cannons salvaged in 1952, the richest haul taken from the ship was its iron ballast, recovered by the ship's blacksmith, who chose to remain on the coast and settle down with two Mpondo wives.

Between May and November, whales with their newborn calves can often be seen offshore, while dolphins are a year-round attraction. This coast also offers some excellent angling opportunities,

BELOW: cows roam along the Wild Coast.

from fishing the Indian Ocean for enormous reef fish such as mussel-cracker, to trying your luck in the rivers and lakes, many of which are full of trout.

On the nature trail

Port Edward marks the start of the splendid **Wild Coast Hiking Trail**, one of South Africa's best. It takes a full two weeks to hike the 200km (160-mile) long route as far as Coffee Bay, though the trip can of course be split up into shorter sections. The southern stretch is the more easy-going and relaxing, thanks to its miles of sandy beaches, while the northern part with its steep cliffs, rivers and ravines is distinctly rugged and difficult.

Here, you can walk for days without seeing another human being. To book permits and accommodation in the basic huts spaced at 12km (8-mile) intervals along the trail, contact Eastern Cape Tourism (tel: 043-701 9600; www.ectourism.co.za).

Largest and finest of the nature reserves scattered along this coast is the 8,000-hectare (19,750-acre) **Mkhambati Nature Reserve ⑯** (www.

ecparks.co.za; daily; charge), created on the site of an old leper colony about 40km (25 miles) north of Port St John's. There are two wide estuaries for canoeing, long stretches of deserted, rocky beach, and accommodation in comfortable bungalows between tall shady trees, or in self-catering rondavels right on the seashore. The flora is wonderfully diverse, too, from mangrove swamps to rare species of palm tree growing in a ravine amphitheatre, and numerous species of wild orchid.

If you'd prefer a smaller retreat, there's **Dwesa Nature Reserve** (www.ecparks.co.z; daily; charge) between The Haven and Qora Mouth, a good place to see wildebeest, eland, monkeys and – if you're very lucky – the Cape clawless otter. Stock up before you travel and plan on being totally self-sufficient during your stay, as there are no shops for miles.

After so much rural tranquillity, arriving in **Port St John's ⑰** is like entering a major metropolis. Here, the mighty

Hut in the Transkei being repaired and repainted. The green color is unique to this region and is made on site by the women who undertake the renovation.

BELOW: sailors named the Wild Coast for its reputation of wrecking ships.

Mzimvubu River – the only navigable river on the Wild Coast – has gouged out an impressive portal for itself as it reaches the sea. The town itself, once a thriving colonial-style outpost, saw an exodus of its white population after Transkei independence. Today, it survives in somnambulent idleness and indifference. Most of its charm lies in this state of semi-decay, the grand old houses having been abandoned or taken over by new tenants. Not surprisingly, perhaps, it is also home to a flourishing artists' colony.

The R61 now leads back inland for 90km (56 miles) to Mthatha (formerly **Umtata**), one-time capital of the defunct Transkei homeland, and today a rather dusty and unprepossessing place. It possesses a few historic buildings dating from 1879, the year the town was founded, namely the Bunga (old Parliament) and the Town Hall.

Coastal resorts

Between Umtata and East London, several side roads wind their way from the N2 down to the coast. Some of the small resorts they lead to – Cintsa, Cefane and Double Mouth among them – are frequented mainly by local farmers, while **Haga-Haga** and **Morgan's Bay** have grown into sizeable resorts with hotels and holiday homes. Their common factors are their small size and situation off the highways. The locals like it this way; it frees some of the pristine lagoons, sun-drenched beaches, and abundant birdlife and fishing resources for their personal enjoyment.

The only surfaced road that branches off this route leads to **Coffee Bay** ⓱ where another dream beach awaits. An 8km (5-mile) walk south along the beach brings you to the giant rock formation known as Hole in the Wall. In Xhosa, this whaleback island with its huge wave- and river-bored tunnel is known as esiKhaleni, or the place of sound – for reasons obvious to anyone who stands on the pebbly beach and listens to the booming echo funnelling through the 20-metre (65ft) hole. But visitors should be forewarned: the rock and the pounding seas that surround it are treacherous and many lives have been lost here by the foolhardy. ❑

The Southern Skies

The glittering African night sky is particularly dazzling in the Karoo and other dry parts of the South African interior – a truly intoxicating experience

South Africa stretches down from the tropics to about 35 degrees south. Visitors from the northern hemisphere will find all the familiar constellations look upside down here.

The most easily recognised constellation is Crucis, or the Southern Cross. Astronomers have determined that, thousands of years ago, this bright constellation was visible from most of Europe. Today, it is visible from just south of 30 degrees north latitude. On a clear night, it is a simple matter to find south by using the Southern Cross and two stars called the Pointers, which are nearly always visible from anywhere in South Africa – bearing in mind that although the stars change their position during the night, the pattern always remains the same. In your imagination, draw a line in the sky linking the two stars on the main axis of the Cross, and another at right angles to the Pointers. The point where they intersect is directly above due south. Take care to distinguish the Southern Cross from the "Diamond Cross" and the "False Cross", lying slightly to the northeast.

The Pointers are the two brightest stars in the constellation of Centaurus. Alpha Centauri, the brighter of the two, is the fourth brightest star of all, and also – at 4.3 light years – the Sun's closest neighbour. Viewed with a small telescope, it resolves rather startlingly into two separate pinpoints of light; viewed with a larger telescope it reveals a third, fainter, companion.

Bright star

Conveniently, the five brightest stars of the Southern Cross are arranged clockwise in order of apparent brightness: Alpha, Beta, Gamma, Delta and finally Epsilon.

The Cross is also a convenient reference point for the Milky Way's two satellite galaxies, the Large and Small Magellanic Clouds. Again, extend the long axis of the Cross by about seven times. On either side of this line, you'll see what resembles two small clouds, except that they do not move or change shape. At roughly 200,000 light years away, they are two of our galaxy's closest neighbours, linked to it not only gravitationally, but via a tenuous bridge of hydrogen gas.

The Large Magellanic Cloud (LMC) came into prominence in 1987 as a result of the massive explosion known as Supernova 1987a. A very bright object, known as S Doradus, is prominent in the IMC and is associated with a gaseous nebula known as the Tarantula Nebula, a remnant of a much earlier supernova event.

Near to the Small Magellanic Cloud, you can spot a hazy white patch with the naked eye. With binoculars it is more prominent; a small telescope resolves it into thousands of stars. This is one of two great globular clusters, consisting of 100,000 stars or more, seen clearly only from the Southern Hemisphere. This one is called 47 Tucanae, and its fellow cluster is Omega Centauri.

Another easily identifiable constellation is Orion, with its belt of three stars. Orion's "shoulder" is the star Betelgeux, a red super-giant star with one of the largest diameters ever measured, 700 times that of the sun.

The Astronomical Observatory at Sutherland in the Karoo is South Africa's best-known astronomical research facility.   ❑

RIGHT: quiver trees underneath the night sky, Richtersveld National Park, Northern Cape.

DURBAN AND THE KWAZULU-NATAL COAST

East meets west in Durban – a cosmopolitan, holiday city set in sugar country and on the edge of a lush subtropical coast

Durban is traditionally South Africa's most popular holiday resort town, thanks to the combination of a seductive subtropical climate (summer temperatures regularly reach 32°C/90°F), alluring beaches, year-round warm seas and excellent facilities – not to mention its relative proximity (about five hours' drive on the nippy N3) to landlocked Gauteng. Durban's bustling beachfront probably hosts South Africa's largest concentration of hotels – unfortunately, many of them of the soulless high-rise variety so beloved of architects in the 1960s and 1970s – and these days it is as popular with black holidaymakers as with its established clientele of white middle-class families from Gauteng.

DURBAN

The site of **Durban** ❶ was one of the first parts of South Africa to appear on European maps, after the Portuguese navigator Vasco da Gama landed there on Christmas Day 1497 and christened it Terra do Natal. The name Port Natal was still in use in 1823, when a party of British traders led by Henry Fynn founded a trading post close to where the city hall stands today, but 12 years later the fledgling city was renamed in honour of the then Governor of the British Cape Colony, Sir Benjamin D'Urban.

With a population of more than 3.5 million, Durban is South Africa's third-largest city, yet it has never been afforded so much as the status of provincial capital. It is also the biggest and busiest port anywhere on the continent, despite its early development having been hampered by a shallow, narrow entrance that caused some 65 shipwrecks prior to 1895, when dredgers were imported from Europe to remove almost 10 million tonnes of sand.

A distinctive feature of Durban is its large community of Indian people –

Main attractions
DURBAN'S "GOLDEN MILE"
USHAKA MARINE WORLD
PORT SHEPSTONE
ORIBI GORGE NATURE RESERVE

PRECEDING PAGES: Durban waterfront.
LEFT: the Wet 'n' Wild Waterworld at uShaka Marine World. **RIGHT:** Durban seafront.

TIP

Take an unusual ride along Marine Parade on one of Durban's famous rickshaws, pulled by a flamboyantly costumed Zulu driver.

around one million strong, of which 70 percent are Hindu, 20 percent Muslim, and the remainder mostly Christian. Descendants of the indentured labourers who arrived in the 1860s to work in the local sugar-cane industry, many Indians in KwaZulu-Natal have been assimilated into the wider South African society, whilst others still maintain a language, religion, dress code and caste system imported from their country of origin.

Metropolitan playground

Set with the municipality of eThekwini ('Place of the Sea' in the local Zulu tongue), metropolitan Durban has the highest population density in the country – a fact that becomes apparent during the peak holiday season, when day-trippers from miles around flock to the bathing beaches stretching in a long golden line north from the harbour entrance. **South Beach** is the most densely packed beach in South Africa; **North Beach** and the adjacent **Bay of Plenty** are also crowded but slightly trendier, lined with bars, cafes and restaurants for surfers and posers.

All the beaches are protected by shark nets and patrolled by lifeguards.

The heart of the resort area is the pedestrianised **O.R Tambo (Marine) Parade Ⓐ** – a brash, busy playground of pools, fountains, amusement arcades and fast-food kiosks, flanked by innumerable luxurious (and not so luxurious) high-rise hotels and apartment blocks. Most of the major tourist attractions are found here, clustered along the strip known as the **Golden Mile**, which actually extends for about 6 sandy kilometres (4 miles) along the coastline running south from the Umgeni River mouth to the main harbour. Although perfect for swimming, sunbathing, surfing and other typical beach activities, the Golden Mile is also dotted with several more manufactured places of interest.

For anybody with an interest in marine wildlife, a certain highlight will be **uShaka Marine World Ⓑ** (www.ushakamarineworld.co.za; daily 9am–5pm; charge), founded opposite New Pier in the 1950s, but reopened in new premises on uShaka Beach, near The Point, in 2004. uShaka comprises

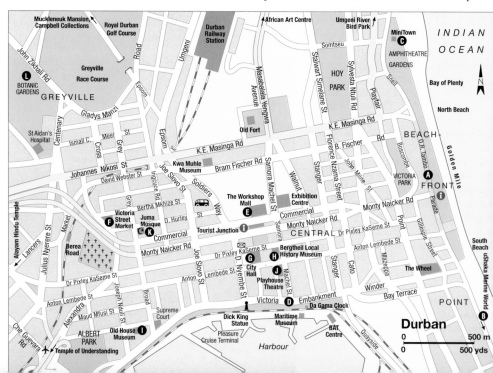

Durban

0   500 m
0   500 yds

two separate parts, of which Sea World is a massive aquarium – probably the largest in the southern hemisphere known for its comprehensive collection of live sharks (the truly bold can hire wetsuits and dive in the tank with them) and daily shows featuring performing dolphins, seals and penguins. The other part of uShaka is the more hedonistic Wet 'n' Wild **Waterworld** which is always packed with thrill-seekers braving the kamikaze water slides and rides.

Also very popular is **MiniTown** ❸ (daily 9.30am–4.30pm; charge), with its miniature railway line and replicas of major city landmarks. A short walk away at Bay of Plenty beach are the **Amphitheatre Gardens**, a tranquil collection of sunken pools, gardens, lawns and fountains.

Victoria Embankment

Situated at The Point, on the harbour end of the Golden Mile, **Victoria Embankment** ❹ is graced with a number of interesting historical features, including **Da Gama Clock** – erected by the Portuguese Government to mark the 400th anniversary of Da Gama's discovery of Port Natal.

To the west of this, also overlooking the harbour, the Dick King Statue commemorates its namesake's heroic 1,000km (600-mile) 10-day horseback ride to Grahamstown, undertaken in 1842 to fetch reinforcements to relieve the Voortrekker-besieged British fort at Durban.

For a less crowded experience, head further afield, to **The Bluff**, the 4km (2½-mile) long ridge that hems in the southern shore of the harbour – known in Zulu as *isiBubulungu*, which translates as "long bulky thing".

Here, **Brighton Beach** is good for body surfing, while at nearby **Treasure Beach** you can explore an unspoilt stretch of tidal pools, with rare corals and marine life. The Durban branch of the Wildlife and Conservation Society (www.wessa.org.za) is based here and it can conduct tours for a small charge.

Otherwise, it's a brief 15km (10-mile) trip north of the city to the up-market resort of Umhlanga Rocks *(see page 233)*, which has a particularly fine stretch of sand.

Durban forms a good base for adventure activities, which can be arranged with ease through any hotel or hostel, or through tourist kiosks along the Golden Mile. Popular with adrenaline seekers are the white water rafting day trips that run on a lively stretch of the Tugela River during the rainy season (typically November–April). A number of scuba-diving schools offer one-off dives, as well as PADI and/or NAUI courses that run over several days. As for surfing, the options are endless, but the readily accessible South Beach offers conditions suitable to novices, while the more experienced might want to head to Dairy Beach on the Golden Mile or Cave Rock on The Bluff.

Craft markets and malls

Situated on Gillespie Street, a vast and rather fancifully designed complex called **The Wheel** (daily 9am–5pm) contains an excellent selection

Dick King's epic 10-day ride to Grahamstown in 1842 – to get help for the British garrison besieged by Boers at Durban's Old Fort – is marked by a statue of him on Victoria Embankment.

BELOW: the Sea World at uShaka Marine World.

The ornate wrought iron curlicues of Da Gama Clock, on Victoria Embankment.

BELOW: just one of the many stalls at Victoria Street Market.

of shops, as well as cinemas, banks, restaurants and bars, and it's the most convenient of Durban's shopping malls, at least if you're based on the Golden Mile. Larger still, but less accessible for most visitors, **The Pavilion** (www.thepav.co.za; daily 9am–7pm) lies just off the N3 in the district of Westville.

But the most interesting downtown mall is **The Workshop** ❸ (99 Samora Machel (Aliwal) Street; www.theworkshopcentre.co.za; Mon–Fri 8.30am–5pm, Sat 9am–5pm, Sun 10am–4pm), which consists of 120 upmarket shops in a converted 1890s railway shed. All these malls offer a few good craft shops along with standard mall-type fare. Directly opposite, **Tourist Junction** – the official tourist information office – is in the old railway station building and can arrange a variety of guided tours and other activities in and around Durban.

By far the most exotic place to shop for curios is **Victoria Street Market** ❻ (Mon–Sat 8am–6pm, Sun 10am–4pm), west of the city centre on Bertha Mkhize (Victoria) Street, where both Indian and African craft markets jostle for space alongside fresh produce stalls. Here, you can spend a morning haggling for Zulu *assegais* (spears) and carved masks, or Indian silver jewellery and leather-work, as well as stocking up on spices (try the potent Mother-in-Law Masala). If you'd prefer to visit with a guide, numerous companies offer city tours which include this market.

A good bet for quality handicrafts and souvenirs is **Essenwood Park** in Berea, which hosts a busy craft market every Saturday (9am–2pm). Then there's the **Heritage Market** (daily; Old Main Road, Hillcrest; www.heritage hillcrest.co.za), with an eclectic range of crafts, antiques and tat housed in a picturesque Victorian building 20 minutes' drive from the city centre. Finally, with more than 750 stalls, the **South Plaza Market** (Sun 9am–4pm) near The Workshop in the city centre is one of the largest flea markets in the country selling crafts, plants and food.

Of particular note to art enthusiasts

is the recently relocated **African Art Centre** (94 Florida Road, Morningside; tel: 031-312 394; www.afriart.org.za; Mon–Fri 8.30am–5pm, Sat 9am–1pm), a non-profit gallery that was founded more than 50 years ago and has long played an important role in exposing the work of talented contemporary South African artists to a wider market.

Mosques and museums

Durban has surprisingly few museums; although each sheds some light on the city's social and natural history, few are exceptional. Make time, nonetheless, for the **Natural Science Museum** (tel: 031-311 2256; Mon–Sat 8.30am–4pm, Sun 11am–4pm; charge), which not only has some interesting wildlife displays (it's especially good on local birds), but is housed in the splendidly neo-baroque **City Hall** ⑤ in downtown Smith Street – built in 1910, it's a near-exact copy of Belfast's City Hall. This is also where you'll find the **Durban Art Gallery** (tel: 031-311 2264; Mon–Sat 8.30am–4pm, Sun 11am–4pm; free), which is worth a visit for its excellent collection of Zulu handicrafts.

A few minutes' walk from the City Hall in Samora Machel (Aliwal) Street is Durban's original Victorian courthouse, now the **Bergtheil Local History Museum** ⑪ (16 Queens Avenue; tel: 031-203 7107 Mon–Fri 8.30am–4.45pm, Sat 8am–noon; free); it tells the story of Port Natal's colonial past.

From here, a short drive west along the Old Fort Road brings you to the leafy suburb of **Berea**, which is set on a ridge, and whose Victorian showpieces include the gracious Muckleneuk Mansion. It houses the worthwhile **Campbell Collections** (220 Gladys Mazibuko (formerly Marriott) Road; tel: 031-260 1720; http://campbell.ukzn.ac.za; Tue and Thur am by appointment only), a museum of rare and valuable Africana which includes books, maps and manuscripts, as well as the Mashu Collection of indigenous Zulu art. Also interesting is the **Old House Museum** ❶ (tel: 031-311 2261; Mon–Sat 8.30am–4pm, Sun 11am–4pm; charge) at 31 St Andrews Street – a

Durban's Victoria Street Market is an excellent place to buy spices and curry powders.

BELOW: Juma Mosque; the Durban area is home to the largest Muslim community in the country.

Name Changes

The renaming of landmarks with negative political associations was an important priority in the post-apartheid era, and many such changes are now well established: Verwoedburg to Centurion, for instance, or Pietersburg to Polokwane, DF Malan Drive to Beyers Naudé Drive, Jan Smuts Airport to O.R. Tambo Airport, or (more cosmetically) Messina to Musina.

The status of other proposed name changes is less clear cut. Indeed, many cities and towns have adopted a kind of dual system wherein the town retains its old name but the controlling municipality has been rechristened – Durban, Pretoria and Port Elizabeth, for example, respectively now fall within the metropolitan municipalities of eThekweni, Tshwane and Nelson Mandela Bay.

The process becomes more controversial where inoffensively titled thoroughfares such as Pietermaritzburg's Long Street are renamed after a partisan political figure, at considerable cost to cash-strapped municipalities and local businesses. And it doesn't help that official name changes have come through in dribs and drabs and largely unpublicised. It can be a messy situation, and while this edition aims to reflect current names as accurately as possible, the process is ongoing and there are bound to be further changes by the time you arrive in South Africa.

TIP

Pleasure cruises round
Durban harbour aboard
the *Sarie Marais* leave
from the Gardiner Street
Jetty. For details, tel:
031-305 4022.

detailed replica of a settler home.

Near the City Hall on the corner of Anton Lembede (Smith) and Acutt streets, the **Playhouse Theatre ❶** (tel: 031-369 9555; www.playhousecompany.com) is the city's major arts venue. It's the place to come for symphony concerts by the now-privatised Natal Philharmonic, as well as performances of ballet, drama and opera. Down on Victoria Embankment just a short walk away, the **BAT Centre** arts complex (tel: 031-332 0451; www.batcentre.co.za) has a concert hall, dance and drama studios, and a particularly nice café overlooking Durban's small crafts harbour. Visit on Friday evenings for the free sundowner jazz concerts.

One of Durban's best-known landmarks is the **Islamic Juma Mosque ❻**, on Grey Street, close to Victoria Street Market. It is the largest place of worship for Muslims in southern Africa, and famous for its enormous golden domes. Further from the city centre, on Somtseu Road, the **Alayam Hindu Temple** (daily; free) is the largest – and the oldest – building of its type in the country.

Parks and gardens

Durban's lush climate supports a healthy number of green spaces and parks. One of the best is the **Umgeni River Bird Park** (tel: 031-579 4600; www.umgeniriverbirdpark.co.za; daily 9am–5pm; bird show Tue–Sun 11am and 2pm; charge), on Riverside Road on the north bank of the Umgeni River. It contains a marvellous collection of over 1,000 mostly exotic birds, including the rhino hornbill, which sports a 30-cm (1ft) long multicoloured beak.

The adjacent **Beachwood Mangroves Nature Reserve** (tel: 083-293 3611; www.kznwildlife.com; entrance through north gate daily; access by appointment only) offers the opportunity to explore a mangrove environment from a wooden boardwalk, walking trail and hide. Look out for the peculiar mudskipper (a type of fish that "walks" on uniquely adapted fins), as well as some interesting indigenous birds such as mangrove kingfisher, pelican and various marine species.

Another attractive retreat from the city centre is the 253-hectare (625-acre)

BELOW: carved tree in Durban's Botanic Gardens.

KwaZulu-Natal
Coast

Kenneth Stainbank Nature Reserve (tel: 031-469 2807; daily 6.30am–6pm; nominal charge), situated in the suburb of Yellowwood Park, where several walking trails lead through a mixture of coastal forest and grassland inhabited by zebra, bushbuck, impala, all three duiker species, vervet monkey and various mongooses. Popular with local bird watchers is the **Bluff Nature Reserve** (tel: 031-469 2807; daily 7am–5pm; nominal charge), where, a short distance south of the city centre, two strategically located hides overlook a reed-lined pan inhabited by the likes of the striking purple gallinule and malachite kingfisher.

The futuristic marble **Hare Krishna Temple of Understanding** (daily; free) just south of the city centre in the suburb of Chatsworth, is the largest of its kind in the southern hemisphere, yet its lush ornamental gardens are a tranquil oasis. It also supports a very good vegetarian restaurant, serving snacks as well as large curries. The **Botanic Gardens ⓛ** (John Zikhale Road; tel: 031-309 1170; www.durbanbotanicgardens.org.za; daily 8.30am–4.30pm; free) in Berea is a more conventional escape from city heat and dust, but it's worth visiting for the collection of rare cycads and the splendid orchid hothouse – to say nothing of the delicious cream teas.

THE SUNSHINE COAST

The Sunshine Coast is the lyrical name given to the lush subtropical coastline that runs parallel to the N2 for about 150km (90 miles) south of Durban, passing through a string of popular seaside resorts – Umzumbe, Banana Beach, Sea Park and Umtentweni among them – before veering sharply inland near Port Shepstone. Some of the country's loveliest beaches grace this stretch of coast, and the associated resorts – which cater mostly to local holidaymakers as opposed to international tourists – tend to be relatively uncrowded except during school holidays, and to offer better value for money than their counterparts on the more publicised Garden Route.

Some of the best scuba diving in South Africa can be had just 22km (14 miles) south of Durban, at **Amanzimtoti ❷**. Here, regular boats depart for the **Aliwal Shoal**, a sandbank roughly 5km (3 miles) from the coast, overgrown with hard and soft coral. At very low tides, passage out to the Shoal may be blocked by a large natural breakwater – but get past that and you can look forward to exploring natural tunnels, caves and reefs up to 43 metres (140ft) below the surface. Two wrecks – the *Nebo* and the *Produce* – lie just north of the northernmost tip of the Shoal, known as the Pinnacles. Around the seaward section nicknamed the Outside Edge you could see ragged-tooth shark, along with manta rays and moray eels. Only experienced divers should attempt the Shoal's dive sites, however, as currents can be very strong; beginners would do better to dive at nearby **Umkomaas**, a further

Durban's Botanic Gardens has a splendid orchid hothouse.

BELOW: the futuristic interior of the Hare Krishna Temple of Understanding.

The wild hibiscus that grows profusely along the road sides between Hibberdene and Port Edward has given the area its name: the Hibiscus Coast.

19km (12 miles) down the coast.

The south coast boasts several excellent golf courses – indeed Selbourne Park and San Lameer are rated among the top 12 in the country. A game at Selbourne Park course can be great fun, thanks to the water obstacles; the fairways at **Scottburgh** also take some getting used to. For a pleasant day trip from Scottburgh, take the R612 heading inland towards Ixopo through sugar and eucalyptus plantations to reach the **Vernon Crookes Nature Reserve ❸** (tel: 039-974 2222; www.kznwildlife.com; Oct–Mar daily 6am–6pm, Apr–Sept daily 6am–5pm; charge), which has a good range of scenery from river valleys and coastal forest to swampland. This range of habitats supports plenty of wildlife – over 300 species of bird, including the rare African broadbill – as well as zebra, blue wildebeest, eland, impala, reedbuck and nyala. If you're visiting in mid-January, there's a good chance of spotting the beautiful snake lily in flower in the reserve's swamp forest.

THE COAST

Known collectively as the Hibiscus Coast, the resorts that lie between Hibberdene and Port Edward – notably Margate, Ramsgate and Southbroom – are hugely popular with South Africans looking for a good-value alternative to the likes of Port Elizabeth, Plettenberg Bay and Knysna in the Cape. Accordingly, in December and January, this stretch of coast can get very crowded indeed, but it's usually pretty quiet at other times of year.

Port Shepstone ❹, the largest town on the Hibiscus Coast, retains a pleasant provincial air. There are several very good (and unbelievably cheap) seafood restaurants here – some specialising in oysters – while the local craft shops are a good bet for high-quality Zulu basketware, hand-crafted beadwork and pottery. Golfers should definitely try out the local course, high above the rocky coast.

Scuba divers, meanwhile, should head down to the bustling seaside resort of **Shelley Beach ❺**, about 5km (3 miles) south of Port Shepstone, where you can arrange to be taken by launch to some excellent shallow-water reef sites – those at Deep Salmon and Bo Boyi reefs are recommended. To see the corals and tropical fish at their best, avoid the summer months – visibility is poor after the seasonal rains. If you're a thrill-seeking diver and fancy getting close to hammerhead and great white sharks, Shelley Beach is also the place to join trips to the deeper waters of Protea Banks, some 9km (6 miles) offshore.

About 12km (8 miles) south of Shelley Beach, **Margate ❻** is a sleepy, small resort whose idyllic white-sand beach, which stretches for 1.5km (1 mile) in front of the town centre, is widely regarded to offer the best swimming conditions in the region. Only 3km (2 miles) north of Margate, a circular

two-hour walking trail runs through the **Uvongo Nature Reserve** (daily; free), which protects a near pristine patch of coastal forest and a diversity of tree, orchid and coastal bird species. Also of interest is the nearby Skyline Nature Reserve (tel: 039-315 0112; www.kznwildlife.com; daily 7am–5pm), whose well-known arboretum harbours about 375 indigenous and 400 exotic tree species. Several self-guided trails are demarcated, and wildlife such as blue and grey duiker are present.

Oribi Gorge Nature Reserve

A highlight of this region is the **Oribi Gorge Nature Reserve** ❼ (tel: 039-679 1644; www.kznwildlife.com; daily 6.30am–7.30pm; charge), which lies some 21km (13 miles) inland of Port Shepstone just off the N2. Here, numerous short hiking trails radiate from an inexpensive cliff-top rest camp into the spectacular euphorbia-studded canyon carved by the Mzimkulwana River, which is also accessible via a steep but surfaced road. The canyon supports a fair bit of wildlife, too – bushbuck and the localised blue monkey lurk in the forested base, black and crowned eagles nest on the cliffs and gaudy agama lizards scuttle around the rocky rim. The part of the gorge outside the reserve has recently caught on with adventure-sport enthusiasts; activities on offer include white water rafting and abseiling alongside a waterfall.

From Oribi Gorge, the N2 continues inland, running roughly parallel to the Eastern Cape border for about 120km (70 miles) until it eventually crosses into that province near **Kokstad**. Although somewhat unremarkable in itself, Kokstad has an attractive location amid the rolling green southern Drakensberg foothills.

The nearby **Mount Currie Nature Reserve** ❽ (tel: 039-727 3844; daily 6am–6pm; charge) is a low-key, pedestrian-friendly retreat where ramblers can expect to encounter a bafflement of small grassland antelope (grey rhebok, oribi, common duiker and mountain

and southern reedbuck are all present) as well as crowned, wattled and blue cranes. By contrast, a network of hiking trails in the **Weza Forest Reserve** – which flanks the N2 between Harding and Kokstad – passes through dense indigenous forest inhabited by bushbuck, duiker and a wide variety of forest birds, including a rare breeding population of Cape parrot.

Back on the coast, situated south of **Port Edward** ❾, lies a jagged series of steep cliffs and deep bays, most of which can only be reached along tiny unsurfaced footpaths such as those that meander through the remote **Umtamvuna Nature Reserve** ❿ (tel: 039-311 2383; daily 6.30am–5.30pm; charge) on the Eastern Cape border. Named after the Umtamvuna River and its wild, forested gorge, this little-known reserve is renowned for its stunning coastal scenery and spring wildflower displays, but it also harbours several rare or endemic plant species, as well as a breeding colony of the endangered Cape vulture and smallish mammals such as bushbuck, red and blue duiker and rock hyrax.   ❑

Rural dwellings in KwaZulu-Natal.

BELOW: Mount Currie Nature Reserve is home to several types of antelope, including grey rheboks.

ZULULAND

From St Lucia's wild waterways to historical Anglo-Zulu battlefields, this compelling region lies at the very heart of the legendary kingdom founded by Shaka Zulu

nformally but ubiquitously referred to as Zululand, the northern part of KwaZulu-Natal (KZN) Province, with its distinct wilderness flavour, numerous fine game reserves and seemingly endless succession of untrammelled beaches, makes for an immensely rewarding destination to self-drive visitors with an interest in natural history.

The main road through the region is the N2 running north from Richard's Bay/Empangeni to Pongola, which forms part of the most popular and straightforward route between Durban and the Kruger National Park, as well as a slower but more scenic alternative to the N3 highway connecting Durban to Gauteng.

The Dolphin Coast

Heading from **Durban** ❶ towards Zululand, the N2 first follows the so-called Dolphin Coast for roughly 140km (87 miles) between Umhlanga Rocks and **Richard's Bay**.

Like the beaches south of Durban, this stretch of the north coast is studded with seaside resorts, though these are generally more upmarket than their southern counterparts, the area is less heavily developed and it's still possible to find wide, unspoilt beaches and sheltered coves fringed with tropical vegetation.

PRECEDING PAGES: a hill village near Eshowe. **LEFT:** giraffe, Shamwari Game Reserve. **RIGHT:** Zulu dwelling.

Bottle-nosed dolphins are plentiful here, and can be spotted from the beaches all year round.

Sharks are also very common; the **KZN Sharks Board** (1a Herrwood Drive; tel: 031-566 0400; www.shark. co.za; Mon–Thur, five times daily; small charge) in Umhlanga Rocks puts on a fascinating audiovisual display on these extraordinary creatures and their importance in the ecological chain in an effort to remove some of the prejudices felt against them.

Umhlanga Rocks ❷ itself is a mid-

Main attractions
UMLALAZI NATURE RESERVE
SHAKALAND
ISIMANGALISO WETLAND PARK
EMAKHOSINI OPHATHE HERITAGE PARK
HLUHLUWE-IMFOLOZI GAME RESERVE
PHINDA RESOURCE RESERVE
TEMBE ELEPHANT SANCTUARY
NCOME MUSEUM

TIP

If you pass through Greytown, on the R74 between KwaDukuza and Ladysmith, do pop into its small museum, set in a 19th century building and boasting a large collection of military memorabilia from all around KwaZulu-Natal.

dling-sized resort with good shopping, magnificent sandy beaches and great watersports facilities.

More remote sections of coast can easily be explored by car. Clearly sign-posted sideroads branching off the N2 lead to a host of pleasant little resorts such as **Tongaat Beach**, **Ballito** and **Shaka's Rock** with its splendid tidal pools – an idyll only briefly interrupted by the unprepossessing industrial sprawl of **KwaDukuza** ❸ (formerly Stanger) on the N2. This sizeable sugar-cane processing centre was founded in 1820 as the the royal kraal of the King Shaka, who named it KwaDukuza ("Place of the Lost Person") in reference to its confusing sprawl of huts. It is here that Shaka was killed by his brothers and rivals Umhlangana and Dingane in 1828; the **Shaka Monument** on Couper Street commemorates his death.

Beyond KwaDukuza

The N2 continues to hug the coast, with good swimming and particularly picturesque scenery at **Blythedale**, 8km (5 miles) away, and little Zink-

wazi. Some 24km (16 miles) north of KwaDukuza, Tugela Mouth marked the southern boundary of Zululand prior to the era of expansionism initiated by Shaka and his successors. Today, the southern bank of the Tugela Mouth is protected within the 100-hectare (247-acre) **Harold Johnson Nature Reserve** ❹ (tel: 032-486 1574; www.kzn-wildlife.com; daily 6am–6pm; charge). Here, 7km of nature walks – including a Muti Trail focusing on traditional medicinal plant usage – through the forested dunes and sea-facing cliffs offer an opportunity to glimpse some of the 200 recorded bird species and forest mammals such as blue and red duiker, and zebra and impala, as well as several historical sites connected to the 1879 Anglo–Zulu War.

At Gingindlovu (Umgungundlovu) just across the river, the R68 leads off to Vryheid, the start of the Battlefield Route *(see page 242)*. For now, we continue along the N2 through the industrial centre of **Empangeni** and then on to the equally ugly **Richards Bay**, some 20km (12 miles) further east down a clearly marked turn-off. Set at

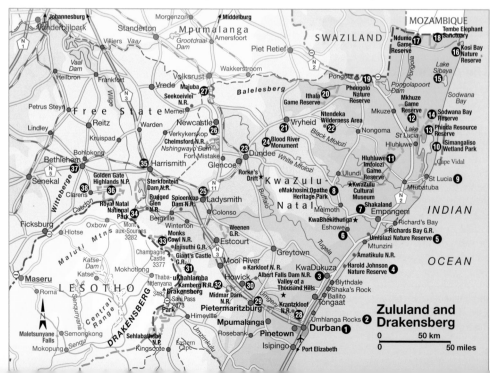

Zululand and Drakensberg

the mouth of the Mhlatuze River, this busy port shifts vast quantities of coal mined in the highveld town of Witbank, and transported here on a seemingly endless series of trains.

Far better to head for the **Umlalazi Nature Reserve ❺** (tel: 035-340 1836; www.kznwildlife.com; daily 5am–10pm; charge) bordering the small resort town of Mtunzini some 50km (30 miles) south of Richards Bay. Set on a near-perfect beach, this suburban reserve protects a remarkable habitat diversity within its small area, attested to by a checklist of more than 300 bird species. The avian highlight of Umlalazi is the country's only breeding population of the striking palmnut vulture, which inhabits a raffia palm swamp that can be explored on a boardwalk. A trio of walking trails twist along the banks of a lagoon, across dunes and into a mangrove swamp, where mudskippers and hermit crabs scuttle around the mud and the localised mangrove kingfisher reveals its presence with a trademark high trilling call.

Eshowe and the Zulu heartland

Offering some respite from the coastal humidity in midsummer, the cosy small town of **Eshowe ❻** is set at an altitude of 500 metres (1,650ft) among lushly forested hills along the R66, just 25km (15 miles) inland of the N2.

Bordering the town centre, the lovely **Dhlinza Forest Reserve** (daily; free) is probably the most accessible patch of mistbelt forest in the country, and its quiet paths are often crossed by the shy blue duiker. The Dhlinza Aerial Boardwalk runs for 125 metres (415ft) through the canopy, culminating in a 29-metre (96ft) high tower that affords a grandstand view over the forest to the Indian Ocean, and provides a great opportunity to see localised forest birds such as Delegorgue's pigeon, spotted ground thrush, grey cuckooshrike and olive woodpecker. Easily visited on foot in combination with the forest, the informative small **Zulu-**

land Historical Museum (Mon–Fri 7.30am–4.30pm, Sat 9am–4pm, Sun 10am–4pm; charge) is housed in Fort Nongqai, built by the British in 1883.

Cultural lodges

Coming from the coastal N2, Eshowe also forms the gateway to a series of cultural lodges and historical sites dotted along or close to the R66 in what was the heart of the Zulu Kingdom during its mid-19th century peak. The best known of the lodges – and for many visitors a highlight of their tour through southern Africa – is **Shakaland ❼** (tel: 035-460 0912; www.shakaland. co.za; daily 7am–8.30pm; main cultural programme 11am–2pm, noon–3pm for day visitors, 4–8.30pm and 9–10am for overnight guests; charge), which lies on the R66 just 15km (9 miles) north of Eshowe, on the site of Shaka's original kraal, which was reconstructed in the 1980s as the set for the television series Shaka Zulu.

Activities at Shakaland, designed to give visitors genuine insight into traditional Zulu culture, include a visit to an *inyanga* (traditional healer),

An *inyanga (traditional healer) at Shakaland.*

BELOW: Umhlanga Lighthouse.

A traditional Zulu beehive hut. The intricately woven thatch ensures it stays cool inside during the summer.

BELOW: the iSimangaliso Wetland Park is home to the largest population of hippos in the country.

spear-throwing and hut-building demonstrations, and – utterly spellbinding – an exuberant drumming and tribal dancing performance set in a traditional dome-shaped auditorium.

Shakaland, it could be argued, has become a victim of its own success, insofar as the sheer volume of tourists that pass through daily has robbed the cultural programmes of some of their immediacy and intimacy. It's a fabulous setup, but those who prefer a more low-key and personalised approach might prefer to try one of two smaller lodges offering a broadly similar experience.

The first of these is **Kwabhekithunga Cultural Lodge**, a small family-run setup founded in the 1970s as a craft centre for the disabled 10km (6 miles) east of the R66 along the R34 to Empangeni. Cultural programmes (tel: 035-460 0057; www.kwabhekithunga.co.za) here are by prior arrangement only, and cater to one group at a time, which means that a personal touch is ensured. A yet more authentic experience is offered by **Simunye Zulu Lodge** (tel: 035-450 0101; www.simunyelodge.co.za;

overnight visitors only) on the R66 about 10km (6 miles) south of Melmoth. Simunye takes a singularly integrated approach to cultural tourism giving visitors the choice of sleeping in a traditional beehive hut situated within a functioning Zulu homestead – your wake-up call here might well amount to having a goat lick your feet – or in more conventional rooms built into a cliff overlooking the Mfule River. Day visitors are not permitted, and the lodge's isolation is underscored by the dense nocturnal chirruping of frogs and insects from the nearby river.

"Valley of Kings"

Sticking to the R66, about 35km (2 miles) past Melmoth you'll reach **Ulundi**, a somewhat nondescript medium-sized town that – rather improbably – served as the capital of the patchwork KwaZulu homeland during the apartheid era. An important site in the vicinity of Ulundi, protected within the 105-sq-km (41-sq-mile) **eMakhosini Ophathe Heritage Park** ❽ (tel: 035-870 2052; www.emakhosini.co.za; daily; charge), is the Zulu "Valley

of Kings", site of the former capital of King Dingane and burial place of King Shaka and the Voortrekker Piet Retief. Accessible from the R66 between Melmoth and Ulundi, eMakhosini Ophathe also includes a wildlife area with rhinos, buffalo, blue wildebeest and other large mammals, and a small but interesting site museum.

The **KwaZulu Cultural Museum** (tel: 035-870 2051; www.zulu-museum. co.za; daily; joint ticket with eMakhosini Ophathe available) lies 5km (3 miles) from Ulundi at Ondoni, the site of the capital founded by King Cetshwayo in 1873 and razed by British troops six years later in what was effectively the last battle of the Anglo-Zulu War.

The hilltop kraal (Ondoni literally means elevated place) was left untouched for almost a century after that defeat, due to a traditional law preventing the re-use of royal land, but partial restoration began in 1981 and the museum now offers what might be termed a low-budget version of the Shakaland experience – complete with affordable accommodation in traditional beehive huts.

St Lucia estuary

Back on the coast, the N2 continues north from Empangeni via Mtubatuba and the R618 to the village of **St Lucia** ❾, which overlooks the mouth of the vast St Lucia Estuary. This is the largest estuarine system in Africa, extending over an area of 325 sq km (125 sq miles), and its shores are protected within a network of small reserves that collectively form the **iSimangaliso Wetland Park** ❿ (tel: 035-590 1340; with the exception of public areas, Oct–Mar daily 5am–7pm, Apr–Sept daily 6am–6pm; charge), a Unesco World Heritage Site since 1999.

Almost 60km (37 miles) long, up to 10km (6 miles) wide and with a maximum depth of just 1.5 metres (5ft), this extraordinary freshwater estuary is fed by the Hluhluwe, Mkhuze and Imfolozi rivers. It harbours an esti-

mated 800 hippos (the largest population in the country) and a similarly impressive crocodile population. The delta is a breeding ground for rare loggerhead and giant leatherback turtles, while an incredible 500 species of bird are known to breed in the vicinity, including pink-backed pelicans, flamingos, spoonbills, fish eagles and Caspian terns.

Hikers have a superb network of routes at their disposal, crisscrossing right across the park along the promontory between the lake and the Indian Ocean through a stunning, lushly forested, sand dune landscape (some of the dunes are as much as 150 metres (500ft) high, among the highest in the world). Divers shouldn't miss the coral reefs and the myriads of colourful fish in the St Lucia Marine Reserve; away from the protected area, the coastline is also hugely popular with anglers. If you hire a powerboat for some lake fishing, however, keep a sharp eye out for hippos; these portly creatures have fixed underwater routes and can become extremely aggressive if their progress is disturbed in any way. One

Grilled mopane worm, an important source of protein for many people in southern Africa.

BELOW: verdant banks along the St Lucia estuary.

This Nile crocodile is one of an estimated 1,500 which inhabit Lake St Lucia; needless to say, swimming in the lake is forbidden.

BELOW: looking for spoor is one way to track animals.

of the best and safest ways to observe them is to join a guided tour of the estuary aboard an 80-seater launch.

There's plenty of self-catering and hotel accommodation in St Lucia village, which makes for an excellent base for exploring the immediate vicinity as well as for day trips to some of the other reserves in the area.

The village is also one of the few urban areas in South Africa where you can still see wildlife – hippos occasionally wander through town, while a great little walking trail through the bordering reserve offers the opportunity to see zebras and various antelope on foot.

A more rustic option, however, is to stay at one of the several overnight camps operated by Ezemvelo KZN Wildlife, which include huts and camp sites at Charter's Creek, Fanie's Island, Mapelane and Cape Vidal, as well as campgrounds at the St Lucia Estuary. For keen walkers, the trails at Charter's Creek are particularly recommended – warthog, vervet monkeys and nyala are common, and you might also catch a glimpse of the shy red duiker on a forest clearing.

Hluhluwe-Imfolozi Game Reserve

Just 25km (18 miles) west of St Lucia lies another important conservation area – the **Hluhluwe-Imfolozi Game Reserve ⓫** (tel: 035-562 0848 for Hluhluwe, tel: 035-550 8476 for Imfolozi; Oct–Mar daily 5am–7pm, Apr–Sept daily 6am–6pm; charge). Originally proclaimed in 1897, making them the second-oldest game reserves in Africa after Phongolo, Hluhluwe (pronounced *shloo-shloo-ee*) and Imfolozi (formerly Umfolozi) were originally discrete entities, but they are now linked by a corridor of state-owned land to create a combined area of roughly 1,000 sq km (390 sq miles) that is jointly administered by Ezemvelo KZN Wildlife. A public link road (the R618) passes through the central section of the reserve and leads north as far as Nongoma. The animals seem to have become quite accustomed to this arrangement and happily cross the asphalt all the time.

Hluhluwe is best known for the success it achieved in saving the white (or wide-lipped) rhino from extinction. By the early 1930s, only about 150 white rhinos were left in southern Africa having been shot almost to extinction.

A breeding programme here has succeeded in raising the population to more than 1,000, while a further 4,000 of these magnificent animals have been exported to parks around the world. Today, a similar battle is underway to save its cousin, the black rhino – distinguishable only by its narrow upper lip. A total of 81 mammal species occur in the reserve, with several of the larger species having been reintroduced relatively recently. Elephant, giraffe, warthog, impala and the localised nyala are all common, and lion, leopard, cheetah, hyena and hunting dog are also present.

Imfolozi's celebrated **Wilderness Trail** was established in 1957, the first of its kind in South Africa, and it is still one of the best ways of exploring the region. Accompanied by experienced

armed rangers who act as guides, these bush walks can last between three and five days. To minimise the ecological impact of visitors to this unspoilt area, numbers are strictly controlled, so booking ahead through Ezemvelo KZN Wildlife is essential, particularly during the busy holiday periods. In addition to mouth-drying encounters with rhino – and possibly elephant or lion – the wilderness trails offer a good opportunity to see a wide range of the 380 bird species recorded in the area.

Mkhuze Game Reserve

Elephant, rhino, leopard, giraffe and nyala are among the game that can be spotted in Ezemvelo KZN Wildlife's **Mkhuze Game Reserve** ⑫ (tel: 035-573 9001; Oct–Mar daily 5am–7pm, Apr–Sept daily 6am–6pm; charge), which borders the iSimangaliso Wetland Park to the east and covers some 36,000 hectares (89,000 acres).

Mkhuze is best known for its tropical bird life, which includes such rarities as Neergard's sunbird and the African broadbill. Because the bush vegetation is so thick, the best place to spot game is from one of the several hides that overlook the park's waterholes, which can also be highly rewarding for wildlife photography. Another draw at Mkhuze, situated on the eastern edge of the reserve, is Nsumo Pan, whose shores are attractively encircled by yellow fever trees and low hills, and support a good range of water-associated birds including pelicans. Sadly, the 3km (2-mile) trail through the fig tree forest bordering the pan had to be closed after elephants were reintroduced to the reserve. The three-night wilderness trail, which must be booked in advance, is a good option if you really want to get back to nature.

Better still for spotting big game are private reserves such as the 17,000-hectare (42,000-acre) **Phinda Resource Reserve** ⑬ (tel: 011-809 4300; www.andbeyondafrica.com; access to overnight visitors only), which is supported by a number of wealthy trusts. Part neglected farmland, part hunting concession before the land was bought up by CCA in 1991, the newly created reserve was immediately subjected to a massive clean-up operation in which

Traditional carved masks are a popular souvenir.

BELOW: taking a siesta.

15,000kg (15 tons) of scrap metal was removed, followed by an even more ambitious programme of reintroductions to boost the then-skittish resident populations of leopard, nyala and other antelope.

The range of accommodation is exclusive, luxurious and definitely not cheap. Phinda today provides an upmarket safari experience to compare with anywhere in Africa; it's particularly good for cheetah and rhino, but lion, leopard, and elephant are also regularly observed. A less luxurious but more affordable alternative, harbouring a similar range of wildlife, is the neighbouring Zulu Nyala Lodge.

Northern Maputaland

North of the St Lucia Estuary, the iSimangaliso Wetland Park protects a narrow belt of pristine coastline that runs north to the Mozambican border, where it is dotted with remote beach-front camps, most of which are accessible by dirt road only. The best-known and busiest of these, serviced by a small resort-like village of the same name, is **Sodwana Bay** ⓮ (daily 24 hrs; charge).

The offshore coral reefs at Sodwana are widely regarded as providing the best snorkelling and scuba diving anywhere in South Africa (for which reason it can become rather crowded during South African school holidays), while endangered turtles regularly land on the beaches to lay eggs.

The terrestrial part of the reserve consists of swamp and dense jungle where fig and milkwood trees can grow as high as 40 metres (130ft). The rest camp and camp site are in a reliable location for the lovely blue monkey, as well as various small forest antelope, and birdwatching is excellent. Beware of snakes in this park, by the way, and make sure you bring mosquito nets and repellent for the nights. It's important that you begin a course of anti-malaria tablets several weeks before visiting the area, too.

Further north still, **Lake Sibaya** ⓯ separated from the ocean by a thin strip of wooded dunes, is South Africa's largest freshwater body at 77 sq km (30 sq miles) and home to prodigious numbers of hippo and crocodile, as well as a varied avifauna that includes the highly localised pink-throated longclaw and Woodward's batis, along with various herons and storks. Somewhat remote from the N2, Sibaya – like Sodwana Bay – only forms a realistic destinaton if you plan to overnight at one of a handful of pricy lodges in the vicinity. Sibaya and Sodwana Bay are both reached via the R22, a surfaced road that branches northeast from the N2 at the town of Hluhluwe.

About 50km (30 miles) north of Hluhluwe, just past the town of Mkuze, a surfaced road running northeast from the N2 leads to three of South Africa's wildest, most remote parks – Kosi Bay Nature Reserve, Tembe Elephant Sanctuary and Ndumo Game Reserve – all of which are nestled up against the border with Mozambique.

Set on a dramatic stretch of pristine Indian Ocean beach front, **Kosi Bay Nature Reserve** ⓰ (tel: 035-592 02... daily 6am–6pm; charge) consists of

BELOW: a purple gallinule.

network of lakes which are home to hippos and crocodiles as well as an extraordinary variety of aquatic birds, including black egret, fish eagle and jacana. As far as accommodation goes, various comfortable thatched cottages, bungalows and huts accommodate house visitors; there are also caravan and camp sites. While the camp area is accessible to all vehicles, sandy terrain makes a four-wheel-drive essential to reach The Mouth, 5km (3 miles) from the camp site; visitors who don't have such a vehicle can book a guided tour.

The 10,000-hectare (25,000-acre) **Ndumo Game Reserve** ⑰ (tel: 035-591 0058; Oct–Mar daily 5am–7pm, Apr–Sept daily 6am–6pm; charge) was established in 1924 to protect a lush section of the Pongola River floodplain and an associated network of seasonal waterways and fever tree-lined perennial pans. Black rhino and white rhino are often seen here, along with giraffe, nyala and other antelope. But the reserve is best known for its birdlife – indeed, many dedicated birdwatchers regard it to be the single most alluring destination in the country – which includes several species rare elsewhere in South Africa. Boat trips through the swamp offer the chance to seek out the localised Pel's fishing owl, lesser jacana and pygmy goose, interrupted by close encounters with crocs and hippos. A long list of "specials" associated with terrestrial thickets includes African broadbill, Narina trogon, Neergard's sunbird, pink-throated twinspot and grey waxbill.

Sadly, despite being listed as a Ramsar wetland, this reserve is one of the most underdeveloped and vulnerable in South Africa, and there has been a spate of rhino poaching and land encroachment since 11km of perimeter fence was cut down in May 2008.

Tembe Elephant Sanctuary

A more recent creation, proclaimed in 1983 and opened to the public seven years later, the **Tembe Elephant Sanctuary** ⑱ (tel: 035-592 0001; Oct–Mar daily 5am–7pm, Apr–Sept daily 6am–6pm; 4x4 only) protects a herd of roughly 180 elephant that once ranged freely between this part of South Africa and neighbouring Mozambique. Man-

A measure of iSimangaliso's ecological significance is that it protects four of South Africa's 17 Ramsar Wetlands: Kosi Bay, Lake Sibaya, the Turtle Beaches & Reefs of Tongaland and, of course, St Lucia Estuary itself.

BELOW: blue wildebeest.

Beaded dolls, such as this sangoma *(traditional healer) one, are made by Zulu women.*

BELOW: a village healing ceremony in Eshowe.

aged by Ezemvelo KZN Wildlife in conjunction with the local Tembe people, this sanctuary operates much like a private reserve – the only accommodation consists of an upmarket private lodge that runs guided 4x4 drives to seek out the region's legendarily large elephants. Other wildlife at Tembe includes buffalo, rhino, lion, leopard, nyala and the tiny suni antelope, and the birdlife is almost the equal of Ndumo. Long term plans include the creation of the Lubombo Transfrontier Park, which will link Tembe to Mozambique's Maputo Special Reserve via an ancient elephant migration corridor.

From the junction with the road to Kosi Bay, the N2 leads northwards through the Lebombo Mountains along the border with Swaziland, following the Pongola River to the eponymous dam and nature reserve.

It comes as a surprise to learn that **Phongolo Nature Reserve** ⑲ (tel: 034-435 1012; Oct–Mar daily 5am–7pm, Apr–Sept daily 6am–6pm; charge) – developed for tourism but still a somewhat obscure destination – has the distinction of being the oldest

game reserve in Africa and second-oldest in the world, proclaimed in 1894 by Paul Kruger to curb the activities of commercial hunters. Wildlife includes white rhino, giraffe, kudu, blue wildebeest and a recently introduced herd of tsessebe, as well as some 300 bird species. The dam, overlooked by a small campsite, is popular with game fishermen for its combative tigerfish – indeed an annual tigerfish competition is held here every September.

From Phongolo, it is just 50km (31 miles) to the **Ithala Game Reserve** ⑳, (tel: 034-893 2540; Oct–Mar daily 5am–7pm, Apr–Sept daily 6am–6pm; charge), yet another fine reserve run by Ezemvelo KZN Wildlife. The scenery in this 30,000-hectare (75,000-acre) reserve is breathtaking, with dramatic granite cliffs, rolling hills, open savannah, dense forests and romantic rivers all blending together to form a fabulous game-viewing environment. Nor does the wildlife disappoint: it includes elephant, white and black rhino, giraffe, leopard, cheetah and eland. A wide range of accommodation is available, from luxury lodges and fully-equipped self-catering chalets, to simple rondavels and bush camps. There is also a small campsite located beside the Thalu River.

The Battlefield Route

From northern Zululand, visitors heading for Mpumalanga and the Kruger Park have the choice either of travelling directly through Swaziland or else taking a slightly more circuitous route through Piet Retief and Barberton, while Gauteng-bound travellers normally follow the R29 through Piet Retief, Ermelo and Bethal.

Whichever route you choose, it's also possible to divert to the small town of **Vryheid** ㉑, which lies 100km (60 miles) southwest of Ithala in the heart of KwaZulu-Natal's historic battlefield area. Plenty of blood was shed round here in the 19th century, first due to conflicts between the British and the Zulus (1879) and then between the

British and the Boers (1880 and 1881). Vryheid was also briefly the capital of the short-lived Boer New Republic (1884–88), a small piece of land granted to a band of 500 Voortrekkers by the Zulu king, Dinizulu. You can learn more at the **Vryheid Museum** (Landdrost Street; tel: 038-981 2133; Mon–Fri 7.30am–4pm; charge), which consists of the New Republiek Museum in the old Raadsaal (parliament building), the Carnegie Library and Lukas Meijer House.

On the hilly northern outskirts of Vryheid, the tiny **Vryheid Hill Nature Reserve** (tel: 034-983 2098; www.kznwildlife.com; daily 6am–6pm; free on weekdays) is a pleasant place to take a stroll among zebras and various antelope, while the combination of protea bush, grassland and montane forest provides suitable habitats for 175 bird species.

Situated about 60km (35 miles) along the R618 east of Vryheid, the pristine indigenous forest protected within the underrated **Ntendeka Wilderness Area** ㉒ (daily; nominal charge) is where King Cetshwayo laid low for seven weeks after his capital at

Ondoni was razed by the British. Some 40km (25 miles) of hiking trails offer the opportunity to see some of the forest's impressive strangler figs, as well as giant tree ferns, various epiphytic orchids (more than half of South Africa's species are present), troops of blue monkey, porcupine quills and many colourful butterflies. Accommodation is limited to one rustic campsite near the entrance gate.

Dundee

About 65 (40 miles) southwest of Vryheid along the R34 and R33 the coal-mining town of **Dundee** ㉓ lies at the epicentre of several of the most important battlefield sites and is a good base for exploring the region.

On 20 October 1899, the first shots of the Anglo-Boer War were fired at Talana Hill, on the northern outskirts of town, a skirmish that forced the British troops amassed in the town to retreat 100km southwest to Ladysmith. The battle site now houses the superb **Talana Museum** (tel: 034-212 2654; www.talana.co.za; Mon–Fri 8am–4.30pm, Sat–Sun 9am–4pm; charge)

Many Zulu dwellings are constructed of a wattle and daub cylinder with a thatched roof.

BELOW: the church at Rorke's Drift.

The Battle of Rorke's Drift

In 1879, with the centre column of the British Army engaged in attacks on the Zululand border, troops under Lieutenant John Chard of the Royal Engineers were left to guard the post at Rorke's Drift, a tiny Swedish mission church, storehouse and hospital. On 22 January, news of the disastrous defeat of the 24th Regiment at Isandlwana reached the garrison. Even more alarming was the report that a large Zulu force was approaching at speed. Lieutenant Chard gave orders that Rorke's Drift would stand and defend itself, and arranged for a barricade to be constructed, although biscuit tins and mealie bags were the only materials to hand. Just 139 men were present on 23 January (of whom 35 were sick) when, soon after 4pm, a force of some 4,000 Zulu warriors appeared. One furious charge after another was launched, often resulting in hand-to-hand combat against the barricades, in an attack which continued until dawn.

The Zulu forces were supremely confident – yet incredibly, Rorke's Drift proved unassailable, the British defending their position with immense bravery. That terrible late afternoon and night left 17 British dead, while Zulu losses were estimated at a minimum of 500. Eleven Victoria Crosses were awarded to the defenders. Today, a memorial and small museum mark the site.

whose 10 hectares of neatly tended grounds include the original farmhouse built by Peter Smith, detailed displays on the key skirmishes that took place around here and the area's industrial heritage of coal mining and glassmaking. In the grounds are graves of British soldiers who died in the Battle of Talana. In 2010, the **Kwakunje Cultural Village** (tel: 076-488 4907; daily 9am–4pm; charge), offering tours of a recreated traditional Zulu village, opened behind the museum.

Blood River

Dundee is the closest town to the site of Blood River, the 1838 battle in which a troop of 468 Boers, armed with rifles and cannons, defeated a 10,000-strong Zulu army. The Zulu short spear proved no match for such firepower and more than 3,000 warriors were killed, many of them shot while fleeing across the Ncome River (*see page 40*). Two monuments mark the site. The dour **Blood River Monument** ❷❹ (daily 8am–4.30pm; charge), an apartheid-era relict of life-size sculpted ox-wagons arranged in a circular laager

as they were on the day of the conflict, was privatised in 1994 and is now operated by an organisation dedicated to the preservation of the Afrikaner cultural heritage. By contrast, the newer and more balanced **Ncome Museum** (tel: 034 271 8121; www.ncomemuseum. co.za; daily 9am–4pm; no charge), on the opposite side of the river, explores the conflict from a Zulu perspective, and is shaped like the "buffalo horn" attacking formation first implemented by King Shaka. To reach either site from Dundee, follow the R33 northeast for 20km (12 miles), then follow the signposted dirt turn-off to the right for another 20km or so.

Two of the most famous battles of the Anglo-Zulu War occurred in the green hills about 50km (30 miles) southeast of Dundee, and are now preserved as heritage sites.

The **Battle of Isandlwana** (Mon–Fri 8am–4pm, Sat–Sun 9am–4pm; charge), the first major conflict, on 22 January 1879, is widely regarded to be one of the greatest embarrassments ever inflicted on the British army, as a well-organised Zulu army launched

a surprise attack on a British military camp below Isandlwana Hill, killing 1,357 of the 1,800 troops present.

It's only a 15 minute drive from here to Rorke's Drift (*see box, page 243*).

Our route now continues past meadows and fields towards **Ladysmith** 25 (named after the wife of Cape governor Sir Harry Smith), handy gateway for trips into the uKhahlamba-Drakensberg. Established by Voortrekkers in 1847, Ladysmith later came under the control of the British, who would be besieged here by Boer forces in October 1899, shelled and starved almost to the brink of defeat, only to be relieved by British troops after 118 days. The **Siege Museum** (Mon–Fri 9am–4pm, Sat 9am–1pm; charge) documents life during the Boer War and displays artefacts dating from the siege.

Coal country

Eighty km (50 miles) further north on the N11 is gritty **Newcastle** 26, one of South Africa's major producers of coal and steel. It was founded in 1864 and its chimneys and smoke are a reminder that the Gauteng, the country's indus-

trial nerve-centre, is not far away. A welcome scenic diversion lies 16km (10 miles) to the west of Newcastle on the Muller's Pass road: the Ncandu River waterfall is set amid good hiking territory in a fold of mountains.

Another major battlefield site on our route lies 43km (27 miles) north of Newcastle on the N11 towards Volksrust. **Majuba** 27 was the site of a humiliating defeat for the British by the Boers in 1881, when 285 British troops died in the battle, compared to just two Boers. Today, Majuba Hill, the high ground which was of such strategic importance during the fighting, offers superb views over the surrounding countryside.

In **Volksrust**, a road off the N11 leads through further historic battlefields to Piet Retief, an unremarkable little place named after a leader of the Great Trek whom Zulu Dingane had murdered. Back on the main route, the town of **Standerton** and the Grootdraai Dam come into view. The dam has pleasant hiking possibilities and is a good place to relax before heading to Johannesburg. ❏

A cheetah on the look out.

BELOW: Zulu *inyanga.*

Ladysmith Black Mambazo

The name Ladysmith is strongly associated with its most famous musical sons, a vocal harmony group formed by Joseph Shabalala in 1960 to compete in Isicathamiya choral competitions countrywide. Shabalala's ambition is reflected in the group's name, which alludes to the black ox (a symbol of strength) and mambazo (axe) with which it would chop down the competition. Already a legend at home, the group gained international exposure for its role in Paul Simon's chart-topping 1986 album *Graceland*. It has since been nominated for more than a dozen Grammys, winning in the traditional world category in 1988, 2005 and 2009. Five decades on, still directed by its founder, Ladysmith Black Mambazo shows no sign of flagging, as four of Shabalala's sons now feature in the group.

CROSSING THE DRAKENSBERG

A route winding up from the KwaZulu-Natal midlands to an eagle's view of the uKhahlamba-Drakensberg – then through the rolling Free State highveld to Gauteng

Main attractions
KARKLOOF CANOPY WALK
GIANT'S CASTLE GAME RESERVE
ROYAL NATAL NATIONAL PARK
CHAIN LADDER HIKE
GOLDEN GATE NATIONAL PARK

Compared to the hustle, bustle and sticky coastal heat of Durban, the interior of KwaZulu-Natal, accessible via the nippy N3 highway or a number of more minor roads, can feel refreshingly sedate, rustic and breezy. The lay of the land changes as soon as you get beyond the satellite towns of Hillcrest and New Germany: a signposted turn-off at Kloof leads to the **Krantzkloof Nature Reserve** ㉘ (tel: 031-764 3515; www.kknr.org. za; daily sunrise–sunset; charge) and the **Inanda Dam**, a lushly forested area noted for its cycads and other rare plants, as well as 200 bird species including the imposing crowned eagle. There are some fine walking trails, too, the most spectacular of which brings you to a cliff edge with panoramic views of the Kloof Falls.

Pietermaritzburg

The journey picks up pace as the provincial capital **Pietermaritzburg** ㉙ comes into view, its Dutch and British settler roots evident in the white picket fences, precisely manicured lawns, red-brick paths and neatly trimmed azalea bushes that characterise the leafy suburbia. Founded in 1838 as capital of the Natalia Boer Republic and co-opted into the British Colony of Natal five year later, "Maritzburg" promotes itself as one of the world's best-preserved

Victorian cities. Visitors can follow a self-guided trail through its historic heart, starting from the elaborately decorated **City Hall** (the largest all-brick building in the southern hemisphere), built in 1893 on the site of the old Voortrekker Parliament. Facing the City Hall on Chief Albert Luthuli (Commercial) Road are two other important buildings: the Legislative Assembly and the old Supreme Court with its striking portico. The latter building now houses the **Tatham Art Gallery** (tel: 033-392 2801; www.tatham.

LEFT: taking a dip in the Royal Natal National Park. **RIGHT:** Pietermaritzburg town hall.

Giant insects adorn a neo-classical frieze on the facade of Pietermaritzburg's Natal Museum.

org.za; Mon–Fri 8am–5pm; free), where an impressive collection of paintings by European artists (Matisse, Picasso, Hockney) is exhibited alongside works by South Africans.

The **Voortrekker Msunduzi Museum** (tel: 033-394 6834; www.voortrekkermuseum.co.za; Mon–Fri 9am–4pm, Sat 9am–1pm; charge) incorporates the Church of the Vow, a small, white-gabled building erected in 1841 to commemorate the Boer's victory over the Zulus at Blood River in 1838 *(see pages 40 and 244)*. The museum offers some interesting insights into frontier life in the mid-19th century. Next door is the restored home of the Voortrekker hero, Andries Pretorius. Not far away at 237 Jabu Ndlovu Street, the **Natal Museum** (www.nmsa.org.za; Mon–Fri 8.15am–4.30pm, Sat 9am–6pm, Sun 10am–5pm; charge) has displays devoted to natural history, palaeontology and ethnology, along with an excellent reconstruction of a Victorian street.

Another building of note is the **Victorian Railway Station**, which you'll find – unsurprisingly – on Railway Street. This was where the Indian law-

BELOW: Queen Elizabeth Park Nature Reserve.

yer Mohandas Gandhi (later known as Mahatma, the man who became world-famous for his policy of non-violence, *see page 49*) was forcibly thrown off a train in 1893, simply because he had dared to take a seat in a whites-only carriage. The incident sparked Gandhi's desire to fight for human rights. A statue to his memory was erected opposite the Old Colonial Building as recently as 1993.

Boshoff Street leads out of town to the **Queen Elizabeth Park Nature Reserve** (tel: 033-845 1999; daily; free), where some magnificent old trees and flowerbeds provide a fitting setting for the headquarters and booking office of Ezemvelo KZN Wildlife, the provincial conservation authority responsible for 60-plus protected areas within KwaZulu-Natal. Situated some 8km (5 miles) from the town centre, the park is an attractive place for a gentle stroll through gardens inhabited by zebra, impala, bushbuck and a variety of small mammals and birds. There are several picnic areas. Also of interest is the collection of endangered cycads in the Douglas Mitchell Centre.

Howick and surrounds

A further 28km (15 miles) along the N3, **Howick** ❸⓿ is a small but pretty town distinguished by the Howick Falls, which crash 110 metres (360ft) down a vertical rock face right next to the town centre. Only 5km (3 miles) west of Howick, Ezemvelo KZN Wildlife's **Midmar Dam Nature Reserve** (tel: 033-330 2067/8; Oct–Mar daily 5am–7pm, Apr–Sept daily 6am–6pm; charge) boasts a pleasant waterfront resort, and a small game reserve stocked with rhino, zebra and various antelope species. To the southeast of Howick, the **Albert Falls Dam Nature Reserve** (tel: 033-569 1202; daily; charge) offers endless scope to keen anglers, canoeing enthusiasts and wildlife lovers, though the waterfall itself didn't survive the construction of the dam wall.

About 20km (10 miles) north of town, the **Karkloof Nature Reserve**

(tel: 033-330 2992; daily) protects a 10-sq-km (4-sq-mile) mistbelt forest of towering yellowwood trees harbouring the likes of samango monkey, blue duiker and many forest birds. A popular goal for walks is the attractive Karkloof Falls, while adrenalin junkies won't want to miss the three-hour **Karkloof Canopy Tour** (tel: 033-330 3415; www.karkloofcanopytour.co.za), which involves the horizontal equivalent of abseiling between a series of seven platforms set high in the treetops.

The area around Howick, often referred to as the Natal Midlands, is a relatively cool and moist part of South Africa, and its neatly fenced green meadows often draw comparisons to the English countryside.

This English connection is reinforced as you explore the so-called **Midlands Meander** (tel: 033-330 8195; www.midlandsmeander.co.za), a loosely defined route that runs southeast from Howick to Hilton and northwest to **Mooi River**, and is dotted with dozens of interesting sites from potteries and art studios to dairies and herb gardens selling fresh produce. The midlands is also where

you'll find some of South Africa's finest English country house hotels.

uKhahlamba-Drakensberg Park

The Drakensberg – Afrikaans for Dragon's Mountain – is South Africa's highest and most extensive range, running for 1,000km (620 miles) from Hoedspruit west of the Kruger National Park all the way south to Rhodes in the Eastern Cape, interrupted by just one valley between Harrismith and Barberton. Not only does this gargantuan range span four different provinces, it also extends into the western half of Swaziland and lies at the core of the Kingdom of Lesotho, reputedly the only state in the world to lie entirely above the 1,000-metre (3,300ft) contour.

When South Africans talk about "The Berg", however, they are almost certainly referring to its most spectacular section: the sequence of jagged cliffs and towering peaks that rises from the KwaZulu-Natal midlands to run for 200km (120 miles) along the eastern border with Lesotho. The Zulu people who live in the shadow of this impen-

A Zulu nyanga, traditional healer wearing a beaded headress.

BELOW: a demonstration of how the springbok acquired its name.

Valley of a Thousand Hills

North of the N3 to Pietermaritzburg, the romantically named **Valley of a Thousand Hills** was incised by the Umgeni River, which flows from the Drakensberg mountains to the Indian Ocean. The Zulu call it Mkhabathini (Place of the Camelthorn) and local legend has it that God once grabbed the world here, ready to throw it away, and scrunched it up, giving it the appearance of a vast piece of crumpled green velvet stretching to the horizon.

To get there from Durban, turn right off the N3 onto the R103 at the Hillcrest/Old Main Road turn-off. After 20km (12 miles), a turn-off to Nagle Dam, 4km (2 miles), leads to KwaZulu-Natal's very own 1,000-metre (3,200ft) -high Table Mountain – hike to the summit for breathtaking views.

Climbing a chain ladder on Mont-aux-Sources, the source of three major rivers, the Elands, the Western Khubedu and the Tugela.

etrable sequence of peaks know it as uKhahlamba – The Barrier of Spears – and even today just one solitary road pass, navigable by four-wheel-drive vehicles only, crosses the formidable crags that divide KwaZulu-Natal from Lesotho.

Rock paintings

Today, this central Drakensberg region is protected within a patchwork of reserves, all of which now fall under Ezemvelo KZN Wildlife, and is referred to collectively as the **uKhahlamba-Drakensberg Park**. The area as a whole has an agreeably temperate climate, but temperatures can drop sharply with altitude, and winter nights are often very chilly.

One of the most attractive parts of the uKhahlamba-Drakensberg Park is **Giant's Castle Game Reserve** ㉛ (tel: 036-353 3718; Oct–Mar daily 5am–7pm, Apr–Sept daily 6am–6pm; charge), the main camp of which lies 50km (30 miles) by road from the N3 near **Estcourt**. Originally established to provide sanctuary to the eland, the largest species of antelope,

Giant's Castle is now considered the best place in the country to spot the endangered lammergeyer (or bearded vulture), which occurs here alongside other raptors such as the majestic black eagle, Cape vulture and lanner falcon. A special lammergeyer hide, to which these massive birds are lured by carrion, is open from May to September, and advance booking is required; tel: 036-353 3718.

Scenically dominated by the 3,377-metre (11,076ft) **Champagne Castle** and 3,315-metre (10,873ft) **Giant's Castle** mountains, this reserve is ideal for climbers, and it also has an extensive network of hiking routes, the most demanding of which is the 40km (25-mile) trail leading in a series of bends to the very top of Giant's Castle.

As recently as the mid-19th century, the Drakensberg was inhabited by San (or bushman) hunter-gatherers whose vivid rock paintings, executed from 150 to more than 3,000 years ago, still decorate numerous shelters and caves throughout the range. At least 500 sites containing a total of 40–50,000 paintings are known to exist within the uKhahlamba-Drakensberg Park alone – quite possibly the richest collection of rock art anywhere in the world.

One of the finest panels can be visited at **Main Cave**, just 30 minutes walk from Giant's Castle's rest camp on an inexpensive guided tour that leaves hourly from 9am–3pm daily. This superb panel is dominated by two 60-cm (2ft) tall humanlike creature with animal's heads (a type of figure known as a therianthrope), but ther are also paintings of a snake, a lion and a procession of cloaked figure. Another high-quality panel that's reasonably accessible is Battle Cave in th **Injisuthi Game Reserve** (tel: 036-43 9000; Oct–Mar daily 5am–7pm, Apr Sept daily 6am–6pm; charge) to th north of Giant's Castle (about thre hours on foot from the rest camp which depicts a clash between tw groups of archers, as well as portrai of bushpig, leopard and grey rhebok.

Kamberg and Monks Cowl nature reserves

South of Giant's Castle, the **Kamberg Nature Reserve** ❸❷ (tel: 033-267 7251; Oct–Mar daily 5am–7pm, Apr–Sept daily 6am–6pm; charge) protects another thrillingly scenic stretch of the uKhahlamba-Drakensberg known for its hiking opportunities and trout fishing. Kamberg is also host to an innovative new **Rock Art Centre** where a fascinating DVD presentation on rock-art interpretation is supplemented by a guided visit to the Game Pass Shelter, a panel of such quality and significance it has been described as the Rosetta Stone of ancient rock art. Further south still, the Sani Pass is the only route leading from the east to the independent state of Lesotho – poor road conditions and treacherous hairpin bends make a four-wheel-drive vehicle essential.

North of Giant's Castle, and accessed via Winterton, the area bordering the **Monks Cowl Nature Reserve** ❸❸ (tel: 036-468 1103; Oct–Mar daily 6am–7pm, Apr–Sept daily 6am–6pm; charge) is serviced by a selection of perhaps two dozen resorts catering to all budgets, from four-star luxury hotels and family-orientated self-catering chalets, down to no-frills camping. Hikes and walks in this part of the uKhahlamba-Drakensberg, which is dominated by the peak of Champagne Castle, range from moderately easy to seriously strenuous, while free-standing peaks such as the Bell, the Inner and Outer Horn, and the very demanding Cathkin Peak offer the experienced climber some interesting challenges. It's also here that you'll find the **Ardmore Ceramic Art Studio** (tel: 036-468 1314; www.ardmore.co.za; daily 9am–5pm), whose bold ceramic artefacts have achieved international recognition and are displayed next to the workshop in a small gallery.

Possibly the most scenic part of the uKhahlamba-Drakensberg, however, is the far north, protected in the Royal Natal National Park and adjoining **Rugged Glen Nature Reserve** (tel: 036-438 6310; both daily 6am–10pm; charge), which lie about 60km (37 miles) from Harrismith and the N3 via the spectacular Oliviershoek Pass. This region's dramatic mountain landscape

The Devil's Tooth is a distinctive feature of the Drakensberg's Northern Buttress.

BELOW: Giant's Castle mountains.

The crested guineafowl is a common sight in the Royal Natal National Park.

is dominated by the Amphitheatre, an 8km (5-mile) crescent-shaped stretch of sandstone escarpment providing magnificent views.

Royal Natal National Park ❸ is where you will find the country's highest peak, the 3,282-metre (10,760ft) high **Mont-aux-Sources** (Mountain of Springs), so named because three of the country's major river systems – the Elands, the Western Khubedu (which eventually becomes the Orange) and the Tugela (also known as Thukela) – all have their sources here. Within a few kilometres of its source, the Tugela plunges in a dramatic series of cascades down to the valley floor below into Royal Natal. The combined drop of the **Tugela Falls** (949 metres/3,114ft, over five stages) makes it the second-highest waterfall in the world.

One of the prettiest day hikes in Royal Natal, a flattish five-hour round trip, is the **Gorge Trail**, which follows the pretty gorge cut by the Tugela close to the base of the waterfall, passing through patches of indigenous forest and skirting transparent natural swimming pools en route. Unfortunately,

unless you are dedicated hiker with a few days to spare and suitable equipment, you can't easily access the top of the escarpment from within Royal Natal. However, if you head to Witsieshoek (in the Free State, about one hour away by car), the **Chain Ladder** hike, steep half-day round trip taking in two vertiginous but sturdy chain ladders, brings you to the top of the Amphitheatre above the Tugela Falls – one of the most stunning viewpoints anywhere in Africa!

Other attractions of Royal Natal and surrounds include several rock art site (none quite so impressive as Game Pas Shelter or Giant's Castle's Main Cave) the attractive Woodstock and Sterk fontein dams and wildlife such as grey rhebok, mountain reedbuck, bushbuck and the exquisite malachite sunbird often seen feeding on blooming aloes

Situated in the lower-lying countr to the east of Royal Natal, the **Spic enkop Dam Nature Reserve** (tel: 036 488 1578; Oct–Mar daily 6am–7pm Apr–Sept daily 6am–6pm; charge supports a cover of dense acacia bus offering lovely views across the dar

BELOW: Tugela river gorge, Royal Natal National Park.

to the towering peaks of the uKhahl-amba-Drakensberg. Wild mammals and birds occur here in abundance, but the dam and public resort on its shores also offer a variety of watersport facilities, and canoes can be hired. Conducted tours of the Anglo-Boer War site at Spioenkop – the plug-like hill overlooking the dam – illustrate the ins and outs of this battle in graphic and somewhat depressing detail.

Harrismith and on...

Harrismith ⑮, which lies just across the provincial border in the southern Free State, is the main town in this part of the country and something of a route focus, but otherwise difficult to get excited about. If you're heading to Gauteng, the drive from Harrismith to Johannesburg takes about three hours on the N3, and there's very little to distract you en route. The only real exception (and then only in a generous mood) is the vast Vaal Dam, which is signposted just north of Villiers. The Vaal River, which feeds the dam, is one of the country's largest, forming the natural border between Free State Province and Gauteng. Apart from supplying water to the Witwatersrand, the dam also caters to the recreational needs of local watersport enthusiasts.

Alternatively, follow the N5 and R74 west out of Harrismith for about 60km (35 miles) until you reach the splendid **Golden Gate Highlands National Park** ⑯ (www.sanparks.org; daily; charge). Over the centuries, wind, rain and sunshine have carved the sandstone hills here into bizarre formations that glow golden at dusk to give the area its unique appeal. Located on the border of the Free State and Lesotho, the park is named after its "gate" entrance, composed of two massive sections of sandstone. Hikers are in their element here, as are horse riders: the small Basotho ponies bred in nearby Lesotho have no problems negotiating this terrain. To book accommodation and arrange hiking permits, contact the National Parks Board.

Heading west from Harrismith on the N5, there are three places worth stopping en route to Winburg – where you connect with the N1 between Cape Town, Bloemfontein and Johannesburg. **Bethlehem** ⑰, dotted with distinctive Voortrekker sandstone cottages, was founded in 1864 beside the Jordan River. Today, it's a modern town with restaurants and all the usual tourist amenities, but they jar with the pleasingly simple original architecture. A 30km (19-mile) diversion south on the R711 brings you to pretty **Clarens** ⑱, another Voortrekker village set on the western edge of the Golden Gate Highlands National Park. Named after the Swiss village where Paul Kruger lived until his death in 1904, it's now a thriving artists' colony. Finally, hugging the Lesotho border southwest of Clarens (along the R26 to the Basotho capital of Maseru), sleepy little **Ficksburg** – notable for its old sandstone buildings, Drakensberg backdrop and ubiquitous cherry trees – is definitely worth a diversion in the second week of November when it hosts a popular cherry festival.   ❏

Hiking in the Drakensberg.

BELOW: Zulu women and children on their way to collect water.

VINTAGE TRAIN JOURNEYS

If rail travel in romantic turn-of-the-20th century style is the sort of journey that sparks your imagination, South Africa offers plenty of steam-driven and other options

Electrification of the railways came slowly to South Africa. Because coal was cheap and readily available, the authorities were reluctant to relinquish steam – indeed, in the early 1960s, the South African Railways were still operating a record 2,682 steam trains. The end of main-line steam traction was officially announced in 1991.

All this, of course, is good news for vintage train lovers, who can look forward to travelling on several services that have been preserved as tourist attractions. The best known, covering the 1,600km (1,000 miles) between Johannesburg and Cape Town in 27 hours, is the five-star Blue Train, a "hotel on wheels" that has counted several heads of state among its patrons since it first started up in 1923.

More opulent still is Rovos Rail's *Pride of Africa*, which plies a route from Cape Town to Pretoria and on to the Victoria Falls and back. These upmarket safaris in immaculately restored 1920s and '30s rolling stock – hauled by steam, diesel and electric locomotives at various stages of the journey – truly evoke the Edwardian era of luxury rail travel.

Until the mid-2000s, several local steam train services also catered to the more restricted budgets of most holidaymakers. Sadly, however, the three most iconic of these services – the Outeniqua Choo Tjoe, which worked the spectacular lake and mountain route between George and Knysna, along with the Banana Express out of Margate and the Apple Express out of Port Elizabeth – have all chugged their last breath and are unlikely to be restored to service in the foreseeable future. On a more positive note, occasional trips around Gauteng are still organised by Reefsteamers, while Atlantic Rail runs occasional excursions in vintage carriages on the Cape Peninsula.
See also page 365.

ABOVE: Atlantic Rail operates regular steam train excursions on the scenic Cape Peninsula, using a Class 24 steam locomotive built in 1 and vintage wooden-bodied coaches dating from the 1920s and '30

BELOW: the legendary Outeniqua Choo Tjoe no longer operates ou of George, but train buffs can still enjoy looking at several vintage locomotives at the same town's Outeniqua Transport Museum.

A ROUTE FROM THE CAPE TO CAIRO

It was Cecil Rhodes' most cherished ambition to have a railway line built from Cape Town to Cairo, passing only through British colonies. That way, Britain – rather than her European rivals – would be able to gain possession of Africa's riches. The groundwork for this scheme was laid in 1885, when the first railway trunk routes in South Africa were constructed, linking Cape Town to the Kimberley diamond fields – in which Rhodes' De Beers Consolidated Company just happened to have a very large stake.

Having achieved the wealth that he craved, Rhodes turned to politics, becoming prime minister of the Cape Colony in 1890. By then, however, his aspirations to creating a continuous territorial bloc from the Cape to Egypt were thwarted by the lateral belt of non-British territory comprising the Belgian Congo and German East Africa (present day Tanzania). More locally, the discovery of gold on the Witwatersrand – right in the middle of the Boer South African Republic – was to prove something of a stumbling block. A strong SAR, Rhodes reasoned, would constitute a severe threat to British supremacy. The ensuing struggle for control of the gold fields culminated in the Anglo-Boer War of 1899–1902. Needless to say, Rhodes' Cape-to-Cairo British line never materialised.

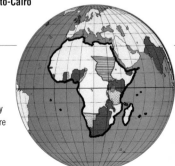

ABOVE AND RIGHT: Cecil Rhodes inaugurates one of the railway lines that he hoped would eventually link Britain's African Empire from Cairo to the Cape.

OVE: billed as the world's most luxurious train service, the Rovos I *Pride of Africa* service runs regularly between Pretoria (Gauteng) I Cape Town, as well as to more far-flung corners of Africa, including ' es Salaam in Tanzania.

GAUTENG

This industrial powerhouse contains
Johannesburg, Pretoria and some of the
country's best museums and galleries –
plus a surprising number of parks

The province of Gauteng – a Sesotho name meaning Place of Gold – accounts for less than 1.5 percent of South Africa's surface area, yet its estimated 12 million residents represent more than a quarter of the country's population and their collective enterprises account for 35 percent of the national GDP. These impressive statistics are attributable to one single factor: the precious metal for which the province is named. Certainly, without gold, the vast urban sprawl that we know as Johannesburg – significantly, the largest city in the world not to be built on a major river – would still be open grassland or farmland. More speculatively, had it not been for the gold boom 50km (31 miles) to its south, Pretoria would most likely be a quaint backwater remembered as the former headquarters of Kruger's 19th-century Zuid-Afrikaansche Republiek (*see page 45*) rather than the capital city of modern South Africa.

Commercial hub

Populous and wealthy as it is, Gauteng doesn't top many peoples' list of must-see places in South Africa. Unsurprisingly, business travellers generate some 70 percent of tourism to the province, which boasts more conference facilities than the rest of the country put

together, while its combination of well-stocked shops and affordability by international standards has made it a popular shopping destination for wealthy residents of other African countries. Much of the remainder of Gauteng's tourism is comprised of incidental transients (O.R Tambo International Airport, east of Johannesburg, remains the regional transport hub) or family visits. And frankly, if your time in South Africa is limited, it would be difficult to make a strong case for dedicating more of it than is necessary

Main attractions
NEWTOWN PRECINCT
MANDELA HOUSE, SOWETO
GOLD REEF CITY & APARTHEID MUSEUM
CRADLE OF HUMANKIND
SUN CITY & PILANESBERG GAME RESERVE
MADIKWE GAME RESERVE

LEFT: Johannesburg is southern Africa's commercial centre. **RIGHT:** giraffe crossing, Madikwe Game Reserve.

The Miners Monument pays tribute to Johannesburg's gold mining origins.

to this least scenic and most industrialised part of the country – no less so because of its unenviable crime rate.

That said, should you spend time in Gauteng, there's no reason to feel downhearted. With its innumerable museums, theatres, musical venues, restaurants, bars and markets, Gauteng vies with Cape Town as the cultural capital of South Africa. For wildlife enthusiasts, several small sanctuaries are dotted around the province, while only slightly further afield, in the otherwise seldom-visited North West Province, the larger and wilder Pilanesberg National Park and Madikwe Game Reserve both support the full quota of Big Five species. Also popular are tours to the vast, modern township of Soweto, while the out-of-town Cradle

of Humankind has been inscribed as a Unesco World Heritage Site in recognition of its wealth of ancient hominid fossils and artefacts.

JOHANNESBURG

Its Zulu name is eGoli: City of Gold. **Johannesburg ❶** is the heart of South Africa's industrial and commercial life, where more than a mile below bustling city traffic, miners dig for the world's most precious metal. At street level, stockbrokers and company directors rub shoulders with street vendors and traditional healers. Ultra-modern corporate towers dwarf noisy pavement stalls. It's the official capital of Gauteng Province, and many residents of Jo'burg or Jozi – as it's known informally – regard it to be the ipso-facto

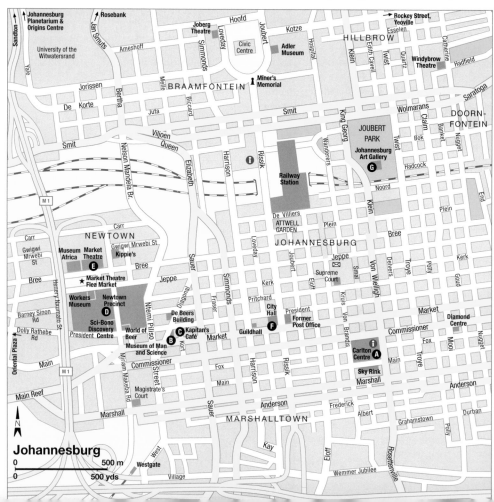

Johannesburg

0 ——— 500 m
0 ——— 500 yds

capital of South Africa, and will fervently defend it against the more obvious charms of places like that sleepy *visdorpie* (fishing village) Cape Town.

Ever since a fateful day in 1886 when George Harrison, a humble prospector, stumbled upon an outcrop of gold-bearing rock, the region's economy and life have been driven by the pulsating rhythm of the mining industry. The effects are inescapable.

Sprawling metropolis

Take an elevator to the 50th floor of the **Carlton Centre** Ⓐ, the tallest building in Africa at 223 metres (730ft), and you see tawny mine dumps and shaft headgears dotting the skyline. Walk the streets of downtown Johannesburg, and you find road and building names vividly evoking the gold-rush days.

Harrison's discovery sparked a gold fever never experienced before or since, anywhere in the world. Prospectors and fortune-seekers descended on the area in search of instant wealth. Makeshift shelters and tents mushroomed all over the tranquil veld. A sprawling, rough and raucous shanty town sprang up

almost overnight. Within three years, Johannesburg was the largest town in South Africa. A rudimentary stock exchange was established. Men outnumbered women three to one. Hotels and canteens, brothels and music halls were erected throughout the town to satisfy the needs of this boisterous new community. But it wasn't long before fledgling mining corporations moved in to take control of the industry and swallow up individual claims. "Randlords" like Cecil John Rhodes, Barney Barnato and Alfred Beit quickly accumulated huge fortunes, imposing a semblance of order on the unruly mining town in their wake.

Today, Johannesburg forms the hub of a sprawling metropolis called the Witwatersrand (Ridge of White Waters), stretching more than 120km (75 miles) from Springs in the east to Randfontein in the west, with a rapidly growing population of at least 5 million. The Witwatersrand is the core of Gauteng and the place where all the country's major industries are based – making this the undisputed powerhouse of sub-Saharan Africa.

Huge cockroaches known as Parktown prawns are a familiar sight in Jo'burg gardens (and living rooms). They can grow up to 7.5cm (3ins) long.

BELOW: view from the Carlton Centre.

*Carlton Centre
shopping mall.*

BELOW: one of the
imaginative
displays in Museum
Africa.

A diverse and divided city

By global standards, Johannesburg is a
medium-sized city, at least in terms of
population, though it must rank as one
of the world's most spread-out urban
centres, due to a tendency towards lateral rather than vertical growth. And
in the African context, it is a giant,
offering some of the continent's best
nightlife, hotels and shopping opportunities. Yet nowhere are the contrasts
that typify the place so forcefully experienced as in the busy downtown area.

Just eleven blocks west along Com-
missioner Street from the modern
Carlton Centre mall you'll find the
traditional charms of Diagonal Street.
Here, dimly lit herbalists such as the
Museum of Man and Science Ⓑ
(also known as KwaZulu Muti Shop;
tel: 011-836 4470; Mon–Sat 9am–5pm)
sell skins, dried plants and the "magic"
bones thrown by *sangomas* (traditional
healers) during divination, alongside
tiny stores crammed with household
goods and cheap African art with a
kitsch appeal. Where Diagonal Street
meets Kort Street lies one of Johannesburg's best-loved Indian restaurants,

Kapitan's Café Ⓒ. This was once
favourite haunt of young attorne
Nelson Mandela and Oliver Tamb
and it's still serving up some of t
finest curries this side of Asia (lun
time only).

Newtown Precinct

Heading north along West Street, yo
reach one of the city's chief cultur
centres, the enormous **Newtown Pr
cinct** Ⓓ. Here, a conglomeration
warehouses stretching across sever
blocks has been converted into venu
for experimental theatre, live mus
performances, exhibitions and wor
shop courses for students. It also co
tains an entire complex of museums.

Foremost among the Newtown Pr
cinct's museums is **Museum Afri**
(tel: 011-833 5624; Tue–Sun 9am–5p
charge), whose innovative displa
depict scenes from Johannesburg
brief but turbulent history. You'll fin
for example, a cluster of squatter shac
brought from Alexandra township an
painstakingly reconstructed; displa
focusing on the Rivonia Treason Tri
which sentenced Nelson Mandela

life imprisonment on Robben Island; even a fearsome assortment of home-made weapons confiscated from a miners' hostel. Museum Africa also houses a **Geological Museum**, displaying some of the country's unique mineral wealth, and the **Bensusan Museum of Photography**.

Market Theatre

Next door to the Precinct complex, the **Market Theatre** ❺ (Margaret Mcingana Street; tel: 011-832 1641; www. markettheatre.co.za) was the home of protest theatre in the 1970s and '80s, and a renowned cornerstone of the intellectual revolution against apartheid. Today, it is an arts complex in its own right, housing art and photographic galleries, a jazz venue and the legendary Gramadoelas Restaurant, which was founded in 1967 and whose sumptuous pan-African cuisine has attracted the prestigious likes of Queen Elizabeth II and Bill Clinton.

Several other points of interest lie within a block or two of the Market Theatre. These include South African Breweries' **World of Beer** (President Street, tel: 011-836 4900; www.worldof beer.co.za; Tue–Sat 10am–5pm; charge), where 90-minute tours chart the history of beer and modern brewing process, the contrastingly sobering **Workers Museum** (Jeppe Street, tel: 083-4170 555), dedicated to the heritage of the migrant worker system that provided the mines with cheap labour during the apartheid era, and the educational **Sci-Bono Discovery Centre** (Miriam Makeba Street; tel: 011-639 8400; www. sci-bono.co.za; Thur–Sat 9am–4pm; free).

There are also some fine contemporary art galleries in the vicinity – notably **Afronova** (Margaret Mcingana Street; tel: 083-726 5906) and **Art Bank Joburg** (President Street; tel: 011-838 6266) – and music venues such as the Bassline on Henry Nxumalo Street.

The Oriental Plaza lies in Fordsburg, a few blocks west of Newtown Precinct, sandwiched in between Bree Street and Central Avenue. Here, shoppers can bargain for the best prices on everything from silks and spices to herbs and haberdashery, or simply settle down to a leisurely curry. Heading back towards the Carlton Centre, the

Portraits of Nelson Mandela at the Apartheid Museum.

BELOW: the famous Market Theatre complex is housed in an old produce market.

The mine dumps, such a common feature of Jo'burg's cityscape, are fast disappearing – they're being reworked to recover the last traces of gold.

BELOW: Mandela Square is surrounded by shops and restaurants.

elegant **City Hall** on Rissik Street offers a rare glimpse of how this area must once have looked, before the office blocks and concrete flyovers sprang up.

In the 1990s, violent crime became such a problem in downtown Johannesburg that many local businesses relocated to safer suburbs and the upmarket hotels that once graced its streets were forced to close or to convert to low-rental apartment blocks. Since the turn of the millennium, however, central Johannesburg has experienced considerable urban rejuvenation, epitomised by the developments around Newtown, and crime is widely thought to be on the decrease. Still, the safest way to see the city centre is on an organised tour. It's probably inadvisable to walk around the city centre without a local companion who knows the ropes, especially after dark, and – as in any city centre, only more so – it would be inviting trouble to carry a camera, or wear expensive jewellery, or flash a loaded wallet. If you're driving, it's a good idea to keep your car doors locked at all times.

Markets and malls

North of the city centre, the prestigious suburbs of Rosebank and Sandton are the site of many of Johannesburg's most well-known exclusive hotels, and while neither suburb boasts much in the way of formal sightseeing, both are well-known shopping hubs. The centre of retail therapy in Rosebank is the **Rosebank Mall** (Cradock Road, tel: 011-788 5530; www.themallofrosebank. co.za), while its Sandton counterpart is **Sandton City** (Rivonia Road, tel: 011-217 6000; www.sandtoncity.com) and adjoining Nelson Mandela Square (complete with gigantic bronze sculpture of its namesake). Both malls have a plethora of restaurants, chain stores and boutiques, as well as cinema complexes and restaurants to keep you amused on a rare rainy day.

Johannesburg's flea markets attract informal traders from all over Africa, so pickings are rich as far as ethnic handicrafts are concerned. Newtown's **Market Theatre Flea Market** (Mon–Sat) is the city's original – and most bohemian – "flea", with stalls selling everything from street fashion to arty

tat. The fascinating **Mai Mai Market** (Mon–Fri), tucked away on the corner or Berea and Anderson Streets, is also known as *Ezinyangeni* (Place of Healers), as most of its 150-odd stalls are dedicated to the paraphernalia and *muti* (medicine) associated with traditional African healing.

A 15-minute drive northeast of the city centre brings you to **Bruma Lake Flea Market World** (Corner Ernest Oppenheimer and Marcia Streets; tel: 011-622 9648; Tue–Sun 9.30am–5pm; small charge), whose 600 stalls sell handicrafts from all over Africa. So does the Africa Craft Market in Rosebank Mall. Haggling is expected at both markets.

Golden City culture

Celebrating its centenary in 2010, the central **Johannesburg Art Gallery** Ⓖ (tel: 011-725 3130; open Tue–Sun; free), designed by Sir Edwin Lutyens, houses a collection of almost 10,000 artworks representing all styles and era in South African art. Unfortunately, it lies in Joubert Park, one of Johannesburg's most crime-ridden quarters, so

is best not visited on foot.

Johannesburg's commercial galleries are the best in the country and the **Everard Read Gallery** (6 Jellicoe Avenue, Rosebank, tel: 011 788 4805; www. everard-read.co.za) is definitely worth a visit – a huge variety of artists are represented here, from landscape painters to wildlife sculptors and cutting-edge township whizz-kids.

Two other excellent private venues in the Rosebank area on Jan Smuts Avenue are the **Kim Sacks Gallery** (tel: 011-447 5804; http://kimsacksgallery.blog spot.com) and the **Goodman Gallery** (tel: 011-788 1113; www.goodman-gallery. com). All of these places keep normal shopping hours and no entrance fee is charged.

In Braamfontein, immediately north of the city centre, the University of the Witwatersrand's **Gertrude Posel Gallery** (Jorissen Street; tel: 011-717 1365; Mon–Fri 8.30am–4.30pm, free) houses a superb collection of ethnic art from all around southern Africa, including valuable examples of vanishing styles of masks, headdresses and drums.

Only five minutes' walk away, and

Singer and civil rights activist, Miriam Makeba was born in Johannesburg.

BELOW: the forbidding entrance to the excellent Apartheid Museum.

One of Gauteng's celebrated Zola Budd minibus taxis, which provide transport for the majority of local commuters.

BELOW: upmarket restaurant in Melrose Arch.

also part of the prestigious university nicknamed "Wits", the **Origins Centre** (corner of Yale Road and Enoch Sontonga Avenue; tel: 011-717 4700; www.origins.org.za; Mon–Sat 9am–5pm charge), opened by President Mbeki in 2006, is a world-class modern museum that explores the emergence of modern humankind in two related sets of displays. The first is dedicated to human evolution as documented by a wealth of fossils unearthed in Gauteng and elsewhere in Africa, while the second houses what is claimed to be the world's largest collection of prehistoric rock art, including some of the earliest surviving images made by man. This interactive museum is worth at least two hours, whether as a standalone experience or as a primer for a visit to the related Cradle of Humankind west of the city.

Also located in the university, the **Johannesburg Planetarium** (Yale Road; tel: 011-717 1392; www.planetarium.co.za) is a good place to view the southern skies from a fresh angle – check the website for details of current audiovisual shows.

On the wild side

Although the city centre is congested with high-rise buildings, it is surrounded by the interminable sprawl of leafy suburbia that characterises Greater Johannesburg, home to more than 600 parks and open spaces.

One of the biggest is the 100-hectare (250-acre) Delta Park, between Blairgowrie and Victory Park, where the two dams in the lovely **Florence Bloom Bird Sanctuary** (daily; free) host a rich birdlife that can be observed from several specially constructed hides.

One of the nicest of Joburg's green patches is the **Melville Koppies Nature Reserve** (tel: 011-482 4797; www.mk.org.za; daily dawn–dusk; free), just north of Melville suburb, which is of some archaeological interest: finds here include stone-age tools dating back 500,000 years and a prehistoric iron-smelting furnace. It forms the southernmost section of the much larger Jan Riebeeck Park, where you will also find the **Johannesburg Botanical Garden** (tel: 011-782 7064; daily dawn to dusk; free) in Roosevelt Park Extension, half-an-hour's drive from the city centre on the banks of the Emmarentia Dam. This tranquil spot covers 148 hectares (365 acres), and contains a rose garden, a bonsai garden, pools, fountains and oaks; the dam itself is a pleasant stretch of water, popular with rowers, windsurfers and sailors.

More than 3,000 mammals, birds and reptiles – 30 of them on the endangered list – are housed at the **Johannesburg Zoo** (tel: 011-646 2000; daily 8.30am–5.30pm; charge) inside the Herman Eckstein Park in Saxonwold. There are enclosures for big cats, elephants, giraffes and large apes, guarded only by moats and free of iron bars. Popular three-hour night tours are conducted daily, starting at 5.15pm and 6.15pm, and offering the opportunity to see several nocturnal inhabitants in action, but advance booking is required.

Across Jan Smuts Avenue at popular Zoo Lake, also in the park, there are rowing boats for hire, a restaurant and children's playgrounds. Behind the zoo, at the **South African National Museum of Military History** (tel: 011-646 5513; daily 9am–4.30pm; charge), 12 aircraft and a military submarine vie for your attention with armoured flight vehicles, artillery, small arms and uniforms.

One of the best places to admire Johannesburg's Manhattan-esque skyline is **Pioneer Park** (corner of Rosettenville Road and 11th Street; tel: 011-435 0425; daily; free), on the banks of Wemmer Pan in Rosettenville. On the northern bank is **Santarama Miniland** (tel: 011-435 0543; daily 8.30am–5pm; charge), a contrived, but nonetheless very popular, miniature city built to a scale of 1:25, depicting all sorts of South African landmarks, including Kimberley's Big Hole.

Visitors can also explore Greater Johannesburg's remaining streams and ridges on a number of self-guided walking trails (detailed brochures marking sites of historical, archaeological and ecological interest are available from the tourist information office). Hikes include the Bloubos Trail and the Sandspruit Trail; closer to the centre of town, you can admire some of the grand Edwardian homes built for the original gold-rush mining barons – led by appropriately costumed guides – on the Parktown Heritage Tour. Contact the Parktown and Westcliff Heritage Trust (tel: 011-482 3349; www.parktown heritage.co.za).

The premier birdwatching site in the Johannesburg area, **Marievale Bird Sanctuary** (tel: 011-734 3661; sunrise to sunset; free), is a Ramsar Convention wetland set between the old mine dumps near the dreary little town of Nigel, 30 minutes drive south of the city. Worth a visit at any time of year, Marievale is best in summer, when resident waterbirds are frequently joined by migrant rarities such as yellow wagtail, European marsh-harrier and black-tailed godwit.

A fantasy African palace in Sun City.

Soweto

It may seem bizarre to treat a township created by the apartheid govern-

BELOW: the glitzy Sun City complex.

Sun City

South Africa's answer to Las Vegas lies 90 minutes' drive west of Jo'burg, on the fringes of the Kalahari. This glitzy resort – the most luxurious in southern Africa – contains casinos, cinemas, restaurants, a world-class golf course and numerous hotels. Most over-the-top of all is the Lost City complex, in which a spectacular five-star hotel – a fantasy African palace – rises from an imported tropical jungle setting, complete with artificial beach and wave pool. Special effects such as the Bridge of Time – scheduled to shudder and shake every now and again, hypo-allergenic smoke seeping out of its man-made fissures to simulate an earthquake – complete the picture.

Sol Kerzner is the brains behind it all; the flamboyant boxer-turned-businessman whose hugely successful company, Sun International, operates hotels and gaming resorts around the world. Part of Kerzner's financial genius was in recognising the potential of building resorts in the so-called homelands, which were granted independence during the days of apartheid. While South Africa's Calvinist white rulers forbade gambling, you could do pretty much anything in the homelands. Sun City (tel: 014-557 1000; www.suncity.co.za) established itself in the former homeland of Bophutatswana. It is complemented by the nearby Pilanesberg Game Reserve.

Mine shaft at Gold Reef City.

ment as a tourist attraction, but a visit to **Soweto** ❷ (an acronym of SOuth WEstern TOwnships) enables one to see both sides of what is still largely a segregated society. Home at one time to luminaries such as Nelson Mandela, Archbishop Desmond Tutu and Lucas Radebe, Soweto was the setting for many pivotal events during the anti-apartheid struggle, including the tragic 1976 Soweto Uprising, which started as a student protest against the enforced use of Afrikaans in schools, and resulted in more than 500 deaths at the hands of trigger happy police. Now home to around two million people, Soweto is most safely visited on a guided tour, which can be arranged through most operators and hotels in Gauteng.

Several important apartheid-related landmarks are dotted around Soweto, and are visited on most guided tours. In the suburb of Kliptown, **Walter Sisulu Square** (corner of Klipspruit Valley and Union Road; tel 011-945 2200; www.waltersisulusquare.co.za), now a modern shopping mall, stands where the Congress of the People – comprising more than 3,000 representatives of various resistance organisations – met on 26 June 1955 to draw up the celebrated Freedom Charter, foundation stone of the modern South African constitution.

The suburb of Orlando West is the site of the **Hector Pieterson Memorial and Museum** (Pela Street; tel: 011-536 0611; daily 10am–5pm; charge), dedicated to the role played by children in the struggle against apartheid, and named after the 13 year old scholar who became the first person to be killed by police fire in the Soweto Uprising. A block or two away, **Mandela House** (Ngakane Street, tel: 011-936 7754; www.mandelahouse.com; Mon–Fri 9am–5pm, Sat–Sun 9.30am–4.30pm, charge) is a small museum dedicated to the legacy of the Mandela family and located in the house where Nelson Mandela and his family lived prior to his arrest for treason in 1962.

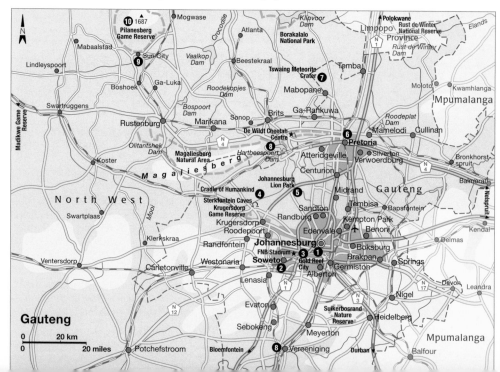

A Legacy of Gold

Wherever you go in downtown Johannesburg, street names reflect the pioneer days – Claim, Prospect, Nugget, Main Reef. But a more evocative reminder of the city's roots as a mining shantytown comes in the form of **Gold Reef City** ❸ (Northern Parkway, 6km (4 miles) south of the city centre, tel: 011-248 6800; www.goldreefcity.co.za; Tue–Sun 9.30am–6pm; charge), which attempts to recreate the rumbustious atmosphere of gold-rush Johannesburg in the form of a Victorian-style theme park, complete with several adrenaline-charged funfair rides and old-style shops and restaurants. Contrived and commercialised it may be, but there are interesting touches, such as the energetic daily demonstrations of *isicathulo* (gumboot dancing) first popularised by migrant workers in the mine hostels.

Guided tours of what was formerly Crown Mine's No. 14 Shaft – once the richest seam of gold in the world – involve taking a lift 200 metres (650ft) underground and watching a reconstruction of the mining process, from the extraction of the ore to the pouring of the molten gold into ingot moulds.

Next to Gold Reef City. the superb **Apartheid Museum** (tel: 011-309 4700; www. apartheidmuseum.org; Tue–Sun 10am–5pm; not suitable for children under 12) illustrates the grim story of apartheid through graphic photographs, film footage and imaginative installations, including an armoured police casspir once used to patrol the townships.

Statue of Robert Broom at the Sterkfontein Caves.

Cradle of Humankind

One of eight Unesco World Heritage Sites in South Africa, the **Cradle of Humankind** ❹ (tel: 014-577 9000; www.maropeng.co.za; daily 9am–5pm; charge) comprises about 20 different archaeological sites to the west of Johannesburg, all of which have yielded hominid fossils dating back millions of years. The main tourist facility in the Cradle is the innovative **Maropeng Visitors Centre** (on the D400 about 50km west of Johannesburg), whose innovative multimedia displays, including an

BELOW: exhibit at the Maropeng Visitors Centre.

FNB Stadium

Africa's largest soccer stadium – and one of the world's ten most capacious – is Soweto's FNB Stadium (aka Soccer City), which holds up to 95,000 spectators. South Africa achieved its famous 2-0 victory over Tunisia in the 1996 Africa Nations Cup final here and it is where the opening ceremony of the 2010 FIFA World Cup took place, along with the final between Spain and Netherlands. Nicknamed the Calabash due to its resemblance to a traditional gourd, it is here that Nelson Mandela made his first Gauteng speech after being released from prison and where the funeral of Chris Hani was held following his assassination in 1993. In 2011, it made its debut as a concert venue, with stars such as U2, Kings of Leon and Neil Diamond performing.

exciting underground boat ride reproducing the geological conditions that shaped our planet, are well worth two hours an provide an excellent background to the paleontological discoveries in the region.

The best known archaeological site in the Cradle is the **Sterkfontein Caves** (10km from Maropeng off the R563; guided tours every hour on the hour; combination tickets for both sites available at Maropeng until 1pm), which were exposed in the late 19th century by lime-quarry blasting, and consist of six chambers and an underground lake that is said to have healing powers. Of more than 500 hominid fossils unearthed in the area, the most famous is a 2.5 million year old skull discovered by Dr Robert Broom in 1936 and nicknamed Mrs Ples (short for *Plesianthropus transvaalensus*, though the skull is now assigned to the species Australopithecus Africanus – and thought to be male). More recent discoveries include a 3.3 million year old male skeleton nicknamed Little Foot, while a near-complete skeleton dating back 3.5 million years, unearthed in 1998 and still *in situ*, is the oldest hominid fossil known from southern Africa.

The area around the Cradle is also the site of several small and rather contrived wildlife sanctuaries that might be alluring to visitors who don't have the time or inclination to visit a proper game reserve. The **Johannesburg Lion Park** ❺ (R114, 12km northwest of Sandton; tel: 011-691 9905; www.lion-park.com; daily, 8.30am–6pm summer, 8.30am–5pm winter; charge per car) is home not only to lions but to a variety of herbivores. The nearby **Rhino and Lion Reserve** (on the R540 north of Sterkfontein Caves; tel: 011-957 0349; www.rhinolion.co.za; daily 8am–3.45pm; charge per vehicle) is a similar set-up but also has an enclosure for rhinos.

PRETORIA (TSHWANE)

Only 50km (30 miles) north of Johannesburg, **Pretoria's** ❻ relatively small size disguises its influence as the centre of political decision-making. All government departments have their head offices here; money may do the

talking in the Golden City, but it is in Pretoria where the strings of power are manipulated. In the past, this gave Pretoria a bit of an image problem: a place where apartheid's most insular strictures were upheld to the letter and a spirit of killjoy puritanism prevailed. But all that has changed and Pretoria now supports a sophisticated international colony of diplomats, politicians and businessmen, and has experienced something of a cultural renaissance, including the emergence of a thriving gay scene. The city now forms part of the greater Tshwane Municipality, but it is still known as Pretoria – or as the Jacaranda City, for reasons that become obvious if you visit in October, when its 50,000-plus jacaranda trees come into bright mauve blossoms.

Historic Pretoria

Many of Pretoria's historic sites commemorate the late 19th-century heyday of Paul Kruger's Zuid-Afrikaansche Republiek *(see page 45)*. In the heart of the city lies **Church Square** Ⓐ, skirted by the Old Raadsaal (seat of the old Republican government); the Palace of Justice and the original South African Reserve Bank. But the chief landmark is a large statue of Kruger himself, flanked by burgher sentries. A short walk down Church Street brings you to Strijdom Square, dominated by a giant bust of a more recent leader of the Volk, former Prime Minister, J.G. Strijdom.

The **Kruger Museum** Ⓑ (Church Street; tel: 012-326 9172; www.ditsong. org.za; daily 9am–4pm; charge) consists of the unpretentious but immaculately restored home occupied by Kruger and his wife between 1884 and 1901. Some of the dour old Calvinist's personal belongings are on display, as well as his private railway carriage and official state coach. Kruger's grave lies nearby at Heroes' Acre.

A 15-minute walk to the southeast brings you to gracious **Melrose House** Ⓒ (tel: 012-322 2805; www.melrosehouse. co.za; Tue–Sun 10am–5pm; charge), in Jacob Maré Street opposite **Burgers Park**. Designed and built in 1886, the

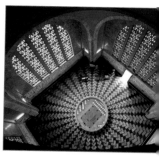

The cenotaph inside the Voortrekker Monument is placed so that on December 16th each year, a shaft of sunlight passes through a small window and sweeps across the inscription "We for thee, South Africa."

BELOW: Paul Kruger Monument in Pretoria's Church Square.

The Cullinan Diamond Mine, 40km (24 miles) east of Pretoria, is famous for the Cullinan diamond, the largest gem diamond ever found.

mansion is one of South Africa's finest surviving examples of Victorian architecture; it is also where the treaty ending the Anglo–Boer War was signed.

Guarding the southern entrance to the city is the **Voortrekker Monument** **D** (Eeufees Road; tel: 012-326 6770; www.voortrekker mon.org.za; daily 8am–5pm; charge), a looming granite structure built to celebrate the centenary of the Great Trek (1834–40), which opened up the country's interior for white occupation

The government's administrative headquarters are situated in the **Union Buildings** **E** (gardens open daily; free) on Meintjieskop Ridge, overlooking the city to the east. The image of this stately red sandstone building, designed by Sir Herbert Baker and completed in 1913, adorns souvenir tray cloths, coffee mugs and biscuit tins nationwide – it was also the setting for Nelson Mandela's historic inauguration on 10 May 1994.

Cultural and outdoor life

The **Pretoria Art Museum** (Arcadia Park; tel: 012-344 1807; Tue–Sun 8am–5pm; charge) houses an impressive collection of work by South African artists. The **National Museum of Natural History** **F** (formerly Transvaal Museum; tel: 012-322 7632; www. ditsong.org.za; daily 8am–4pm; charge), a 10-minute walk away in Paul Kruger Street, opposite the City Hall, houses a collection of fossils, as well as one of the country's largest collections of rock art.

The **State Theatre** **G** (tel: 012-392 4000; www.statetheatre.co.za) on Church Street is the formal centre of cultural life in Pretoria. A grand total of six separate auditoriums in the complex provide facilities for opera, drama, ballet and symphony concerts. As far as more informal entertainment is concerned, some of the liveliest nightlife centres around the suburbs of Hatfield and Sunnyside.

A short drive north of the city centre, the **National Zoological Gardens** **H** (Boom Street; tel: 012-328 3265; www.zoo.ac.za; daily 8am–5pm; charge) is the largest and best in the country.

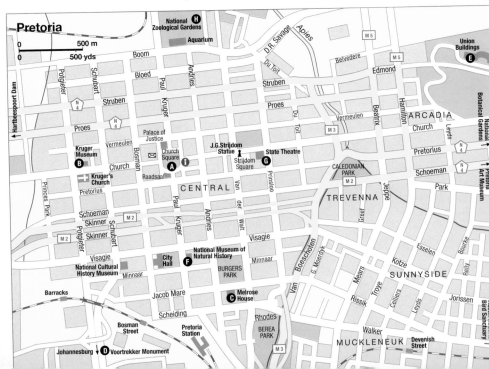

home to about 3,500 southern African and exotic animals; an overhead cableway provides the visitor with a panoramic view of the zoo and the surrounding city. The magnificent **Pretoria National Botanical Gardens** (tel: 012-843 5172; www.sanbi.org; daily 6am–6pm; charge) lie 8km (5 miles) east of the city centre and contain every major type of southern African vegetation. Conducted tours include a slide show and visit to the nursery.

Situated 40km (25 miles) northwest of Pretoria, the **Tswaing Meteorite Crater** ❼ (tel: 012-945 5911; www.ditsong.org.za; daily 7.30am–4pm; charge) protects a 1km (½-mile) wide meteorite crater and the brackish lake on its floor. Facilities are rather limited following a destructive fire in 2009, but the three-hour hike around the crater is a scenic delight and comes with a good chance of seeing kudu, monkeys and a variety of woodland birds.

NORTHWEST PROVINCE

The **Hartbeespoort Dam** ❽, 35km (22 miles) west of Pretoria, set against the backdrop of the Magaliesberg Mountains, is the setting for numerous small holiday resorts – popular weekend retreats for locals – as well as a good snake park. The **De Wildt Cheetah Centre**, off the R513 near Hartbeespoort Dam (tel: 012-504 9906; www.dewildt.co.za; tours by advance booking only) is the first place where the cheetah was successfully bred in captivity and it's also where researchers discovered that the rare king cheetah, whose spots meld together into stripes, is not a separate species, but the result of a recessive gene in both parents.

The N4 running northwest across Hartebeespoort Dam Wall is also the main gateway from Gauteng to the considerably less densely populated Northwest Province – or at least to the part of Northwest that is most commonly visited by tourists, thanks to the presence of the legendary **Sun City** ❾ (see box on page 265) and a pair of malaria-free game reserves that offer the full Big Five experience.

Rather less alluring, it has to be said, is the city of **Rustenburg**, established as a Boer village in 1851, and now home to more than 400,000 people, thanks partly to its proximity to the world's two largest platinum mines. Rustenburg – literally Place of Rest – was the base for the English squad during the 2010 FIFA World Cup and their opening game against the USA was one of six World Cup matches played at the city's Royal Bafokeng Stadium.

North of Hartebeespoort Dam, the 550-sq-km (215-sq-mile) **Pilanesberg Game Reserve** ❿ (tel: 014-555 1600; www.pilanesberg-game-reserve.co.za; daily sunrise to sunset; charge) is noteworthy both as the closest fully-fledged "Big Five" reserve to Johannesburg – about two hours drive in total – as well as providing a back-to-nature facet to the otherwise rather glitzy Sun City on its southern border.

The reserve protects an area of mixed grassland and woodland set within a collapsed volcanic crater whose mountainous rim encloses the central Mankwe Dam. Following an extensive

WHERE

There's no more dramatic way of seeing the Pilanesberg than a dawn hot-air balloon ride, with the sun rising gold over hills studded with elephants and zebras. Tel: 021-433 0142 for details.

BELOW: the grand archway on Hartbeespoort Dam.

A green-backed heron in Pilanesberg Nature Reserve.

BELOW: bathtime at Pilanesberg Nature Reserve.

programme of reintroductions in the late 1970s, the reserve is now one of the best places to see white rhino and elephant, which roam freely alongside lion, leopard, buffalo, zebra and giraffe. There are about a dozen species of antelope and a remarkable checklist of 350 bird species, whose composition reflects the reserve's location in a transitional vegetation zone. Serviced by good internal roads and the full gamut of accommodation options – from camp sites to five-star hotels and luxury tented camps – Pilanesberg is perfect for a one- or two-night self-drive safari out of Gauteng, though most of the lodges also offer guided drives for those who prefer.

Madikwe Game Reserve

For those seeking a more exclusive game-viewing experience, the 550-sq-km (292-sq-mile) **Madikwe Game Reserve** (tel: 018-350 9931; www.madikwe-game-reserve.co.za; access to overnight visitors only) lies about 90 minutes drive northwest of Sun City on the Botswana border. Traversed through by the Great Marico River, the reserve was established as recently as 1991, but an extensive programme of reintroductions over the subsequent decade means it is now home to all of the Big Five – expect great lion, elephant and rhino sightings – as well as being perhaps the most reliable reserve in the country for encounters with the endangered African wild dog. The birdlife includes several species associated with the dry west at the eastern extreme of their range, among them the striking crimson-breasted shrike, violet-eared waxbill, paradise whydah and pied babbler. The overall experience here is very similar to the private reserves bordering Kruger, with around 30 small and exclusive camps offering all-inclusive packages centred on organised game-drives in an open 4x4 with a knowledgeable guide. An important asset of Madikwe is that it is completely free of malaria.   ❑

The Lure of Gold

Gold-mining has been the flywheel of the South African economy since the largest seams known to man were discovered below Johannesburg

Of all the gold mined in the world to date, about half came from the African continent. The bulk of that half gold has come from South Africa, the world's largest annual producer from 1905 to 2007 (with production peaking in 1970 at 1,480 tonnes, 80 percent of the global supply) and second only to China today. Gold is only one of South Africa's many mineral assets: it is also the world's largest platinum producer and an important supplier of diamonds and other gemstones.

Johannesburg grew from the rough-and-ready diggers' camps that mushroomed here when gold was first discovered in 1886. Today's visitors to Gold Reef City (see page 267) – a popular theme park depicting Johannesburg at the dawn of the 20th century – can take a cage some 200 metres (650ft) underground, to see just how the precious metal is wrested from the rock. But gold has little to do with nostalgia or romance for South Africa's 500,000-odd mine workers.

"The wealth of our gold-mining industry is not so much due to the richness of gold as it is to the poorness of Black wages," wrote Alan Paton in the 1960s. Even in the post-apartheid era, despite the minimum wage levels negotiated by the trade unions, the mine worker's life is a tough one.

Below the surface

Most miners begin their day by climbing into the giant metal cages that will take them deep into the belly of the earth for their working shift. Already, South Africa's gold mines probe deeper than their counterparts around the world. In the mid-1980s, for example, the Witwatersrand's Western Deep Levels was mining 3,447 metres (10,300ft) below the earth's surface – a world record.

Working conditions are intensely hot and humid, and despite stringent safety measures, often hazardous. Many of the gold-bearing underground seams are narrow and the shafts or "stopes" in which the miners work little more than 1 metre (3ft)

high. Rock temperatures can reach 55°C (131°F), and even though refrigerated air is constantly pumped through the networks, air temperatures often exceed 32°C (90°F).

Because of the narrowness of the seams, drilling and blasting are usually manual operations. The raw rock is hoisted onto carts which are whisked up to ground level to undergo a series of gold extraction processes – but there is the ever-present danger of rock-bursts or earth tremors.

The mining industry has long relied on contract labour as the backbone of its workforce. In the early 20th century, bleak hostels were built to house the thousands of men who, having been forced off their land, came seeking work in the city of gold. Mineworkers' traditional songs bear testament to the loneliness of their life, to the harsh, crowded conditions in the single-sex hostels and to their longings for faraway families.

Inevitably, perhaps, hostels became flashpoints for political violence in the 1980s and 1990s, fuelled by alienation, bitterness and despair. Since apartheid ended, however, working and housing conditions in the mining industry have improved greatly, partly at the instigation of the ANC (factions of which are currently talking about nationalisation of the mines). Nevertheless, the reality behind the glittering image of gold remains an industry built on back-breaking work in harsh conditions. ❏

RIGHT: pouring molten gold at Gold Reef City.

MPUMALANGA AND LIMPOPO

North and east of Gauteng, the highveld rolls on to a vast escarpment, where wooded cliffs plunge down to the bushveld wilderness of the vast Kruger National Park

Extending northeast from Gauteng to the borders with Zimbabwe and Mozambique, the provinces of Limpopo and Mpumalanga are dominated by the charismatic wilderness of Kruger National Park, which runs for a full 350km (190 miles) along their eastern borders. This game-rich area is larger than Wales or Massachusetts and abutted by private sanctuaries to the west, and by the Zimbabwean and Mozambican components of the Great Limpopo Transfrontier Park to the north and east.

Most Kruger safaris stick to the southern fifth of the park. In part, this is because the southern Kruger has better facilities than the north and offers better game viewing, but another factor is relative proximity to Gauteng and ease of onward road travel to Swaziland and KwaZulu-Natal. Similarly, Mpumalanga's southerly Panorama Route can become rather crowded in season, yet comparably scenic parts of Limpopo Province in the north feel decidedly remote. Logistically, sticking to the south makes sense within the time frame of a standard holiday, certainly if you also intend to visit Cape Town. Nevertheless, with sufficient time – ten days, say – you could travel the full loop out of Gauteng described in this chapter, heading east to Mpu-

malanga, then driving right through the Kruger Park to the far north, and returning via off-the-beaten-track Limpopo Province.

THE HIGHVELD

Leaving **Pretoria** on the N4, or Johannesburg on the N12, the road east rolls steadily on through sun-bleached grassland. Initially, the journey shows little promise of the beautiful eastern escarpment that lies ahead, yet these undulating plains once teemed with herds of wildlife, particularly black wildebeest

Main attractions
PANORAMA ROUTE
PILGRIM'S REST
KRUGER NATIONAL PARK
SABI SAND & MALAMALA
MAPUNGUBWE NATIONAL PARK
MASHATU GAME RESERVE
MODJADJI NATURE RESERVE

PRECEDING PAGES: horseback safari in Limpopo Province. **LEFT:** leopard, Kruger National Park. **RIGHT:** Ndebele villagers.

Nylstroom (Nile Stream), as Modimolle used to be known, was named by a Voortrekker group who attempted to cross Africa in 1886 and were convinced they had reached Egypt when they mistook a river flowing past a pyramid-shaped hill for the Nile.

and zebra. Today, the indigenous wildlife has been displaced by cattle and sheep farming, as well as intensive maize and sunflower monoculture. Occasionally, domesticated blesbok can be seen grazing in game-fenced ranches along the roadside.

The N12 and N4 converge outside **eMalahleni** (formerly Witbank), whose nondescript town centre cannot be seen from the highway and offers little to merit a diversion. As the name eMalahleni ('Place of Coal') suggests, the country's largest coal deposits are found in the area, fuelling several power stations, but also creating growing environmental problems such as air pollution and acid rain.

This region is home to the Southern Ndebele, refugees from Shaka's

Zulu Empire who settled here in the early 19th century and are celebrated today for their colourful decoration. Exquisite examples of geometrically patterned homes and intricately beaded costumes can be seen at the 19th-century **Botshabelo Mission Station ❶** 13km (8 miles) north of **Middelburg**. You can explore on your own or take a guided tour, available from the open-air museum (tel: 013-245 9003; daily; charge). Nearby **Fort Merensky**, built in 1865, is a rather bizarre construction resembling a hybrid of a Gothic castle and the ruined stone city of Great Zimbabwe.

You might want to take a short drive through the adjacent game enclosure, perhaps the most northerly remaining refuge for the endemic black

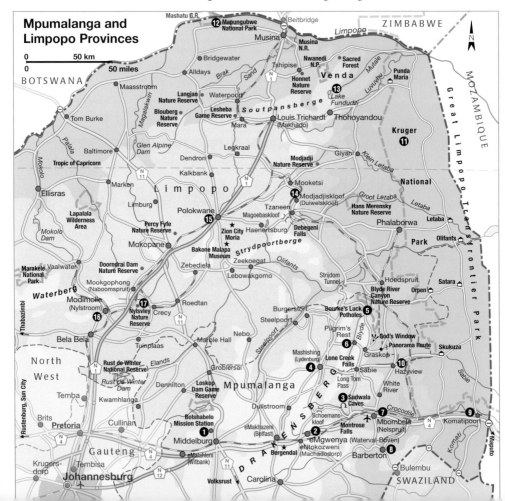

Mpumalanga and Limpopo Provinces

wildebeest. About 15km (9 miles) further north, **Loskop** (Loose Head) **Dam Game Reserve** (Apr–Oct daily 6.30am–6pm, Nov–Mar daily 6am–6.30pm) supports white rhino, giraffe, zebra, buffalo, kudu and over 200 bird species in an area transitional to the highveld and lowveld biomes.

Further east, the N4 bypasses the unremarkable small towns of **eMakhazeni** and **eNtokozweni** (formerly Belfast and Machadodorp), both of which played important roles in the history of the Zuid-Afrikaansche Republiek. After the evacuation of Pretoria in 1900 during the Anglo–Boer War, Kruger moved his government to what was then Machadodorp. Later that year, the last major battle of the war was fought at **Bergendal**, 8km (5 miles) outside Belfast. A small memorial marks the battlefield.

On the edge of the Drakensberg escarpment, the two little railway towns of **eMgwenya** (formerly Waterval-Boven) ❷ and **Waterval-Onder** are (as their Afrikaans names suggest) respectively situated above and below a spectacular 228 metre (745ft) high waterfall on the Elands River. In the mid-1890s, Dutch contractors employed considerable engineering skills in bringing the railway right to the point where the water plunges over the escarpment. You'll pass the steeply inclined tunnel and rack-rail as you drive; a short walk from the roadside leads to lovely views of the waterfall.

A rewarding diversion heading left over the escarpment just before reaching eMgwenya (R539) follows the Crocodile River for 67km (42 miles) through the precipitous Schoemanskloof, then links up with the N4 at the confluence of the Elands and Crocodile rivers which tumble over the beautiful **Montrose Falls**.

The N4 leads on through lush farmland towards Mbombela (Nelspruit) and Kruger National Park, past extensive citrus orchards and wayside stalls selling fruit and curios. Two kilometres (1 mile) beyond the intersection

at Montrose, a turn-off to the north takes you on a 14km (9-mile) drive to the **Sudwala Caves** ❸ (tel: 013-733 4152; www.sudwalacaves.co.za; daily 8.30am–4.30pm; guided 1-hour tour every 15 minutes; charge). Nobody knows why, but the caves' temperature stays at a constant 18°C (64°F) throughout the year. Their full depth has not yet been established, but you can explore the enormous chambers with their weird dripstone formations for about 500 metres (1,600ft) into the mountainside.

Elands River waterfall.

Towards the Escarpment

South Africa's Drakensberg Range swoops down along the entire length of Mpumalanga and KwaZulu-Natal, providing breathtaking views and excellent opportunities for hiking or driving. The craggy Mpumalanga section – known simply as The Escarpment – runs south from Blyde River Canyon for nearly 320km (200 miles). It is criss crossed with many passes pioneered by the transport-riders of

BELOW: Ndebele style.

WHERE

Find out how to pan for gold on a conducted tour with the Pilgrim's Rest Diggings Museum, just outside Mashishing on the Graskop road. Tel: 013-768 1060.

the late 19th century, who provided a vital link between the land-locked Zuid-Afrikaansche Republic and the Portuguese port of Lourenço Marques (Maputo).

One of these intrepid pioneers was young Percy Fitzpatrick, who, disillusioned with his job in a Cape Town bank, opted for a job carting supplies by ox wagon from Delagoa Bay to the highveld goldfields. Fitzpatrick's closest travelling companion was a crossbreed bull terrier named Jock; the tale he wrote about their adventures, *Jock of the Bushveld* (1907), is now a classic.

Useful jumping-off points for exploring the Escarpment include sleepy little **Dullstroom** (proposed new name Emnotweni), 30km (19 miles) north of eMakhazeni (Belfast) on the R540 and set amid one of the few remaining stretches of pristine highveld countryside. Numerous small streams rise in these cool highlands, draining towards the escarpment to the east. All are stocked with trout; fly-fishing is almost as important round here as farming. As most of the trout streams are privately owned, seek advice on good fishing

spots from your hotel reception.

Some 58km (36 miles) further north, **Mashishing** ❹ (formerly Lydenburg, meaning "Town of Suffering") is a beautiful town that belies the name given to it in the 1850s by survivors fleeing malaria-stricken settlements of the lowveld. Later, it became the capital of an independent Boer republic; the town's Dutch Reformed church and old school house were built during this period. In the **Lydenburg Museum** (tel: 013-235 2213; www.lydenburg museum.org.za; Mon–Fri 8am–4pm, Sat–Sun 8am–5pm; charge), you can see replicas of the Lydenburg Heads based on reassembled pottery found in the area. The masks date from AD500 and are one of South Africa's most important archaeological discoveries.

The Panorama Route

From Mashishing, it's 56km (35 miles) east across the Mauchberg via the scenic Long Tom Pass, once used by transport riders, to the forestry town of **Sabie**. Timber plantations cover the surrounding hill sides; most of the country's major paper mills are

BELOW: Bourke's Luck Potholes.

situated here. So dramatic is the road north from here along the Escarpment's edge that it's been named the **Panorama Route**. For once the tourist-board tag is no exaggeration. This is also waterfall country and numerous short drives lead from town to picnic and viewing sites such as **Sabie Falls**, **Horseshoe Falls**, **Lone Creek Falls**, **Bridal Veil Falls** and **MacMac Falls** (so-called after the Scots prospectors who camped in the area during the gold rush). Photographers should note that most of the waterfalls face east and are best visited before midday.

The 86km (54-mile) drive northwards from Sabie via **Graskop** to the **Blyde River Canyon** should be taken at a leisurely pace: the views are exceptional. At **Pinnacle Rock**, **Jock's View** and **God's Window**, you can stop to look out from sheer cliff outposts over the expanse of the lowveld. Other sights include the Lisbon Falls and the Berlin Falls before the road reaches **Bourke's Luck Potholes** ❺, 66km (41 miles) from Sabie. Here, paths and footbridges take visitors to viewing sites overlooking an extraordinary series of water-eroded cylindrical potholes at the confluence of the Blyde (Joy) and Treur (Sorrow) Rivers.

Northwards, the Blyde River has carved a magnificent gorge through the mountains. Viewing sites have been created at points along the canyon, providing superb views of the winding river 800 metres (2,600ft) below. Dominated by three peaks known as the **Three Rondavels**, and by **Mariepskop**, one of the highest points in the region, the canyon is a nature reserve (daily; free) and much of it is accessible on foot only.

Starting from the rest camp at the entrance gate, well-marked trails of varying lengths lead through the canyon's lush riverine flora of evergreen trees, prehistoric-looking cycads, giant ferns and orchids. Particularly worthwhile is the **Kadishi Trail**, which visits a waterfall notable for the stalactite-like tufa (calcium carbonate) formations that

have formed below it. Large mammals are seldom seen, but the bird life is excellent including the endemic bald ibis and Gurney's sugarbird.

An alternative trip from Sabie is over Bonnet Pass along the R533 for 35km (22 miles) to **Pilgrim's Rest** ❻, one of the oldest gold-mining towns in South Africa. Legend ascribes the discovery of gold in this valley (in 1873) to Alec "Wheelbarrow" Patterson, so called because he roamed the hills pushing all his possessions in a wheelbarrow. He stumbled across what was, at the time, the richest known deposit of alluvial gold on the subcontinent, and within no time at all a large and motley assortment of fortune-seekers had flocked to the area.

Yet within a decade, most of the alluvial deposits had been worked out and mining operations were taken over by larger companies. In 1883, the independent diggers migrated south to the new fields at Barberton. Underground mining continued at Pilgrim's Rest until the 1920s, but today the entire town has been restored as a national monument and living museum.

Long Tom Pass got its name during the Anglo–Boer War. The Boers tried to slow the advance of the British here with the help of two mighty 150-mm Creusot field guns, nicknamed Long Toms.

BELOW: Pilgrim's Rest.

Hiking trails

Some of the most rewarding views of this picturesque countryside are to be had on foot, for the Escarpment is crisscrossed by a network of impressive hiking paths. The **Fanie Botha Trail** was the first National Hiking Way trail to be opened, in 1973. It covers almost 80km (50 miles) of magnificent mountain countryside between the Ceylon Forest near Sabie to God's Window north of Graskop. Short sections of the five-day trail can be taken one at a time.

At God's Window, the Fanie Botha Trail merges with the 65km (40-mile) **Blyderivierspoort Hiking Trail**, offering a series of much more leisurely walks along the canyon, ending up at the Three Rondavels.

The region's early mining history can be traced along the **Prospector's Hiking Trail**, which links up with the Fanie Botha Trail at MacMac Falls and leads northwards for 70km (43 miles) through Pilgrim's Rest and north to Bourke's Luck Potholes. Pilgrim's Rest is also the starting point for a selection of shorter walks.

THE LOWVELD

Mbombela (formerly Nelspruit) **❼**, set at the escarpment base 355km (220 miles) east of Johannesburg, has a hot and humid atmosphere reflecting its low altitude. The capital of Mpumalanga, one of the country's smallest and least-populated provinces, Mbombela is quite a pretty place, its streets festooned with bougainvillaea and frangipani. The real showpiece is the **Lowveld National Botanical Garden** (tel: 013-752 5531; www.sanbi.org; daily Sep–Mar 8am–6pm, Apr–Aug 8am–5pm; charge), set in lush subtropical scenery 3km (2 miles) outside town at the confluence of the Nels and Crocodile River, where there is an attractive waterfall. Rare plants include a comprehensive cycad collection, as well as a large baobab and several fig species.

The lowveld was once the site of the major pre-Witwatersrand gold rush **Barberton ❽**, 45km (28 miles) south of Mbombela, near the Swaziland border, is the product of those wild days of fortunes made and lost overnight. Founded in 1883, it expanded rapidly as rich gold deposits were found in

BELOW: recycling in style.

the surrounding hills. The Barberton Museum on Crown Street has exhibits relating to the gold rush days and other aspects of local history, and the town is dotted with Victorian relicts, including an Anglo-Boer War Blockhouse, Stopforth House and the Lewis & Marks Building. Nearby Sheba was once the world's richest mine, and a separate town, Eureka City, grew up beside it. Eureka is now a ghost town and a half-hour drive from Barberton leads to the ruins past old excavations and mining gear.

Mbombela is a mere 105km (66 miles) west of the Mozambique border and the gateway town of **Komatipoort** ❾, sweltering in the confluent valleys of the Komati and Crocodile rivers. During the 20 years of civil war in Mozambique, Komatipoort lay dormant but for sporadic gunfire. Since then, however, the Mbombela-Maputo road has been completely rebuilt and the area is now a vibrant economic corridor of agriculture, industry and communications.

A 16km (10-mile) drive north of Mbombela on the R40 brings you to the attractive little town of **White River**. The lowveld climate here is ideal for the cultivation of exotic subtropical fruit and you'll notice banana, papaya and mango plantations lining the roadside. Avocados, litchis, citrus and passion fruit are all farmed here, too.

After a further 24km (15 miles), the R40 reaches **Hazyview** ❿, a once rather down-at-heel village that has flourished over the past few years thanks to its proximity to the Kruger Park's **Numbi** (20km/12 miles) and **Paul Kruger Gates** (45km/27 miles). Equipped with several supermarkets and restaurants, Hazyview is the site of a coterie of lodges catering to visitors who can't get bookings within the park, or want more upmarket accommodation, and day access was further improved a few years ago with the opening of the **Phabeni Gate** next to the **Albasini Ruins** (where the Portuguese ivory hunter Joao Albasini maintained a trading post in 1846–8) only 10km (7 miles) from the town centre.

Kruger National Park

In a roundabout way, it was the mosquito and the tsetse fly which helped

The Impala Lily is endemic to Kruger National Park.

BELOW: the Three Rondavels, Blyde River Canyon.

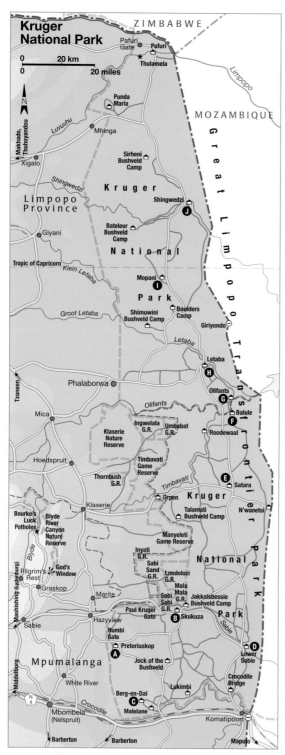

Kruger National Park

0	20 km
0	20 miles

N

ZIMBABWE
Pafuri Gate
Pafuri
★ Thulamela
Punda Maria
MOZAMBIQUE
Mhinga
Makhado, Thohoyandou
Luvuvhu
Xigalo
Sirheni Bushveld Camp
Shingwedzi
Kruger
Shingwedzi **J**
Limpopo Province
Giyani
Bateleur Bushveld Camp
National
Tropic of Capricorn
Klein Letaba
Mopani **I**
Park
Groot Letaba
Shimuwini Bushveld Camp
Boulders Camp
Giriyondo
Letaba
Letaba **H**
Phalaborwa
Olifants **G**
Mica
Olifants
Balule
Ingwelala G.R.
Umbabat G.R.
Roodewaal **F**
Tzaneen
Klaserie Nature Reserve
Hoedspruit
Timbavati Game Reserve
Thornbush G.R.
Timbavati
Orpen
E Satara
Kruger
N'wanetsi
Klaserie
Talamati Bushveld Camp
Bourke's Luck Potholes
Blyde River Canyon Nature Reserve
Manyeleti Game Reserve
Inyati G.R.
National
Mashishing (Lydenburg)
Pilgrim's Rest
God's Window
Blyde
Graskop
Sabi Sand G.R.
Londolozi G.R.
Mala Mala G.R.
Park
Marite
Sabi Sabi G.R.
Jakkalsbessie Bushveld Camp
Paul Kruger Gate
B Skukuza
Sabie
Hazyview
Numbi Gate
Sabie
Pretoriuskop **A**
D Lower Sabie
Mpumalanga
Jock of the Bushveld
Crocodile Bridge
Middelburg
White River
Lukimbi
Berg-en-Dal **C**
Malelane
N4
Mbombela (Nelspruit)
Crocodile
Komatipoort
Barberton
Barberton
Maputo

Great Limpopo Transfrontier Park

safeguard South Africa's herds of w
game, the highlight of any visit to t
country today. Thanks to the mala
and deadly nagana cattle sickness whi
these insects spread, hunting part
had to be restricted to the disease-fi
winter months, while all attempts
settle or civilise the area were doom
By the end of the 19th century, ho
ever, this was no longer enough to p
tect the land from farmers with th
fences and "sportsmen" with th
guns, who between them took a dev
tating toll of the area's game. Finally
1898, despite considerable oppositi
from his contemporaries, Preside
Kruger granted the proclamation
the Sabie Game Reserve to conser
the area's dwindling wildlife. This w
the core of what was to become t
much larger **Kruger National Pa**
⑪ (tel: 012-428 9111; www.sanpar
org; daily Nov–Feb 5.30am–6.30p
Mar, Oct 5.30am–6pm, Apr, Aug, Se
6am–6pm, May–Jul 6am–5.30p
charge), with boundaries approxim
ing the part of the park that lies to t
south of the Sabie River.

Diverse wildlife

The Kruger National Park has a
extraordinarily rich and diverse anim
life, which together with its treme
dous size makes it one of the worl
great game reserves. Some 147 ma
mal species have been recorded (t
second-highest tally for any Afric
national park), including lion, leopa
cheetah, wild dog, spotted hyena, e
phant, black and white rhino, hipp
zebra, giraffe, warthog, buffalo and
antelope species.

The bird checklist of 517 species
particularly strong on raptors, alo
with several other large birds no
rare outside of protected areas, su
as ground hornbill, saddle-billed sto
and kori bustard. Of the other vert
brate classes, 114 reptile, 34 amphibi
and 49 fish species have been recorde
while the more conspicuous invert
brates include the dung beetle (oft
seen rolling elephant dung along th

road), a variety of butterflies, and – somewhat less endearing – significant numbers of mosquitoes in summer.

Most of Kruger's game is spread fairly evenly throughout the park, but the frequency of sightings will obviously be determined by topography and vegetation. Game densities are generally highest in the south and hippo, elephant, crocodile, buffalo and small herds of giraffe are often spotted around rivers and watering holes near camps such as **Skukuza**, **Pretoriuskop**, **Lower Sabie** and **Crocodile Bridge**.

The central parts, around Satara, Olifants and Letaba camps, are inhabited by large herds of antelope and zebra, which in turn attract the larger predators such as lion and cheetah.

Game spotting

In the north, around **Shingwedzi** and **Punda Maria**, large herds of elephant and buffalo are often spotted, as well as leopard and the elusive nyala.

Kruger is among the largest reserves in Africa, extending over 19,000 sq km (7,340 sq miles). The park's effective area has increased significantly over the past two decades, thanks to the dropping of fences with several private reserves, and the creation of **Great Limpopo Transfrontier Park**, which amalgamates Kruger with Gonarezhou in Zimbabwe and Mozambique's Limpopo National Park to cover a total area of 35,000 sq km (13,670 sq miles).

An important practical landmark in the development of the Transfrontier Park, the opening of the Giriyondo border post, 45km (28 miles) northeast of Letaba, in 2006 allows for direct access between the Kruger and Limpopo National Parks.

Although the park is served by an extensive network of roads and rest camps, this infrastructure barely affects the natural wildness. Some of the regulations governing activities may seem onerous, but they are directed mainly at the well-being of the wildlife. For example, the strictly enforced speed limit of 40km/h (25mph) on dirt roads and 50km/h (30mph) on surfaced roads is designed to limit the number of road kills (and wrecks) that might otherwise

Anopheles mosquito, the malaria carrier. Malaria kills more than a million people every year in Africa alone.

BELOW: white rhino, Kruger National Park.

A marker on the Jock of the Bushveld Road, a scenic 12km (8-mile) route through the Kruger National Park once used by transport riders such as Percy Fitzpatrick and his dog, Jock.

result from collisions between traffic and wildlife – in any event, even at these speeds it's difficult to spot well-camouflaged wildlife, and you'd see nothing if you went any faster.

Kruger practicalities

Eighteen national park rest camps are scattered around the park, varying in size and character, and all are bookable through the National Parks website. The larger camps have restaurants and in most cases also supermarkets, and all accommodation provides the option of self-catering using kitchens and/or open-air barbecues. Fuel is sold at the larger camps, and some even have ATM facilities and internet access. The five smallest camps – Boulders, Mopani, Jock of the Bushveld, N'wanetsi and Roodewaal – are strictly self-catering, accommodate up to 15 people and must be taken in their entirety by a single party. There are also four small bushveld camps without restaurant or shop facilities (which can provide an exciting experience of self-catered camping in the wild).

At the other extreme, the last decade has seen the opening of about a dozen private concessions within the park, all of which offer luxurious "bush" accommodation and an activities package similar to the private game reserves outside the park.

Coach tours are available, but game viewing from a private car is just as enjoyable – and you can go at your own pace. The best game-viewing is in the morning until about 10am and in the late afternoon. Camps open at dawn (ranging from 4.30am in mid-summer to 6.30am in winter) and it is well worth rising early to get the best sightings of predators, which are generally most active at this time of day. The sweltering midday hours are best spent enjoying a picnic at a waterhole, or in the camps, some of which have swimming pools.

Camp gates and park entrance gates close at sunset (6.30pm in summer and 5.30pm in winter) and late comers are fined. Frustratingly, this early closing time often means abandoning a game drive just when it holds most promise. However, night drives in special vehicles with knowledgeable driver-guides

are on offer in the larger camps.

The South African cognoscenti try to visit the park during the dry winter months of May to September, when temperatures are relatively moderate, mosquito activity (and the risk of contracting malaria) is very low and the thinner vegetation improves the odds of picking up predators. The very best time to visit is towards the end of the dry season, from August into early October, when the lack of any other standing water forces the wildlife to concentrate around perennial waterholes and rivers, where they can more easily be spotted.

Paradoxically, tourist numbers in the Kruger Park actually peak during the hot, wet summer months of October to April, which is favoured by international visitors as it's the best time to visit Cape Town and it coincides with the European winter. Fortunately, spring and summer are not without their attractions – the trees and flowers are at their best, bird life is abundant thanks to an influx of migratory species and many of the animals are nursing newborn young.

Wilderness hiking trails – where face-to-face encounters with big game are a real possibility – are conducted under the supervision of experienced rangers. Trails operate out of six base camps; they last three nights and two days, starting either on Sunday or Wednesday. The number of hikers on each trail is usually limited to 10, so book well in advance.

Southern Kruger

Most of the larger rest camps lie to the south of the Olifants River, which also forms the boundary between Mpumalanga and Limpopo provinces. **Orpen, Malelane** and **Crocodile Bridge** are entry-gate camps, used most often as a first base by visitors arriving shortly before the park gates close for the night. But don't let that put you off: the road between Orpen and Satara must rank as one of the very best for lion, spotted hyena and other large predator sightings, while the immediate vicinity of Crocodile Bridge is the most reliable part of the park for rhinos.

Deeper into the park, **Pretoriuskop** **A**, set in the thick acacia woodland of the southwest, is the oldest camp in the park, with a large and welcoming swimming pool – the surrounding roads are good for rhino and the localised sable antelope. **Skukuza B** is the biggest and busiest camp, a bustling village in its own right, but it also lies at the heart of some of the best game-viewing roads. The up-market, modern design of **Berg-en-Dal C** near the southern border of the park is quite unlike the traditional African rondavels of other camps. Set in a hilly landscape overlooking the Matjulu Dam, its extensive, well-fenced grounds are one of the few places where you can walk in the park and enjoy the flora at close quarters.

A firm favourite with many Kruger aficionados is **Lower Sabie D**, a relatively small camp set attractively on the banks of a dam on the Sabie River, in the heart of a prime viewing area. Elephants are numerous and can often

A hot-air balloon ride is a magnificent way to experience the landscape.

BELOW: sheltering from the midday sun.

Because the Kruger Park's population of elephants is culled every year, it has amassed a large ivory stockpile.

BELOW: buffalos at dawn.

be seen from the camp as they visit the Sabie River, or at the small water hole on the Skukuza Road about 1km (½ mile) from camp. The drive along the river towards Skukuza should reward you with sightings of buffalo and bushbuck. It can also be good for lion and leopard, and the opportunities for birdwatching are excellent. Unfortunately, this road also carries the densest traffic in the park – if it gets too much, try the quieter but often very rewarding road loop to and from Crocodile Bridge.

Further north, **Satara** ⓔ is a large camp set in the open savannah of the park's central region. Scenically, it's not very interesting, but several good game-viewing roads emanate from it, and cheetah and lion are regularly seen within a 10km (6-mile) radius of camp. Large seasonal concentrations of wildebeest and zebra may be seen on the road towards Nwanetsi, and if you have no intention of staying at the more northerly camps, then do try to fit in a day trip northwards as far as Olifants. The most northerly camp in Mpumalanga is the tiny but highly rec-

ommended **Balule** ⓕ, which consists of just ten huts and a similar number of campsites about 5km (3 miles) south of the Olifants River.

Northern Kruger

Unquestionably the most scenic of the Kruger camps, **Olifants** ⓖ is set on a high cliff overlooking the northern bank of the eponymous river. The game viewing from the comfort of the restaurants and public verandas here can be simply superb – ne'er was a river more aptly named than the Olifants (Elephants) – and the surrounding roads offer reliable game viewing.

Only 30km (18½ miles) further north, **Letaba** ⓗ is named after the meandering seasonal river upon whose southern bank it lies, and can also offer good in-house game viewing (elephants on the river, bushbuck in the riparian forest and some wonderful bird life in the shady fig trees). A speciality of this area is the uncommon roan antelope. Since 1993, the camp has housed an elephant exhibition that includes the 3 metre (10ft) long, 50-plus kg (100lb) tusks of the

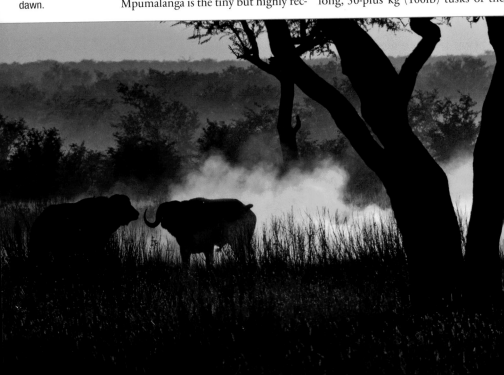

so-called Magnificent Seven – a group of immense bulls who roamed the area for decades before they died of old age in the 1980s.

Coming from the south, the area around Olifants and Letaba feels pretty quiet in terms of tourist traffic. Head further north still, into the part of the park that was first proclaimed in the 1920s, and things start to take on a genuine wilderness atmosphere – amazingly, only three public camps lie in the half of the park north of Letaba, with a combined bed space far smaller than that of Skukuza alone. **Mopani** ❶, the first camp you reach coming from Letaba, is one of the newest in the park, set in an area of dry mopane woodland that can offer rather indifferent game viewing, but it makes for a convenient overnight stop.

Far more reliable for wildlife is **Shingwedzi** ❶, a medium-to-small camp set attractively on the stretch of the eponymous river above the Kanniedood Dam. The best game drive here follows the river for about 10km (6 miles) south of the camp, through an area favoured by elephants, buffalo

and handsome male kudus, to the dam wall. The birdlife here is among the best in the park – look out for open-billed, yellow-billed and woolly-necked storks near the water, and the spectacular broad-billed roller in the riverine woodland. Further north still, **Punda Maria** is a small camp ideally placed to explore the superb and remote Pafuri game-viewing circuit on the Luvuvhu River near the Zimbabwe border. The camp also offers guided tours to **Thulamela Heritage Site**, where you can wander through the substantial ruins of a stone-wall royal village, built on a hilltop overlooking the south bank of the Luvuvhu in the 16th century, following the abandonment of Great Zimbabwe.

Kruger concessions

Nine private concessions, populated by a total of about 15 small exclusive camps and lodges, now operate within the Kruger. These concessions are tracts of land in which the concessionaire enjoys exclusive traversing rights, allowing them to offer a similar experience – centred on guided game

Intricate thatching on a traditional hut.

BELOW: view from Olifants camp.

*Elephants rarely use
the park's designated
crosswalks.*

drives in open 4x4s – to the private reserves discussed under the next heading.

As a rule, accommodation and guiding standards at the concession lodges is comparable to their counterparts at Sabi Sands, but animals tend to be less habituated to vehicles, so that game viewing is comparatively erratic. On the plus side, the concessions are much larger than most private reserves, they possess more of a wilderness feel, and guides focus less obsessively on chasing the Big Five based on radio alerts from other vehicles.

Among the more interesting concession lodges are the riverside Pafuri Camp and clifftop The Outpost *(see Travel Tips pages 344–5)*, both of which lie in **Makuleke Contractual Park**, a 235-sq-km (90-sq-mile) wedge of land bounded by the rivers Luvuvhu and Limpopo in the park's far north. The concession is named after the Makuleke people, who were forcibly evicted from their land when the apartheid government decided to incorporate it into the Kruger in 1969,

BELOW: on safari at
Mala Mala.

but regained it 30 years later in a successful land claim.

Instead of resettling, the Makuleke decided to develop the land for sustainable tourism by contracting game management to the national park authorities, and leasing two sites for lodge development. The most biodiverse and most tropical part of the Kruger, the area is legendary among South African birdwatchers thanks to the presence of rarities such as Pel's fishing owl, racket-tailed roller, crested guinea-fowl and triple-banded courser. Other sites of interest include notably the brooding fever tree forest at Crooks Corner (the confluence of the two rivers), the spectacular Lanner Gorge and Thulamela Heritage Site *(see page 289)*.

It is difficult to single out other concession lodges – they are all in the ballpark of superb – but a usefully located option for time-restricted visitors to the far south is **Lukimbi Safari Lodge**, *(see Travel Tips page 344)* only 25km (15 miles) from Malelane Gate, and with exclusive traversing rights across a 150-sq-km (58-sq-mile) tract of wilderness

that supports plentiful lion, elephant, black rhino and white rhino. For top-of-the-range quality and style, the two award-winning **Singita** lodges, set in a vast concession on the Lebombo foot-hills, are peerlessly chic.

Also highly recommended, albeit for more down-to-earth reasons, is **Rhino Walking Safaris** (*see Travel Tips page 345*), an unpretentious set-up whose main focus is foot safaris on a concession that shares a 15km (9-mile) unfenced boundary with MalaMala and Sabi Sands. Foot safaris are also the main activity at **Machampane Wilderness Trails**, which lies across the border in Mozambique's Limpopo National Park (daily pick-ups from Letaba rest camp are offered) and also offers an exciting selection of canoeing safaris on the Olifants River (*see Travel Tips pages 344–46*).

Private reserves bordering Kruger

In the 1970s, several drought-stricken cattle farms adjacent to southern Kruger were transformed into private game reserves, granting them a fresh lease of life that gained added impetus when fences with the national park were dropped in the 1990s, allowing wildlife to move freely between them.

The most famous and arguably best of these private entities is **Sabi Sand Game Reserve**, which abuts the Kruger north of Skukuza, and incorporates the iconic lodges of Londolozi, Singita and Sabi Sabi among others.

The largest individual private reserve, formerly part of Sabi Sands but now managed independently, **Mala Mala** boasts exclusive traversing rights over 130 sq km (50 sq miles) of prime wild-life territory with 20km (12 miles) of river frontage. Other top private reserves include Timbavati, Manyaleti, Thornybush and Kapama, the latter the only place in the region to offer elephant-back safaris.

The main experiential difference with the Kruger is that game viewing is exclusively undertaken on organised

drives in open 4x4 vehicles led by expe-rienced guides, who are allowed to go off-road for special sightings. Not only does this mean that more game is likely to be seen than in the Kruger itself (two or three nights in most private reserves comes with a near guarantee of seeing all the Big Five), but you also get to learn about animal behaviour, how to track spoor and how different spe-cies integrate into their environment. The less obvious things – trees, geol-ogy, small mammals and birds – are also shown and explained. Night drives are integral to the private game reserve experience and come with your best chance anywhere in Africa of spotting the elsewhere elusive leopard, along with other nocturnal oddities such as bushbaby, serval, genet and civet.

Lodges

Lodges in the private reserves all offer luxurious bush-style accommodation to go with the spectacular game-watch-ing and prices are generally on a par with five-star hotels, but then so is the service. In most cases, the wining and dining is world class, too, with dinner

The yellow-billed hornbill lives off a diet of seeds, insects, spiders and scorpions.

BELOW: Mala Mala lodge.

Chacma baboon and young.

BELOW: king of the beasts, Kapama Private Game Reserve.

often being eaten under the stars in a traditional *boma*, where guests can exchange their experiences of the day around the campfire.

One factor that will affect the quality of the experience is whether you are at a lodge that shares traversing rights with neighbouring reserves, or one that has exclusive use of its land – in the latter case, game drives can get a bit like a production line, as guides from different lodges wait in turn to join sightings they have picked up on the radio. From this perspective, Singita, Londolozi and MalaMala offer the most exclusive experiences in the region.

Baobab country

Upon exiting the Kruger's northerly Punda Maria or Pafuri gates, follow the R524 or R525 to connect with the N1, the 2,000km long highway that runs northeast from Cape Town to the Zimbabwe border post of **Beitbridge**. Spanning the Limpopo, Beitbridge is the only direct road link between South Africa and Zimbabwe, situated a few kilometres north of the rather dull little town of **Musina,** which is

rescued from visual anonymity by the impressive stands of baobab trees that surround it.

In medieval times, the Limpopo Valley lay at the centre of a wealthy empire that supplied gold, copper and ivory to Swahili merchants on the east African coast, following a set of ancient trade routes whose cultural and economic impact is only now beginning to be understood by historians.

The district is rich in archaeological relics, none more significant than Mapungubwe Hill, which lies near the confluence of the Limpopo and Shashi rivers in **Mapungubwe National Park** ⓬ (tel: 015-534 3545; www.sanparks.org; daily Sept–Mar 6am–6.30pm, Apr–Aug 6.30am–6pm; charge), some 75km (45 miles) west of Musina.

Proclaimed a World Heritage Site in 2003, the flat top of **Mapungubwe Hill** served as the royal capital in the 13th century, when some 5,000 people lived there, and it formed the precursor to the more impressive stone ruins of Great Zimbabwe to the north. Many interesting artefacts have been unearthed, among them a pair of

gold-plate rhino sculptures. Guided visits to the hill leave daily from the park headquarters and a network of internal roads offers great views over the Limpopo and the surrounding baobab-studded hills, as well as the opportunity to see large mammals such as elephant, kudu and klipspringer, as well as numerous birds.

Pontdrift border post, immediately west of Mapungubwe National Park, offers access to one of Southern Africa's best-kept game viewing secrets, the private **Mashatu Game Reserve** (tel 011-442 2267; www.mashatu.com; access to overnight visitors only), which forms part of the transfrontier Tuli Block. Although it lies within Botswana, Mashatu is most easily and commonly visited from the South African side, either directly by air, or by parking at the border post and then crossing the Limpopo on a hand drawn cable-car. Once there, guests enjoy an all-inclusive guided safari package similar to those on offer at the private reserves abutting Kruger, but with far less tourist traffic. The game viewing is superb: large herds of elephant haunt the sandy river beds, lion and leopard sightings are on a par with Sabi Sands, and there's no better place in southern Africa for wild dog sightings.

Land of the Rain Queen

About 100km (60 miles) along the N1 south of Musina, nondescript **Louis Trichardt**, named after an important Voortrekker leader, was officially known as Makhado from 2003 until 2007, when the name change was reversed by Supreme Court appeal. The area to the east of this is home to the Venda, skilled miners and masons possessing close historical and cultural links to the people of southern Zimbabwe.

Traditional rituals continue to survive in this remote area, where ancestral spirits guard many of the beautiful pools and forests. Most important of the holy places is **Lake Fundudzi** ⑬, which can be reached by road, or by following the four-day **Mabudashango Hiking Trail** through the sacred Thathe Vondo Forest, the burial place of many Venda chiefs, about 70km (42 miles) northeast of Louis Trichardt. Visitors to these holy forests and lakes

Duiwelskloof means devil's gorge – a reference to the hazards these muddy slopes posed to transport riders and wagon trains in the rainy season. Thankfully today conditions have now improved.

BELOW: view of the Waterberg massif.

The Rain Queen of Venda

The Modjadji, or Rain Queen, of Balobedu, the figure upon whom the adventure novelist Rider Haggard based the novel *She* (1887), is one of the few matrilineal rulers in southern Africa. A mysterious and remote figure, the Modjadji traditionally holds an annual rainmaking ceremony in her own compound every November, but otherwise she avoids public functions, communicating to the outside world only through a group of male councillors who also select suitable sexual partners to ensure her children are of pure royal lineage.

The origin of the Modjadji lineage is uncertain. Some oral sources date the dynasty to the 16th century, when the ancestral spirits of a chief in a drought-stricken part of present-day Zimbabwe told him that by impregnating his own daughter, he would create a child with rainmaking skills. The Modjadji is a hereditary title, passed on to the incumbent's eldest daughter upon her death. The popular fifth rain queen Mokope Modjadji ruled from 1981 to 2001, to be succeeded by her daughter Makobo, who died in mysterious circumstances aged 27 in 2005. Some observers fear that this premature loss will signal the end of the royal line, as Makobo's only daughter, Masalanabo, born four months before her death, is fathered by a commoner and may be regarded as ineligible when she comes of age.

should always take care to respect the beliefs of the local people, and swimming and washing in the lakes is forbidden.

About 100km (60 miles) southeast of Louis Trichardt, **Modjadjiskloof** (formerly Duiwelskloof) is the gateway to Balobedu, homeland of the Lobedu people, a Venda clan traditionally ruled by the Modjadji "Rain Queen" for whom the town is named *(see tint box page 293)*. Set within the the heart of Balobedu, the 5-sq-km (2-sq-mile) **Modjadji Nature Reserve**, home to several generations of Rain Queen, protects what is reputedly the world's largest concentration of cycads, odd prehistoric gymnosperms that date back to the age of dinosaurs. The Modjadji cycad, *Encephalartos transvenosus*, endemic to Limpopo Province, is one of the giants of the genus, growing up to 12 metres (40ft) tall and bearing cones that weigh up to 35 kilograms (70lb).

The well-wooded slopes around **Tzaneen**, 20km (12 miles) south of Modjadjiskloof, form the northernmost reaches of the same escarpment as the

Panorama Route. The showpiece this area is the spectacularly beautif **Magoebaskloof**, set in the lush indig nous forest that covers the slopes of th Wolkberg Range. An enchanting 3k (2-mile) walk through the forests fro the main road brings you to **Debege Falls**, which tumble about 25 metr (80ft) into a deep, pot-like natur swimming pool. This is also a prospe ous fruit-farming region; tea and tir ber plantations are abundant, too.

The 52-sq-km (20-sq-mile) **Ha Merensky Nature Reserve**, which li on the southern banks of the Gro Letaba River about 70km (43 mile east of Tzaneen, has plentiful gam including zebra, warthog, giraffe an various antelope, and walking is pe mitted due to the absence of dange ous game. Also of interest within th reserve is the **Tsonga Kraal Open A Museum** that displays the Tsonga w of life and where craftsmen demor strate their arts.

THE BUSHVELD

Heading south from the Venda are in the direction of Pretoria, the N

is flanked by of hot, yellow plains – classic cattle-ranching country. Some 112km (70 miles) south of Louis Trichardt, you pass through plain, dusty **Polokwane ⓯**, capital of Limpopo Province, then about 70km (45 miles) further comes nondescript **Mokopane**; while pressing on a further 90km (56 miles) through sleepy Mookgophong (formerly Naboomspruit) brings you to the agricultural settlement of **Modimolle ⓰** (formerly Nylstroom).

The birdlife around Modimolle is among the richest in South Africa, in terms of both numbers and variety. The little **Nylsvley Nature Reserve ⓱** (tel: 014-743 1074; www.nylsvley.co.za; daily 6am–6pm; charge) conserves some of the marshland 16km (10 miles) north of the town. This key wetland attracts more than 400 species of bird, notably one of the greatest concentrations of waterfowl in South Africa, and 70 mammal species are present in the reserve.

Aeons ago, the Great Rift Valley in East Africa cracked open, pumping masses of molten rock southwards and eventually creating the Igneous Bush-

veld Complex – today regarded as one of the world's richest mineral areas. Traces of these ancient seismic events are still evident around the town of **Bela Bela**, founded near the largest of several hot mineral springs which erupt from the flat savannah.

Driving along the N1, it's impossible to ignore the distant mountain massif on the western horizon. This is the Waterberg, an isolated mountain range long used for cattle ranching which has only recently opened up to tourism. Various ranches offer horse-riding safaris and other kinds of activity holiday, and there are also three luxurious private reserves within the **Lapalala Wilderness Area** (tel: 014-755 4395; www.lapalala.com), some 130km (80 miles) from Modimolle. Nearby **Marakele National Park** (tel: 014-777 6929; www.sanparks.org) has been restocked with indigenous game and is now home to the world's largest breeding colony of endangered Cape vultures as well as elephant and both black and white rhino; the rich diversity of plant species includes the rare Waterberg cycad.   ❏

The southern tree agama has a distinctive cobalt blue head.

BELOW: Cape vultures.

The Bulbous Baobab

African legend has it that in a light-hearted moment, the gods planted the first baobab upside down. Yet the role of these monster trees is more important than their weird shape suggests. Because their fibrous wood allows them to store huge volumes of water, they can offer critical relief in times of drought – to humans as well as animals. This perpetual supply of water ensures an abundance of leaves every spring, providing both shade and nourishment to animals and insects alike. The soft, well-insulated stems are ideal for hole-nesting birds such as barbets and hornbills. After these have been vacated, the nests are often re-employed as beehives, or retreats for snakes and lizards, so that every baobab is always abuzz with the comings and goings of its many residents. People of the Limpopo River Valley attribute fertility properties to the fruits, filled with seeds embedded in a refreshing white "cream-of-tartar" pulp; rock paintings in the region often portray women with baobab fruits instead of breasts.

Baobabs can live for 3,000–4,000 years. When they die, the end is swift and dramatic. After a few months, the ancient fibres completely disintegrate and the tree simply collapses in on itself, disappearing so suddenly that it was once thought that baobabs ignited spontaneously and burned away.

TWO ROUTES TO CAPE TOWN

Two overland routes from Johannesburg to
Cape Town – a journey from vast, sunburned plains
to fertile valleys graced with historic wine farms

Few tourists undertake the long overland trek through the interior between South Africa's two largest cities. And understandably so. The most direct route, the N1 via Bloemfontein, entails a daunting 1,400km (875-mile) drive through a landscape of open farmland and semi-desert that has its apologists but offers limited opportunities for sightseeing, and the same might be said for the slightly longer deviation along the N12 via Kimberley. But while the most efficient route between Johannesburg and Cape Town is undoubtedly the aerial one, the long drive along the N1 and N12 will hold some appeal for lovers of wide open spaces, or road movies – with the historic cities of Kimberley and Bloemfontein and more southerly Karoo National Park offering worthwhile stops en route.

Open horizons

For those with time to spare and a love of open horizons, a third inland road route between Gauteng and Cape Town is also worth considering. True, the N14 and N7, which run via Springbok through the arid heart of the thinly populated Northern Cape, won't hold out much appeal to agoraphobics, or to visitors seeking the sort of tropical beach nirvanas that proliferate on the east coast. Furthermore, advocates of the N12/7 who bang on about it being only 200km (120 miles) longer than the N1 are begging the question somewhat, since it would scarcely be worth undertaking this additional mileage unless you also made a few diversions that would double the total driving distance and require at least a week, and better, 10 days to complete. Make that commitment, however, and you'll be amply rewarded. The Northern Cape accounts for almost one-third of South Africa's surface area, but supports less

Main attractions
KIMBERLEY'S BIG HOLE
KAROO NATIONAL PARK
KGALAGADI TRANSFRONTIER PARK
AUGRABIES FALLS NATIONAL PARK
RICHTERSVELD NATIONAL PARK
NAMAQUALAND

PRECEDING PAGES AND RIGHT: Karoo National Park. **LEFT:** statue of Boer Christiaan de Wet, Bloemfontein.

Kimberley's Big Hole, once the world's richest diamond mine.

than 5 percent of the national population; its wide-open spaces and perennial blue skies are possessed of an austere beauty and spirit-enriching tranquillity that reaches its apex in the fantastic granite moonscapes of Augrabies Falls National Park and the soulful red dunefields of the remote Kgalagadi Transfrontier Park on the Namibia/Botswana border.

ROUTE ONE: BLOEMFONTEIN

Travelling southwards from Johannesburg along the N1 for about 300km (180 miles) brings you to the turn-off to the 120-sq-km (47-sq-mile) **Willem Pretorius Game Reserve** (tel: 057-

651 4003; daily 6am–6pm), which lies between the identikit highveld towns of Kroonstad and Winburg. This underrated reserve harbours the largest extant herd of black wildebeest (some 600), as well as introduced populations of giraffe, buffalo and white rhino. The **Allemanskraal Dam** extends over about one-fifth of the reserve's surface area when full, and many of the 220 recorded bird species can be seen in its vicinity. Boat trips are organised and the fishing is good.

Heading further south along the N1 for another 100km (60 miles) or so, you'll reach **Bloemfontein ❶** – or more accurately a series of off-ramps that lie a few kilometres northwest of the city centre. The long-serving capital of Free State Province, Bloemfontein means

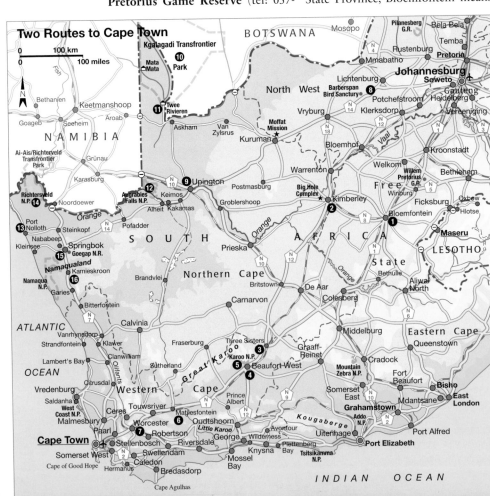

Two Routes to Cape Town

"spring of flowers", a name which dates back to 1840 when the Voortrekker Johannes Nicolaas Brits built his *hartbeeshuisie* (a simple thatched dwelling with a dung floor) here, at the site of a spring encircled by clover. Today it forms part of the Municipality of Mangaung (a seSotho name meaning "Place of the Cheetah").

Bloemfontein briefly served as capital of the Old Republic of the Free State before it was occupied by the British forces of Lord Roberts during the Anglo-Boer War (1899–1902). The occupation was a mixed blessing. The descendants of the Voortrekkers, who had braved the dangers of the wild unknown to escape the British Empire, had nothing but contempt for the Union Jack hoisted over their town. But British occupancy protected the town from the ravages of war, ensuring that its architectural heritage remained well preserved as it is to this day.

Anglo-Boer War

For a better understanding of the war and its background, the excellent **Anglo-Boer War Museum** (tel: 051-

447 3447; www.anglo-boer.co.za; Mon–Fri 8am–4.30pm, Sat 10am–5pm, Sun 11am–5pm; charge) stands alongside the National Women's Monument, which was unveiled in 1913 to commemorate the Boer women who died in British concentration camps.

Stroll down **President Brand Street**, which is widely regarded as one of South Africa's most beautiful streets. Most of the historic buildings are open to the public apart from the **Fourth Raadsaal**, once the parliamentary building of the Boer's Orange Free State Republic and now the provincial legislature. The Old Government Building on the corner of President Brand and Maitland streets houses the **Afrikaans Literature Museum** (tel: 051-405 4034; Mon–Fri 8am–4pm, Sat 9am–1pm; free), with displays on all the leading lights of Afrikaans literature from the brilliant Eugene N. Marais *(see page 80)* to anti-apartheid novelist André Brink. Continue down to the corner of St Georges Street to

Bloemfontein's imposing City Hall.

BELOW: friendly faces in Bloemfontein.

Statue at the entrance to Bloemfontein's Anglo-Boer War Museum.

BELOW: the Supreme Court of Appeal, Bloemfontein.

reach the **Old Presidency** (tel: 051-448 0949; Mon–Fri 8am–3pm; free), and the **First Raadsaal** (tel: 051-447 9609; Mon–Fri 10am–1pm, Sat–Sun 2–5pm; free), the city's oldest surviving building.

The British side to Bloemfontein often surprises visitors – the Free State is, after all, an Afrikaner heartland. Yet sites such as **Naval Hill** and **Queen's Fort** (Mon–Fri), as well as the Edwardian Ramblers cricket ground with its Edwardian clubhouse, preserve the colonial heritage. Bloemfontein also holds a very significant place in black South African history, for this was the birthplace in 1912 of the South African Native National Congress – known after 1923 as the African National Congress, or ANC.

Diamond country

Situated some 470km (295 miles) southwest of Johannesburg along the N12, **Kimberley** ❷ is also accessible from Bloemfontein following the almost dead straight 150km (90-mile) N8 along a road bordered by vast sun-flower fields. Kimberley is distinctly past its prime; indeed, when you consider that this was the country's fastest-growing town in the 1870s, its present-day atmosphere of somnolence is astonishing. Unfortunately for modern residents of Kimberley, their hometown's former prosperity was based entirely on diamonds, the supply of which petered out in the 1930s. The local economy has been boosted considerably since Kimberley was chosen over Upington as the capital of the Northern Cape, despite lying right on the eastern border of this vast province.

Whether it's worth making a special effort to visit Kimberley is debatable, but passers-through will find that the partially open-air **Big Hole Complex** (Tucker Street; tel: 053-830 4417; www.thebighole.co.za; daily 8am–5pm; charge) does a good job of reincarnating the city as it looked in its colourful heyday. Here you can see a collection of 40 reconstructed buildings such as Barney Barnato's Boxing Academy and the Diggers' Tavern, along with a private railway coach, custom-built for

the directors of the all-powerful De Beers mining group. You'll also find an exquisite collection of uncut stones here, along with a copy of the largest diamond in the world (616 carats). The museum also includes a viewing platform over the Big Hole, the source of all the stones in on display here. As you survey the 800-metre (2,600ft) deep, 470-metres (1,500ft) wide hole, its base now filled with water, its towers derelict, it is incredible to think that this giant gash in the earth yielded some 2,722kg (5,988lbs) of diamonds between 1871 and 1914.

In the city centre lies an unexpected treat – the **William Humphreys Art Gallery** (tel: 053-831 1724; www.whag.co.za; Mon–Fri 8am–4.45pm, Sat 10am–4.45pm, Sun 2–4.45pm; charge), which contains one of South Africa's best collections of 16th- and 17th-century Flemish and Dutch Old Masters as well as South African works. On the eastern edge of town you'll find the wealthy suburb of Belgravia, where the diamond barons built their grand houses on Lodge Road. A very different relict of the city's diamond-mining

days is housed in the **Duggan-Cronin Gallery** (tel: 053-842 0099; Mon–Sat 9am–1pm, daily 2–5pm; donations requested) on Egerton Road. Exhibits include a collection of photographs of mine labourers taken between 1919–39 by Alfred Duggan-Cronin, a nightwatchman for De Beers.

Outside Kimberley on the Barkley West Road is the **Wildebeest Kuil Rock Art Centre** (tel: 053-833 7069; www.wildebeestkuil.itgo.com; Mon–Fri 9am–4pm, Sat–Sun 10am–4pm; charge), where several prehistoric rock engravings of animals can be admired in-situ. The self-guided tour includes a 25-minute introductory film and short walking trail with 10 listening posts providing audio commentary.

The Central Karoo

Southwest of Kimberley and Bloemfontein, the N12 and N1 run roughly parallel to each other for approximately 550km (330 miles), passing through an eastern extension of Northern Cape Province, before finally they converge at Three Sisters on the border with Western Cape Province. Once little

BELOW: you can hitch a ride on this old train at the Kimberley Mine Museum.

Many old farmsteads in the Karoo have been abandoned during hard times.

BELOW: Beaufort West, "Capital of the Karoo".

more than a dot on the map, **Three Sisters** ❸ – which is named after a nearby trio of dolerite-capped hills – is now distinguished by one of those one-stop garage/supermarket/fast-food complexes that punctuate the highways of South Africa, and the first opportunity to stretch your legs and refuel you'll have had in a while.

Land of the Great Thirst

Three Sisters lies in the heart of the Great Karoo, the name of which derives from a San phrase meaning "Land of the Great Thirst". For most visitors – and even for South Africans – these wide, rocky plains are often seen as a natural obstacle, something to overcome en route to the lush winelands or frenetic Gauteng. Yet the Karoo's bleakness has a beauty all its own. Dotted with flat-topped *koppies* (hills), it is somehow reminiscent of the South Dakota badlands; a spaghetti-western setting enhanced at sunset when the *koppies* – peculiarly light-sensitive –

change colour from warm red and ochre to purple and blue. At night the cool, clear air tempts you outside to gaze at the brilliant stars of the southern hemisphere.

The origin of the Karoo is still a mystery. It is known that the soft sandstone and shales here were created some 200 million years ago, when vast quantities of mud, clay and sand were first washed into the low-lying, marshy Karoo basin. As the climate gradually warmed, the area was invaded by an ocean, trapping the remains of a temperate forest and creating significant deposits of coal, which are now mined in the northern part of the system. The entire sequence was capped some 130 million years ago by a massive volcanic outpouring of basalt lava. The softer sandstone layers underneath gradually eroded, while the hard volcanic dolerite remained, creating those characteristic flat-topped hills.

It is ironic that what was once a gigantic freshwater swamp is today drought-stricken and almost devoid of surface water. Rainfall is quite unpredictable – when it does rain, torrents

fall in fierce thunderstorms, often causing destruction and erosion as the water cascades into normally dry water beds. Keep an eye out for that trademark of the Karoo, its creaking wind pumps. This ingenious but simple contraption forms the backbone of the region's economy. Erected at a borehole and then left to its own devices, the wind pump continuously churns up water from deep underground into drinking troughs for livestock.

Beaufort West

About 75km (45 miles) southwest of Three Sisters lies the self-styled "Capital of the Karoo", the small town of **Beaufort West ❹**, whose dry climate once made it a popular winter holiday resort for asthmatic and otherwise wheezy Capetonians. Those days are long gone, but Beaufort West is still studded with its fair share of guesthouses and hotels, most of them rather modest crash pads geared towards tired Capebound motorists. In the town itself you can visit three neo-Gothic churches and the **Town Hall** (daily), built in 1867. A wing of the latter is now a museum, which includes in its exhibits a section dedicated to the town's most famous son, the pioneering heart surgeon Dr Christiaan Barnard.

Beaufort West lies at the hub of a rich farming district known primarily for its merino sheep, a breed that was first brought to the country from the Netherlands in 1789. Today, more than 35 million of the animals graze on a diet of semi-desert shrubs, herbs and succulents, which creates the utterly distinctive taste of Karoo mutton – well worth trying should you decide to stop over for lunch or dinner in the area.

Comparatively more interesting than Beaufort West itself is the **Karoo National Park ❺** (tel: 023-415 2828; www.sanparks.org; daily 5am–10pm; charge), the main entrance to which lies about 5km (3 miles) west of town along the N1. Established in 1979, the park covers almost 33,000 hectares (81,500 acres). Early hunters and explorers recounted tales of a land

Self-catering chalets in Karoo National Park.

BELOW LEFT: monument commemorating the foundation of the South African Republic, Beaufort West. **BELOW RIGHT:** Karoo National Park.

The Fossil Trail in Karoo National Park provides a fascinating insight into the region's geological history.

where thick swathes of grass stood shoulder-high and where the teeming herds of springbok were so huge that wagons had to be unharnessed for two or three days to allow the herd to pass by. But "civilisation" brought with it hunters and guns and ploughs and fences and fires. Two animal species – the zebra-like quagga and the bluebok antelope – were shot to extinction, and other herds were decimated and driven into the remotest regions of the arid interior. Today, nature reserves like the Karoo National Park are trying their utmost to preserve some of that fauna and its typical Karoo habitat.

Park life

The park currently supports large numbers of antelope, including an estimated 1,500 oryx, 1,400 red hartebeest and 700 kudu, along with springbok, klipspringer and smaller predators such as caracal, black-backed jackal and African wild cat. A unique feature is the great concentration of tortoises, of which the world's largest and smallest species can both be spotted here – these are the leopard tortoise, which weighs in at 45kg (100lb), and *Homopus s. signatus* (Namaqualand speckled padloper), which is just 100mm (3ins) long and weighs 150 grams (5oz). The park also forms the major stronghold for the riverine rabbit, an endangered Karoo-specific species that's now thought to number just 1,500 in the wild. The successful introduction of eight lions in 2010 represents the first step in transforming this oft-neglected park to a Big Five safari destination, and elephant, buffalo and rhino are likely to follow within the next few years.

In spring, the dusty landscape is covered with a colourful carpet of wildflowers. This is a particularly rewarding time to tackle the demanding three-day 27km (17-mile) **Springbok Hiking Trail**, which closes between November and February because of the excessive heat, (and may well close on a more permanent basis if the park becomes a Big Five reserve). If you prefer to restrict your walking tour to just a few hours, you can undertake an excursion into prehistory along the **Fossil Trail**, where fossilised remains over 50 million years

old can be seen. The path is also suitable for the blind and for those in wheelchairs.

Scheduled to open on a 200 hectare site off the R61 outside Beaufort West in 2011, the **Biggest Painting in the World** (www.biggestpainting.com) will be an immense collage of one million paintings from all 54 African countries as well as from communities of African descent elsewhere in the world. The site will also include villages representing various African cultures, as well as outlets for local art and music, and a variety of food and drinks.

Continuing southwest for some 240km (150 miles), the N1 skirts **Matjiesfontein ❻**, a lovely little Victorian town that has been declared a National Monument in its entirety. An enterprising Scotsman, Jimmy Logan, was the first to make profitable use of the railway station here, a refilling point for steam locomotives about to embark on the long haul north to Pretoria through the parched Karoo. It wasn't long before he was supplying the trains with water and the passengers with cold drinks and hot lamb chops. Logan's business prospered to such an extent that he was soon able to build the elegant **Lord Milner Hotel**. You can still spend the night here if you wish, and the Karoo lamb still tastes as good as it did in Logan's times.

During the Boer Wars the little town was a British garrison and the hotel served as a military hospital, with a lookout post in the tower. Today, Matjiesfontein is a popular stopover on the route between Johannesburg and Cape Town; the famous luxury Blue Train also pulls in here.

About 100km (60 miles) past Matjiesfontein, the N1 leaves the Karoo to cross the Hex River Pass and descend into the strikingly different landscape of green mountains and cultivated river valleys that characterise the southwestern Cape. Another 30km (18 miles) brings you to the champion winelands centre of **Worcester ❼**, from where you can either head straight on to Cape Town, some 80km (55 miles) distant, or divert towards the Boland and wine-production centres such as **Stellenbosch** or **Franschhoek** (*see Winelands pages 176–180*).

TIP

Matjiesfontein is a little Victorian gem. Keep a look out for items such as lampposts – shipped all the way from London.

BELOW: park warden.

The crescent-shaped pods of the camel thorn tree are a valuable source of food for many species of animal in the Kgalagadi Transfrontier Park.

BELOW: camel thorn tree, Kgalagadi Transfrontier National Park

ROUTE TWO: TOWARDS UPINGTON

The otherwise memorable journey from Gauteng to Cape Town through the heart of the Northern Cape starts less than auspiciously with a 350km (210-mile) haul west along the N14 to **Vryburg**. The only attraction of note along this flat stretch of road is **Barberspan Bird Sanctuary ❽** (tel: 053-948 1854; www.tourismnorthwest.co.za; daily 6am–7pm; charge), an important wetland that flanks the northern side of the N14 between Sannieshof and Delarayville and often harbours flocks of up to 20,000 flamingos as well as large numbers of other water birds.

As for Vryburg (Afrikaans for "Freetown"), it started life as the capital of a breakaway Boer Republic called Stellaland in 1882 – and nothing much of note seems to have happened there since that republic was disbanded three years later.

Some 150km (90 miles) further west,

the pretty town of **Kuruman** owes its existence to the large freshwater spring that empties a remarkable 50,000 litres (227,000 gallons) of crystal-clear water daily into a lily-covered, tree-fringed pool in the town centre. The **Moffat Mission** (tel: 053-712 2645; Mon–Sat 8am–5pm; charge), which lies 6km (4 miles) from Kuruman along the Hotazel Road, was established in 1821 by the Scots missionary Robert Moffat. Oddly reminiscent of a misplaced English village, the mission is centred on the attractive stone church – built in 1838 and still in active use – where Moffat's daughter Mary married a budding young explorer named David Livingstone.

Upington

Situated on the N14 roughly 260km (155 miles) southwest of Kuruman – about 8–10 hours' drive from Gauteng if you're thinking of pushing through in one day – **Upington ❾** is the second-largest town in the Northern Cape after Kimberley, and (although it probably receives fewer international tourists annually than Table Mountain would

on a quiet day) it is also an important regional tourist centre.

Direct flights from Cape Town or Johannesburg shorten the journey here considerably; if you're planning to head off into the Kalahari, this is a good place to rent a four-wheel-drive vehicle, or even a mobile home. At the entrance to the Eiland Holiday Resort there's an impressive 1,041-metre (3,415ft) long date-palm avenue – indeed, coming after the increasingly arid landscapes passed through on the N14, much of Upington feels unexpectedly green and leafy, thanks to its location on the banks of the Orange River, the country's largest waterway.

Kgalagadi Transfrontier Park

The remote, immense and utterly absorbing **Kgalagadi Transfrontier Park ❿** (tel: 054-561 2000; www.sanparks.org; daily dawn–dusk; charge) was created in 1999 when South Africa's 9,600-sq-km (3,750-sq-mile) Kalahari Gemsbok National Park merged with its larger but less-accessible cross-border counterpart, the Gemsbok National

Park in Botswana. Characterised by red sand dunes interspersed with sandy river beds, Kgalagadi is strikingly reminiscent of Australia's Simpson Desert, but with a more varied fauna, including all three of Africa's large felines as well as an impressive selection of smaller predators such as black-backed jackal, bat-eared fox (very visible in winter when it is more diurnal), Cape fox, caracal, suricate and yellow mongoose.

The only entrance to the park, and the site of the largest camp, is at **Twee Rivieren ⓫** (Two Rivers), which lies close to the confluence of the Auob and Nossob rivers – or, more normally, river beds, since the Auob might go three or four years without flowing, and the Nossob several decades. It's the rainwater that collects beneath the light sand of the river beds that ensures the vegetation along them is relatively lush, attracting surprisingly large concentrations of wildlife. It's not unusual to witness a cheetah running down a springbok along the Nossob's dry bed, or a large herd of handsome oryx with their rapier horns silhouetted against a sky bruised by thunderclouds. Heavily

The swallow-tailed bee-eater has an unmistakeable forked tail.

BELOW: jackal on the prowl in Kgalagadi Transfrontier Park.

maned Kalahari lions escape the mid-day heat beneath thorn bushes, while brilliantly spotted leopards take refuge in the tall camel thorn trees.

The park's 280 bird species are sure to impress most visitors – highlights include the brilliant swallow-tailed bee-eater and the noisy but sometimes elusive crimson-breasted shrike, while a wide array of raptors is most visibly represented by Bateleur, pale chanting goshawk and the shrike-sized pygmy falcon. The large camel thorn trees (*Acacia erioloba*) that define the river's course are the life-giving source of the region, providing nesting sites for sociable weavers and the many other birds, and offering shade to game and domestic stock. The tree's large crescent-shaped pods also make for nutritious food when they fall. The gum is eaten by animals and used in traditional medicine by local communities. Giraffes, which were reintroduced to the park in the late 1990s after several decades absence, can wrap their long prehensile tongues around the thorny branches and strip the leaves with seeming immunity to the cruel spikes.

The best time of the year to visit is between February and April, at least that is the case in years with a good amount of rainfall, as large herds of game concentrate along the river beds (don't forget to protect yourself against the pesky mosquitoes who also thrive on the damp environment). Some, however, might prefer the cooler winter months of June to September, when daytime temperatures are generally comfortable to warm, but the nights are very cold. The month of May would be an excellent compromise. Accommodation in the park is sometimes booked solid well in advance (booking 13 months in advance is normal).

Main camp

The relatively comfortable main camp is located at Twee Rivieren, but you can also spend the night at **Mata Mata Camp** (118km/73 miles to the northwest, after a particularly attractive trip), located not far from the Namibian border which is, however, closed at that point. **Nossob Camp**, 152km (94 miles) to the north and on the border with Botswana, is less attractive. There

are now also several unfenced wilderness camps in the park, of which Grootkolk and Bitterpan each consist of just four double chalets apiece and overlook a water hole.

The closest town and normal springboard for visits is **Upington**, from where a bizarrely quiet 190km (114-mile) surfaced road leads through some impressive dunes to Askham, after which it's 60km (100 miles) on dirt to Twee Rivieren. Coming from Johannesburg, a more direct route runs north from Kuruman through Van Zylsrus, but this involves 358km (222 miles) of manoeuvring on dirt roads. Either route is do-able in an ordinary saloon car, provided you drive sensibly, but the Van Zylsrus route is exhausting and, without suitable experience, there's a real risk of losing control of the vehicle or getting stuck in the sand. Whichever route you use, leave in time to get there before the gate closes.

The Orange River

Back in Upington, the N14 continues westward along the banks of the **Orange River** (also sometimes known by its old Nama name "Gariep"), which dominates the entire region as it makes its inexorable way to the Atlantic Ocean like a giant serpent. Carrying almost a quarter of the volume of South Africa's entire river system, the 2,000km (1,240-mile) long Orange is the life-giving source of the entire region.

The tiny **Tierberg Nature Reserve** (daily; free) on the outskirts of **Keimos**, 50km (30 miles) west of Upington, offers a good view over the river and surrounding cultivated area, and also contains some excellent specimens of the striking kokerboom (quiver tree), a type of tree aloe whose bark was used by the San to make quivers for their arrows.

Just past Kakamas, 40km (24 miles) west of Keimos, a side road branches north from the N14 and follows the bank of the Orange River to **Augrabies Falls National Park** ⑫ (Apr–Sept 6.30am–7.30pm, Oct–Mar 7.30am–5pm; charge; tel: 054-452 9200; www.sanparks.org). Here, overlooked by a gem of a rest camp, the Orange thunders spectacularly over a 56-metre (185ft) cliff into a deep gorge carved

Striped ground squirrel feeding.

BELOW: Augrabies Falls National Park.

Orange River Wines

Artificially irrigated vineyards and orchards line the Orange River valley between Upington and Kakamas, and the green river banks, cultivated with cotton, fruit and grapes, stand in stark contrast to the arid surrounds.

The region is famous for its sultanas, and it produces many of the table grapes exported from South Africa to Europe. It is also South Africa's most remote winelands, dominated by the massive Orange River Cellars co-operative (tel: 054-337 8800; www.orangeriverwines.com), which has cellars in Upington, Keimos and Kakamas. The local dessert wines and sherries are justly celebrated, and there's an ever-improving range of dry whites and reds too. Tasting hours in all three cellars are Mon–Fri 8am–5pm, Sat 8.30am–noon; Sun 9am–noon.

TIP

Refuse offers from locals who offer to sell you cheap diamonds. Not only are they trading illegally but the stones often turn out to be worthless lead crystal.

out of the granite bedrock. Crashing down a further 35 metres (115ft) over a series of secondary falls and cataracts, the water sends a vast column of spray into the air, enveloping the area in a heavy mist. Two large pools at the base of the falls are thought to be at least 130 metres (425 ft) deep and contain a great wealth in diamonds carried from the vicinity of Kimberley and washed over the edge – unfortunately, it is difficult to explore or extract the gems from underneath a waterfall.

The park contains a great deal more than just the waterfall. Colourful Cape flat lizards bask conspicuously around the rocky rest camp, from where you can wander or drive along a small road network and see springbok, klipspringer, rock hyrax and a variety of dry-country birds. The route to Arrow Point is particularly recommended; there's a great view from here over two canyons simultaneously. More ambitiously, the popular three-day **Klipspringer Hiking Trail** (40km/23 miles) is almost always booked solid during school holidays, and it closes during the extreme heat of summer.

Night drives and black rhino tours to otherwise inaccessible parts of the park can be booked at the rest camp – as can white water rafting excursions along an 8km (5-mile) long stretch of river with five sets of grade 2–3 rapids.

The Diamond Coast

From Kakamas, a lonely 250km (150-mile) trip along the N14 leads via **Pofadder** – a good place to stop for petrol and a cold drink, to the medium-sized town of **Springbok** at the junction of the N7 between Cape Town and Namibia. Here, you'll most probably want to head south, towards Cape Town. but it's also possible to follow the N7 northwards to Steinkopf (52km/32 miles) and turn onto the asphalt-surfaced R382 leading over the 950 metre (3,100ft) high Annienous Pass, down to the coast and **Port Nolloth ⓭**. The biggest attraction here is the sunsets – utterly magnificent when they aren't obscured by rising sea fog. Port Nolloth used to be a copper port, but today the primary source of income is fishing – and not just for crayfish, either. Diamonds are

BELOW: windmills still power many of the country's farms.

West Coast Diamonds

Diamonds were discovered near Port Nolloth almost by accident when a British officer, Captain Jack Carstens, undertook an exploratory dig while visiting his parents there in 1926. The geologist Hans Merensky later claimed to have found 487 diamonds under one stone, and in a single month he recovered 2,762 diamonds near Alexander Bay. As the news spread, fortune-seekers descended on the area in droves, prompting the government to ban private prospecting. Today, the coast between Kleinsee and Oranjemund is controlled by De Beers Consolidated Mining Company – founded by Cecil John Rhodes in 1880 – and the public isn't allowed off the main road.

This stretch of coast is continually worked over and shifted by the world's largest armada of earth-moving equipment and a vast wealth of diamonds is recovered each year. The desert-besieged fishing and diamond towns of the northwest coast are still real frontier places and the only resorts are to be found much further south at Strandfontein near the Olifants River mouth and at the Port Nolloth extension, McDougall's Bay. These are rudimentary places as resorts go, catering almost exclusively for fishermen and the rough-and-ready local sheep-farming communities. If there is such a place as the end of the line, then Port Nolloth is surely it.

sucked off the seabed here in large quantities by giant vacuum cleaner-like devices. On its journey past Kimberley, the Orange River gathers up diamond-rich sediments before spewing its precious load up and down the Northern Cape coastline, thus creating the world's richest deposits of alluvial diamonds.

From Alexander Bay, an unsurfaced road leads to the **Richtersveld National Park** ⓫ (tel: 027-831 1506; www.sanparks.org; Oct–Apr 7am–7pm, May–Sept 7am–6pm; charge), which amalgamated with its Namibian counterpart in 2003 to form the Ai-Ais/Richtersveld Transfrontier Park. Richtersveld is a wild and remote semi-desert region that was accessible to campers only prior to 2005, when a self-catering rest camp was built. Winter is the only time it rains here, and in summer the temperature can rise to an unbearable 50°C (122°F). It's hard to believe that so much grows in such a harsh environment, but the diversity of succulents here is so rich that botanists are struggling to get them all classified and described.

Namaqualand

Back on the N7, **Springbok** ⓯ is the principal town of a vast region of sandveld known as Namaqualand, which extends northwards from the Olifants River as far as Pofadder, and is renowned for its spring wildflower displays. For most of the year, these stony plains cannot hide the wrinkles and cracks of their age-old skin, or the tattiness of their drab green-grey cover. But come spring, fields burst forth in colours gay and dazzling. Nature favours these semi-arid scrublands with one youthful flush of wildflowers that draws people from all over the world for a few days in August or September each year. Indeed, the daisies of Namaqualand are one of South Africa's greatest natural attractions.

Springbok owes its existence to the rich copper reserves in the region (some mines are open to the public), and to something much rarer round here: a spring of fresh water. The big attraction, however is the **Goegap Nature Reserve** (daily 8am–4pm; charge), about 15km (9 miles) to the east. It is absolutely stunning during

The yellow mongoose is widespread throughout southern Africa.

BELOW: Oryx grazing, Namaqualand.

The bark of the quiver tree was used by the San people to make quivers for their arrows.

the flowering season, and worth a visit even outside that time of year. In the Hester Malan Wild Flower Garden, which forms part of the reserve, you can admire over a hundred species of aloes and succulents, many of which are indigenous to the area. It's a 17km (10-mile) long round trip if you decide to explore the reserve in your own car, but it's actually more rewarding to book the three-hour guided tour when you arrive; it will take you to more remote and exciting corners. Caracal, oryx, springbok and South Africa's only population of Hartmann's mountain zebra are just a few of the animals you may encounter.

Wildflower show

The Namaqualand wildflower extravaganza lasts for only a short time each year and never erupts in the same place all at once, so make sure you listen to the weather forecast before you plan your trip (Cape Town flower hotline: 083-910 1028) and bear in mind there are no flowers without rain. One of

the most reliable sites for wildflowers is **Kamieskroon** ⑯, 68km (42 miles) south of Springbok, which consists of little more than a petrol station, a shop, and the Kamieskroon Hotel (a seasonal hotel if there ever was one) – the latter often booked solid by wildflower enthusiasts right through from July to September.

About 20km (12 miles) west of Kamieskroon, the pedestrian-friendly **Namaqua National Park** (tel: 027-672 1948; www.sanparks.org; daily 8am–5pm; charge), now extends over 1,400 sq km (545 sq miles) following the addition of the coastal strip between the Groen and Sproeg in 2008. The park protects more than 1,000 bulb floral species and a rich variety of dry country birds, and it also incorporates the Skilpad Wildflower Reserve, which is known for its fine spring flower displays. Further south, only small corrugated-iron hamlets such as Garies, Bitterfontein and Vanrhynsdorp add variety to the dusty-brown wilderness before you arrive at Citrusdal and the moister southern section of the West Coast (*see pages 171–74*). ❏

Dorps

The South African landscape is dotted with idiosyncratic villages and hamlets – locally referred to as dorps – Afrikaans for "little town"

Tranquil and traditionally-minded, often poor and distinctly down-at-heel, most dorps are just pinpoints on the map – yet they can be well worth the effort it takes to track them down. There's a timeless quality to these dusty verandahs and sun-baked stone cottages set back in wide main streets, where the rhythms of life are seductively slow and measured. Here, locals greet each other by name, and everything – even the corner café – closes for lunch.

Take the time to delve behind the sleepy facade and you'll find most dorps steeped in romance and folklore, still proudly bearing testament to the colourful cast of characters – outlaws, fortune-seekers, missionaries and pioneers – who helped to shape the country over the past 100 years.

Bathurst in the Eastern Cape has a particularly fine collection of classic old buildings, built by British settlers in the 1820s. Here, the Pig & Whistle – the country's oldest pub – still resounds with bawdy laughter. Lazy creepers climb the walls of the old stone churches which sheltered settler women and children when the town became the focus of a series of bloody frontier wars with the Xhosa.

Time-warp dorps

One of the strangest places anywhere in South Africa is Die Hel (The Hell), an isolated hamlet in the remote Karoo valley of Gamkaskloof. First settled by farmers during the Great Trek of 1837, residents contrived to avoid contact with the outside world for more than 50 years. It was only when Boer War guerrillas fleeing the British stumbled across the valley that they were discovered – some 20 families, speaking an archaic form of High Dutch, clad in goat skins and only vaguely aware that there was a war on. It took until 1963, 126 years after the settlement was established, for a road connecting the valley to the outside world to be built (until then, all provisions were brought in by pack donkey over a mountain track).

The Northern Province settlement of Modimolle,

formerly Nylstroom (Nile Stream), was named by a break-away sect of Voortrekkers on a mad mission to reach the Holy Land. Having driven their wagons all the way from the Cape, the day came when the doughty trekkers saw up ahead what they thought was a pyramid (actually, a solitary hill) and assumed they were in Egypt – and that the large, flooding river before them was the Nile.

Like so many dorps in the far north of the country, Leydsdorp began life as a mining camp at the turn of the 20th century, part of a colourful wild-west culture where the local stagecoaches travelling on to Pietersburg were pulled by zebra. Today, in the local cemetery, gravestones bear silent witness to the deadly plague of malaria and blackwater fever which brought the thriving little settlement to its knees in 1924 – and condemned it to the status of a dorp forever.

Arid, isolated and thinly populated, the Karoo and Northern Cape are scattered with their fair share of sleepy dorps. Some, like Matjiesfontein or Prince Albert, make a conscious virtue of their time-warped atmosphere, actively marketing themselves as tourist attractions. Others, like Leeu-Gamka or Pofadder, are – well – just there.

Either way, a short time spent in any South African dorp will expose you to a side of South Africa remote from cosmopolitan metropolises such as Cape Town or Johannesburg. ❑

RIGHT: the Victorian village of Matjiesfontein.

SWAZILAND AND LESOTHO

These two tiny kingdoms, one fully surrounded within South Africa, the other bordered by it on three sides, have a great deal to offer the adventurous traveller

The landlocked Kingdoms of Swaziland and Lesotho are somewhat anomalous in modern Africa. Neither has ever been subject to sustained outside rule, though both are former British Protectorates with strong economic and political links to the neighbour that encloses Lesotho entirely and Swaziland on three sides. Both nations are unusual in their ethnic homogeneity and monarchies, though the King of Lesotho is largely a ceremonial figure whereas his Swazi counterpart remains highly politically active.

Lesotho dates back to the time of the first Basotho king, Moshoeshoe. He founded the Basotho nation, uniting a medley of vanquished clans after inter-tribal clashes convulsed much of southern Africa during the 1820s and 1830s. From his celebrated mountain stronghold, Thaba Bosiu (Mountain of the Night), he went on to repel countless attacks by Zulu, Boer and British invaders. Finally, tired of fighting, Moshoeshoe turned to Britain in 1851. His kingdom became a British protectorate, and it remained one until 1966 when it became an independent democracy with a titular king.

The shape of the nation

Swaziland's history has much in common with Lesotho's. The Swazi nation started to take shape in the late 1600s under a powerful chief, Dlamini. He forged a nation of Nguni-speaking clans, closely related to the Zulus further south.

The Boers subjugated the Swazi for several decades, but when Britain won the Anglo–Boer War at the turn of the 20th century, it inherited Swaziland. Mswati III now presides contentiously over one of the world's last absolute monarchies – political parties are banned and ministers are hand-picked by the king.

Main attractions
SIBEBE ROCK
MANTENGA NATURE RESERVE
MLILWANE WILDLIFE SANCTU
MKHAYA NATURE RESERVE
HLANE ROYAL NATIONAL PAR
RAFTING THE GREAT USUTU R
PONY-TREKKING IN LESOTHO
SEHLABATHEBE NATIONAL PA

PRECEDING PAGES: Sani Pass. **LEFT:** reed dance in honour of the King of Swaziland. **RIGHT:** one of Africa's most aggressive beasts.

Highland peaks, wild lowveld

Compared to Lesotho, Swaziland has a good, predictable infrastructure and is a much simpler country to negotiate. The main road through the country also forms the least circuitous route between Zululand and the Kruger Park, so that it slots neatly into any itinerary that includes both of these areas. Once in Swaziland, it's easy to organise guided tours or to rent a car for self-drive trips, and travel conditions are safe too (in Lesotho, even the weather conspires against you) – though drivers should be aware that livestock quite often wanders onto the road.

The country's attractions divide fairly neatly into two categories: the comforts of the Ezulwini Valley, with its numerous smart hotels, restaurants, casinos and craft markets; and then the impressively well-stocked and managed game reserves.

Many of the key sights are ranged on either side of the capital, **Mbabane ❶**, which lies in the northwest of the country on the South African border. Founded in the mid-1880s, Mbabane has a temperate climate that made it attractive to British settlers, and it was made capital of the protectorate in 1903. Today, it's a bustling little city of perhaps 100,000 residents, but rather lacking in charm or any unique character – indeed, a few international embassies aside, there's little to distinguish Mbabane from any similarly sized South African town. The closest thing to a tourist attraction in the city centre is the main market, on Msunduzu Street, which offers good craft bargains but also attracts its fair share of pickpockets.

Craft-hunters should head for the **Ngwenya Glass Factory** (tel: 442 4053; www.ngwenyaglass.co.sz; daily 9am–5pm), which manufactures decorative and functional glassware from recycled bottles, and Endlotane Studios (tel: 442 4196; www.endlotane. net), a craft workshop best known for the woven tapestries based on San rock art and bird designs produced by **Phumalanga Tapestries**. Both are found in Ngwenya, near the Oshoek Border, 23km (14 miles) northwest of Mbabane.

BELOW: a Swazi woman demonstrates traditional craft skills.

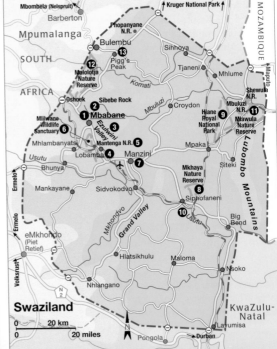

Sibebe Rock

A 15-minute drive north from Mbabane, **Sibebe Rock ❷** is the largest exposed granite dome in the world. Sibebe rises in lunar splendour from the surrounding green valleys like Africa's answer to Ayers Rock (Ulura), and it's even more impressive when you realise it's merely the tip of a batholith that extends for a full 15km (9 miles) below the earth's surface. Not for the faint of heart or giddy of head, Swazi Trails offers a guided three-hour ascent of the main face that's billed as the steepest commercial walk (more accurately, slow-motion wobble) in the world – difficult to verify, but thus far, they claim, nobody's returned with sufficient breath left to argue the point.

About 15km (9 miles) southeast of Mbabane on the MR3, at the end of a tortuous descent down Malagwane Hill, is the lovely **Ezulwini Valley ❸**, the centre of most tourist activity in Swaziland. The 30km (18-mile) valley ends at **Lobamba ❹**, the traditional seat of the Swazi monarchy and modern site of parliament. The fascinating **National Museum** (tel: 416 1516; www.sntc.org.sz; daily; charge) houses several displays relating to the royal lineage and an absorbing collection of monochrome photographs from late 19th century onwards.

Also of cultural interest is the nearby **Mantenga Nature Reserve ❺** (tel: 416 1151/1178; www.sntc.org.sz; daily 7am–6.30pm; charge), whose lush riverine scrub and attractive waterfall are leered over by the foreboding Execution Rock (over which convicted murderers were shoved in pre-colonial times). As well as good tented accommodation, the reserve contains a meticulously reconstructed traditional Swazi village offering cultural tours and virtuoso musical performances.

Elsewhere in the valley, there's a good range of hotel accommodation, offering just about every holiday activity short of a beach. As well as golf, bowls, tennis, horse riding and a health centre, there are a few glitzy casinos and strip clubs that pay sleazy homage to the days when visiting Swaziland

Road sign in Mlilwane Wildlife Sanctuary.

BELOW: Swazi men watch the annual reed dance.

In 2008 huge celebrations were held in Swaziland in honour of King Mswati III's 40th birthday..

BELOW: on safari.

was practically synonymous with indoor pursuits frowned on by the apartheid government. You will also find plenty of opportunity to buy Swazi crafts, both at the road side (bargaining is expected) and in more organised shops. Soapstone sculpture and wood carvings, beadwork and woven articles are the cream of the curios, while the brilliantly coloured Swazi candles – shaped like animals – are the pick of the crafts.

Midway along the valley is the **Mlilwane Wildlife Sanctuary ❻** (tel: 528 3944; www.biggameparks.co.sz; daily 6am–6pm; charge), a patch of former farmland that has now been regenerated and re-stocked with game, though it remains compromised by the abundance of exotic trees, eucalyptus in particular. You can see white rhino, hippo, giraffe, crocodile, kudu, nyala and eland here, among other animals, although the only large predators are leopards, which are rarely spotted. Birdwatching hides have been built overlooking the dams (240 species of bird have been recorded here, includ-

ing plum-coloured starlings and blue cranes). As there are few predators in Mlilwane, you can explore it in your own vehicle, on horseback, or even by mountain bike, as well as taking game drives or guided walks with park rangers. Mlilwane is an easy day trip from Mbabane; there is also a pleasant rest camp if you wish to stay longer.

Swaziland's main industrial hub is **Manzini ❼**, which lies about 40km (24 miles) southwest of Mbabane at the opposite end of the Ezulwini Valley. Founded in 1889 as Bremersdorp, Manzini served as the capital of Swaziland before it was usurped by Mbabane in 1903, and it remains the country's largest town. Although not overly endowed with character, Manzini has a bustling central market – an excellent place to buy traditional handicrafts – and on Thursday it hosts a macabre traditional medicine market.

The interior – myriad landscapes

Private and exclusive **Mkhaya Nature Reserve ❽** (tel: 528 3944; www.biggameparks.co.sz; overnight visitors only) lies

Swazi Crafts

Swaziland is well known for its handicrafts. The famous Swazi candles come in all shapes and colours – a squatter and more psychedelic version of the conventional cylindrical shape, moulded to resemble anything from a guineafowl to a giraffe. The best producer, a Fair Trade organisation, is simply called Swazi Candles (tel: 528 3219; www.swazicandles.com). In Ngwenya, near the Oshoek Border, 23km (14 miles) northwest of Mbabane, the Ngwenya Glass Factory (tel: 442 4053; www.ngwenyaglass.co.sz; daily 9am–5pm), manufactures decorative and functional glassware from recycled bottles, while Endlotane Studios (tel: 442 4196; www.endlotane.net) is a craft workshop whose woven tapestries are based on San rock art and bird designs produced by Phumalanga Tapestries.

about 90km (55 miles) southeast of Mbabane, past scenery which changes from the forestry plantations of the highveld and the rolling grasslands around Manzini to dry, flat plains, dotted with thatched huts. Mkhaya itself is set in classic acacia bushveld and offers excellent game viewing, whether you choose guided walks or drives with the rangers. It is one of the best places in southern Africa to see both white rhino and the more reticent black rhino, while the likes of crested guineafowl, Narina trogon and paradise flycatcher inhabit the luxury river-front lodge.

You'll pass through much the same range of landscapes en route to Swaziland's other chief game reserve, the **Hlane Royal National Park 9** (tel: 528 3944; www.biggameparks.co.sz; daily, 24-hour access to rest camp; charge), about 110km (68 miles) east of Mbabane on the MR3. Hlane, pronounced shlane, covers 70,000 hectares (173,000 acres) of bushveld, spread among the toes of the Lebombo Mountains. Hlane was designated as a royal hunting ground since colonial times, but has been privately managed as a certified game reserve since 1967 – though it's still owned by King Mswati, who passes by on ceremonial occasions to bag the customary impala. Game includes hippo, elephant, white rhino, giraffe, zebra, impala and – the big news round these parts – lion, successfully reintroduced here for the first time in the country. This is a good place for birdwatching, and for raptor-watching in particular. Hlane is popular with young independent travellers because its rest camp is readily accessible from the main road and it's one of the few reserves in southern Africa offering inexpensive, no-booking-required, game walks that come with a high chance of encountering rhino and the like on foot.

Great Usutu River

Another highlight for thrill-seekers is the white water rafting run by Swazi Trails on the **Great Usutu River 10** southeast of Manzini (tel: 416 2180; www.swazitrails.co.sz). The series of Grade I–IV rapids on this river is probably the most challenging stretch of southern

BELOW: mother and baby elephant in Mkhaya Nature Reserve.

African white water that can safely be tackled in unguided two-berth crocodile rafts. Navigable all year through, the turbulent river runs through a starkly beautiful valley of black volcanic outcrops hemmed in by wooded hills, an excellent location for abseiling – which, if your legs are feeling up to it, can be tagged on to the rafting to make a full-day excursion.

The wild north

The contiguous **Mbuluzi, Mlawula** and **Shewula nature reserves** ⓫, set in the far northeast, cover the slopes of the Lebombo Mountains and associated river valleys on the Mozambique border. Mbuluzi and Mlawula protect similar habitats of dense acacia woodland, coursed through by the forest-fringed subtropical rivers after which they are named.

Large mammals are present in both reserves – giraffe, kudu, zebra – but nothing dangerous enough to inhibit exploration on foot, while the checklist of 350 bird species approaches Zululand's more publicised Ndumo and Mkhuze Game Reserve in stature and

species composition. Altogether different, Shewula is the only community-owned reserve in Swaziland – running village tours that reflect modern rather than traditional rural culture out of a rustic rest camp set on a ridge offering breathtaking views across the surrounding lowveld.

Spectacular **Malolotja Nature Reserve** ⓬ (tel: 442 4241; www.sntc.org.sz; daily 6.30am–6pm in winter, 6am–6.30pm in summer; charge), about 35km (22 miles) north of Mbabane on the road to Pigg's Peak, is Swaziland's other northern gem. Wildlife is not the main attraction here, although game includes the endemic blesbok and black wildebeest, as well as impala and oribi antelope. The varied birdlife includes a breeding colony of the rare bald ibis on the cliffs above the Malolotja Falls. Above all, this is superb hiking country, from deep, forested ravines and waterfalls to high plateaux, most of which are only accessible on foot (there are some 200km/125 miles of trails).

The reserve also contains the ancient Lion Cavern, believed to be the world's

Moshoeshoe asked Queen Victoria to annex Lesotho in 1851 so that his people might be as "the lice in the blanket of the great Queen" – a reference to the all-embracing protection of the British Empire.

BELOW: Sotho man.

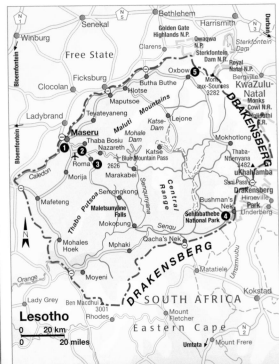

oldest mine. Radiocarbon dating techniques have shown that red oxides and haematite were being dug out of the earth here as long ago as 41,000 BC. It is situated about 16km (10 miles) from the park entrance, near the still-active Ngwenyan iron ore mine.

Run by the National Trust Commission, accommodation at Malolotja is in log cabins, adequately equipped with cooking facilities. There is a shop selling basic supplies and a camp site. Further afield, the historic mining village of **Pigg's Peak** ⓑ (about 24km/14 miles further north from the reserve on the MR1) is set amid green, rolling hills covered in pine and eucalyptus plantations; it makes an interesting half-day excursion.

Lesotho – African Switzerland

This tiny mountain kingdom is an adventurer's dream. Saw-tooth ridges and deep, precipitous valleys glittering with tumbling rivers and falls; mud-and-thatch villages where herders watch over their flocks – it's an African Switzerland, on African time.

The best time to go is between March and April, before it gets too cold to swim, or from October to November, before the summer rains turn the rivers to torrents. These are also good times to see wildflowers – the white and mauve cosmos which creates great bands of colour across the landscape in autumn, and the delicate Afro-alpine species which twinkle on the grassy hills throughout spring and summer. One of the most popular modes of travel through the rugged interior is by sturdy Basotho pony (but be warned – this does require a certain level of stamina and stoicism). Trekking centres organise tours for horse riders through breathtakingly beautiful mountain scenery, in accommodation ranging from hotels to village huts. Here, conditions are fairly basic, but perfectly adequate once you get used to no running water, no flush toilets and no electricity. The other way to get round Lesotho is by four-wheel-drive

Heavy snowfalls can occur in the highland areas of Lesotho.

BELOW: the magestic Maletsunyane Falls.

The sturdy Basotho pony is the product of careful breeding from bloodstock captured by the Sotho during the Eastern Cape's Frontier Wars over a century ago.

vehicle, either on a self-drive basis or on a guided trip with a tour operator.

Mountain cities of the west

Most visitors will pass through or be based in **Maseru** ❶, the capital. Just across the border from the South African town of Ladybrand, it may be twice as big as its South African neighbour, but it's also twice as ugly. Nonetheless, the gift and craft shops here serve as a good introduction to the styles of local craftsmanship you'll encounter throughout the country.

Thaba Bosiu ❷, King Moshoeshoe's majestic mountain stronghold, lies about 10km (6 miles) east of Maseru on the B20. You can visit the ruins of the king's residence and his grave after tackling the short, steep climb to the summit. It is compulsory to hire a guide (a small fee is charged) from the Tourist Information Centre at the base of the mountain.

Also worth a visit is the picturesque sandstone town of **Roma** ❸, about 35km (22 miles) southeast from Maseru on the A3 route. Home of the National University of Lesotho, Roma

was first established as a mission centre in 1863. Educational and spiritual matters aside, it is set in a lovely wooded valley, surrounded by mountains that are often snowcapped in winter.

Lesotho's topography consists of a skirt of sandstone crowned by a massive wedge of volcanic basalt (no point in the country has an altitude less than 1,000 metres/3,300ft). Pocking the soft sandstone are hundreds of caves, once home to those diminutive hunter-gatherers, the San – many are vividly decorated with their paintings.

One of the best-preserved rock-art sites is at Ha Baroana, about 20km (12 miles) north of Roma near the mission settlement of **Nazareth**. This drive follows a road that winds up from the lowlands into the foothills of the Maluti Mountains, offering dramatic views back over Roma. From Nazareth, it's a 5km (3-mile) walk from a signposted turn-off to the site. The curator charges a small fee to open the gate.

Peaks and dramatic passes

East from Maseru, a series of magnificent passes soar over the Maluti Moun-

BELOW: Basotho round house.

tains, penetrating deep into the heart of Lesotho. The Thaba Tseka road via **Marakabei** is especially scenic; **Bushman's Nek** (2,268 metres/7,440ft) and the dramatic **Blue Mountain Pass** (2,626 metres/8,615ft) are just two of the highlights. In between lies a pass called Molimo Nthuse (Sesotho for "Gold Help Me"!), at the top of which is the **Malealea Lodge & Pony Trek Centre**, from which ponies may be hired and excursions planned.

South from here lie **Semongkong** and the Maletsunyane Falls, at 192 metres (630ft), the longest single-drop waterfall in southern Africa. You could fly to Semongkong from Maseru in about an hour, but it takes three days to ride there from the trekking centre at Molimo Nthuse Pass. By four-wheel-drive track from Roma, you could spend anything from a few hours to a few days, depending on the weather. That's Lesotho, and that's why it's such an adventurer's dream.

Isolated, inaccessible and spectacular, **Sehlabathebe National Park ❹** the only one in Lesotho, is earmarked to form a transfrontier park with the contiguous uKhahlamba-Drakensberg in KwaZulu-Natal. There's very little game there except for the occasional mountain reedbuck, grey rhebok or oribi, although it's an excellent place to see the rare lammergeyer (bearded vulture) and black eagle.

Situated in the far southeast of the country on the South African border, you can reach the park by four-wheel-drive from **Qacha's Nek** (about 100km/60 miles), or by walking or pony-trekking from the South African border post at Bushman's Nek. Either way, there's nothing there but miles of rugged wilderness.

Europeans may find the ski resort at **Oxbow ❺** a bit of a joke, although there's usually a foot or two of snow in midwinter. Reached via Butha Buthe, about 100km (60 miles) northeast of Maseru on the Sani Pass road, accommodation is rudimentary. Summer visitors can take advantage of the fine trout fishing in the Malibamatso River here – there's a good site near the Oxbow Lodge, which will advise on permits as well as arrange local guides and treks. ❑

One of Lesotho's main exports is mohair from the angora goat.

BELOW: the Sani Pass, on the border with South Africa.

ℤINSIGHT GUIDE | TRAVEL TIPS
SOUTH AFRICA

T RANSPORT

GETTING THERE
AND GETTING AROUND

GETTING THERE

By Air

The majority of international flights land at **OR Tambo International Airport** (formerly Johannesburg International), which lies to the east of Gauteng, about 30 minutes drive from the city centre or popular suburb of Sandton, and which also services Pretoria and lies within about four hours' of the southern Kruger National Park. From here, you can fly to pretty much every substantial city in South Africa, as well as to other African and Indian Ocean destinations, for instance Angola, Botswana, Ethiopia, Kenya, Madagascar, Malawi, Mauritius, Namibia, Reunion, Tanzania, Zambia and Zimbabwe.

A limited selection of international flights also land at **Cape Town International Airport**, **King Shaka International Airport** (outside Durban) and **Kruger Mpumalanga International Airport** (near Mbombela/Nelspruit), all of which are more convenient options for those with no specific reason to pass through Johannesburg.

Most larger airports in the country are managed by Airports Company South Africa; check their website www.acsa.co.za for detailed information about all available services at an airport, or tel: 0867-277 888 for flight information. For details of Kruger Mpumalanga International Airport visit www.mceglobal.net.

The national carrier **South African Airways** (SAA; tel: 021-936 1111; www.flysaa.com) connects South Africa

to most European and many African capitals, as well as to the USA, South America, Asia and Australia. Visit their website for details and timetables.

Dozens of other international airlines fly to South Africa, among them **British Airways** (www.british airways.com), **Singapore Airlines** (www.singaporeair.com), **KLM Royal Airlines** (www.klm.com), **Lufthansa** (www.lufthansa.com), **Virgin Atlantic** (www.virgin-atlantic.com), **Emirates** (www.emirates.com), and **Delta Air** (www.delta.com). A little bit of research on the internet or via your travel agent will be able to provide information about cheaper deals through African carriers such as **Kenya Airways** (www.kenya-airways.com), **Ethiopian Airlines** (www.ethiopian airlines.com) and **Egypt Air** (www.egyptair.com).

Direct flights between Europe and South Africa typically take 10–12 hours, longer if a stop-off is involved, which will always be the case if you use another African airline. Flights to the USA, Australia and most Asian destinations take longer. Airport taxes are levied at all South African airports (as they are elsewhere in the world) but they are now always included in the final fare.

By Sea

The days when you could take one of the weekly mail boats from Cape Town to Southampton in England for far less than the price of a flight are no more. Now the only option is **RMS St Helena** (tel: 021-425 1165 or (UK) 020-7575 6480; www.rms-st-helena.com), which carries up to 128 passengers on its Portland (UK) to Cape Town route, via Tenerife, Ascension Island and St Helena,

though it usually only sails from the UK once or twice annually. A number of cruise companies offer Cape Town as a port of call, including Crystal Cruises, Princess Cruises and Silversea Cruises.

By Rail

It is possible to enter South Africa by train from Namibia with **Trans-Namib** (tel: +264 (0)61 298 2175; www.trans namib.com.na), which is based in the Namibian capital of Windhoek, and operates a twice weekly service to Upington via Keetmanshoop. The train leaves Windhoek at 7.40pm on Tuesday and Friday, while the return trip sets off from Upington at 5am on Sunday and Thursday and takes around 26 hours one-way.

By Long-distance Bus

This is faster and cheaper than the train, but distances are substantial and you should be ready for lengthy, if comfortable, periods sitting down and braced for rally-style bus drivers. **Intercape Mainliner** (tel: 0861-287 287; www.intercape.co.za) covers the routes between Cape Town, Windhoek (Namibia) and Livingstone (Zambia) as well as between Johannesburg, Mbombela/Nelspruit and Maputo (Mozambique). Services to Zimbabwe have been suspended for some years now. Harare–Bulawayo–Johannesburg services have been suspended due to fuel shortages in Zimbabwe. **Greyhound** (tel: 083-915 9000; www.greyhound.co.za) and **Translux** (tel: 0861-589 282; www.translux.co.za) also run coach services between Johannesburg, Mbombela and Maputo (Mozambique).

By Car

For reasons of insurance and security, you can't go to or from South Africa by way of Zimbabwe and Mozambique in a hired car.

In Botswana, you can only drive hired cars on paved roads (except four-wheel drive vehicles).

To go to or from Namibia, Botswana, Lesotho or Swaziland you need a written statement from the hire company authorising you to take the car over the border.

GETTING AROUND

Internal Flights

There is plenty of competition between carriers on South Africa's most popular domestic routes so it is worth shopping around online for the best deals, especially on busy routes such as Johannesburg to Cape Town, where flights might range from R400 to R2,000 one-way, depending on when you book and the airline. The main players for cheap fares are **Kulula** (tel: 0861-585 852 within South Africa, +27 11 921 0500 from outside; www.kulula.com), **Mango** (tel: 011-359 1222; www.flymango.co.za), **1time** (tel: 011-086 8000; www.1time. co.za), and **SA Express** (tel: 011-978 9905; www.flyexpress.aero), the latter a cheaper affiliate of SAA. Book online with any of these airlines, and you can also arrange well-priced hotel accommodation and car rental as part of the deal.

To and From the Airport

OR Tambo International Airport lies about 25km (15 miles) from the city centre, 35km (22 miles) from the northern suburbs and 60km (35 miles) from Pretoria. Plenty of metered taxis stand outside the arrivals hall, and you can expect to pay a fare of R200–500, depending on how far away you are headed. A cheaper option is the **Magic Bus** shuttle (tel: 011-548 0822; www.magic bus.co.za), which will take you to the hotel of your choice, The only viable public transport is the recently opened **Gautrain** (www.gautrain.co.za), a high-speed rail service that started running between the airport and Sandton in 2010 and should also connect to the city centre, Rosebank, Midrand and Pretoria by the end of 2011. All major car rental agencies are represented at the airport too,

including Avis, Budget, Hertz and Imperial. For those on a brief overnight stop, another option is one of several chain hotels situated within a kilometre or two of the airport – most of them also have prominently signposted free shuttle buses. For further information, contact the Gauteng Tourism Authority, which is open from 6am–10pm daily in the international terminal.

Cape Town International Airport is also about 25km (15 miles) east of the city centre, and about 30km (18 miles) from Stellenbosch in the heart of the Cape Winelands. Many upmarket hotels around Cape Town offer free airport transfers, but there are also metered taxis and shuttle buses, of which Randy's Tours (tel: 021-934 8367; www.randystours.com) or the Backpacker Bus (tel: 021-439 7600; www.backpackerbus.co.za) are recommended. Several car rental companies are represented and Cape Town Tourism has a jacked-up information desk in international arrivals.

King Shaka International Airport, about 35km (20 miles) north of Durban, opened in 2010, replacing the old international airport to the south of the city centre. As with other major airports, there are metred taxis, car rental agencies and airport shuttles (for the latter, contact 086-661 1707; www.airportshuttle.co.za).

For information about getting to and from other airports, check www.acsa.co.za.

Specialised Charter and Sightseeing Flights

If you'd like to visit South Africa's remotest corners, a light aircraft or helicopter flight could be your best bet, making the journey as much of an adventure as the destination.

Obviously, chartering an aircraft will work out cheaper if you can fill every passenger seat. Specialist operators in Johannesburg include **Jetair Charter** (tel: 011-880 8800; www.jetair. co.za) and **Air Charter Service** (tel: 010-590 1098; www.aircharter.co.za), while a good option in Cape Town, for planes and helicopters, is **Civair** (tel: 021-419 5182; www.civair.co.za).

By Rail

In 2010, operation of South Africa's long-distance "Shosholoza Meyl" passenger services was transferred from Spoornet to the Passenger Rail Agency of South Africa (PRASA), the state-owned enterprise that already ran the country's metropolitan rail services. Although several intercity routes were suspended in late 2010, there remains a service linking Cape Town to Johannesburg and Pretoria via Kimberley and Beaufort West, while other routes connect Cape Town to Durban via Port Elizabeth, Johannesburg to Durban via Ladysmith and Pietermaritzburg, Johannesburg to Mbombela, and Johannesburg to Port Elizabeth via Bloemfontein.

PRASA also operates the faster Premier Classe service between Johannesburg and Cape Town, Johannesburg and Durban, Johannesburg and Mbombela, and Cape Town and Port Elizabeth. Timetables can be downloaded from the (somewhat temperamental) website www.prasa.com. This should also soon have online booking facilities; until that happens, enquiries and reservations for Premier Class or Shosholoza can be directed to tel: 086-000 8888; or to the respective email addresses info_premierclasse@prasa.com and info_shosholozameyl@prasa.com.

BELOW: water taxi, Kalk Bay.

For extreme luxury there is the privately owned Rovos Rail (tel: 021-421 4020; www.rovos.com). Its beautifully restored trains consist of four royal suites and 32 de luxe suites, accommodating a maximum of 72 passengers, and routes include a two-day trip between Cape Town and Pretoria, a 24-hour journey between Cape Town and George, and irregular trips further north into Africa, as far as Tanzania.

An alternative is the famous Blue Train (tel: 021-449 2672/2991; www.bluetrain.co.za), with its swish sleeper compartments. It offers two scheduled routes: Cape Town to Pretoria or vice versa (one day, one night) and Cape Town to Port Elizabeth (the Garden Route), taking one day and two nights.

By Long-distance Bus

South Africa's most comprehensive formal public transport network consists of the various upmarket-ish coach services that link major towns countrywide. The most popular routes covered by these coaches include the N1 between Johannesburg and Cape Town, the N2 between Cape Town and Durban, and the N3 between Durban and Johannesburg. Other routes covered include Upington to/from Johannesburg and Cape Town, and Johannesburg to/from Musina, Mbombela (Nelspruit), Port Elizabeth and East London.

Online booking services and full timetables are included on the following websites: Greyhound (tel: 083-915 9000; www.greyhound.co.za), Translux (tel: 0861-589 282; www.translux.co.za) or Intercape Mainliner (tel: 0861-287 287; www.intercape.co.za). As an example, the 1,400km trip (870-mile) from Cape Town to Johannesburg takes about 18 hours by coach, and tickets cost up to R500.

The hop-on, hop-off Baz Bus (tel: 021-439 2323; www.bazbus.co.za) runs about thrice weekly from Cape Town to Johannesburg via KwaZulu–Natal and the uKhahlamba-Drakensberg or Kruger and Swaziland. It's popular among backpackers and younger travellers because you can get on and off as often as you like along the route.

Taxis

Taxi cabs are generally metered though some prefer to work to a fixed fare for specific routes. Either way, you are usually looking at around R10 per kilometre, depending on traffic conditions. Taxi ranks are not as

Automobile Association

It is worth noting that services of the **Automobile Association of South Africa** (queries: 083-843 22; emergency breakdown 0800 111 998; www.aa.co.za) are free to international AA members, on presentation of a valid membership card, and, for a fee, to non-members.

common as in the UK or Europe, and where they do exist it is usually outside four or five-star hotels. More normal, however, is to call a cab, which any hotel can do on your behalf. Failing that, recommended operators in the major cities include **U-Cabs** (Durban; tel: 031-561 1846), **Intercab** (Cape Town; 021-447 7799; www.intercab.co.za) and **Rose Taxis** (Johannesburg; tel: 011-403 0000; www.rosetaxis.com). Also worth singling out as something of a Cape Town institution is **Rikki's** (tel: 0861-745 547, www.rikkis.co.za), a shared taxi service that works out cheaper than using private cabs, but is just as safe. It is worth noting that in South Africa the term taxi is also and most commonly used to refer to the manically driven and rather unsafe shared minibuses that form the main means of getting around for locals without private transport.

Car Rental

South Africa has a total road network of around 750,000km (470,000 miles) and almost all roads likely to be used by tourists are surfaced, the exception being in parts of the Northern Cape and in most game reserves. However, these unsurfaced roads are usually in good condition and can be covered in an ordinary saloon car. Travelling overland, visitors will enjoy the low traffic densities outside urban areas. South Africa drives on the left-hand side of the road. Traffic laws are strictly enforced. Speed limits are generally well signposted. The maximum speed on motorways is: 120km/h (74mph); rural roads: 100km/h (62mph); in built-up areas: 60km/h (37mph). Seat belts must be worn at all times by both the driver and passengers.

Traffic casualties are high in South Africa due to reckless and high-speed driving. It's advisable to drive more carefully than you would at home and to be wary of other road users doing the unexpected – minibus-taxi or "combie" drivers have a particularly

bad reputation in this regard. When driving through any rural area, particularly in Swaziland, be careful of cattle, goats and sometimes even pedestrians wandering blithely into the road. Most roads are poorly lit at night, when you ought to be careful of cyclists and also of pedestrians.

If you will be driving in national parks and reserves, bear in mind that speed limits vary from 25km/h (15mph) to 50km/h (30mph) and are strictly enforced. Because of stops for photography and the like, you should reckon on an average speed of 30–35km/h (18–21mph) at a push on the asphalt roads, and 25–30km/h (15–18mph) on gravel. More realistically, assuming that game viewing takes priority over hurtling around for the sake of it, would be to work on the basis of covering around 20km (12 miles) per hour. Maps showing the distances from point to point can be bought at the entrance gates. Note that in most game reserves it is forbidden to get out of the vehicle except in designated areas.

Remember to take your driving licence with you if you wish to rent a car (an international licence is not required for short stays, provided that your normal licence is written in English or includes an English translation). UK drivers may be required to produce an EU-style photo-card licence as opposed to the old-style green paper licence. Car rental firms offer a wide variety of vehicles; mileage charges are usually extra. Check with the rental firm for details. With major international car rental companies, it is often cheaper to arrange your car hire from home, but many local companies offer extremely competitive rates once you are in the country. Most of the budget airlines listed (see page 331) also offer good online car rental deals through reputable rental companies – it's difficult to find a serviceable saloon car for around R200 (£20/US$30) including insurance and 200km (124 miles) free daily usage. Most car rental companies place a minimum age restriction of between 21 and 25 on renters and it can be problematic to rent a car without a credit card.

Vehicles of all types can be rented from major car companies such as Avis (tel: 086-1021 111; www.avis.co.za), Budget (tel: 086-102 6622; www.budget.co.za), Hertz (tel: 021-935 4800; www.hertz.co.za) and Europcar (tel: 086-113 1000; www.europcar.co.za). Car rental desks can be found inside the International and Domestic Arrival terminals at all major airports.

A CCOMMODATION

HOTELS, YOUTH HOSTELS, BED & BREAKFAST

Choosing a Hotel

Visitors to South Africa can expect a good choice of accommodation, from exclusive five-star hotels to modest city guesthouses, efficient motorway motels to tranquil country inns, rustic rondavels (thatched huts) in game reserves to farmhouses offering bed and breakfast. As South Africa is such an outdoor-loving nation, there's also an excellent range of camping and caravan sites, although national park and in-town campground sites are not necessarily the cheapest accommodation options. For the budget traveller, there is a superb network of private backpacker hostels.

A hotel's star rating is a good guide to its quality and price range. Luxury hotels of four or five stars cost over £200/US$300 per night for a double room, while budget hotels of one star cost less than £80/US$120. The rest fall somewhere in between, though many hotels in the three-star category will offer special rates at not significantly higher than budget hotels when you visit out of season. It is not an indication of poor quality if a hotel has no star rating: such hotels are simply those not listed by the tourist board. Guesthouses and hostels fall into moderate and budget accommodation, while backpacker hostels typically charge around £8/US$12 per person for dormitory accommodation and around £25/US$40 for a double room.

There are many hotel booking agencies on the Internet. In addition to the sites listed below, check out www.southafrica.net for information on all kinds of accommodation, or www.bedandbreakfast.co.za.

Hotel Chains

Southern Sun

One of the largest hotel operators in South Africa, Southern Sun, manages several different chains, ranging from its flagship Sun hotels (several of which are rated five star) through to the upmarket but somewhat characterless Holiday Inns, right down to the budget-friendly Garden Court and StayEasy chains. For further details and online bookings visit; www.southernsun.com. Alternatively dial 0861-447 744 toll-free (within South Africa) or 011-461 9744.

Protea Hotels

This long-serving chain owns, manages or franchises more than 100 hotels countywide, including several units in all major cities as well as hotels in some fairly out-of-the-way places. Overall standards are high, and special offer deals are available. Full details from; www.proteahotels.co.za. Alternatively dial 0861-119 000 toll-free (within South Africa) or 021-430 5300, or email info@proteahotels.com.

City Lodges

City Lodges is aimed squarely at local business travellers, but also offers comfortable accommodation and

Budget Travellers

Coast to Coast is an excellent information and booking service aimed at backpackers and other budget travellers. Its regularly updated 320-page *Coast to Coast* booklet lists practically every backpacker hostel countrywide, while a user-friendly website (www.coastingafrica.com) has links and/or booking facilities for most such establishments.

good value to tourists. Its flagship range of hotels is the rather plush Courtyard chain, while City Lodges, Town Lodges and Road Lodges are each another rung down and priced accordingly. Tel: 011-557 2600; toll-free: 0861-563 437; www.citylodge.co.za.

Portfolio Collection

This is a loosely affiliated collection of individually selected owner-managed guesthouses, bed & breakfasts and game lodges. With over 800 establishments countrywide, Portfolio covers practically every corner of the country and offers online booking through www.portfoliocollection.com. Enquiries can be directed to tel: 021-689 4020; or email: res@portfolio collection.com.

National Parks and Reserves Accommodation

SANParks

Formerly the National Parks Board, SANparks is the authority responsible for the country's 20 national parks, including the Kruger and Kgalagadi. All accommodation, camping and other overnight facilities within these national parks can be booked online through www.sanparks.org or through the head office in Pretoria (tel: 012-428 9111; email: reservations@sanparks.org).

KZN Wildlife

The most important of South Africa's provincial conservation bodies, KwaZulu-Natal's Ezemvelo KZN Wildlife, manages 66 game and nature reserves in Zululand, the Drakensberg and elsewhere in the province. Bookings for practically all accommodation and camping within these reserves (the exception being a handful of upmarket private franchises) can be made at www.kzn wildlife.com, or tel: 033-845 1000.

ACCOMMODATION LISTINGS

CAPE TOWN AND CAPE PENINSULA

Central

Ashanti Lodge
11 Hof Street, Gardens
Tel: 021-423 8721
www.ashanti.co.za
This long-standing and perennially popular backpackers hostel has units in Gardens and Green Point, excellent facilities, and a good travel centre. **$**

Avatara Guesthouse
25 Leinster Road, Green Point
Tel: 021-433 0341
www.avatara.co.za
Situated in funky Green Point, this comfortable and good-value owner-managed guesthouse is set in a restored Victorian homestead and consists of five individually decorated rooms, some with wooden floors and balcony. Breakfast is served in a quiet courtyard. **$–$$**

Breakwater Lodge
Portswood Road, V&A Waterfront
Tel: 021-406 1911
www.breakwaterlodge.co.za
This converted 19th-century prison offers comfortable rooms with all mod cons at very reasonable rates directly opposite the popular V&A Waterfront and its excellent selection of shops, restaurants and other facilities. **$–$$**

BELOW: elegant decor at the Cape Grace Hotel

Cape Grace Hotel
West Quay Road, V&A Waterfront
Tel: 021-410 7100
www.capegrace.com
As a member of the Leading Small Hotels of the World, the Cape Grace combines world-class service and standards with an understated elegance and charm. The hotel's 122 rooms and suites are luxuriously furnished and well supplied with the usual treats. With views of the harbour and Table Mountain, it includes a spa that incorporates various facets of African traditional healing. Have a drink downstairs at the Bascule whisky bar and wine cellar, followed by a gourmet meal at one.waterfront. **$$$$**

Cape Town Hollow Boutique Hotel
88 Queen Victoria Street, City Centre
Tel: 021-423 1260
www.capetownhollow.co.za
Despite its quiet location opposite the Company's Garden, this small and well-run hotel is well located for museum enthusiasts or those who want to be close to the lively nocturnal scene on Long Street. The rooms are very comfortable at the price, and several have views of the gardens to the mountains. **$$**

Daddy Long Legs Art Hotel
134 Long Street, City Centre
Tel: 021-422 3074
www.daddylonglegs.co.za
A unique, arty backpackers hotel with a difference. Each of the 13 rooms has been individually decorated by a well-known Cape Town artist. Well-priced and central to all the hotspots and tourist attractions. **$**

Derwent House
14 Derwent Road, Tamboerskloof
Tel: 021-422 2763
www.derwenthouse.co.za
Combining classical elegance with contemporary

African decor, this owner-managed boutique hotel wins the affections of all who stay there, thanks to the excellent service, relaxed ambience, top-notch facilities, overall attention to detail and useful location within walking distance of dozens of restaurants. The rates are very competitive for this level of quality. **$$**

Westin Grand Cape Town Arabella Quays
1 Lower Long Street, City Centre
Tel: 021-412 9999
www.starwoodhotels.com
The former Sheraton is an ultra-cool glass-and-granite structure situated opposite the Cape Town International Convention Centre. There's a good selection of restaurants and bars nearby to suit your mood. **$$$$**

Kensington Place
38 Kensington Crescent, Higgovale
Tel: 021-424 4744
www.kensingtonplace.co.za
With only eight rooms, this is arguably the best small hotel in the city. Chic is a byword for the style of the rooms and of the guests. Centrally located. **$$$–$$$$**

Mount Nelson Hotel
76 Orange Street, Gardens
Tel: 021-483 1000
www.mountnelson.co.za
Traditionally one of the "Big Five" luxury hotels in Cape Town and still the grande dame of Cape Town's historic hotels. Illustrious past visitors include Sir Winston Churchill and Lady Colefax. Luxury, opulence, world-class service and out-of-this-world food make this a favourite among celebrities, world leaders and royalty. **$$$$**

Peninsula All-Suite Hotel
313 Beach Road, Sea Point
Tel: 021-430 7777
www.peninsula.co.za
Situated on the city's Platinum Mile, this large,

modern hotel comprises 110 large, luxurious, sea-facing rooms and suites, some with two bedrooms and all with self-catering facilities, making it especially well-suited to families. Its restaurant offers a wide range of international and Cape Malay cuisine. **$$$–$$$**

The Village Lodge
49 Napier Street, De Waterkant
Tel: 021-421 1106
www.thevillagelodge.co.za
A 15-bedroom boutique hotel, a private villa and several fully furnished self-catering town houses in this trendy and centrally located area. The rooftop pool at the main lodge is a highlight. **$$**

The Cape Peninsula

Andros Boutique Hotel
Corner Phyllis and Newlands Road, Claremont
Tel: 021-797 9777
www.andros.co.za
Situated in an elegant 100-year old Cape Dutch homestead designed by Sir Herbert Baker, this sedate hotel comprises 12 rooms and one suite set in leafy gardens around a swimming pool. The rather isolated location is unsuitable for those without a vehicle, but otherwise it's the perfect retreat. **$$$**

The Bay Hotel
69 Victoria Road, Camps Bay
Tel: 021-430 4444
www.thebayhotel.co.za
Clean white lines, cool tiled floors, light, bright and airy – this is a refreshingly

modern alternative in a town where it's almost obligatory for luxury hotels to double up as listed monuments. Every room enjoys a spectacular sea or mountain view. **$$$$**

Cape Point Cottage
59 Cape Point Road, Castle Rock, Simon's Town
Tel: 021-786 3891
www.capepointcottage.co.za
Only five minutes from the Cape of Good Hope sector of Table Mountain National Park, the two isolated cottages here can be taken on a self-catering or bed-and-breakfast basis. It's a perfect spot for nature-lovers. **$**

The Cellars-Hohenort
93 Brommersvlei Road, Constantia
Tel: 021-794 6561
www.cellars-hohenort.com
Graceful hotel converted from the 17th-century cellars of the former Klaasenbosch wine farm. Set in large landscaped

gardens bordering Kirstenbosch Botanical Garden. Noted restaurant and cellar, too. Swimming pool, tennis and walking trails. **$$$$**

The Constantia
Spaanschemat River Road, Constantia
Tel: 021-794 6561
www.theconstantia.com
Spacious, well-appointed rooms are a feature of this plush hotel set in the heart of the Constantia Winelands. Here you can enjoy country-style accommodation with all the frills, from air conditioning to heated towel rails and a full English breakfast. It's just a short drive to local shopping centres and beaches. **$$$$**

Green Elephant
57 Milton Road, Observatory
Tel: 021-448 6359
www.greenelephant.co.za
This stalwart backpacker hostel lies in the trendy

suburb of Observatory and is ideal for travellers who value laid-back socialising as much as active sightseeing – though a great selection of day trips and activities are also offered. Colourful murals adorn each guest room. **$**

Lord Nelson's Inn
58 St George's Street, Simon's Town
Tel: 021-786 1386
www.lordnelsoninn.co.za
This delightful small but long-serving inn offers unpretentious, homely and very reasonably priced accommodation and meals within walking distance of Boulders and its penguin colony, and a short drive from the Cape of Good Hope Nature Reserve. **$$**

Simon's Town Boutique Backpackers
66 St George's Street, Simon's Town
Tel: 021-786 1964
www.capepax.co.za

Situated within walking distance of a railway station, several historic buildings and good but inexpensive restaurants, and the iconic Boulders Beach, this boasts one of the most scenic and convenient locations of any of the 40-odd backpacker hostels in and around Cape Town. **$**

Twelve Apostles Hotel
About 2km (1½ miles) south of Camps Bay on the Hout Bay road
Tel: 021-437 9000
www.12apostleshotel.com
Gold-listed as one of Condé Nast Traveler's "Best Places to Stay in the World" for 2010, this elegantly laid-back hotel has a variety of chic sea-view rooms. The spa offers indulgent treatments inside a cave-like space, with flotation tanks and steam rooms. South African food is served at the Azure restaurant, overlooking the ocean. **$$$$**

WESTERN CAPE

Saldanha

Saldanha Bay Protea Hotel
51B Main Road, Saldanha
Tel: 022-714 1264
www.proteahotels.com
This comfortable harbour-front hotel is well-equipped and makes a useful upmarket base from which to explore the nearby West Coast National Park. **$$**

Cape Columbine Nature Reserve

The Beach Camp
Tel: 082-926 2267
www.beachcamp.co.za
This private camp offers inexpensive tented and A-frame accommodation, along with guided sea-kayak

trips, dive training, boat trips to nearby seal and seabird colonies and hiking. **$**

Lambert's Bay

Lambert's Bay Hotel
72 Voortrekker Street
Tel: 027-432 1126
www.lambertsbayhotel.co.za
This comfortable 47-room hotel facing the old harbour is the best option in a quaint village known for its bird colonies and fine seafood. **$$**

Cederberg

Bushmans Kloof
43km (27 miles) from Clanwilliam, towards Wupperthal through Parkhuis Pass
Tel: 027-481 1860
www.bushmanskloof.co.za
This award-winning ultra-luxurious oasis, set in the middle of nowhere, offers tranquillity, gourmet cuisine, game drives, and hiking through unspoilt vistas that hide a full 130 different

prehistoric rock art sites. Enjoy some serious pampering in the sumptuous spa. **$$$$**

Kagga Kamma
Between Citrusdal and Ceres
Tel: 021-872 4343
www.kaggakamma.co.za
This private reserve in the southern Cederberg is less notable for its game perhaps than its craggy scenery, rock art and resident San village. Accommodation is in luxury chalets or tents and there's a restaurant and swimming pool. **$$$$**

Stellenbosch

Devon Valley Hotel
Devon Valley Road, 6km (4 miles) from Stellenbosch
Tel: 021-865 2012
www.devonvalleyhotel.com
Set on the Sylvanvale Estate (a boutique vineyard known for its Pinotage reserve and vine-dried Chenin Blanc), this medium-sized hotel has a scenic winelands

atmosphere, two fine restaurants, good facilities for disabled guests, and a pool. **$$$**

D'Ouwe Werf
30 Church Street,
Tel: 021-887 4608
www.ouwewerf.com.
Established in the heart of old Stellenbosch in 1802, this plush inn is a real gem – notable for its authentic Cape Dutch architecture, period decor, personal service, sumptuous traditional Cape cuisine and quality wine list. **$$**

Lanzerac Hotel and Spa
Lanzerac Street
Tel: 021-887 1132
www.lanzerac.co.za

Map showing South Africa with Johannesburg, SOUTH AFRICA and Cape Town labelled.

PRICE·CATEGORIES

Price categories are for a double room without breakfast:
$ = under R1,000
$$ = R1,000–2,000
$$$ = R2,000–3,000
$$$$ = over R3,000

This 300-year-old manor house is set amongst award-winning vineyards, beautifully landscaped gardens and centuries-old oak trees. Five-star suites, Cape Malay cuisine and a wellness centre and spa. Check the website for specials. **$$$–$$$$**

Stumble Inn
12 Market Street
Tel: 021-887 4049
www.stumbleinnstellenbosch.hostel.com
This lively, central and well-established backpacker hostel sprawls over two houses and facilities include a swimming pool, satellite TV and discounted wine-tasting tours. **$**

Franschhoek

Franschhoek Manor
Dassenberg Road, about 1km (½ mile) from central Franschhoek
Tel: 021-876 4455
www.franschhoekmanor.co.za
This tranquil owner-managed boutique lodge is set in a lovely Cape Dutch manor with period decor, sprawling attractive riverfront gardens and a small army of friendly cats. The four spacious rooms are all decorated with flair and individuality and the breakfast is superb. Despite the rural location, it's less than five minutes' drive to some of the country's top restaurants. Good value. **$$**

Le Quartier Francais
16 Huguenot Road
Tel: 021-876 2151
www.lequartier.co.za
An exceptional upmarket guesthouse set in the heart of this scenic village. It's small and built round a garden courtyard with a pool. Well placed for tours of the winelands, and the restaurant is highly acclaimed. **$$$$**

Paarl

Grande Roche Hotel
Plantasie Street
Tel: 021-863 5100
www.granderoche.com
A superb vineyard setting, luxury accommodation, good service, fine food and prize-winning cellar (plus swimming pool, tennis and gym) place this restored 18th century Cape Dutch homestead among the best hotels in South Africa. **$$$$**

Picardie Guest Farm
Laborie Street
Tel: 021-863 3357
www.picardie.co.za
A small farm at the foot of Paarl Mountain with three types of accommodation: B&B, self catering or a more informal backpackers unit is available. **$**

Roggeland Country House
Roggeland Road, Northern Paarl
Tel: 021-868 2501
www.roggeland.co.za

A superb eight-bedroom Cape Dutch-style guesthouse set in the shadow of the Drakenstein Mountains. The atmosphere, the restaurant and the service have placed it firmly in the ranks of the 50 best country-house hotels in the world. The cuisine is South African. **$$**

Hermanus

Harbour Vue Guesthouse
84 Westcliff Road
Tel: 028-312 4860
www.harbourvue.co.za
Overlooking the new harbour and only 50m/yds from the cliff paths used by whale-watchers, this small friendly guesthouse boasts good sea views from the first floor, neat spacious rooms with kingsize beds, and good facilities including free WiFi, a swimming pool and two lounges. **$–$$**

The Marine Hermanus
Marine Drive
Tel: 028-313 1000
www.marine-hermanus.co.za
Expanded and renovated on several occasions since it spearheaded Hermanus's first tourist boom back in 1902, this superb cliffside hotel now has 42 individually-decorated bedrooms and suites with views across Walker Bay or the Kleinriviersmond Mountains. **$$$$**

Agulhas

Arniston Spa Hotel
Beach Road
Tel: 028-445 9000
www.arnistonhotel.com
This unpretentious, friendly hotel doubles as a meeting place next to the sleepy fishing village of Kassiesbaai. The large airy rooms mostly come with a sea view. Enjoy a gin and tonic on the terrace overlooking the ocean. **$–$$**

De Hoop Collection
Tel: 021-422 4522
www.dehoopcollection.co.za
A variety of self-catering accommodation in the underrated De Hoop Nature Reserve east of Agulhas. With campsites, cottages and rest camps, there's something to suit most tastes and budgets. **$–$$$**

Swellendam

Klippe Rivier
Off the R60, about 3km (2 miles) out of Swellendam
Tel: 028-514 3341
www.klipperivier.com
Set in a fine 1820 Cape Dutch homestead that has been converted to luxury suites, this charming retreat also comprises a secluded honeymoon cottage, lovely gardens and a swimming pool. The relaxed three-course dinner is a good introduction to Cape fusion cuisine. **$$**

GARDEN ROUTE

Mossel Bay

The Point Hotel
Point Road
Tel: 044-691 3512
www.pointhotel.co.za
This four-star hotel dominates the rocky Mossel Bay seafront, and while its presence is somewhat intrusive, the views from the rooms are lovely. The location is excellent for exploring the town's museums and walking trails. **$$**

Protea Hotel Mossel Bay
Corner Church and Market streets
Tel: 044-691 3738

www.proteahotels.com
Built as a warehouse in 1846, this historic hotel has an attractive waterfront location in the town centre and consists of 30 smartly decorated rooms with all the usual modern amenities. The attached Café Gannet serves good seafood. **$$**

George

Acorn Guest House
4 Kerk Street
Tel: 044-874 0474
www.acornguesthouse.co.za
A renovated Victorian house

conveniently situated near the best restaurants and sights of George. The guesthouse has comfortable bedrooms, a pool deck and Wi-fi. Good value. **$**

Oudtshoorn

Eight Bells Mountain Inn
Situated on the R328 between Mossel Bay and Oudtshoorn
Tel: 044-631 0000
www.eightbells.co.za
This family-run four-star country inn, set amid stunning scenery south of

Oudtshoorn combines character with comfort and a variety of sports. **$$**

Protea Hotel Riempie Estate
Baron Van Rheede Street
Tel: 044-272 6161

www.riempieestate.co.za
Cosy country atmosphere and tranquil setting in the heart of ostrich country. **$$**
Rosenhof Country House
Baron Van Rheede Street
Tel: 044-272 2232
www.rosenhof.co.za
Set in a Victorian townhouse dating to the days of the ostrich boom, this five-star guesthouse has large rooms with ancient yellowwood beams and modern facilities, and a wellness centre, swimming pool, bar and country-style restaurant are attached. **$$$–$$$$**

Wilderness/Knysna

Eden's Touch
Off the N2 east of Knysna
Tel: 083-253 6366
www.edenstouch.co.za
This idyllic retreat on the road towards Plettenberg Bay consists of just five large wooden chalets set on a *fynbos*-covered slope fringed by privately protected indigenous forest. **$$**
Knysna Backpackers
42 Queen Street, Knysna
Tel: 044-382 2554
www.knysnabackpackers.co.za
Set in a Victorian manor, this is among the more sedate of the half-dozen backpacker hostels scattered around central Knysna, and it offers private rooms as well as dorms. **$**
Knysna River Club
Sun Valley Drive, Knysna
Tel: 044-382 6483
www.knysnariverclub.co.za

The recipient of several awards, this small resort consists of 35 fully equipped and serviced self-catering log chalets perched on the grassy verge of Brenton Lagoon. Facilities include a restaurant, swimming pool and canoeing. **$$–$$$**
Lake Pleasant Living
Off the N2 between Wilderness and Knysna
Tel: 041-407 1000
www.lakepleasantliving.com
Idyllically located on the banks of the freshwater Lake Groenvlei. Facilities include a health spa and bistro, and activities include golf, birdwatching, bass-fishing and boating. **$$**
Moontide
Touws River Road
Tel: 041-877 0361
www.moontide.co.za
With a shady deck set below an ancient milkwood tree overlooking the pretty Touws River, this owner-managed eight-room guesthouse has a setting to match its individualistic character and attractive rates. **$$**
Views Boutique Hotel
South Street, Wilderness
Tel: 044-877 8000
www.viewshotel.co.za
Part of the excellent Mantis Collection hotel group, this stylish hotel has fabulous views over the beach from most rooms. Facilities include a heath spa, two restaurants and a large swimming pool where you can retire with a cocktail

ABOVE: Storms River Mouth Rest Camp, Tsitsikamma.

when the ocean is too rough. **$$$–$$$$**
Wilderness Rest Camp
Tel: 044-302 5600
www.sanparks.org
Camping sites and affordable self-catering cabins and chalets are available at this idyllic rest camp (also known as Ebb & Flow) on the Touws River. **$**

Plettenberg Bay

Albergo For Backpackers
6–8 Church Street
Tel: 044-533 4434
www.albergo.co.za
This relaxed hillside backpacker hostel, set within walking distance of the central shopping area and beach, offers dorms, camping and private rooms, while the attached "one-stop action shop" is a good place to arrange local activities and day trips. **$**
Bitou River Lodge
Tel: 044-535 9577
www.bitou.co.za
This luxurious owner-

managed guesthouse consists of just five rooms set along the forested banks of the Bitou River – canoes available – about 10km (6 miles) from Plettenberg Bay. **$$$**
The Plettenberg
40 Church Street
Tel: 044-533 2030
www.plettenberg.com
Arguably the grandest hotel along the Garden Route, this iconic hotel combines English country-house decor with superb food, memorable sea views and five-star amenities. **$$$$**

Tsitsikamma

Storms River Mouth Rest Camp
Tel: 044-302 5600
www.sanparks.org
Magnificently sited on the rugged coast of the Storms River estuary, this rest camp has beachfront campsites and a variety of comfortable, but very affordable, self-catering chalets. **$–$$**

EASTERN CAPE

Addo Elephant National Park

Addo Rest Camp
Tel: 042-233 8600
www.sanparks.org

Reasonably-priced chalets and rondavels, camping and caravanning and a restaurant, shop and petrol are available at this rest camp at the main entrance gate to Addo Elephant National Park. **$–$$$**
Kwandwe Game Reserve
160km (100 miles) from Port Elizabeth on the R67
Tel: 046-603 3400
www.kwandwereserve.com
An excellent malaria-free upmarket safari destination

is this Big Five reserve bordering Addo Elephant National Park. Four stunning lodges are scattered around the reserve, with the thatch-and-stone River Lodge, on the euphorbia- and aloe-studded banks of the Great Fish River, being a top-notch example of a classic safari accommodation. The hillside Ecca Lodge is more architecturally playful and innovative, though the

funky interior of the suites is complemented by wide wooden decks and tall glass front windows. **$$$$**

ABOVE: white rhinoceros, Shamwari Game Reserve.

Port Elizabeth

Brighton Lodge
Brighton Drive, Summerstrand
Tel: 041-583 4576
www.brightonlodge.co.za
Set in a quiet neighbourhood only one block from the beach, this convenient and sensibly-priced guesthouse has comfortable rooms with kitchenettes and it offers easy access to shops and restaurants. $–$$

City Lodge Port Elizabeth
Corner of Beach and Lodge Road, Summerstrand
Tel: 041-584 0322
www.citylodge.co.za
This value-for-money chain hotel overlooking Humewood Beach has air conditioning, facilities available for disabled guests, restaurant and pool. $$

Hippo Backpackers
14 Glen Road, Richmond Hill
Tel: 041-585 6350
www.thehippo.co.za
This popular backpacker hostel has a central location, the choice of dorms and single or double rooms, and a good selection of excursions including safaris to Addo Elephant National Park. $

Shamwari Game Reserve
Tel: 041-407 1000
www.shamwari.com
This exciting private game reserve has won numerous international awards for its superior accommodation and guided game drives. An excellent malaria-free alternative to the Kruger,
with seven small air-conditioned luxury lodges on the property. $$$$

Cradock

Mountain Zebra National Park
Tel: 048-881 2427
www.sanparks.org
The rest camp here offers pleasant and affordable self-catering accommodation, as well as camping facilities. $$

Die Tuishuise
Market Street, Cradock
Tel: 048-881 1322
www.tuishuise.co.za
Exuding old-world charm, this unusual establishment comprises a row of restored craftmen's houses, along Market Street, decorated in Victorian style. Plenty of character and great value. $

Graaff-Reinet

Buiten Verwagten Guesthouse
58 Bourke Street
Tel: 049-892 4504
www.buitenverwagten.co.za
This characterful owner-managed four-star guesthouse, set in a handsome 1840 mansion is easily the most appealing option in the town. It is close to several restaurants and shops, and facilities include a heated and unheated pool, and health spa. $$

Urquhart Caravan Park
Stockenstroom Street
Tel: 049-892 2136
Email: graaffreinetcpark@wam.co.za
Set on the R63 fringing the town centre, this attractive municipal resort offers camping facilities, as well as comfortable and inexpensive huts and chalets. $–$$

Nieu-Bethesda

Owl House Backpackers
Martin Street
Tel: 049-841 1642
www.owlhouse.info
An inexpensive B&B is available near the idiosyncratic Owl House, the staff of which can also point you to some good local hiking and rock-art sites. $

Grahamstown

The Cock House
10 Market Street
Tel: 046-636 1287/95
www.cockhouse.co.za
Set in a restored 1820s building, this popular award-winning guesthouse is ideally located for exploring the City of Saints' many historical sites and museums. $$$

Makana Resort
Grey Street
Tel: 071-167 3042
www.makanaresort.co.za
Formerly the municipal caravan park, this privatised resort offers good value camping and affordable self-catering accommodation in gardens on the southwestern edge of the town centre. $

Hogsback

Away With The Fairies
Ambleside Close
Tel: 045-962 1031
www.awaywiththefairies.co.za
Set in spacious grounds inhabited by monkeys and various colourful birds, this excellent backpacker hostel has rooms, dorms, camping space and a restaurant – a great base for exploring the forested Amatola Mountains on a budget. $

Hogsback Inn
Main Road
Tel: 045-962 1006
www.hogsbackinn.co.za
With a cosy highland atmosphere, this old-fashioned, sensibly-priced country inn offers good hotel accommodation, plus a self-catering log cabin. Activities available include horse riding, fishing and birdwatching. $–$$

Port Alfred

Halyards Hotel
Albany Road
Tel: 046-624 8525
www.riverhotels.co.za
The centrepiece of the Royal Alfred Marina, this highly regarded hotel is a fine example of Cape Cod architecture and most of its smart, comfortable rooms have sea views. $$

East London

East London Backpackers
11 Quanza Street, Quigney
Tel: 043-722 2748
www.elbackpackers.co.za
Popular and long-serving backpacker hostel close to the beach front esplanade. $

Esplanade Hotel Beachfront
Tel: 043-722 2518
Simple yet comfortable accommodation on the main beach front. $$

Hemingways Hotel
Corner Western Bypass and Two Rivers Drive
Tel: 043-707 8000
www.southernsun.com
Part of the Southern Sun chain of luxury city hotels, this hotel combines Key West architecture with colourful modern decor reflecting its African location. A casino, gym and restaurant are attached. $$

Premier Hotel King David
Corner Currie Street and Inverleith Terrace
Tel: 043-722 3174
www.kingdavidhotel.co.za
This hotel is convenient for both East London's city centre and its beaches. The 80 well-equipped rooms and suites include air conditioning and telephones. Popular with business travellers because of its proximity to the business district. $$

Wild Coast

Cremorne Riverside Holiday Resort
Port St Johns
Tel: 047-564 1110
www.cremorne.co.za
Rustic log cabins with a superb location on the lush banks of the Umzimvubu River, opposite Port St Johns. Good facilities. $–$$

Kob Inn Beach Resort
Quigney
Tel: 047-499 0011
www.kobinn.co.za
This comfortable family-oriented hotel has a beach front location at the Qora River mouth. Well-situated for beach activities, fishing and country walks. $$

TRANSPORT

DURBAN AND KWAZULU-NATAL (KZN) COAST

Durban

Essenwood House
630 Stephen Dlamini (Essenwood),
Berea
Tel: 031-207 4547
www.essenwoodhouse.co.za
This colonial-era
homestead, set in large
gardens overlooking the city
centre and ocean, offers
personalised service and a
high standard of
accommodation in its six
en-suite rooms. **$$**

Goble Palms
120 Smiso Nkwanyana (Goble)
Road, Morningside, Durban 4001
Tel: 031-312 2598
www.goblepalms.co.za
Luxurious owner-managed
four-bedroom guesthouse
set in a Victorian homestead
with great sea views. **$$**

Royal Hotel
267 Anton Lembede (Smith) Street
Tel: 031-333 6000
www.theroyal.co.za
The bland modern exterior
of this award-winning hotel
hides a large, luxurious and
comfortable interior that
prides itself on offering the
"Last Outpost of the British

Empire" experience. Four
restaurants, including the
Ulundi which specialises in
fabulous curries. Air
conditioning, fitness centre
and pool. Check the website
for specials. **$$**

Southern Sun Elangeni
63 Snell Parade
Tel: 031-362 1300
www.southernsun.com
This beach front hotel offers
breathtaking views of
Durban's Golden Mile. It
also has three excellent
restaurants and all-luxury
hotel and business
facilities. **$$**

**Tekweni Backpackers
Hostel**
169 Ninth Avenue, Morningside
Tel: 031-303 1433
www.tekwenibackpackers.co.za
One of the oldest and best
backpacker hostels in
Durban, the Tekweni
sprawls over three houses
near to Florida Road and
offers a good selection of
rooms and dorms. It's the
home of Tekweni Ecotours,
who have a varied
programme of cultural and
wildlife tours. **$**

KZN Coast

Beach Lodge Hotel
Marine Drive, Margate
Tel: 039-312 1483
www.beachlodge.org.za
Comfortable rooms and
self-catering apartments.
The restaurant serves
traditional German cuisine.
Swimming pool. A few
minutes' walk to the beach.
$

Oribi Gorge Camp
Tel: 039-679 1644
www.kznwildlife.com
This small rest camp,
commanding an impressive
view of Oribi Gorge, and
comprises six twin cottages
and a seven-bed chalet
aimed at budget self-
caterers. **$**

Oribi Gorge Hotel
Fairacres
Tel: 039-687 0253
www.oribigorge.co.za
This moderately-priced
country hotel offers
comfortable rooms in pretty
grounds that afford a
wonderful view over Oribi
Gorge, and a good range of
outdoor activities. **$$**

**Protea Hotel Karridene
Beach**
Old South Coast Road, Illovo Beach
Tel: 031-916 7228
www.karridene.co.za
A modern hotel with good
sports facilities. The rooms
have air conditioning and
telephone. Facilities for the
disabled. Swimming pool
and restaurant on site. **$$**

Selborne Hotel
Spa and Golf Estate, Pennington
Tel: 039-688 1800
www.selborne.com
Just 40 minutes' drive south
of Durban, this smart
country house-style hotel is
decorated with antiques
and fine oil paintings and
set in tropical gardens that
are a bird-spotter's delight.
Good golf course, too. **$$$**

ACCOMMODATION

ZULULAND

Umhlanga Rocks

Beverley Hills Hotel
54 Lighthouse Road
Tel: 031-561 2211
www.southernsun.com
This luxurious, child-friendly
hotel stands right on the
beach, only 10 minutes'
drive from Durban. Rooms
are spacious and have a sea
view, and there are also
luxury suites with butlers.
Facilities include a fitness
centre, restaurant,
swimming pool and
complimentary DVD library.
$$$–$$$$

The Oyster Box
2 Lighthouse Road
Tel: 031-514 5000
www.oysterbox.com
Reopened in 2009 after two
years' closure for
renovations, this iconic five-
star hotel started life as a

lighthouse in 1869 and
opened as a hotel in the
1930s. Quiet, comfortable
and ultra-luxurious, it also
has three restaurants,
renowned for their seafood,
and an immense infinity pool
overlooking the beach. **$$$$**

Tugela Mouth

**Harold Johnson Nature
Reserve**
Tel: 032-486 1574
www.kznwildlife.com
Camping and caravan site
on the river mouth. **$**

Richards Bay

Protea Hotel Richards Bay
Corner Davidson and Launder Lanes
Tel: 035-753 1350
www.proteahotels.com
Pleasant, if unexceptional,
beach front hotel with 66

comfortable rooms and
services geared primarily
towards business travellers.
$$

Mtunzini

Umlalazi Nature Reserve
Tel: 035-340 1836
www.kznwildlife.com
A string of 13 five-bed log
cabins set in the coastal
forest, and there's also a
campsite. **$–$$**

Eshowe

George Hotel
36 Main Street
Tel: 035-474 4919
www.eshowe.com
Committed to several local
community projects, this
country-style hotel is the
pulse of tourist activity in
Eshowe. In addition to

comfortable mid-range
accommodation in the main
building, it offers
backpacker rooms and
dorms in an annexe, while
the on-site Zululand

PRICE CATEGORIES

Price categories are for a
double room without
breakfast:
$ = under R1,000
$$ = R1,000–2,000
$$$ = R2,000–3,000
$$$$ = over R3,000

ACTIVITIES

A – Z

EATING OUT

Eco-Adventures offers a variety of day/overnight tours and activities. Facilities include a pool and restaurant. **$**

Eshowe Caravan Park
Saunders Road
Tel: 035-474 1141
The municipal campsite has a wonderful location on the edge of the Dhlinza Forest Reserve. **$**

Cultural Lodges

KwaBhekithunga Cultural Lodge
R34 between Empangeni and Melmoth
Tel: 035-460 0057
www.kwabhekithunga.co.za
Low-key family-run cultural lodge offering cosy accommodation in beehive huts and a most worthwhile cultural programme that places substance over style. **$$$**

Shakaland
R66 near Eshowe
Tel: 035-460 0912
www.shakaland.co.za
Commodious traditional beehive huts with air conditioning, en-suite bathrooms and other modern amenities, which compliment an excellent cultural programme that starts at 4pm for overnight visitors. **$$–$$$**

Simunye Zulu Lodge
R66 near Eshowe
Tel: 035-450 0101
www.simunyelodge.co.za
This fabulous (albeit somewhat rustic) lodge has a down-to-earth bush feel and a great Zulu cultural programme – starting at 3.30pm when visitors are transported there by ox-cart from a meeting point on the R66. **$$$**

St Lucia

Bibs International Backpackers
310 McKenzie Street,
St Lucia Village
Tel: 035-590 1056
www.bibs.co.za
Long-standing and popular backpacker hostel offering dorms, private rooms, camping and various

excursions in the leafy heart of St Lucia village. **$**

Cape Vidal Resort
On the coast about 30km (18 miles) north of St Lucia village
Tel: 035-590 9012
www.kznwildlife.com
Located on a beautiful cape covered in tall dunes and coastal forest, this rest camp consists of 33 rustic but well-equipped log cabins sleeping from 2–20 each, as well as space for 50 tents. **$–$$**

Elephant Lake Hotel
Mackenzie Street, St Lucia Village
Tel: 035 590 1001
www.elephantlakehotel.co.za
Situated above the estuary, this long serving hotel is the smartest option in the village, with 28 en-suite rooms facing the water, and a deck where you can eat to an accompaniment of chorusing frogs and grunting hippos on warm summer evenings, **$$**

St Lucia Wetlands Guesthouse
Kingfisher Street
Tel: 035 590 1098
www.stluciawetlands.com
Excellent, good value four-star B&B with a quiet location in a pretty garden that attracts plenty of birds from the nearby forest. The friendly owner-managers are a great source of local travel information. **$**

Hluhluwe-Imfolozi

Bonamanzi Game Park
10km (6 miles) south of Hluhluwe village
Tel: 035-562 0181
www.bonamanzi.co.za
This private reserve offers accommodation in tree houses and various lodges, as well as guided walks and 4x4 drives in a game area harbouring hippo, zebra and a variety of antelope. **$$**

Hilltop Camp
Hluhluwe Game Reserve
Tel: 035-562 0848
www.kznwildlife.com
This modern, motel-like rest camp consists of 65 en-suite chalets and huts set on a rise offering expansive views across green hills dotted with wildlife. A good

restaurant and shop are attached. **$–$$$**

Isinkwe Backpackers Bushcamp
Situated at Bushlands about 20km (12½ miles) from Hluhluwe Game Reserve
Tel: 035-562 2258
www.isinkwe.co.za.
This tranquil budget bush camp offers self-catering chalets, backpacker rooms and dorms, camping space, meals and day trails, as well as operating excellent guided 4x4 trips into Hluhluwe-Imfolozi on a twice-daily basis. **$–$$**

Mpila Camp
Imfolozi Game Reserve
Tel: 035-550 8476/7
www.kznwildlife.com
This rustic self-catering camp offers a variety of hutted accommodation. The elevated safari tents regularly receive nocturnal visits from spotted hyena, porcupine and other small carnivores. The shop has limited supplies, so it's best to bring whatever food you need with you. **$–$$**

Mkhuze Game Reserve and surrounds

Mantuma Resort
Mkhuze Game Reserve
Tel: 035-573 9001
www.kznwildlife.com
Set in the heart of the game reserve, this acacia-shaded camp consists of a variety of huts, chalets and cottages catering for 2–7 people each. There's also a camp site at the reserve entrance gate. **$–$$**

Phinda Resource Reserve
Bordering Mkhuze Game Reserve
Tel: 011-809 4314
www.phinda.com
The four immaculate luxury lodges within this superb private game reserve all offer 4x4 excursions with knowledgeable guides, and a good chance of close encounters with lion, cheetah, leopard, elephant, rhino and much else besides. The food is world-class. **$$$$**

Zulu Nyala Safari Lodge
Tel: 035-562 0177

www.zulunyala.com
This private game reserve borders Phinda and supports many of the same species. Accommodation in either of its two upmarket tented camps includes guided 4x4 drives and good food. **$$–$$$**

Maputaland

Kosi Forest Lodge
Tel: 035-474 1473
www.isibindiafrica.co.za
Set in sand forest overlooking Lake Shengeza in the Kosi Bay wetlands, this relaxed bush camp is popular with birdwatchers and offers excursions to hippo-infested Lake Amanzamnyama Kosi Bay mouth. **$$$$**

Rocktail Bay
Tel: 011-257 5111
www.rocktailbay.com
Set on the pristine and practically deserted coast line south of Kosi Bay, this small, upmarket beach resort must be just about the most remote in South Africa. **$$$–$$$$**

Sodwana Bay
Tel: 035-571 0005
www.kznwildlife.com
This beachfront rest camp consists of 33 log cabins sleeping 5–8 adults apiece, as well as 350 camping sites. **$$**

Tembe Elephant Park
Tel: 031-267 0144
www.tembe.co.za
Packages at this small privately-run luxury tented campsite within KZN Wildlife's Tembe Elephant Park include all meals and guided 4x4 drives to seek out the park's elephant, rhino, lion and other wildlife. **$$$$**

Thonga Beach Lodge
Tel: 035-474 1473
www.isibindiafrica.co.za
Operated in conjunction with the local Mabibi community, this appealing "bush meets beach" lodge has chic but organic architecture and a pristine beach location. Snorkelling, fishing, deep-sea diving and kayak excursions onto Lake Sibaya are offered. **$$$$**

Ithala and Phongola Game Reserves

Ntshondwe Resort
Ithala Game Reserve
Tel: 034-983 2540
www.kznwildlife.com
This large modern rest camp in Ithala Game Reserve consists of a full-service restaurant with fantastic views and a variety of huts and chalets overlooking the sweeping plains below. **$$**

Pongola Country Lodge
14 Jan Mielie Street, Pongola
Tel: 034-413 1352

www.pongolacountrylodge.com
This homely and affordable hotel in the village of Pongola is ideally situated for exploring Phongola Nature Reserve and other local attractions. **$**

Battlefield Route

Babanango Valley
About 80km (x miles) southeast of Dundee on the R68
Tel: 035-835 0062
www.bbanangovalley.co.za
This stylish small country lodge, set in scenic farmland between the

historic sites of Isandlwana and Ulundi, is an easy place to settle into for a few days. It offers top-class guided tours to the many battlefields in the area. **$**

Royal Country Inn
61 Victoria St, Dundee Road
Tel: 034-212 2147
www.royalcountryinn.com
Founded in 1886, this homely and good-value three-star hotel in the heart of Dundee is a useful base from which to explore the Battlefields Route. The English pub-style bar, and plentiful military

paraphernalia in the public rooms create a strong sense of place. **$**

Three Tree Hill
Off the R616 between Ladysmith and Bergville
Tel: 036-448 1171
www.threetreehill.co.za
This hilltop lodge, adjacent to the Spionkop Battlesite and Nature Reserve, has luxurious suites with wonderful views to the dam. Excellent country style food, and enthusiastic owner who is knowledgeable about the various nearby battlesites. **$$$**

DRAKENSBERG

Pietermaritzburg

Protea Hotel Imperial
224 Jabu Ndlovu Street
Tel: 033-342 6551
www.proteahotels.com
This Victorian gem offers comfortable accommodation and good food in the heart of the historic city centre. **$–$$**

Howick

Hartford House
Summerhill Stud Farm, Mooi River
Tel: 033-263 2713
www.hartford.co.za
Superb five-star guesthouse situated on a large estate on the Drakensberg foothills near Mooi River, horse riding, walking, birdwatching, trout fishing and top-notch country cooking. **$$$–$$$$**

Howick Falls Hotel
2 Main Street, Howick
Tel: 033-330 2809
www.howickfallshotel.co.za
This historic three-star hotel, built in 1872, hosted the likes of Mark Twain, Cecil John Rhodes and Paul Kruger in its early days. It is centrally located for viewing Howick Falls and exploring the quaint town centre, and its spacious modern rooms are good value. **$$**

Midmar Public Resort and Nature Reserve
Tel: 033-330 2067
www.kznwildlife.com

Situated on Midmar Dam, this resort offers 63 cottages/huts, camping and caravan sites, restaurant and bar, swimming (no bilharzia), fishing, sailing, water-skiing, tennis, squash, bowls and riding. **$–$$**

Zuvuya Farm
Tel: 033-234 4032
www.zuvuya.co.za
This alternative eco-friendly community, with riverfront setting in the hills around Dargle, has dorm accommodation and regular musical, drum circles and other happenings, usually coinciding with solstices or other significant celestial events. **$**

uKhahlamba-Drakensberg Park

Amphitheatre Inkosana Lodge
Champagne Valley
Tel: 036-468 1202
www.inkosana.co.za
Offering double rooms, dorms and camping facilities at backpacker-friendly rates, Inkosana, with its knowledgeable staff, is a perfect base from which to hike the central Drakensberg on a budget. **$**

Ardmore Guest Farm
Champagne Valley
Tel: 036-468 1314
www.ardmore.co.za

This small, homely and very friendly owner-managed guesthouse lies on grassy green farmland overshadowed by the peaks of Champagne Castle. It's attached to the celebrated Ardmore Ceramic Art Studio, which is well worth a look. The superb home-cooked four-course meals are very reasonably priced. **$–$$**

Champagne Castle Hotel
Tel: 036-468 1063
www.champagnecastle.co.za
Set right at the base of the "barrier of spears" topped by Champagne Castle Peak, this spacious hotel is ideally located for hiking, horse riding and exploring the rock art at nearby Didima. **$$–$$$**

Drakensberg Sun
Champagne Valley
Tel: 036-468 1000
www.southernsun.com
A spectacular upmarket mountain resort in the central Drakensberg. **$$–$$$**

Giant's Resort
Giant's Castle Game Reserve
Tel: 036-353 3718
www.kznwildlife.com
The main camp here consists of 45 huts and cottages of various sizes, ideally placed for trout fishing, hiking and viewing the nearby rock art. **$–$$**

Orion Mont-aux-Sources Hotel
Bordering Royal Natal Park

Tel: 036-438 8000
www.oriongroup.co.za
Situated at the entrance to Royal Natal Park, arguably the most scenic piece of real estate anywhere in the Drakensberg, this quiet hotel also has good sports facilities, and the surrounding slopes are rich in walking possibilities. **$$**

Sani Pass Hotel
Sani Pass Road
Tel: 033-702 1320
www.sanipasshotel.co.za
Set at the foot of the Sani Pass in 800 hectares (2,000 acres) of southern Drakensberg countryside. Good for sports and activity holidays, facilities include sauna, swimming pool, golf, horse riding, tennis and squash courts. **$$**

PRICE CATEGORIES

Price categories are for a double room without breakfast:
$ = under R1,000
$$ = R1,000–2,000
$$$ = R2,000–3,000
$$$$ = over R3,000

Sani Lodge Backpackers
Sani Pass Road
Tel: 033-702 0330
www.sanilodge.co.za
This enduringly popular backpacker lodge has a superb location at the base of Sani Pass, and the owner-manager is a mine of information about neighbouring Lesotho. A variety of package tours include two-day guided hikes to South Africa's highest peak; a regular road shuttle from Durban and Pietermaritzburg. **$**

Free State Highlands

278 on Main
278 Main Street, Clarens
Tel: 082-556 5208
www.278onmain.co.za
Situated in a quiet part of pretty Clarens, opposite the old sandstone church, this owner-managed four-star guesthouse offers accommodation in four large and airy individually decorated suites or a two-bedroom apartment. An imaginative breakfast is

included in the rates. **$**
Cranberry Cottage
37 Beeton Street, Ladybrand
Tel: 051-924 2290
www.cranberry.co.za
Delightful guesthouse in a renovated Victorian home. Very good food, too. Well-placed for a stopover if you're doing the Eastern Highlands Route. **$**
Glen Reenen Rest Camp
Golden Gate Highlands National Park
Tel: 058-255 1000
www.sanparks.org
Lodge, chalets, huts;

caravanning and camping; restaurant and shop; swimming pool, tennis, golf, bowling, horse riding; one overnight and half a dozen shorter trails. **$–$$**
Mount Nebo Holiday Farm
Nebo Farm, outside Ficksburg
Tel: 051-933 3947
Email: simon.nebo@gmail.com
Two-bedroom thatched cottage accommodation set in an Old English-style rose garden on this large cherry estate. Telephone in rooms, restaurant, sports facilities and swimming pool. **$$**

GAUTENG

Johannesburg

Airport Backpackers
3 Mohawk Street, Kempton Park
Tel: 011-394 0485
www.airportbackpackers.co.za
This well-established hostel offers good facilities close to the airport, free airport pick-ups and a good travel centre. It is also a popular Baz Bus collection point. **$**
Aloe Ridge Hotel
Muldersdrift, 40km (25 miles) north of Johannesburg
Tel: 011-957 2070
www.aloeridgehotel.com
Luxury hotel set in a game reserve with semi-authentic Zulu village. Air conditioning, telephones, restaurant. Fishing, squash, tennis courts and pool.
$$$–$$$$
Backpackers Ritz
1a North Road, Dunkeld West
Tel: 011-325 7125/2520
www.backpackers-ritz.com
The oldest backpacker lodge in the city, and still a reliable and convenient base, offering dorms, double rooms and free pick-up from anywhere in Jo'burg. **$**
Garden Court/Tambo Airport Hotel
2 Hulley Road, Isando
Tel: 011-392 1062
www.southernsun.com
Only 1km (½ mile) from the airport and connected to it by a regular shuttle, this is very convenient for short overnight stops in

Johannesburg. Air conditioning, telephones, facilities for the disabled, swimming pool. **$–$$**
The Grace
54 Bath Avenue, Rosebank
Tel: 011-280 7200
www.africansunhotels.com
Luxurious little country-house-style hotel with impeccable service; handily placed for the shopping and nightlife facilities of Rosebank. **$$$$**
Heia Safari Ranch
Muldersdrift, about 30km (18 miles) northwest of Johannesburg, PO Box 1387, Honeydew 2040
Tel: 011-919 5000
www.heia-safari.co.za
Comfortable hotel set in a nature reserve, 40km (25 miles) from Johannesburg. Telephones, restaurant, fishing, swimming pool, tennis court. **$$$**
Michelangelo Towers
Nelson Mandela Square, Sandton
Tel: 011-245 4000
www.michelangelotowers.co.za
This stylish and prestigious five-star hotel overlooking Nelson Mandela Square, in the heart of Johannesburg's most exclusive business and residential suburb, has 194 spacious suites, and excellent facilities include a heated indoor pool and spa.
$$$$
Protea Hotel Balalaika
20 Maude Street, Sandton
Tel: 011-322 5000
www.balalaika.co.za
Established in 1949, this

unexpectedly countrified hotel is one of the most tranquil places to stay in the exclusive suburb of Sandton, a popular area with business travellers and shopaholics. **$$**
Crowne Plaza Johannesburg – The Rosebank
Corner Tyrwhitt and Sturdee avenues, Rosebank
Tel: 011-448 3600
www.therosebank.co.za
This prestigious 318-room hotel lies in the attractive old suburb of Rosebank, close to a good selection of shops and restaurants, and only 10 minutes drive from the city centre or Sandton. Three restaurants are backed by excellent facilities for business and leisure travellers. **$$–$$$**
Saxon Boutique Hotel
36 Saxon Road, Sandhurst
Tel: 011-292 6000
www.thesaxon.com
This prestigious and ultra-expensive hide-out near Sandton was favoured by Nelson Mandela in his globetrotting days. Set in vast gardens, the high-class decor and cuisine are complemented by rooms the size of aircraft hangars and superb facilities. **$$$$**
Ten Bompas Hotel
10 Bompas Road, Dunkeld West
Tel: 011-341 0282
www.tenbompas.com
A rambling family home in one of the city's leafiest

suburbs has been transformed into a funky boutique hotel, where each of the 10 suites has a different African theme. Swimming pool and garden. **$$$$**
The Westcliff
67 Jan Smuts Avenue, Westcliff
Tel: 011-481 6000
www.westcliff.co.za
Spread out over a ridge (chauffeured golf cars provide transport), here is opulence and luxury in slightly self-conscious "neo-African" surroundings. Wonderful views from the terrace and pool over the lush northern suburbs.
$$$–$$$$

Pretoria

Farm Inn Country Hotel
Lynnwood Road next to Silverlakes Golf Estate
Tel: 012-809 0266
www.farminn.co.za
Four-star accommodation in an African stone-and-thatch palace in a private game sanctuary. Telephones, restaurant. Hiking trails,

fishing, horse riding and swimming pool. **$$–$$$**

Protea Hotel Hatfield
1141 Burnett Street, Hatfield
Tel: 012-364 0300
www.proteahotels.com
This agreeable good-value hotel a short drive east of the city centre has comfortable rooms in the trendy, low-crime suburb of Hatfield, opposite a major shopping mall and within a block of a dozen restaurants. **$–$$**

Lesedi African Lodge
R512 southwest of Pretoria
Tel: 012-205 1394
www.lesedi.com
Comfortable accommodation based on traditional African architecture in Lesedi Cultural Village in Broederstroom on the road towards Hartebeespoort Dam. **$$–$$$**

La Maison Guesthouse
235 Hilda Street, Hatfield
Tel: 012-430 4341
www.lamaison.co.za
This homely five-bedroom guesthouse has excellent facilities and a reputation for top-notch Portuguese cuisine, prepared by the hands-on owner-manager, a qualified chef. **$**

Sheraton Pretoria Hotel
Corner Church and Wessels streets, Arcadia
Tel: 012-429 9999

www.starwoodhotels.com
This exclusive chain hotel is probably the largest in the city centre, boasting 175 rooms, and also the only one to meet five-star standards. **$$$$**

Southern Sun Pretoria
Corner of Church and Beatrix streets, Arcadia
Tel: 012-341 1571
This modern multi-storey hotel lies right in the centre of Pretoria. It has all the facilities you would expect of a top class business hotel, and the online special rates are often superb value. **$–$$**

Word of Mouth Backpackers
430 Reitz Street, Sunnyside
Tel: 012-343 7499
www.wordofmouthbackpackers.com
Popular backpacker hostel in a central location, with good facilities, including free airport pick-up, and comfortable dorms and rooms. **$**

Sun City and Pilanesberg Game Reserve

Kwa Maritane
Southeast entrance gate to Pilanesberg
Tel: 011-806 6800
www.legacygroup.co.za
This reasonably-priced 90-room lodge lies within

the Pilanesberg, overlooking a waterhole that attracts plenty of elephants, only 10-minutes drive from glitzy Sun City. The food is excellent, especially the bush dinners, and you have the option of self-drive or guided excursions into the reserve, including night drives. **$$**

The Palace of the Lost City
Sun City
Tel: 014-557 1000
www.suninternational.com
Critics deplore its flamboyant, glitzy presence in one of the poorest regions of the country. A top-class hotel in an imported "tropical jungle" setting, complete with artificial beach and wave pool. **$$$$**

Madikwe Reserve

Buffalo Ridge Safari Lodge
Access via the R49 from Zeerust
Tel: 011-805 9995
www.buffaloridgesafari.com
Possibly the most idyllically sited lodge in Madikwe, community-owned Buffalo Ridge straddles a tall wooded rise offering views down to a waterhole and beyond, all the way into Botswana. The hilltop swimming pool is superb, and rates include all game

drives. It is one of the better value set-ups in a reserve where accommodation is uniformly pricey, and it offers good deals for longer stays. **$$$$**

Makanyane Safari Lodge
Makanyane Gate, on the dirt road between Sun City and Derdepoort
Tel: 014-778 9600
www.makanyane.com
Set on private land, this attractive bush lodge comprises eight large suites carved into the riparian woodland fringing the Marico River. Guided game drives offer reliably good wildlife sightings, and there's great food complemented by a good value wine list. Facilities include a swimming pool, spa and gym. **$$$$**

Tuningi Safari Lodge
Access via the R49 from Zeerust
Tel: 011-805 9995
www.tuningi.com
Consisting of just eight ultra-spacious villas with air conditioning and attractively sited bathrooms, this five-star lodge in the hilly western half of Madikwe is notable for its enthusiastic staff. Facilities include a game viewing deck overlooking a waterhole, two swimming pools, and a spacious dining/lounge/bar area with an award-winning wine list. **$$$$**

MPUMALANGA AND LIMPOPO

Middelburg

Forever Resort Loskop Dam
Loskop Dam Game Reserve
Tel: 012-423 5600
www.foreversa.co.za
This well-managed resort has a variety of self-catering accommodation as well as space for offering

PRICE CATEGORIES

Price categories are for a double room without breakfast:
$ = under R1,000
$$ = R1,000–2,000
$$$ = R2,000–3,000
$$$$ = over R3,000

caravan and camping. **$–$$**

Sabie

Jock-Sabie Lodge
Main Road, Sabie
Tel: 013-764 2178
www.jock.co.za
Named after Jock of the Bushveld, this central resort has camping space, dorm accommodation and chalets catering to budget travellers. **$**

Villa Ticino Guesthouse
Louis Trichardt Street, Sabie
Tel: 013-764 2598
www.villaticino.co.za
This small bed and

breakfast offers comfortable accommodation and good food and is surrounded by lush gardens only 100 metres/yds from the town centre. **$**

Blyde River Canyon

Blyde Canyon Forever Resort
Off the R532 between Graskop and Tzaneen
Tel: 0861-226 966
www.foreverblydecanyon.co.za/
With 75 chalets, caravanning and camping sites, two restaurants, a shop, sport facilities and several walking trails, this is

an excellent base from which to explore the Panorama Route. **$–$$**

Swadini Forever Resort
On the Lowveld side off the R531 from Acornhoek to Hoedspruit
Tel: 015-795 5141
www.foreverswadini.co.za
This low-key resort consists

of self-catering chalets, a campsite, and a restaurant and shop perched scenically on the east side of the canyon. **$–$$**

Pilgrim's Rest

Mount Sheba Forever Resort
Lydenburg Road,
near Pilgrim's Rest
Tel: 013-768 1241
www.mountsheba.co.za
Situated in the mountains above Pilgrim's Rest, this four-star thatched lodge boasts wonderful views, walking trails through forested slopes alive with small game and superb four-course meals by candlelight. **$$–$$$**

Royal Hotel
Main Street
Tel: 013-768 1100
www.pilgrimsrest.org.za
This atmospheric hotel offers accommodation in converted miners' cottages, decorated in period style, as well as forming a useful base for exploring the Panorama Route. **$$**

Tzaneen

The Coach House Hotel and Spa
Old Coach Road, outside Tzaneen
Tel: 015-306 8000
www.coachhouse.co.za
Set in lushly forested countryside, this elegant, luxury country-house style hideaway has won several awards, and has a highly

regarded restaurant. **$$$**

Magoebaskloof Hotel
On the R71 west of Tzaneen
Tel: 015-276 5400
www.magoebaskloof.co.za
This friendly 68-room hotel has been going since the 1950s and it remains a gem for wildlife lovers, offering the opportunity to see the rare blue monkey and a host of forest birds in the company of knowledgeable local guides. Facilities include a good restaurant and a swimming pool. **$$**

Mbombela (Nelspruit)

Crocodile Country Inn
On the N4, 20km (12 miles) west of Mbombela
Tel: 013-733 3040
www.crocinn.co.za
Set in leafy grounds around a large swimming pool, this country-style hotel offers comfortable accommodation and good food, and is only a 45-minute drive from the Kruger Park. **$$$**

Hazyview and White River

Big 5 Backpackers
On the R40, 3km (2 miles) from Hazyview
Tel: 013-737 8000
www.big5backpackers.co.za
This well-established backpackers' haunt near Hazyview offers dorms, private rooms and camping in a house with great views

towards the Kruger Park. It also runs affordable day and overnight trips into Kruger Park. **$**

Böhm's Zeederberg Country House
On the R536, 17km (10½ miles) west of Sabie
Tel: 013-737 8101
www.bohms.co.za
Set in the Sabie Valley, 20 minutes' drive from the Kruger Park, this owner-managed country style hotel comprises ten rooms set in lush gardens around a swimming pool. The restaurant serves German, French and African fusion cuisine using fresh herbs from the garden. **$$**

Hazyview Protea Hotel
On the R40, 7km (4 miles) from Hazyview
Tel: 013-737 9700
www.proteahotels.com
This comfortable hotel lies about 15km (10 miles) from the Kruger National Park. It has a swimming pool, sauna and tennis court. **$$**

Pine Lake Inn
Main Hazyview Road, White River
Tel: 013-751 5036
www.africanskyhotels.com
A high-quality resort set in beautiful countryside, this offers fishing, a golf course, a swimming pool, hiking trails, horse riding, a bowling green, and squash and tennis courts. **$$**

Sabie River Sun
Main Sabie Road, Hazyview
Tel: 013-737 7311
www.southernsun.com
Sprawling along the banks

of the Sabie River, this luxury resort hotel lies 15 minutes' drive from the Kruger National Park, where there is a fair amount of wildlife on site, notably hippos and birds. Facilities include fishing, a golf course, a swimming pool, a bowling green, and squash and tennis courts. **$$**

Kruger Park

The numerous rest camps in this vast park are described in the Places section on pages 289–292. Bookings for all camps are through SANParks (www.sanparks.org), which can also provide up-to-date details of rates and facilities. There are also several private concessions within the park, including the following:

Hamiltons 1880 Tented Camp
50km (30 miles) from Orpen Gate
Tel: 011-516 4367
www.hamiltonstentedcamp.co.za
This stylish camp in the Imbali concession consists of just six en suite canvas-walled units that combines Edwardian decor with modern facilities. Set in lush riparian woodland along the seasonal Nwatsitsonto River, it offers access to the game-rich acacia woodland between Skukuza and Satara. **$$$$**

Lukimbi Safari Lodge
25km (15 miles) from Malelane Gate
Tel: 013-635 8000
www.lukimbi.com
Set in the far south, overlooking a permanent pool on the seasonal Lwakhale River, this camp enjoys exclusive traversing rights on a concession that supports good populations of lion, elephant, black rhino, white rhino and regular African wild dog visits. A split-level dining and sitting area, decorated in African style, is connected by wooden walkways to the spacious suites. **$$$$**

The Outpost
Makuleke Contractual Park,
near Pafuri Gate
Tel: 011-245-5704

BELOW: it is easy to forget your wild environs when you're tucked away in a luxury lodge.

www.theoutpost.co.za
This one-off designer lodge, set in the remote northern Kruger, consists of 12 innovative open-fronted steel, canvas and aluminium suites that are entirely open to the elements except for the rock face they appear to grow out of. The sunrise view over the Luvuvhu floodplain is stunning. Game viewing is less rewarding than in the south, but the isolated setting of this lodge gives it an appeal all its own. **$$$$**
Pafuri Camp
Makuleke Contractual Park, near Pafuri Gate
Tel: 011-257-5111
www.pafuri.com.
Managed by the lauded Wilderness Safaris, this unpretentious bush camp on the forested banks of the Luvuvhu river offers accommodation in 20 tented units connected by a 2km (1½-mile) raised wooden boardwalk that offers some great opportunities for wildlife watching. As with The Outpost, the wilderness setting (and birding opportunities) are a stronger selling point than the game viewing, which doesn't compare to southern Kruger.
Rhino Walking Safaris
About 15km (9 miles) north of Skukuza Rest Camp
Tel: 011-467-1886
www.isibindi.co.za
Bordering the renowned MalaMala Game Reserve, this 12,000 hectare (29,640 acre) concession concentrates mainly on game walks, offering welcome respite from the motorised approach taken by other lodges, assuming you're prepared for a daily regime of 4-5 hours on foot. Walks are based out of two small lodges, Rhino Post and Plains Camp, and while you tend to see less game than from a vehicle, the sensation of exploring the African bush on foot is truly exhilarating.
Shishangani Lodge
25km (15 miles) from Crocodile Bridge Gate

Tel: 013-735-3300
www.threecities.co.za
Set in the extreme southeast bordering the Crocodile River, this is the largest of three lodges set in a concession famed for rhino sightings, but also good for the rest of the Big Five. Under the same management and also worth considering is the more intimate Camp Shawu, which has one of the most compelling settings of any concession lodge, overlooking a dam that attracts plentiful wildlife.
Singita Lebombo & Sweni
In the far east, about 50km (30 miles) from Satara Rest Camp
Tel: 021-683 3424
www.singita.co.za
This pair of award-winning designer lodges – whose vast open-plan stilted suites use wraparound glass walls to enhance the views – have attracted several movie stars and other celebrities. Despite the chic atmosphere, the game viewing here in the rugged Lebombo foothills is probably the best of any of the Kruger concessions and the quality of guiding is as good as it gets. Between the two lodges, "The Village" features a spa, a gym, some craft and gift stores, and even a wine-tasting facility. **$$$$**

Private Reserves

Camp Jabulani
Kapama Game Reserve, near Hoedspruit
Tel: 015-793 1265
www.campjabulani.com
This top lodge in Kapama, a fenced private reserve best known for its elephant-back safaris, an activity that offers a unique perspective over the African bush and its inhabitants. The lodge comprises six spacious wood, stone and thatch cottages, all with private deck and plunge pool, and other features are the Relais and Château cuisine, and visits to the associated Hoedspruit Endangered Species Centre. The

nocturnal elephant-back trips below a glittering African night sky are truly wondrous. **$$$$**
Honeyguide Tented Safari Camps
Manyeleti Game Reserve
Tel: 011-341 0282
www.honeyguidecamp.com
Situated between Timbavati and Sabi Sand on the western boundary of Kruger Park, this 230-sq-km (88-sq-mile) reserve operates two camps, Khoka Moya Camp and Mantobeni Safari Camp, both of which lie 20km (12 miles) from Kruger Park (Orpen Gate), and offer open-car safari drives by day and night, and hiking trails to view the abundance of game. **$$$$**
Inyati Game Lodge
Sabi Sand Game Reserve
Tel: 011-880 5907
www.inyati.co.za
Overlooking the Sand River in the western Sabi Sand, this is one of the more unpretentious and affordable lodges in the reserve, but it shares traversing rights with several others. Dinner is served in "bush bomas", while dancers accompanied by drums perform traditional ceremonies. **$$$$**
Kings Camp
Timbavati Game Reserve
Tel: 011-793 1123
www.kingscamp.com
This exclusive lodge lies in Timbavati, a 750-sq-km (290-sq-mile) private reserve on the western boundary of Kruger Park between Phalaborwa and Orpen Gates. The reserve is famed for its white lions, a rare morph that appears here once or so in every leonine generation, but geneal game viewing is comparable to Sabi Sands, with all the Big Five likely to be seen over the course of a 2–3 night stay. **$$$**
Londolozi Lodges
Sabi Sand Game Reserve
Tel: 011-280 6655
www.londolozi.co.za
Five different lodges are scattered around this large section of Sabi Sand, which retains exclusive traversing

rights, and is famed for its leopard sightings – though all the Big Five are likely to be seen over a 2–3 night stay. The lodges overlook the Sand River, and renowned are for top-of-the-range quality, comfort and service. **$$$$**
MalaMala Game Reserve
Tel: 011-442 2267
www.malamala.com
This internationally-renowned safari destination, sandwiched between Sabi Sand and the Kruger Park, is the largest private reserve in the country. Guests at the two lodges enjoy exclusive traversing rights across this area, which includes some 20km (12 miles) of river frontage, and which has in recent years notched up the full Big Five on all but around 10–20 days annually. Main Camp, though very comfortable, remains delightfully unpretentious, with the emphasis being firmly on quality game-viewing and guiding, rather than top end safari chic. **$$$$**
Sabi Sabi Luxury Safari Lodges
Sabi Sand Game Reserve
Tel: 011-447 7172
www.sabisabi.com
This large private reserve in southern Sabi Sand maintains more-or-less exclusive traversing rights for its four lodges, albeit over a far smaller area than MalaMala and catering to almost twice the bed capacity. Its post-millennial flagship is the futuristic Earth Lodge, an architecturally bizarre opinion-divider that feels like it has been built into the ground, but those seeking more conventional safari accommodation can choose between the large Bush

PRICE CATEGORIES
Price categories are for a double room without breakfast:
$ = under R1,000
$$ = R1,000–2,000
$$$ = R2,000–3,000
$$$$ = over R3,000

TRANSPORT · ACCOMMODATION · EATING OUT · ACTIVITIES · A – Z

Lodge or the smaller and relatively affordable Little Bush Camp or Selati Lodge. $$$$

Mapungubwe and Mashatu

Leokwe Camp
Mapungubwe National Park, 15 minutes from the entrance gate
Tel: 015-534 2014
www.sanparks.org.
Set in the eastern section of the park, near Mapungubwe Hill, this camp stands in a valley by spectacular sandstone hills and offers accommodation in self-catering huts with air-conditioning, and a shared pool. $

Mashatu Main Camp
Mashatu Game Reserve
Tel: 011-442 2267
www.mashatu.com
Comprising 14 luxury bush suites overlooking a busy waterhole, this camp is of interest mainly for exploring the superb Mashatu Game Reserve, whose remarkably low volume of tourist traffic is complemented by some fine Big Five and other game viewing (cheetah and African wild dog are regular). The only other accommodation in the reserve, the smaller and more exclusive Mashatu Tent Camp, is under the same management.

Modimolle

Shangri-La Country Hotel
Eersbewoond Road
Tel: 014-718 1600
www.shangri-la.co.za
The best of the limited options around Modimolle is this agreeable 42-room three-star hotel, all with en-suite bathrooms, set in lush gardens with a swimming pool towards Bela-Bela. $$

OVERLAND ROUTES

Bloemfontein

Bishop's Glen
Tel: 051-861 2210
15km (10 miles) north of Bloemfontein following the Glen/Maselpoort turn-off from the N1
www.portfoliocollection.com
Good-value and atmospheric accommodation in a 19th-century mission set on a working stud farm (with adjacent game ranch). $–$$

Innes Guesthouse
29 Innes Avenue
Tel: 051-433 1555
www.innes.co.za
This peaceful ten-bedroom guesthouse is set alongside a small nature reserve, and offers the rare opportunity to watch wildlife wander past the veranda only 5 minutes' drive away from the city centre and all its amenities. $$

Liedjiesbos Guesthouse
13 Frans Kleynhans Road, Groenvlei
Tel: 083-282 5701
www.liedjiesbos.co.za
Situated about 3km (2 miles) from the city, this inspirational guesthouse combines airy contemporary architecture with African and eastern influenced decor reflecting the tastes of the attentive owner-managers. The accommodation is excellent value, and the indigenous garden set on the edge of town and superb food are added bonuses. $

Southern Sun Bloemfontein
Corner Nelson Mandela Boulevard and Melville Drive
Tel: 051-444 1253
www.southernsun.com
This well-managed chain hotel is set right in the city centre. It has 147 rooms, with air conditioning, facilities for the disabled, a restaurant and pool. $$

Kimberley

Gum Tree Lodge
Old Bloemfontein Road (R64)
Tel: 053-832 8577
www.gumtreelodge.com
Historic backpacker hostel, lies about 5km (3 miles) from the city centre and can host up to 200 people in its dorms and private rooms (some en suite). Facilities include a good restaurant and swimming pool. $

Milner House
31 Milner Street, Belgravia
Tel: 053-831 6405
www.milnerhouse.co.za
Comfortable and friendly six-bedroom guesthouse, set in lush gardens in the old suburb of Beaconsfield, and lies close to most tourist attractions and amenities. $$

Protea Hotel Diamond Lodge
124 Du Toitspan Road
Tel: 053-831 1281
www.proteahotels.com
This small, central hotel offers rooms with air conditioning and telephones, facilities for disabled guests and bar. $–$$

Karoo

Haus Holzapfel
6 Langenhovenstreet
Tel: 023-414 4434
www.hausholzapfel.com
This small German owner-managed place has large brightly decorated rooms with good facilities, and the owners are passionate about promoting the areas' oft-neglected tourist attractions. Good value. $

Lemoenfontein Game Lodge
Off the N2 about 2km (1 mile) Beaufort West
Tel: 023-415 2847
www.lemoenfontein.co.za
This game farm with 13 chalets is set amid wild Karoo rockscapes and harbours more than 20 game species. $

Lord Milner Hotel
Matjiesfontein
Tel: 023-561 3011
www.matjiesfontein.com
There is no better place to break up a long drive than this atmospherically restored Victorian resort, whose period character is rendered somewhat surreal by its isolation amid open arid plains. $

Main Rest Camp
Karoo National Park
Tel: 023-415 2828
www.sanparks.org
This excellent faux-Cape Dutch rest camp lies only a few kilometres from the N1, five minutes' drive south of Beaufort West. Facilities include en suite chalets with air-conditioning, camping

facilities, restaurant, shop and various walking and hiking trails. $

Upington

Die Eiland
Palm Avenue
Tel: 054-334 0288
www.kharahais.gov.za
Excellent municipal resort offering comfortable chalet accommodation and camping space on a wooded island on the Orange River. $

Kgalagadi Transfrontier Park
Tel: 054-561 2000
www.sanparks.org
There are three main rest camps: Twee Rivieren (the South African entrance to the park), Mata-Mata and Nossob. All three have hutted accommodation, camping sites, cooking facilities, and reasonably well-stocked shops. There's also a restaurant (advance booking sometimes necessary) and swimming pool at Twee Rivieren. $–$$

Le Must River Manor
12 Murray Avenue
Tel: 054-332 3971
www.lemustupington.com
This absolute gem consists

of a lovingly restored and lavishly decorated Cape Dutch homestead set in flowering gardens that run down to the banks of the Orange River. **$$**
Protea Hotel Upington
24 Schroder Street
Tel: 054-337 8400
www.proteahotels.com
Centrally-located and blandly comfortable accommodation, with a good restaurant, bar and swimming pool. **$–$$**

Augrabies Falls National Park

Augrabies Rest Camp
Main Entrance Gate
Tel: 054-452 9200
www.sanparks.org
This excellent rest camp overlooking the main falls offers a variety of chalet and hutted accommodation, as well as camping. Facilities include a restaurant and shop, while the front desk can

arrange night drives and rafting trips on the Orange River. **$–$$**
Kalahari Outventures
Tel: 082-476 8213
www.kalahari.co.za
Situated 10km (6 miles) from the park entrance, this rafting operation operates a good value river camp, as well as rafting excursions, extended Karoo trips and safaris to Kgalagadi Transfrontier Park. Clean, comfortable rooms. **$**

Namaqualand

Kamieskroon Hotel
Old National Road, Kamieskroon
Tel: 027-672 1614
www.kamieskroonhotel.com
This family-owned hotel in the heart of Namaqualand specialises in eco-tourism and amateur and professional photographic workshops during wildflower season (August and September). 24 en suite rooms and pool. **$**

SWAZILAND AND LESOTHO

International dialling code +268 (Swaziland) or +266 (Lesotho)

Mbabane

Mountain Inn
PO Box 223, Mbabane
Tel: 404 2781
www.mountaininn.sz
This attractively-located hotel on the outskirts of town consists of 60 en suite rooms and a good restaurant set in green gardens overlooking the Ezulwini Valley. **$$**

Ezulwini Valley

Mantenga Tented Camp
Tel: 416 1049
www.mantengalodge.com
This superb bush-style tented camp is great value, consisting of about 15 en suite thatched units tucked unobtrusively into thick riverine woodland on the Mantenga River. A coffee shop serves great snacks and meals. **$**
Mlilwane Rest Camp
Mlilwane Wildlife Sanctuary
Tel: 528 3944
www.biggame.co.sz
Overlooking a water hole with resident hippo, the rest camp in the centre of this small reserve offers a variety of inexpensive accommodation, as well as camping. A good restaurant is attached. **$**
Royal Swazi
Ezulweni and Lugogo Suns
Tel: 011-780 7800 (South Africa)

www.suninternational.com
This trio of glitzy upmarket hotels is most popular for its casinos – bookings and enquiries can be directed through Sun International's head office in South Africa. **$$$**
Sondzela Backpackers
Mlilwane Wildlife Sanctuary
Tel: 528 3944
www.biggame.co.sz
A popular stopover on the Baz Bus route, this rustic backpacker hostel sits on the border of Mlilwane Wildlife Sanctuary and is under the same management. Private rooms and camping **$**

The Interior

Ndlovu Camp
Hlane Royal National Park
Tel: 528 3944
www.biggame.co.sz
Comfortable and very affordable hutted accommodation, campsites and decent restaurant, set in spacious, bird-filled grounds overlooking a water hole where rhino come by on a daily basis. **$–$$**
Stone Camp
Mkhaya Game Reserve
Tel: 528 3944
www.biggame.co.sz
Excellent, luxury-tented camp consisting of just half-a-dozen luxurious open-air "rooms" with en suite facilities strung along a thick stand of riverine scrub. Rates include all meals and game drives. **$$$$**

The North

Malolotja Nature Reserve
Tel: 442 4241
www.sntc.org.sz
Inexpensive log cabins and camping in a compelling, hiker-friendly montane wilderness running along the South African border. **$**
Mbuluzi Game Reserve
Tel: 383 8861
www.mbuluzigamereserve.co.sz
Accommodation within this reserve consists of just a handful of isolated but luxurious self-catering chalets overlooking the Mbuluzi River in the foothills of the Lubombo Mountains. It offers great opportunities to view rare birds and watch big game on foot. **$$$**
Phophonyane Ecolodge
Tel: 437 1319
www.phophonyane.co.sz
Situated on what is in effect a private sanctuary abutting Malolotja Nature Reserve, this comfortable self-catering lodge protects a spectacular waterfall and a long stretch of riverine forest in an area rich in bird life. **$$**
Piggs Peak Hotel & Casino
Piggs Peak
Tel: 437 1104
www.piggspeakhotel.com
This smart hotel is just across the Swazi border in richly forested high country to the north of Malolotja Nature Reserve. **$$**
Shewula Mountain Camp
Tel: 605 1160
www.shewulacamp.com

The rustic accommodation here has fantastic views into the riverine valleys and is part of a community project offering insights into contemporary rural Swazi culture. **$**

Lesotho

Lesotho Sun
Tel: 011-780 7800 (South Africa)
www.suninternational.com
Modern, comfortable and central. **$$$**
Malealea Lodge
Tel: 082-552-4215 (South Africa)
www.malealea.com
This self-catering lodge situated in the central Thaba Putsoa Range also offers facilities for backpackers and campers, It specialises in pony treks, but the staff can organise just about anything you want to do in Lesotho. **$**

PRICE CATEGORIES

Price categories are for a double room without breakfast:
$ = under R1,000
$$ = R1,000–2,000
$$$ = R2,000–3,000
$$$$ = over R3,000

E ATING OUT

RECOMMENDED RESTAURANTS, CAFÉS AND BARS

What to Eat

When it comes to eating out, South Africa – especially larger cities such as Cape Town, Johannesburg and Durban – caters to every taste and pocket. Thanks to the significant Portuguese and Italian communities, there are plenty of unpretentious Mediterranean-style cafés, which transplant ideally to this predominantly sunny climate. And in trendier suburbs such as Pretoria's Hatfield, Johannesburg's Norwood and Melville, or Cape Towns V&A Waterfront and Tamboerskloof, you'll find a veritable United Nations of eateries, collectively representing almost every conceivable global cuisine, with something to suit all budgets.

Cape Malay Cuisine

Particularly in the Western Cape, there is also a growing culinary trend towards serving specialist Cape Malay cuisine or associated fusion dishes. This style of cooking is derived from Malaysian cuisine – a legacy from the 17th century, when Indonesian slaves imported by the Dutch were often used as cooks in white households. The result is a sweet-and-sour cuisine whose distinctive flavour results from the combination of mild Malay spices and fruit such as apricots and sultanas.

Indian Influences

In Durban and the surrounding area, the cuisine has a distinctly Indian flavour. Indentured labourers imported from India to work in the sugar-cane trade in the 1860s brought with them their wonderful curries – spicy casseroles made of vegetables, legumes, lamb, chicken or beef on saffron rice. They're accompanied by such condiments as bananas, tomatoes, chutneys, and particularly grated coconut, which is said to take away some of the bite of very hot curries.

South Africa is also increasingly good as a place to sample various cuisines from elsewhere on the continent, whether it be spicy Ethiopian stews eaten with sour injera pancakes, deliciously tangy Mozambican chicken piri-piri, Swahili-style coconut stews or Arabian-influenced Egyptian dishes.

Drinking Notes

South African wines are among the best in the world, and cheaply priced by international standards, particularly in and around Cape Town and the adjacent Winelands, where the wine is produced.

Beer, almost exclusively light lagers of the climatically appropriate "best served chilled" variety, is brewed prolifically; popular brands include SABMiller's Castle, Carling Black Label and Amstel, and the Namibian Windhoek and Windhoek Light.

The usual **spirits** are widely available and it is easy to become addicted to the creamy liqueur, Amarula, made locally from the Maroela fruit. The legal drinking age is 18.

Tap water is fine to drink unless you are explicitly informed otherwise (for instance at some remote game lodges) but sparkling and still mineral water are sold everywhere.

Dining Out

A feature of South Africa's better restaurants is that ingredients tend to be relatively organic. Meat in particular generally comes from large ranches whose cattle range freely by comparison to their European counterparts.

Even the smallest towns in South Africa can be relied upon to have one decent grill-style restaurant. Medium to large towns will typically have a wide variety, ranging from fast-food outlets such as Kentucky Fried Chicken, McDonalds and similar (as well as Nando's, a local chain specialising in Mozambique-style spicy peri-peri chicken) to proper sit-down restaurants specialising in grills, seafood and Italian dishes. The restaurants in and around the main cities that are listed below reflect the rich diversity of cuisines available in modern South Africa.

Opportunities for dining out in most safari and wilderness destinations – a category that includes the Kruger Park, much of Zululand and the uKhahlamba-Drakensberg region, and the likes of Pilanesberg, Madikwe, Mapungubwe or Addo – are usually somewhat limited. This is because you'll almost invariably be staying in a private game lodge whose package includes meals, or at public rest camps with a restaurant and/or self-catering facilities – and in either case you cannot leave the camp after dark, nor are there any standalone restaurants in the immediate vicinity. When you visit public rest camps in game reserves and national parks, it's best to check ahead that restaurant facilities exist, or whether you will need to book for self-catering.

RESTAURANT LISTINGS

CAPE TOWN AND THE CAPE PENINSULA

Cape Town

Addis In Cape
41 Church Street
Tel: 021-424 5722
www.addisincape.co.za
Situated just off Long Street, this welcome addition to Cape Town's culinary scene is the ideal place to try Ethiopia's little-known but delicious cuisine. Vegetarians are well-catered for here, but there is a good selection of meat dishes too, all at what are rock bottom prices for Cape Town. **$**

Anatoli Turkish Restaurant
24 Napier Street
Tel: 021-419 2501
www.anatoli.co.za
The dining here is mostly about meze. Countless tasty morsels are brought to your table on vast trays, accompanied by chunks of hot bread for dunking into various Middle Eastern dips. The restaurant is built around a tiny internal courtyard. Dinner only. **$$**

The Atlantic Restaurant
The Table Bay Hotel, V&A Waterfront
Tel: 021-406 5918
The decor and ambience are rather overbearing in this smart hotel restaurant. The food, however, is worth coming for, particularly on a special occasion. It's fine dining with silver service, but expect interesting twists on old favourites. **$$$$**

Aubergine Restaurant
39 Barnet Street, Gardens
Tel: 021-465 4909
www.aubergine.co.za
Situated in a restored 19th century mansion, this classy restaurant has received numerous accolades for its innovative cuisine, which fuses elements of South African, French and Asian cooking to sublime effect. **$$$$**

Baía
V&A Waterfront, Shop 6262, Upper Level Victoria Wharf
Tel: 021-421 0935
www.baiarestaurant.co.za
A tourist-crowded venue where the food and drink will set you back a small fortune. However, the choice of seafood here is legendary, most of it caught locally, with a wine list to match. **$$$$**

Balducci's
Lower Level, Victoria Wharf, V&A Waterfront
Tel: 021-421 6002
www.balduccis.co.za.
Popular vegetarian-friendly café-bar-restaurant has a great terrace for people watching. There is a wide range of options, from South African game to Thai green curry or sushi. There's also great coffee and a popular wine list. **$$$**

Beluga
The Foundry, Prestwich Street
Tel: 021-418 2948
www.beluga.co.za
This is a busy, high-profile American-style venue for smart, young professionals. Menu varies from steaks, ostrich and game to freshly caught fish and big seasonal salads. The emphasis of the main menu is South African specialities and shellfish, and there's a separate Pacific Rim menu. **$–$$$**

Belthazar Restaurant and Wine Bar
Victoria Wharf, V&A Waterfront
Tel: 021-421 3753
www.belthazar.co.za
Popular with wine-lovers – it claims to have the world's biggest selection of wine by the glass – this place has also won several awards. Steaks are the specialty, but there's good seafood too. **$$–$$$**

Biesmiellah
Corner Wale and Pentz Street, Bo-Kaap
Tel: 021-423 0850
This restaurant is a must. In fact it's a private house, and you come here to eat well-prepared and authentic Cape Malay cooking. No alcohol. **$**

Bukhara
33 Church Street
Tel: 021-424 0000
www.bukhara.com
Possibly the best curry restaurant in town, Bukhara is noisy and busy, so be sure to make a reservation. The food is authentic and delicious – the butter chicken is the all-time favourite – and vegetarians have plenty of choice. **$$$$**

The Cape Colony
Mount Nelson Hotel, Orange Street, Gardens
Tel: 021-483 1948
www.mountnelson.co.za
Smart dining at its finest in Cape Town's favourite old colonial-style hotel. Dress up and enjoy chic Afro cuisine – with a strong emphasis on seafood and game meat. Dinner only **$$$$**

Chef Pon's Asian Kitchen
12 Mill Street, Gardens
Tel: 021-465 5846
www.chefponsasiankitchen.co.za.
Everybody knows Chef Pon's Asian Kitchen, with its eclectic selection of spicy dishes from Vietnam, Mongolia, Japan, Thailand, China and elsewhere, not least of which are the aromatic crispy duck and tom yum soup. The Asian beers are a treat. **$**

City Grill
Shop 155, Victoria Wharf, V&A Waterfront
Tel: 021-421 9820
www.citygrill.co.za
Fresh seafood and a wide range of venison are the speciality of this relaxed restaurant, which overlooks the harbour. **$$$**

Col'cacchio
42 Hans Strydom Avenue
Tel: 021-419 4848
www.colcacchio.co.za.
This is just outside the CBD, at the junction of Hans Strijdom Avenue and Loop Street. Proper pizzas are the order of the day and the toppings are generous and varied. Big barn of a place with a rapid turnover. There are also pastas and salads. **$**

Den Anker
Pierhead, V&A Waterfront
Tel: 021-419 0249
www.denanker.co.za
Prominently situated on the Pierhead, Den Anker has great views of the passing scene, including the comings and goings of the fishing boats and yachts. It is a large, bustling place, serving Belgian food such as marrow on toast and bowls of mussels and fries. **$$$$**

Emily's
202 Clock Tower, V&A Waterfront
Tel: 021-421 1133
Occupying the famous Victorian Clock Tower near the Pierhead, this famous Cape Town establishment serves inventive South African dishes that impress and amaze. Classics have been updated and typical South African dishes have been borrowed from the kitchen table and smartened up. **$$$**

Frieda's on Bree
15 Bree Street
Tel: 021-421 2404
www.friedasonbree.co.za
Come in for a quick snack or for a long lazy breakfast on a Saturday morning. Unfussy and kitted out in retro kitchen equipment, it is popular with a youngish crowd who pop in here after trawling the vintage clothing stores on Long Street. **$**

Ginja
70 New Church Street
Tel: 021-426 2368
Fusion-style food with some good South African-inspired dishes. The food is delicious, the wine list extensive and the venue has a boho chic that attracts a sophisticated crowd. **$$$**

PRICE CATEGORIES

Price categories are for a three-course meal for one with a half-bottle of house wine, except $ which covers a main course and a drink:
$ = under R100
$$ = R100–200
$$$ = R200–350
$$$$ = over R350

ABOVE: Savoy Cabbage restaurant, Cape Town

Gold Restaurant
96 Strand Street
Tel: 021-421 4653
www.goldrestaurant.co.za.
Part of the Gold of Africa Museum, this is a great place to sample cuisine from all over Africa, and the multiple course set menu dinner is complemented by a fine wine list, vibrant drumming and Dogon masked dancers. **$$$$**

Haiku
33 Church Street
Tel: 021-424 7000
www.haikurestaurant.com
This is a hotspot new-age Asian tapas venue in sexy surroundings. The wide menu includes five-spice calamari, translucent steamed dumplings filled with spinach and cream cheese, and their famous Peking duck. Pricey but worth every cent. **$$$–$$$$**

Jardine
185 Bree Street
Tel: 021-424 5640
www.jardineonbree.co.za.
An exceptional fine-dining experience. Sit and watch George Jardine take action inside his open-plan kitchen and prepare specials that include a beetroot tart or a seared sirloin with béarnaise sauce. Optional wine pairing with each course. **$$$$**

Mama Africa Restaurant and Bar
178 Long Street
Tel: 021-426 1017
www.mamaafricarest.net.
This energetic, funky restaurant serves a good selection of South African dishes, including Malay style curries and venison grills. **$$**

Mesopotamia
Corner Long and Church streets
Tel: 021-424 4664
www.mesopotamia.co.za
The only Kurdish restaurant in South Africa. Recline on floor cushions to eat authentic Kurdish food and smoke hookah pipes. It's always busy, mostly with a young crowd. Dinner only. **$$**

Noon Gun Tearoom
273 Longmarket Street, Bo-Kaap
Tel: 021-424 0529.
Specialising in Cape Malay cooking, the Noon Gun Tearoom serves set lunches and dinners and teas. No alcohol. **$–$$**

Nyoni's Kraal
98 Long Street
Tel: 021-422 0529
www.nyoniskraal.co.za
A traditional South African dining experience in funky surroundings. Try its signature pap and meat towers made from steamed corn discs layered with tender steak, spinach, creamed butternut, whole kernel sweetcorn and smothered in beef gravy. **$$**

Savoy Cabbage
101 Hout Street
Tel: 021-424 2626
www.savoycabbage.co.za
This is one of the oldest fine dining venues in Cape Town, with modern warehouse-style decor in an historical setting. The emphasis is on fresh local ingredients. **$$$**

Toni's Portuguese Restaurant
88 Kloof Street, Tamboerskloof
Tel: 021-423 6717
This quiet Mozambican style eatery is excellent value, and the food is fantastic – try the trademark Mozambican chicken peri-peri or grilled prawns. **$$**

Constantia and the Southern Suburbs

Barristers Grill and Café on Main
Corner Kildare and Main streets, Newlands
Tel: 021-671 7907
www.barristersgrill.co.za
Barristers has been long revered for its large and succulent steaks, but it's also strong on fish. Offers relaxed eating at its best. **$$$**

Buitenverwachting
Klein Constantia Road, Constantia
Tel: 021-794 3522
www.buitenverwachting.co.za
The name means "beyond expectation" and that's a fair description of this wonderful restaurant set on a stunning wine estate. Impressive wine list. Closed Mondays and in August. **$$$$**

The Cape Malay
Cellars-Hohenort Hotel, 93 Brommersvlei Road
Tel: 021-794 2137
www.cellars-hohenort.com
Probably the region's leading specialist in Cape Malay cuisine, this is housed in a Cape Dutch mansion with attractive period decor in the grounds of this five-star hotel on the eastern slope of Table Mountain. **$$$$**

Catherina's Restaurant
Steenberg Hotel, Tokai Road, Constantia
Tel: 021-713 2222
www.steenberghotel.com
Come here for a close-up view of Steenberg, the oldest farm in the Constantia Valley. The architecture is Cape colonial, the decor African, and the cuisine is strong on venison dishes. **$$$$**

La Colombe
Constantia Uitsig Estate, Spaanschemat River Road
Tel: 021-794 2390
www.constantia-uitsig.com.
The decor is unpretentious and simple, while the set menu meals are rooted in French country cooking, but also very experimental and aimed at discerning foodies with a generous budget. **$$**

Constantia Uitsig
Spaanschemat River Road, Constantia
Tel: 021-794 4480

www.constantia-uitsig.com.
One of the most expensive restaurants in Cape Town, and winner of many awards, this is arguably the best place to eat in Constantia. It is essential to book in advance. The fusion menu draws from Italy, Asia and elsewhere, and there's an extensive wine list. **$$$$**

Jonkerhuis
Groot Constantia Estate, Groot Constantia Road, Constantia
Tel: 021-794 6255
www.jonkershuisconstantia.co.za.
The renovated interior to this Cape Dutch farmhouse on Groot Constantia is an ideal setting for family lunches. The simple country fare is complemented by a good menu of salads and Cape Malay dishes. **$$$**

Melissa's
Cardiff Castle, Kildare and Main streets, Newlands
Tel: 021-683 6949
www.melissas.co.za.
A casual vegetarian-friendly deli which sells the very best open sandwiches, salads and chicken pie. Eat as much as you like and pay by weight. **$**

River Café
Constantia Uitsig Farm, Spaanschemat River Road
Tel: 021-794 3010
www.constantia-uitsig.com.
A relaxed, laid-back and informal sort of place, with rooms opening on a courtyard and a garden. Try the Eggs Benedict for breakfast, or have a glass of Constantia Uitsig wine for lunch. **$**

Wijnhuis
Kildare Road, Newlands
Tel: 021-671 9705
www.wijnhuis.co.za.
As you would expect of somewhere called Wijnhuis (wine house), it offers an extensive list of wines to go with good, modern Italian food. Has a relaxed atmosphere with comfy sofas for post-prandial lounging. **$$**

Cape Peninsula

Bertha's
1 Wharf Road, Simon's Town

Tel: 021-786 2138
www.berthas.co.za
This harbourside restaurant specialises in seafood but it is also good for burgers, pasta and salads. With its big open deck by the water, it gets very busy at the weekends. **$$**

Blues
The Promenade, Victoria Road, Camps Bay
Tel: 021-438 2040
www.blues.co.za
Californian-style cuisine in a spacious, airy room overlooking one of the world's most beautiful beaches. Always packed so book ahead. **$$$**

Brass Bell
Kalk Bay Station
Tel: 021-788 5455
www.brassbell.co.za
If you want to see the whales (May–Nov), come to the Brass Bell. To get here, pass under the railway line and climb up the steps to a warren of old station

buildings. Ask them to grill the fish and serve it with oil and lemon. **$$–$$$**

Codfather Seafood Emporium
37 The Drive, Camps Bay
Tel: 021-438 0782
www.codfather.co.za.
Come here for the seafood and sushi. Customers select what they fancy from the counter, where it is weighed and then cooked while they wait. **$$**

Fish on the Rocks
Hout Bay Harbour
Tel: 021-790 0001
Very basic, but serving superb fish and chips. The calamari and kingklip are especially good. Sit inside or out on the grass. **$**

Fogey's Railway House
177 Main Road, Muizenberg
Tel: 021-788 3252
www.fogeys.co.za.
Set in a defunct railway station, this serves contemporary South African cuisine and really good line-

fish, all at very competitive prices. **$**

Harbour House
Kalk Bay Harbour
Tel: 021-788 4133
www.harbourhouse.co.za
Perched above rocks and crashing waves serving up simple seafood. Perfect for a lazy lunch. **$$$**

Olympia Café and Deli
134 Main Road, Kalk Bay
Tel: 021-788 6396
Really great food in a bohemian atmosphere. For brunch, take the papers, order a jug of coffee and settle down with poached eggs and smoked salmon. **$**

The Roundhouse
The Glen, Camps Bay
Tel: 021-438 4387
www.theroundhouserestaurant.com.
Situated in a historic building on the slopes above Camps Bay, this restaurant has an inventive menu and a wine cellar of note. Dinner is a costly but sumptuous multi-course set menu eaten

indoors, while lunch is a more casual and affordable al fresco affair. **$$$$** (dinner), **$–$$** (lunch)

Salt
Ambassador Hotel, Victoria Road, Bantry Bay
Tel: 021-439 7258
www.newmarkhotels.com
Possibly the best seat on the Atlantic Seaboard if you want spectacular sea views (diners are suspended over the ocean) and good food. Delicious local wines by the glass that are affordable too. **$$$$**

Tibetan Teahouse
2 Harrington Street, Seaforth
Tel: 021-786 1544
www.sopheagallery.com
Part of the Sophea Gallery, on the main road connecting Simon's Town to Boulders, this is an excellent lunch venue, both for light, tasty and inexpensive Tibetan-style vegetarian fare, and for the superb view over False Bay. Lunch only. **$**

WESTERN CAPE

Stellenbosch and Surrounds

Blaauwklippen Wine Estate
R44 south ofStellenbosch
Tel: 021-880 0133
www.blaauwklippen.co.za.
Upmarket, yet informal dining in the winelands. Simple, yet modern bistro dining with a German flavour and some South African specials. **$$$–$$$$**

De Oewer
Aan-de-Wagen Road
Tel: 021-886 5431
www.volkskombuis.co.za
Idyllically situated on the willow-lined banks of the Eersterivier. The light, alfresco Mediterranean meals here are accompanied by good local wines. **$$$**

D'Ouwe Werf
30 Church Street
Tel: 021-887 4608
www.ouwewerf.co.za
This atmospheric small restaurant is located in South Africa's oldest inn (founded in 1802). It serves

quality Cape and Continental food, with an excellent wine list. The breakfast is excellent. **$$$**

Terroir
Kleine Zalze Wine Farm, off the R44
Tel: 021-880 8167
www.kleinezalze.co.za
An earthy, reed-roofed farmhouse restaurant, with terracotta floor tiles and crisp white linen tablecloths. Chef Michael Broughton's ever-changing menu celebrates seasonal, locally sourced ingredients, elegantly presented and delicious to eat. **$$$$**

Tokara
Hellshoogte Pass
Tel: 021-808 5959
www.tokara.co.za.
Set in a beautiful space overlooking vineyards and mountains. Quality ingredients with the emphasis on fish and game dishes. **$$$$**

Vergelegen Estate
Off the R44 near Somerset West
Tel: 021-847 1346
www.vergelegen.co.za

Arguably the most beautiful wine estate in the Cape, Vergelegen is home to the the superb Lady Phillips Restaurant known for its adventurous Continental menu, as well as a cosy coffee shop. Closed in the evenings. **$$$–$$$$** (restaurant); **$** (coffee shop)

Wijnhuis Stellenbosch
Corner Church and Andringa streets
Tel: 021-887 5844
www.wijnhuis.co.za
Top-notch Continental cuisine complemented by legendary wine list – connoisseurs can sample up to six different wines over the course of a meal for a sensible set fee. Many of the wines are from the Stellenbosch area. **$$$–$$$$**

Franschhoek and Surrounds

Boschendal Restaurant
R310 towards Stellenbosch
Tel: 021-870 4272
www.boschendal.com

Situated on the lovely wine estate of the same name, this fine-dining restaurant offers first-class South African cuisine amid elegant surroundings. A cheaper and equally popular option is to enjoy one of their famous Pique-Nique hampers on the shady lawn. **$$$**

Bread & Wine
Moreson Winery, Happy Valley Road, La Motte
Tel: 021-876 3692
www.moreson.co.za.
Idyllically set among the estate's vineyards and orchards, Bread & Wine is a great place to stop for lunch. Freshly prepared

PRICE CATEGORIES

Price categories are for a three-course meal for one with a half-bottle of house wine, except $ which covers a main course and a drink:
$ = under R100
$$ = R100–200
$$$ = R200–350
$$$$ = over R350

dishes are made with top-quality ingredients. **$$$**

La Petite Ferme
Franschhoek Pass Road
Tel: 021-876 3016
www.lapetiteferme.co.za
This award-winning restaurant boasts an attractive terrace overlooking the Franschhoek Valley, a reasonably-priced wine list, and a menu rooted in the Mediterranean. **$$$**

The Tasting Room
Le Quartier Français,
16 Huguenot Street
Tel: 021-876 2151
The Tasting Room at Le Quartier Français does a set five- or eight-course menu with a degustation option that involves tasting a different wine with every course. The cuisine reflects the influence of the region's original French settlers. Dinner only. **$$$$**

Paarl and Surrounds

The Goatshed
Fairview Wine Farm,
Suid Agter Paarl Road, Suider-Paarl
Tel: 021-863 3609
www.fairview.co.za
A charming, barn-style restaurant with a huge image of a goatherd on the wall. Choose from cheese and meat platters and daily specials, accompanied by carafes of the estate wine. It is one of the best lunching spots in the county. **$$**

Kostinrichting Coffee Shop
19 Pastorie Avenue
Tel: 021-871 1353
The aroma of fresh coffee permeates the oak-shaded courtyard of this restored Victorian school hostel next to the Paarl Museum. Offers a range of light meals. **$**

Noop Restaurant & Bar
127 Main Road
Tel: 021-863 3925
www.noop.co.za.
This popular eatery has a central location, a relaxed modern ambience and a varied menu specialising in sushi and other seafood, as well as steaks and pizzas. **$$**

Paddagang Restaurant
23 Church Street, Tulbagh
Tel: 023-230 0242
www.paddagangrestaurant.com
Known for its excellent wine list, the Paddagang – literally "Frogmarch" – serves wholesome South African fare in a restored Cape Dutch building. **$$**

Hermanus and the Overberg

Agulhas Country Lodge
Main Road, L'Agulhas
Tel: 028-435 7650
www.agulhascountrylodge.com
The nicest place to eat in Agulhas, this lodge has a restaurant and tea room serving tasty unpretentious fare indoors or on a terrace with ocean views. **$$**

Savannah Café
25 High Street, Hermanus
Tel: 028-312 4259
Affordable snacks and meals in a beachfront setting opposite the old railway station. **$**

Seafood at the Marine
Main Drive, Hermanus
Tel: 028-313 1000
www.marine-hermanus.co.za
A luxury dining room with a fresh, modern appeal in the world-class Marine Hotel. Its small menu focuses solely on fish and other seafood, and it's superb. **$$$–$$$$**

West Coast

Evita se Perron
Darling Station, Darling
Tel: 022 492 3930
www.evita.co.za
Light snacks with a traditional Cape touch, dinners are accompanied by the one-man show performed most weekends by the legendary drag artist and socio-political satirist Pieter Dirk Uys. **$$$**

Die Strandloper
Saldanha Road, Langebaan
Tel: 022-772 2490
www.strandloper.com.
This legendary and informal West Coast restaurant serves delicious and very filling seafood buffets in the open on the beach. Opening time depends on demand so ring or check website in advance. **$$**

GARDEN ROUTE

Mossel Bay

Bahia dos Vaqueiros
Diaz Strand Hotel, Beach Boulevard
Tel: 044-692 8400
www.diazbeach.co.za
Great for its views and sounds of the ocean. An interesting menu, with unusual combinations like ostrich babotie spring rolls with fruit chutney and mint sauce. **$$$**

Café Gannet
Church Street
Tel: 044-691 1885
Part of the Bartolomeu Dias Museum Complex, this popular café is known for its excellent and good value seafood. **$**

George

La Laconda
124a York Street
Tel: 044-874 7803
www.lalocanda.co.za
Possibly the finest Italian
along the Garden Route, this central restaurant has acquired a great reputation for thin pizzas and homemade pasta since it opened in 2007, and the meat and seafood dishes are pretty good too, as is the wine list. **$$**

Oudtshoorn

Jemima's
94 Baron von Rheede Street
Tel: 044-272 0808
www.jemimas.com
Robust, generous portions of Karoo fare, including a selection of ostrich dishes. A focus on seasonal ingredients with a fun, modern twist. **$$$**

Knysna

East Head Café
Knysna Heads
Tel: 044-384 0933
www.eastheadcafe.co.za
A memorable location on the waterfront makes this a great spot for a relaxed and inexpensive breakfast or a lunchtime sandwich. **$$**

Il de Pain Bread & Café
10 The Boatshed.
Thesen Harbour Town
Tel: 044-302 5707
www.theboatshed.co.za
The best freshly baked breads and pastries on the Garden Route. Munch on croissants, quiches and sandwiches layered with local cheeses, meats and home-made relishes. **$**

JJ's Restaurant
Knysna Waterfront
Tel: 044-382 3359
www.jjsrestaurant.co.za
This relaxed restaurant is arguably the leading light on Knysna's waterfront, has a great quayside location, and an equally good seafood and venison menu, with a varied wine list to go with it. **$$$**

Plettenberg Bay

Mugg & Bean
Market Square
Tel: 044-533 1486
This affordable coffee house has a great sandwich and snack menu. **$**

Sand at the Plettenberg
The Plettenberg Hotel
Tel: 044-533 2030
www.plettenberg.com
Set in one of the most prestigious hotels on the Garden Route, Sand offers a great à la carte selection of contemporary South African and seafood dishes. **$$$$**

PRICE CATEGORIES

Price categories are for a three-course meal for one with a half-bottle of house wine, except $ which covers a main course and a drink:
$ = under R100
$$ = R100–200
$$$ = R200–350
$$$$ = over R350

EASTERN CAPE

Port Elizabeth

34° South
Boardwalk Complex,
Summerstrand
Tel: 041-583 1085
www.34-south.com
This laid-back venue serves
oyster platters, freshly
grilled line fish, seafood
paella and Mediterranean-
style meze. **$$$**

Natti's Thai Kitchen
Park Lane
Tel: 041-373 2763
This Thai eatery serves great
mini-platters for those
wanting to sample a bit of
everything. Good selection
for vegetarians. No alcohol
served, but you can bring
your own bottle. **$$**

Royal Delhi Restaurant
10 Burgess Street
Tel: 041-373 8216
This family-run Indian
restaurant has been serving
the best curries in town
since the early 1990s.
Strong on seafood and
vegetarian fare. **$$**

Graaff-Reinet

Gordon's Restaurant
Andries Stockenström Guest
House, 100 Cradock Street
Tel: 049-892 4575
www.asghouse.co.za
Specialising in typical local
fare – Karoo lamb and
ostrich – this small
restaurant is *the* place for a
fine dining experience. **$$$$**

Grahamstown

**Norden's at the
Cockhouse**
10 Market Street
Tel: 046-636 1295
www.cockhouse.co.za
Set in an 1820s mansion,
this traditional restaurant
has a regularly revised
menu of country-style meat
and fish dishes. **$$$**

The Rat & Parrot
59 New Street
Tel: 046-622 5002
Popular haunt with
Grahamstown's substantial
student population, this
sociable spot is a great
place for inexpensive and
filling pizzas or decent pub
grub. **$**

East London

Grazia Fine Food
Upper Esplanade, Beach Front
Tel: 043-722 2009
www.graziafinefood.co.za
Contemporary Italian
cuisine, pizzas and delicious
seafood are the specialities
at this stylish waterfront
restaurant. **$$–$$$**

Smokey Swallows
Chess Galleria, Devereaux Street
Tel: 043-727 1349
This funky favourite with
East London gourmets
specialises in imaginative
pan-Asian fusion cuisine,
and the knowledgeable staff
will guide you through the
extensive wine list.
$$$–$$$$

DURBAN

Aangan
86 Denis Hurley (Queen) Street
Tel: 031-307 1366
Excellent South Indian
vegetarian restaurant with
an informal atmosphere. **$**

Jewel of India
Southern Sun Elangeni Hotel,
63 Snell Parade
Tel: 031-362 1300
www.southernsun.com

One of the city's longest-
serving and finest Indian
eateries, situated in the
beach front Elangeni Hotel.
$$$

Joe Kool's
137 O.R. Tembo Parade (Lower
Marine Parade), North Beach
Tel: 031-332 9697
Popular beach front bar and
restaurant. Where Durban's

surfers come when there's
no surf. **$**

Moyo
uShaka Marine World
Tel: 031-332 0662
www.moyo.co.za
Serving an imaginative and
varied selection of dishes
from all over Africa, this
conveniently located
restaurant has a good

vegetarian selection.
$$$–$$$$

Oyster Bar & Zenbi Sushi
Victoria Embankment
Tel: 031-307 7883
Specialising in prawns,
sushi, oysters and other
seafood, this open-plan
harbour front restaurant has
a great view and a quality
wine list. **$$–$$$**

ZULULAND AND uKHAHLAMBA-DRAKENSBERG

St Lucia Village

Alfredo's Restaurant
Mackenzie Street
Tel: 035-590 1150
Situated near the bridge
end of town, this long-
serving restaurant
specialises in pasta, pizza
and other Italian dishes.
$$–$$$

Pietermaritzburg
and The Midlands

Rosehurst Cafe
239 Boom Street, Pietermaritzburg
Tel: 033-394 3833
This peaceful cafe is set in a
Victorian redbrick
homestead. The chalkboard
menu seldom stays the

same for long, but it
invariably includes a
Mediterranean-influenced
selection of salads,
sandwiches, cakes and egg
dishes. **$**

Yellowwood Café
Shafton Road, Howick
Tel: 033-330 2461
This out-of-town restaurant
is housed in a characterful
hillside farmhouse built in
the 1870s. Country-style
cuisine is the order of the
day. **$–$$**

Northern Berg

Bingelela Restaurant
R74 5km (3 miles) north of
Bergville
Tel: 036-448 1336

Long renowned for its
steaks, Bingelela also
serves good salads, pasta
and local trout, and has
recently added a gourmet
pizza selection to the menu.
$$–$$$

Tower of Pizza
Off the R74 on the approach road
to Royal Natal Park
Tel: 036-438 6480
Situated in a small copse in
farmland, this informal and
popular family-run
restaurant serves great
pizzas. **$**

Central Berg

Thokozisa Mountain Café
R600 west of Winterton
Tel: 036-488 1273

Situated in a small open-air
shopping mall on the R600,
this popular café serves a
selection of light meals,
pasta dishes and cakes, to
be eaten indoors or on the
shady veranda. **$$**

Valley Bakery
R600 west of Winterton
Tel: 036-468 1257
This has a pleasant
inexpensive coffee shop set
on a forested farm. **$**

Waffle Hut
R600 west of Winterton
Tel: 036-488 7085
Part of the KwaZulu
Weavers complex, this
popular eatery opens daily
for breakfasts, light lunches,
and a selection of sweet
and savoury pancakes. **$**

TRANSPORT

ACCOMMODATION

EATING OUT

ACTIVITIES

A–Z

GAUTENG

Johannesburg

Cranks
Rosebank Mall
Tel: 011-880 3442
www.themallofrosebank.co.za
Funky decor, an informal
vibe, large portions and
reasonable prices are a
hallmark of this justifiably
popular Thai restaurant. **$$**

Da Vincenzo
29 Montrose Road, Kyalami
Tel: 011-466 2618
www.davincenzo.co.za
Authentic home-made
Italian cuisine in a thatched
house with a country setting
a short drive north of
Sandton. **$-$$**

**Gramadoelas at the
Market Theatre**
Bree Street, Newtown
Tel: 011-838 6960
www.gramadoelas.co.za
Established in 1967, this
has long been a magnet for
overseas visitors and
adventurous locals thanks

to the superb South African
cuisine and convenient
location in trendy Newtown.
$$$-$$$$

Le Canard
163 Rivonia Road, Sandton
Tel: 011-884 4597
www.lecanard.co.za
Award-winning French and
international cuisine in a
gracious house and garden
setting. Also with a notable
wine list. **$$$-$$$$**

Moyo
Melrose Arch
Tel: 011-664 1477
www.moyo.co.za
Sumptuous pan-African
cuisine from both sides of
the Sahara complemented
by a superb and varied list
of local wines make this one
of Johannesburg's most
innovative fine-dining
venues. **$$$-$$$$**

Osteria Tre Nonni
9 Grafton Avenue, Craighall Park
Tel: 0861-222 532
www.osteriatrenonni.co.za

Unpretentious and good
value, this place is always
abuzz with Italian families
tucking into authentic
dishes from Tuscany and
Umbria. **$$**

Wandie's Place
Makhalamele Street, Soweto
Tel: 011-982 2796
www.wandies.co.za
A mandatory lunch-time
stop on most Soweto tours,
Wandie's has a lively
informal atmosphere and
offers a self-service buffet of
popular local African dishes.
$$

Pretoria

Café Riche
Church Square, City Centre
Tel: 012-328 3173
Open from 6am until after
midnight, this laid-back
street café has a historic
location on Church Square.
The extensive menu of
pastries, snacks and meals

has a strong South African
character. **$**

La Madeleine
122 Priory Road, Lynwood Ridge
Tel: 012-361 3667
www.lamadeleine.co.za
This Pretoria institution has
been serving sensational
Provençal food for more than
30 years. The menu changes
regularly, but simplicity is
always the watchword of
Daniel Leusch's cooking. The
Sunday three-course set
menu is great value.
$$-$$$

**Prue Leith's Chef's
Academy**
262 Rhino Street, Hennops Park,
Centurion
Tel: 012-654 5203
www.prueleith.co.za
Presided over by one of
South Africa's best known
chefs, the award-winning
restaurant has a strong pan-
African flavour to the menu,
and several vegetarian
selections. **$$**

MPUMALANGA AND LIMPOPO

Panorama Route

Canimambo
Corner Louis Trichardt and Hoof
streets, Graskop
Tel: 087-802 5288
www.canimambo.za.net
This is a superb
Mozambican-style
Portuguese restaurant,
serving delicious chicken
piri-piri, lemon butter
prawns and a traditional

Mozambican bean stew for
vegetarians. **$$-$$$**

Harrie's Pancakes
Corner Louis Trichardt and Church
streets, Graskop
Tel: 013-767 1273
www.harriespancakes.com
Founded in 1992 and now
something of a Graskop
institution, Harrie's is still
the place to stop for a light
lunch of sweet or savoury
filled pancakes. **$**

Salt
Bagdad Centre, R40, White River
Tel: 013-751 1555
The pick of a cluster of
eateries in White River's
adjacent Bagdad and
Casterbridge Centres, this
modern and airy restaurant
combines classic-
contemporary decor with an
interesting Continental and
South African fusion menu.
$$$

Mbombela (Nelspruit)

Chez Vincent
56 Ferreira Street
Tel: 013-744-1146
www.chezvincent.co.za
Mediterranean and South
African fusion cuisine are
the speciality at this French
owner-managed guest
house and restaurant in the
town centre. **$$**

OVERLAND ROUTES

Bloemfontein

Seven on Kellner
7 Kellner Street
Tel: 051-447 7928
www.sevenonkellner.co.za
Set in a historic mansion,
Bloemfontein's most
celebrated fine dining venue
has something for everyone,
ranging from exotic
Moroccan fare to wood-fired
pizzas. **$$-$$$**

Kimberley

Butler's Restaurant
The Estate Hotel, Lodge Street
Tel: 053-832 2668
www.theestate.co.za
Part of an internationally-
recognised chef training
school since 2009, this
formal restaurant
specialises in hearty but
imaginative venison and
other meat dishes. **$$$**

Upington

Le Must
11 Schröder Street
Tel: 054-332 6700
www.lemustupington.com
The finest restaurant in the
Northern Cape combines
elegant old-world decor with
traditional and fusion Cape
cuisine dominated by the
meats for which the Karoo
is famous: lamb and

springbok. Not to be missed
if you are in the vicinity. **$$$**

PRICE CATEGORIES

Price categories are for a
three-course meal for one
with a half-bottle of house
wine, except $ which covers
a main course and a drink:
$ = under R100
$$ = R100–200
$$$ = R200–350
$$$$ = over R350

A CTIVITIES

FESTIVALS, THE ARTS, NIGHTLIFE, SHOPPING, OUTDOOR ACTIVITIES AND SPECTATOR SPORTS

FESTIVALS

January

Cape Town Minstrel Carnival. Cape Town's biggest and most raucous carnival sees the city celebrating the advent of the New Year with festivals, competitions and extravagant parades. **Jazzathon**, Cape Town V&A Waterfront Tel: 021-696 6961 www.jazzathon.co.za Highly recommended music festival held over several days in mid-summer. Free entry.

February

Cape Town Pride Festival Tel: 021-425 6461 www.capetownpride.co.za The most flamboyant date on Cape Town's gay calendar, Pride Parade Day is the centrepiece of a fortnight-long festival that includes pageants, balls, wine-tasting sessions, tea parties and a season of gay movies.

March

Cape Town Festival Tel: 021-465 9042 www.capetownfestival.co.za A wave of sizzling talent comes to 20 different venues throughout the region during March.

April

Splashy Fen Music Festival Tel: 031-563 0824 www.splashyfen.co.za Coinciding with the Easter weekend,

and celebrating its 21st in 2011, this is South Africa's answer to Glastonbury, with as good selection of local talent playing over 4-5 nights in the small town of Underberg in the uKhahlamba-Drakensberg foothills.

May

Pink Loerie Mardi Gras www.pinkloerie.com Set in the Garden Route town of Knysna, this lively carnival is second only to its Cape Town counterpart on the country's gay calendar.

June

National Arts Festival www.nafest.co.za Sometimes starting in late June, this ten-day festival in the old settler town of Grahamstown is South Africa's oldest arts festival.

July

Encounters South African Independent Documentary Festival Cinema Nouveau, V&A Waterfront, Cape Town Tel: 021-465 4686 www.encounters.co.za An interesting programme of documentaries from top film-makers.

August

Oppikoppi Bushveld Festival www.oppikoppi.co.za Excellent three-day alternative music festival held in the middle of North West Province's bushveld. **Joy of Jazz Festival** www.joyofjazz.co.za Held at the end of August,

Johannesburg's premier musical festival is a multi-venue affair showcasing jazz musicians from home and abroad, **V&A Waterfront Winter Food Fair** Market Square, V&A Waterfront, Cape Town Tel: 021-556 8200 www.waterfront.co.za A feast of hot and tasty local cuisine and wine. Mid-August.

September

Arts Alive, Johannesburg www.artsalive.co.za This multi-faceted arts festival takes place over three weeks, with everything from comedy and drama to music and dance hosted at a number of venues around Johannesburg **Cape Town Comedy Festival** Tel: 021-425 5792 www.comedyfestival.co.za The world's leading stand-up comics share the stage with top local talents. first three weeks.

December

Mother City Queer Parade www.mcqp.co.za Another highlight of Cape Town's gay calendar.

THE ARTS

Theatre

Although it's restricted to the main population centres, particularly Cape Town and Johannesburg, South Africa has an active and varied theatrical scene, with something to please

TRANSPORT
ACCOMMODATION
EATING OUT
ACTIVITIES
A – Z

ABOVE: band performing at the Cape Town festival

everyone, from light-hearted comedy and musicals to serious drama. Going to the theatre is also an affordable night out on the town, in comparison to London's West End or New York's Broadway strip.

Barnyard Theatre Chain
Tel: 021-914 8898
www.barnyardtheatres.co.za
This popular chain of theatre/restaurant venues specialises in nostalgic musical revues. There are several branches in and around Johannesburg, as well as in Durban, Pretoria, Cape Town, Franschhoek, Mossel Bay and Plettenberg Bay.

Cape Town and Peninsula

Artscape Theatre Centre
DF Malan Street, Foreshore
Tel: 021-410 9800/01
www.artscape.co.za
Box office: Mon–Fri 9am–5pm, Sat 9am–12.30pm.
This theatre might stage anything from an Andrew Lloyd-Webber musical extravaganza to contemporary African dance, classical ballet or opera. It is also home to the **Cape Philharmonic Orchestra** (tel: 021-410 9809, www.cpo.org.za), **Cape Town City Ballet** (tel: 021-650 2400, www.capetowncityballet.org.za), **Cape Town Opera** (tel: 021-410 9807, www.capetownopera.co.za) and the modern dance company **Jazzart Dance Theatre** (tel: 021-410 9848, www.jazzart.co.za).

Baxter Theatre Complex
University of Cape Town, Main Road, Rondebosch
Tel: 021-685 7880
www.baxter.co.za
There are two main venues at this buzzing venue: the Main Theatre and Concert Hall. Productions include light musicals, dramas and comedy.

Little Theatre
Hiddingh Campus, Orange Street
Tel: 021-480 7129

www.uct.ac.za/about/arts/littletheatre
Stages classical, contemporary and experimental student productions in association with the University of Cape Town's Drama Department.

The Fugard Theatre
Corner of Harrington and Caledon streets
Tel: 021-461 4554
www.thefugard.com
Cape Town's newest theatre is named after the eminent playwright Athol Fugard. Situated in District Six, in the handsomely restored Sacks Futeran Building, it has a very pleasant roof terrace and is a good place to see arty local productions.

Theatre on the Bay
Link Street, Camps Bay
Tel: 021-438 3301
www.theatreonthebay.co.za
This vibey theatre definitely has the best setting in Cape Town. It's situated on the trendy strip on Camps Bay, where you can enjoy a light drink or supper before making your way to the show.

On Broadway
88 Shortmarket Street
Tel: 021-424 1194

Cinema Scene

There are cinema complexes in most main shopping malls, operated either by Ster-Kinekor (www.sterkinekor.com) or by Nu-Metro (www.numetro.co.za).

Full listings are advertised on the websites and in local newspapers, with mainstream Hollywood movies dominating. European and alternative films are screened at a handful of **Cinema Nouveau** complexes in the large cities (see also www.sterkinekor.com) and at Cape Town's independent **Labia Theatre** (www.labia.co.za).

www.onbroadway.co.za
This central dinner-theatre features brilliant drag shows, cabaret and stand-up comedy shows.

Kalk Bay Theatre
52 Main Road, Kalk Bay
Tel: 073-220 5430
www.kbt.co.za
The oldest theatre in Cape Town is situated in a Victorian church hall in the quaint village of Kalk Bay.

Durban

Elizabeth Sneddon Theatre
Mazisi Kunene (South Ridge) Road
Tel: 031-260 2296
www.sneddontheatre.co.za
Part of the University of KwaZulu-Natal, this established venue hosts a variety of student performances as well as outside productions.

Playhouse Theatre
231 Anton Lembede (Smith) Street
Tel: 031-369 9555
www.playhousecompany.com
The city's premier theatre hosts a varied selection of drama and dance.

Gauteng

Joburg Theatre
Loveday Street, Braamfontein
Tel: 011-877 6800
www.showbusiness.co.za
Formerly the Civic Theatre, this huge venue has four auditoria: The Mandela, The Fringe, The Peoples and space.com, the latter a versatile "black box" environment.

The Market Theatre
Market Theatre Complex, Bree Street, Newtown
Tel: 011-832 1641
www.markettheatre.co.za
The home of South African protest theatre contains three stages: the Main Auditorium, the Barney Simon Theatre and the Laager Theatre.

State Theatre
Church Street, Pretoria
Tel: 012-392 4000
www.statetheatre.co.za
Set in the heart of Pretoria, this has seven auditoriums with everything from symphony orchestras and opera to contemporary drama.

Victory Theatre
105 Louis Botha Avenue, Orange Grove
Tel: 011-728 9603
www.victorytheatre.co.za
This dinner-theatre specialises in musicals and cabaret acts.

Windybrow Theatre
Nugget Street, Hillbrow
Tel: 011-720 0003
www.windybrowarts.co.za
Known for alternative and fringe dramas.

Classical Music

The Cape Philharmonic Orchestra
(tel: 021-410 9809 www.cpo.org.za) is a
full-time professional symphony
orchestra that often hosts
internationally known conductors and
soloists, and performs over 100
concerts each year. They play most
Thursday nights at Cape Town City
Hall, on Darling Street, opposite the
Grand Parade. Also worth checking
out, with details of pending
performances posted on their
websites, are the Pretoria-based
Chamber Orchestra of South Africa
(tel: 012-420 2249; www.cosa.co.za),
Durban's **KwaZulu-Natal
Philharmonic** (tel: 031 369 9438;
www.kznpo.co.za) and the **Johannesburg
Philharmonic** (tel: 011-789 2733;
www.jpo.co.za).

Dance

Traditional African dances are
frequently performed informally at
wildlife lodges and more formally in
the form of musicals staged at some
of the theatres listed above. **The
Cape Town City Ballet** (tel: 021-650
2400; www.capetowncityballet.org.za),
based in the Artscape Theatre
Complex *(see Theatre)* also performs
at other events in and around Cape
Town. In addition to classical ballets,
it stages more contemporary
productions mixing dance, opera and
rock singers.

Its Johannesburg counterpart,
based in the Joburg Theatre, is the
South African Ballet Theatre (tel:
011-877 6898; www.saballettheatre.co.za).
More oriented to traditional African
and contemporary dance
performances is the **Jazzart Dance
Theatre** (also based in Artscape, tel:
021-410 9848; www.jazzart.co.za), and
private **Cape Dance Company** (tel:
021-701 0599; www.capedancecompany.
co.za). For detailed listings of all types
of dance performances countrywide,
check the website www.dancedirectory.
co.za.

Comedy

Stand-up comedy is thriving in South
Africa, much of it highly satirical in
character, demonstrating the country's
newfound ability to laugh both at itself
and its politicians. The trend was
pioneered by the internationally
acclaimed female impersonator Pieter
Dirk Uys, whose celebrated alter-ego
Evita Bezuidenhout, originally created
to satirise government policies in the
apartheid era, now thrives as the

hostess of her own comedy venue
Evita Se Perron (tel: 022-492 3930;
www.evita.co.za) in the small town of
Darling, a short drive north of Cape
Town. Other prominent figures in the
movement include Marc Lottering,
David Kau and Loyiso Gola.

Good venues for stand-up comedy
include Cape Town's **Jou Ma Se
Comedy Club** (tel: 021-447 7237;
www.kurt.co.za), **Zula Bar** (Monday
evenings; Long Street; www.zulabar.co.za)
and the **Purple Turtle Bar** (Thursday
evenings; Long Street; 021-424 0811;
www.thepurpleturtle.co.za).

In Johannesburg, **Parkers Comedy**
(Montecasino Boulevard; Corner
William Nicol and Witkoppen roads;
tel: 011-511 0081; www.parkerscomedy.
com) claims to be the only purpose-
built comedy club in Africa.

Jazz Music

Performed in both the American and
distinctive South African styles – as
well as fusions thereof – jazz is very
popular in South Africa, partially due to
its strong association with the early
years of the anti-apartheid struggle,
before such popular icons as Hugh
Masakela, Abdullah Ibrahim (Dollar
Brand) and Miriam Makeba opted for,
or were forced into, overseas exile.
The scene still thrives today, and there
is regular live jazz at venues such as
Johannesburg's Bassline (10 Henry
Nxumalo Street, Newtown; tel: 011-
838 9142; www.bassline.co.za) and
Katzy's (The Firs Shopping Centre,
Oxford Road, Rosebank, tel: 011-880
3945; www.katzys.co.za) and Cape Town's
Green Dolphin (V&A Waterfront; tel:
021-421 7471) and **Dizzy Jazz Café**
(The Drive, Camps Bay; tel: 021-438
2686; www.dizzys.co.za).

NIGHTLIFE

South Africa is primarily an outdoor
destination and it lacks the sort of
cosmopolitan nightlife one associates
with cities such as London, Paris or
Sydney. but there are plenty of
opportunities for night owls to enjoy
themselves, particularly in Cape Town
and, to a lesser extent, Johannesburg.

Johannesburg

Johannesburg has a rather diffused
nightlife scene, thanks partly to the
city centre's reputation for crime, and
it lacks a focal point equivalent to, say
Long Street in Cape Town.

Well worth an evening, however, is

the cluster of venues in the revitalised
Newton Precinct (www.newtown.co.za),
whose focal point is the Market
Theatre and the adjacent
Gramadoelas Restaurant. A legendary
live venue here is **Kippies**, named for
1950s sax player Kippie Moeketsi,
and specialising in township jazz.
There's also **The Bassline** (10 Henry
Nxumalo Street, tel: 011-838 9142;
www.bassline.co.za), which hosts a good
variety of live music, from jazz and
reggae to afrobeat and kwaito.

Clubs and Bars

The best venues are dotted in and
around the trendy northern suburbs of
Melville, and to a lesser extent,
Rosebank. Probably the greatest
concentration of such hangouts is
along Melville's Fourth Avenue and
Seventh Street – try **Xai-Xai** (tel: 011-
482 6990) at the northern end of
Fourth Road for a glass of wine and
typical Mozambican selection of
seafood and spicy peri-peri dishes, or
Cool Runnings (tel: 011-482 4786;
www.coolrunnings.co.za) at the other end
for a relaxed outdoor beer, or **Ratz** (tel:
011-726 2019, www.ratz.co.za),
Unplugged on 7th (tel: 011-482
5133) and the **Tokyo Star** (tel: 011-
486 334; www.tokyostar.co.za) in-between,
for trendy (sometimes live) music.

For those based in upmarket
Sandton, **The Blues Room** (Village
Walk, Rivonia Road, tel: 011-784
5527; www.bluesroom.co.za) is a good all
round live music and dance venue,
with a more varied and contemporary
selection of music than its name
might suggest – some of the country's
top DJs, rock, hip-hop and dance acts
have performed here, and there is
sometimes comedy too. Popular
venues in the northern suburbs
include **Latinova** (60 Jan Smuts Ave,
Rosebank, tel: 011-447 1006; www.
latinovasa.com), **FTV Sandton**
(Michelangelo Towers, Sandton, tel:
011-783 1866; www.ftvsandton.co.za)
and **E.S.P** (84 Oxford Road, Ferndale;
tel: 011-792 4110).

Cape Town

Unlike Johannesburg, Cape Town still
has a vibrant city centre with several
focal points for nightlife. The most
important is backpacker-oriented
Long Street and Kloof Nek, in the
heart of the city centre, which has so
many bars, eateries and music
venues you can easily just explore at
whim. There is also the more westerly
Green Point and De Waterkant, known
for its flourishing gay scene, and the
slicker V&A Waterfront.

ABOVE: Cape Town nightlife.

Cocktails, Clubs and Bars

For sophisticated pre-dinner cocktails in the city centre, try the **Planet Cocktail Bar** (Mount Nelson Hotel; 76 Orange Street, Gardens; tel: 021-483 1737; www.mountnelson.co.za; 5pm–late daily), where you can expect to find a mix of young and mature, locals and tourists, tapping their feet to the funky music. At the other end of the scale, **Rafiki's** (13 Kloof Nek Road, Tamboerskloof; tel: 021-426 4731; www.rafikis.co.za), is a good place to hang out with a mixed bunch of locals and backpackers. On Long Street, there's none more vibey than **Cape to Cuba** (227 Long Street tel: 021-424 2330; www.capetocuba.com), an all-rounder with a mellow mood, Cuban-style decor and indoor or balcony seating. For a more historic setting, nowhere better than the **Fireman's Arms** (Corner Buitengracht and Mechau streets; tel: 021-419 1513; www.firemansarms.co.za), the city's oldest pub, dating to 1864, with unpretentious homely decor complemented by large screen TVs for sports events and a good sound system.

Altogether less grungey than Long Street is the V&A Waterfront where the most sophisticated drinking hole is the **Bascule Whisky Bar and Wine Cellar** (Cape Grace Hotel; tel: 021-410 7100) which offers more than 400 whiskies, an extensive wine list, plush leather sofas, breathtaking views of Table Mountain and tasty nibbles. Although you might break the bank with a single glass of icy Sauvignon Blanc. For a more affordable and down-to-earth night out, visit **Ferryman's Tavern** (tel: 021-419 7748; www.ferrymans.co.za), which has graced the V&A Waterfront since 1989 and has cosy indoor seating, a beer garden, and a good selection of local beers and inexpensive pub grub. Right next door

is **Mitchell's** (tel: 021-425 9462; www.mitchellsseafront.co.za), which serves a range of ales and beers from in its own Knysna-based brewery.

A host of buzzing cocktail bars lines the main road through trendy Camps Bay on the Western Seaboard, a short drive from the city centre. The evergreen **Café Caprice** (tel: 021-438 8315; www.cafecaprice.co.za), with the feel of Ibiza-meets-Cannes, spills out onto the pavement across from the beach; arrive early to grab a table and enjoy the often spectacular sunset. Another institution for casual sundowners is **La Med** (tel: 021-438 5600; www.lamed.co.za), where you should come early to get a spot on the deck overlooking the ocean, before hitting the late-night dance floor that opens later.

The Sand Bar (31 Victoria Road. Tel: 021-438 8336; www.sandbar.co.za; daily 9.30am–late) is a pavement bar with great views but none of the pretentiousness that you'll find elsewhere on the strip.

For a pub-like atmosphere, Kalk Bay has two options: the **Brass Bell** (waves practically wash over it on a stormy night, 021 788 5455. www.brassbell.co.za) and the **Polana** (tel: 021-788 4133, www.harbourhouse.co.za; until 3am), where you can eat or curl up in an old leather armchair.

Recommended nightclubs and dance music venues around Cape Town include **Hemisphere** (31st floor, ABSA Building, 2 Riebeek Street; tel: 021-421 0581; www.hemisphere.org.za), **Mercury Live and Lounge** (43 De

Villiers Street; tel: 021-465 2106), **Chrome** (6 Pepper Street; tel: 083-700 6078; www.chromect.com), **Fiction** (226 Long Street, tel: 021-424 5709; www.fictionbar.com) and the **Bang Bang Club** (70 Loop Street, tel: 021-426 2011; www.thebangbangclub.co.za).

For live music in the city centre, try the **Zula Sound Bar** (196 Long Street; tel: 021-424 2442; www.zulabar.co.za) or **The Assembly** (61 Harrington Street, District Six; tel: 021-465 7286; www.theassembly.co.za).

Alternatively, head out out of town to Muizenberg for the **Acoustic Café** (Corner Main and Camp roads, tel: 021-788 1900; http://acousticcafe.tripod.com) or the Melting Pot (15 Church Street, tel: 021-788 9791).

SHOPPING

Shopping Malls

South Africa's cities are scattered with shopping malls hosting dozens or even hundreds of chain stores and boutiques selling a range of goods comparable to any mall in Europe or North America. Among those most convenient to tourists are Cape Town's **V&A Waterfront** (www.waterfront.co.za), Johannesburg's **Sandton City** (www.sandtoncity.com) and **Rosebank Mall** (www.themallofrosebank.co.za), and Durban's **Gateway** (www.gatewayworld.co.za). Details of other malls near to your hotel can be obtained from the receptionist.

Spas and Treatments

Many upmarket hotels and game lodges now have wellness centres or spas offering massages, beauty treatments and such, and those that don't can usually make arrangements for guests elsewhere. There are also several dedicated spas in the country, most centred on natural hot springs. Some of the best known are as follows:

Bela Bela, 100km (62 miles) from Pretoria on the N1, in Limpopo Province, is a renowned mineral resort with a modern health complex that includes various pools and hydrotherapy facilities. There is also a nature reserve (with a variety of game) where you can take lovely walks. Accommodation is in chalets, flats, a caravan park and camping site. Contact Bela Bela Tourist Information, tel: 014-736 3694; www.belabelatourism.co.za.

To get to the **Cradock Spa** (tel:

048 881 2709; www.cradock-spa.co.za), 5km (3 miles) outside the town of the same name on the Eastern Cape, take the N10 between Port Elizabeth towards Middelburg. There are lovely trails and paths through this area. Also, in Aliwal North, on the N6 between Bloemfontein and East London, the **Fish Eagle Spa** (tel: 051 633 3777, www.fisheaglespa.co.za) has mineral springs and thermal baths, plus open-air and indoor pools, a bio-kinetic centre and a children's water playground.

Montagu Springs (tel: 021-614 1050; www.montagusprings.co.za) have been touted for their curative powers for more than 200 years. These mineral springs are located almost 3km (2 miles) north of Montagu, in the Cogmans Kloof (Gorge) Nature Reserve, Western Cape. There are many hiking trails in the vicinity.

Arts and Handicrafts

For many tourists, the most interesting shopping in South Africa is for arts and handicrafts made locally or imported from elsewhere in Africa. These are usually best bought at one of a few specific craft markets, listed below, or if you are a more serious collector from specialist shops. Cape Town excels for craft and memento shopping, with Long Street in particular being lined with quirky shops selling everything from East African CDs to West African fabrics.

In rural areas, the **Ndebele** paint their houses with certain specific patterns, and produce magnificent beaded jewellery as well as copper and bronze bracelets; while the filigree-like chains of **Zulu** beadwork have an entirely different character. The **Venda** produce brightly coloured clay pots while in **Mpumalanga**, along the Panorama Route, you can find leiklip, a soft, shale-like stone with light and dark layers, which is used to make ashtrays and animal carvings.

Making a Purchase

When considering a purchase, you should ask about the item's provenance. Old (antique) South African beadwork and San (Bushman) curios, for instance, are very rare. It is also ethically unacceptable and illegal to buy products made of ivory or associated with plants or other animals listed by CITES (The Convention on International Trade in Endangered Species of Wild Fauna and Flora; www.cites.com).

As for other shopping practicalities, bargaining over prices isn't really the norm in South Africa, the one significant exception being when buying crafts from market stalls or from the side of the road. There are no hard-and-fast rules or magical formulas in this situation – sometimes the initial asking price may be slightly inflated, at other times grossly so – but you can probably expect to knock at least a third off that price, sometimes more, through good-natured negotiation.

Western Cape

African Music Store
134 Long Street, Cape Town
Tel: 021-426 0857
This is the best specialist African CD shop on the continent, with knowledgeable staff and racks stacked with everything from local kwaito to the latest sounds from Mali, Congo or Ethiopia.

Clarke's Bookshop
211 Long Street, Cape Town
Tel: 021-423 5739
www.clarkesbooks.co.za
Established in 1956, this excellent second-hand bookshop is highly rated by serious collectors for its specialist collections of Africana and tomes about South African art.

Galerie Ezakwantu
Village Centre, Huguenot Road, Franschhoek
Tel: 021-876 2162
www.ezakwantu.com
One of the top galleries of its type in the region, this will delight ethnic arts and crafts enthusiasts with its superb collection of quality African artworks.

Greenmarket Square Flea Market
Corner Shortmarket and Burg streets, Cape Town
Mon–Sat 9am–4pm
This daily market is the city's best one-stop for African crafts, and the vendors here are as varied in African origin as their wares.

Mali South Clothing
90 Long Street, Cape Town
Tel: 021-426 1519
www.malisouthclothing.co.za
Malian designer Maiga Abdoulaye uses the colourful cloths traditional to West Africa as the basis for an innovative range of men's, women's and children's clothing.

Pan-African Market
76 Long Street, Cape Town
Tel: 021-426 4478
Mon–Sat 8.30am–5.30pm
Sprawling across three floors, this is a wonderful place to dig around for carvings, textiles, beadwork, ceramics, tableware, clothes, shoes, baskets, jewellery and CDs from all over Africa.

Tribal Trends
72–74 Long Street, Cape Town
Tel: 021-423 8008
sales@tribaltends.co.za
This owner-managed store has the finest selection of African crafts, artworks and antiques you're likely to encounter anywhere.

Vaughan Johnson's Wine Shop
V&A Waterfront, Cape Town
Tel: 021-419 2121
The eponymous owner-manager of this long-serving emporium is one of the country's leading wine experts, and it's a good place to sample and stock up on Cape wines – which can be shipped to anywhere in the world.

KwaZulu-Natal

Amphimarket
O.R Tambo (Lower Marine) Parade, Durban
Tel: 031-301 3080

The Amphitheatre is transformed into a flea market where you can also watch Zulu dancers. Every Sunday 9am–4pm.

Church Square Flea Market
City Hall, between Dr Pixley KaSeme (West) and Monty Naicker (Pine) streets
Tel: 031-392 1400
Curios, clothing – a little bit of everything. Daily 8am–4.30pm.

Essenwood Craft Market
Essenwood Park, Stephen Dlamini (Essenwood) Road, Berea
Tel: 031-208 1264
www.essenwoodmarket.com
Every Saturday arts and crafts, plus tea garden and live music, 9am–2pm.

Victoria Street Market
Corner Denis Hurley (Queen) and Bertha Mkhize (Victoria) streets, Durban
Haggling is expected here: you can get discounts of up to 30 percent when buying jewellery, wood-carvings, hand-embroidered clothing or Indian spices. Mon–Sat 6am–5pm, Sun 10am–3pm.

Gauteng

African Craft and Rooftop Market
Rosebank Mall, Johannesburg
Tel: 011-880 2096
www.themallofrosebank.co.za
One of the best in Johannesburg for African artefacts and crafts – from as far afield as the Ivory Coast and Ghana. Craft market open 9am–5pm daily; rooftop market Sun only.

Bruma Flea Market
Corner Ernest Oppenheimer and Marcia avenues, Johannesburg
Tel: 011-622 9648
Hundreds of stalls to choose from – including plenty selling good-quality African crafts. Tue–Sun 9am–5pm.

Michael Mount Organic Village Market
Bryanston Road, Johannesburg
Tel: 011-706 3671
Around 100 stands selling hand-sewn clothes, jewellery, African batik and pearl creations, minerals and crystals, glass, leather, woodwork, and even organically grown vegetables. Thur–Sat 9am–3pm; Tuesday nearest the full moon, 6–9pm.

Market Theatre Flea Market
Market Theatre, Johannesburg
Tel: 085-586 8687
Sat 9am–4pm. The best-known bazaar in Johannesburg, worth a visit for people-watching.

Mpumalanga

Promenade Centre Flea Market
Louis Trichardt Street, Mbombela

White River just north of Mbombela (Nelspruit), is home to a number of well-known South African wildlife artists including sculptors, woodcutters, weavers and potters. Contact the regional tourist office *(see page 371)* for further information. Sat 8am–1pm; moonlight markets last Friday of the month 6–10pm.
Casterbridge Lifestyle Centre
White River
Tel: 013-751 1540
www.casterbridge.co.za
There's plenty of interesting craft and boutique shops in this pretty outdoor centre on the northern outskirts of White River.

Limpopo Province

Liberty Gardens Flea Market
Polokwane
First and last Saturday of the month, set in the Library Gardens, 9am–5pm.

Free State

Cinderella Castle
Clarens
Curio shop in a building made of beer bottles.
Westdene Flea Market
Brill Street, Bloemfontein
Second Saturday of the month 8am–1pm.

OUTDOOR ACTIVITIES

Hiking

The best way to explore South Africa's lofty mountains, long, sandy beaches, indigenous forests and plantations is on foot. Opportunities range from short rambles suitable for families with young children to week-long expeditions and guided wilderness trails in big-game country. A network of self-catering overnight hiking trails traverses the country from the **Augrabies Falls National Park** in the Northern Cape to the **Western Cape mountains** and the **Soutpansberg** in Limpopo Province. While some trails follow the coastline, others traverse challenging peaks which are often covered in snow during the winter. Some wind through the aromatic *fynbos* vegetation of the Western Cape, others through the grasslands of the Free State. Hiking trails vary in length from two to eight days, although shorter alternatives are usually available on long routes.
    Heading the list of South Africa's most popular trails is the **Otter Hiking**

Trail along the southern Cape coast, while the **Blyderivierspoort** and **Fanie Botha hiking trails** in Mpumalanga are other favourites. Of the several wilderness areas available to outdoor enthusiasts seeking solitude and tranquillity, those in the **uKhahlamba-Drakensberg Park** are the most dramatic. Although footpaths exist, backpackers are not obliged to stick to a particular route, nor are any facilities provided.
    Backpacking requires a degree of experience and self-reliance and, depending on weather conditions, nights are spent either under the stars, in caves or, in many instances, in a small backpacking tent. Other wilderness areas include the **Cedarberg**, **Groot-Winterhoek** and **Boesmanbos** (Western Cape), the **Baviaanskloof** and **Groendal** (Eastern Cape), **Ntekenda** in KwaZulu-Natal and the **Wolkberg** in the north. For many hikers, however, the ultimate outdoor experience is a **guided wilderness trail** such as those conducted in Kruger National Park and several game reserves in KwaZulu-Natal.
    For guided wilderness trails and the more popular hiking trails, advance planning is essential, since it is almost impossible to get a booking at short notice. For details of booking hiking trails in the national parks and KwaZulu-Natal, see the websites www.sanparks.org and www.kznwildlife.com respectively. Alternatively, visit www.sahikes.co.za which provides detailed descriptions of contact details for more than 300 routes countrywide, as well as listing most local hiking clubs in the country, and providing excellent information about hiking preparation and first aid on the trail.
    Johannesburg-based **Drifters** (tel: 011-888 1160; www.drifters.co.za) has been organising multi-day hikes to

various parts of South Africa since the 1980s.

Mountaineering

South Africa's mountains and marvellous cliff formations are particularly inviting to mountain climbers, who will find details of the best areas for climbing and contact details for the 14 regional branches of the Mountain Club of South Africa on its website www.mcsa.org.za.
    Popular sites for climbing include the **Magaliesberg Mountains**, which lies less than two 2 hours by car from Johannesburg. On the range's north side, the rock faces have been eroded in places into picturesque gorges, lined with clear mountain brooks and giant trees (difficulty rating up to 8b on the French scale). Limpopo Province also offers tempting and difficult faces with walls up to 400 metres (1,300ft) high. For information, contact the Magaliesberg section of the Mountain Club of South Africa, tel: 087-808 3729.
    KwaZulu-Natal's **Drakensberg Mountains** have a more Alpine character; there are several 3,000-metre (9,800ft) peaks to scale. The highest mountain in the range is just over the Lesotho border, the 3,482 metre (11,386ft) Thabana Ntlenyana. Most of the climbing mountains in KwaZulu-Natal lie within the uKhahlamba-Drakensberg Park (www.kznwildlife.com); before beginning, climbers have to register at the relevant park entrance gate.
    Montesiel, between Durban and Pietermaritzburg, is held to be the best region in South Africa for hobby climbers.
    Cape Province contains the most popular and best-known mountains for climbers. Leader among these is

BELOW: South Africa offers some stunning trails for walkers and bikers.

Table Mountain (1,084 metres/ 3,556ft), which boasts more than 500 routes. Northwest of Cape Town, the **Cedarberg Range** enchants visitors with its wonderful rock formations. Along the Garden Route, the **du Toits Kloof Mountains** (Bain's Kloof and Sir Lowry's Pass) are also climbers' favourites.

Rock climbers incline towards Limpopo Province, or the Cedarberg or du Toits Kloof Mountains in the Cape. Often, the best mountains for climbing are privately owned. For more details, visit the website of Climb ZA (www.climb.co.za).

Four-wheel Drive Camping

Four-wheel drive vehicles are advisable for journeys into Botswana or the more remote beaches of northern KwaZulu-Natal. Rental vehicles are available fully equipped with a long-distance tank, special jack, fridge, one or two tents on the roof rack and camping requisites (bedding, cutlery, gas stove and gas lamps). The rental price normally includes insurance and unlimited mileage. In general it is safer to use international companies or to follow recommendations from friends.

As camping equipment is seldom available for rent, tents are best brought from home. Alternatively, it can be bought cheaply at South African chain stores such as Makro (tel: 0860-300 999; www.makro.co.za) or Cape Union Mart (tel: 021-464 5800; www.capeunionmart.co.za).

Rental companies include **Campers Corner Rentals** (tel: 011-793 3536; www.campers.co.za) and **U-Drive-Rent-a-Car** (tel: 011-392 5852; www.udrive.co.za).

Gliding

The north of the country is renowned for its good gliding conditions – endless blue skies, stable weather all year round with lots of sunshine and thermals that facilitate very long glides. Gliding tours are offered and clubs may be helpful in organising equipment privately; there are no commercially organised hiring facilities. For further information contact the **Aero Club of South Africa** (tel: 011-082 1100; www.aeroclub.org.za) or **Magaliesberg Gliding Club** (www.mgc.org.za).

Hang-gliding

To practise hang-gliding in South Africa, you need to be a member of the South African Aero Club (see above), thereby incurring a liability insurance, but temporary membership is available. Also, check whether your licence system is valid here. Equipment may be a problem if you need to hire it. Clubs may be able to help, but there are no regular hiring facilities. For further information, contact the **South African Hang Gliding and Para-gliding Association** (tel: 074-152-2505; www.sahpa.co.za).

Cycling

As there are no cycling paths, the sport is more hazardous than in Europe. However, traffic on the smaller roads is not heavy. Despite the distances involved, people do cycle from Johannesburg to Cape Town, from Durban to Johannesburg, along the Garden Route and most of all around the Western Cape, which is wonderfully suited for fun cycling as it has magnificent scenery and there is no rain during the summer months (October–April).

Useful organisations include **Cycling South Africa** (www.cyclingsa.com), the official cycling body in South Africa, and **Mountain Biking in South Africa** (www.mtbonline.co.za) whose website has news and links to local mountain bike clubs.

Bike Hire

Downhill Adventures
Corner Kloof and Long streets, Cape Town
Tel: 021-422 0388
www.downhilladventures.com

Golf

Some 300 registered golf courses are scattered around the country, offering a wide range of challenges. Many also incorporate the natural habitat to stunning effect. Most of the leading courses are reviewed on the website www.southafricagolf.com

From the **Milnerton** or **Mowbray** greens, you have a splendid view of Table Mountain, while the **Wild Coast Course** is laid out with sea water, dunes and plants. The **Royal Cape** and **Royal Johannesburg** are graced by beautiful old trees, dating from 1882 and 1890 respectively. The **Royal George** and the **Durban Country** are said to be the most beautiful golf courses. It's advisable to call the club secretary and ask for a confirmed starting time and dress codes.

For further information – possibly the planning of a golf safari – contact **South African Golf Tours**, tel: 021-712 1949; www.southafricangolftours.com.

Horse Riding

The diversity and spaciousness of the South African landscape, together with the temperate climate, lends itself well to horse riding. Riding is within reach of many more people here than in Europe since it is more affordable.

Trails are available throughout the country, offering visitors a chance to experience it at a "grass-roots level" where the sensations of what South Africa is about are really immediate and alive. For more details, contact the Association for Horse Trails and Safaris in Southern Africa, tel: 011-788 3923.

Trails in the Drakensberg take you through scenic grandeur, across natural streams and grassy plains along the escarpment. The area appears untouched by the 21st century. You may come across rural dwellings or Basotho (the people of Lesotho) pursuing the rhythm of their traditional lifestyle.

Drifters, PO Box 484, Roosevelt Park 2129, tel: 011-888 1160; www.drifters.co.za.

Hollybrooke Farms (tel: 082-552 1285; www.hollybrooke.co.za) offers horseback excursions along the Magalies River in the untrammelled thornbush of the Skeerpoort Valley, less than an hour's drive from Johannesburg or Pretoria. A range of other activities are available, as is accommodation.

Equus Horse Safaris (tel: 014-721 0063; www.equus.co.za) and **Horizon Horseback** (tel: 27083-419 1929; www.ridinginafrica.com), both offer horse riding holidays in the craggy, isolated Waterberg range, 2 hours' drive north of Pretoria.

Trails in the Cape are equally scenic but offer a very different landscape that includes lush green surroundings, rolling hills, forests and vineyards.

Sleepy Hollow Horse Riding (tel: 021-789 2341, www.sleepyhollowhorseriding.co.za), gives you the chance to ride in the beautiful surroundings of the Noordhoek Valley. Join their sunset and champagne rides, moonlight rides with an evening meal, morning rides with a hearty farmhouse breakfast afterwards and lessons. The 2-hour beach ride is highly recommended in winter.

Marathons

Road running – ranging in distance from 10 to 90km (6 to 55 miles) – is one of South Africa's most popular sports. Events are held in most major towns and cities at weekends.

TRANSPORT

ACCOMMODATION

EATING OUT

ACTIVITIES

A – Z

The highlight of the year is the 90km (55-mile) **Comrades Marathon** (www.comrades.com) which alternates annually between Durban and Pietermaritzburg on 31 May. The race has an 11-hour time limit and attracts over 10,000 participants. The runners have to endure a 700-metre (2,300ft) altitude difference. The 50km (31-mile) **Two Oceans Marathon** (www.twooceansmarathon.org.za) on the Cape Peninsula every Easter Saturday also attracts many runners. Another popular event is the **City to City Marathon** from Johannesburg to Pretoria.

For details of other events contact Athletics South Africa (tel: 011-880 5800; www.athletics.org.za).

Canoeing

South Africans engage with enthusiasm in all forms of canoeing: white water, slalom, sprint and long distance. Olympic canoeists and trainers regard the Highveld as a good training area because of the sunny climate and high altitude (Johannesburg lies at 1,700 metres/yards). There are also some very challenging rivers in South Africa. Some clubs hire out equipment. For information, visit the **Canoeing South Africa** website www.canoesa.org.za.

River Rafting

This is another popular way to enjoy the many large African rivers, especially the Orange River. For 4–6 days let this gentle giant take you in rubber rafts or canoes through the most spectacular, unspoilt Richtersveld. The wonderful thing is that no canoeing experience is required and even children can take part (especially in the rubber-raft trips).

Rafting and Canoeing Trips

Felix Unite
(Tugela, Orange and Breede rivers – canoes)
Tel: 021-702 9400
www.felixunite.com
This is the very best agency for finding out all you need to know about rafting and canoeing in South Africa.

Diving

Diving South Africa's coastal waters is a great way to explore the rich marine life (2,000 species) from the icy west coast (the Benguela current of the Atlantic) to the subtropical east coast (the Agulhas current of the Indian Ocean).

On the Atlantic coast, divers can harvest rock lobster (crayfish), perlemoen, black mussels and others. Where the warm Agulhas current can be felt further up the Eastern Cape coast, the marine life changes: flame coral, starfish, feather stars and other exotic and colourful sea creatures abound. People without diving experience might consider making use of diving courses offered here to acquire diving qualifications.

The best area for diving is the northern part of the iSimangaliso Wetland Park, running northward from Cape Vidal (on the level of St Lucia Lake) via Sodwana Bay to the Mozambique border, where an aquatic reserve stretches for 5km (3 miles) out into the sea to protect the world's southernmost coral reefs and its colourful marine life. A recommended operator here, offering courses as well as single dives, is **Sodwana Bay Lodge Scuba Centre**, tel: 035-571 0117; www.sodwanadiving.co.za.

The region between Umhlanga Rocks and Salt Rock, with its shallower reefs close to the coast, lends itself especially to spear fishing. Vetch's pier is more for beginners.

Based in Umkomaas, just south of Durban, **Aliwal Dive Centre** (tel: 039-973 2233; www.aliwalshoal.co.za) organises dives to the Aliwal Shoal 4km (2 miles) off the coast.

In the Tsitsikamma Section of Garden Route National Park, east of Plettenberg Bay, a snorkelling trail and a scuba-diving trail have been established so you can explore this silent world. For more information, see www.sanparks.org.

The numerous rugged stretches of coast in the southwestern Cape make diving a fascinating proposition almost everywhere. You may well discover old wrecks between Danger Point and Waenhuiskrans; more information can be obtained from the Cape Overberg Tourism Association (tel: 021-405 4500; www.tourismcape overberg.co.za). Closer to Cape Town, Cape Hangklip is another popular diving area.

Fishing

Trout fishing is pursued by many South Africans all over the country. You need a licence – not transferable from province to province – which is issued by a magistrate's court or (sometimes) by the office of the nature reserve where the stream is located. Obviously, you also require the prescribed trout tackle. The season is all year round, peaking in

autumn and spring. In the north, the favourite areas are Dullstroom, Pilgrim's Rest, Graskop, Sabie and Lydenberg, all in Mpumalanga.

The KwaZulu-Natal trout areas are all along the Drakensberg Escarpment and rivers in the Umgeni and Himeville districts. In the Cape, popular trout fishing areas are around Stellenbosch, La Motte, Bain's Kloof and Maden Dam near King Williams Town.

For information, contact the **Federation of South African Fly Fishermen**, tel: 011-467 5992; www. fosaf.org.za.

Rock and Surf Angling

This is a favourite pastime all along South Africa's interesting coastline with its varied conditions concerning water temperatures, winds and currents, all of which affect the type of marine life. Fishing permits are required for particular areas such as Table Bay (obtainable from harbour authorities). No licences are required to fish off the KwaZulu-Natal coast or in estuaries, but taking rock life such as crayfish does.

Popular coastal strips include Durban Harbour, North and South Pier, St Lucia, Mapelane, Cape Vidal, Mission Rocks, Umfolozi and Sodwana Bay. The best season here is June–November.

The Garden Route coastline, the peninsula coastline and False Bay and from Gordon's Bay around Cape Hangklip are popular areas. The season is all year round.

Game and Deep-sea Fishing

This has a special thrill for many anglers. June marks the famous Sardine Run which is accompanied by hundreds of game fish, while in the Cape the two main runs are the tunny run in October and the runs of snoek in autumn and winter. The best areas of the KwaZulu-Natal coast include the south coast, off Durban harbour and the north coast at Sodwana, Richards Bay and St Lucia (season December–June). Cape areas include Hout Bay, Simon's Town and Hermanus, where the season stretches mid-October–November and March–mid-May. In KwaZulu-Natal the best season for marlin and sail fish is November–April, while in the Cape the long fin and yellow-fin tunny are in season September–April.

Sailing

With an almost 3,000km (1,860-mile) coastline of sandy beaches, bays, lagoons, cliffs and rock shorelines, the South African seas offer the sailing enthusiast the full spectrum of challenges in conditions from the Cape of Storms to calm seas bathed in sunshine. On average the winds are in the 15–25 knots range.

Yacht-club facilities are excellent, from clubs with 50 to those with 3,000 members. Most yachts in South Africa belong to the cruising category in the 10–15-metre (50–80ft) range, of which the majority are built locally to stringent standards. Offshore sailing requires that you belong to a recognised yacht club and that you comply with harbour regulations (licence, permits, registration, etc.). Local yacht clubs include the following:

Royal Cape Yacht Club
PO Box 772, Cape Town 8000
Tel: 021-421 1354
www.rcyc.co.za
Point Yacht Club
3 Maritime Place, Durban 4000, KwaZulu-Natal
Tel: 031-301 4787
www.pyc.co.za
The following listed organisations offer courses in sailing, scenic chartered tours, and activities such as fishing:
Good Hope Sailing Academy
PO Box 32296, Camps Bay 8040
Tel: 021-424 4665
www.goodhopesailingacademy.co.za
They offer everything from lunch and sunset charters to five-day cruises in 13 metre (45ft) and 16 metre (53ft) sailing boats off the Cape coast and in the best wetland and wildlife sanctuaries.

Dinghy Sailing
Dinghy sailing (that is, sailing in a boat under 6 metres/20ft with raisable centreboard) is popular mainly on the inland dams. Clubs welcome visitors and may be helpful in getting you a sail. The Vaal Dam is the largest venue (420km/260 miles), with 700km (430 miles) of shoreline, and the season is year round. The major event is the Lion Week Vaal Dam in October.
SA Sailing Northern Region
www.sailrsa.org.za

Surfing

South Africa has beautiful sandy beaches and great surf. Durban, South Africa's surfing centre, hosts most of the surfing competitions since weather and water are warm all year round. Further south lies Jeffrey's Bay, well known for its dangerous but exhilarating waves. Even more

challenging are the St Francis Bay waves known as "Bruce's". However, they are not as consistent as the waves at Jeffrey's Bay; many only work on a few winter days a year. West of Port Elizabeth, the long breakers abound right down to Cape Town's big solid waves. While the landscape is spectacular, the waters are freezing. Equipment and information on local conditions is available from surf shops in urban centres.
Surfing South Africa
Tel: 021-674 2972
www.surfingsouthafrica.co.za

Windsurfing

South Africa's sunny weather, together with the many beautiful sandy beaches and the huge expanses of water of the inland dams, offer many opportunities for the windsurfing enthusiast. Not only are temperatures ideal, wind conditions, too, facilitate the sport. Access to the water is very good and South Africa's rescue operations are very well organised. All you need worry about is whether you can handle the strength of the wind. Some areas require permits for offshore windsurfing. For information, contact Windsurfing Africa, www.windsurfingafrica.com. Below are some of the popular areas in Mpumalanga, KwaZulu-Natal and the Western Cape.
The North: Bona Manzi Dam (near Bronkhorstspruit), Vaal Dam, Ebenezer Dam (near Tzaneen).
KwaZulu-Natal: Midmar Dam; suitable coastal areas are few: Warner Beach (Scottburgh), Amanzimtoti (for experienced windsurfers), lagoon at Zinkwazi, northern Richards Bay, lagoon at Mtunzini.
Cape: Plettenberg Bay, Struisbaai, Swartvlei (inland, near George) and many more.

Inland Water Sports

Sailing, windsurfing, speed-boating and water-skiing can be enjoyed at the Midmar Dam, northwest of Pietermaritzburg on the N3, and at the Hartebeespoort Dam, north of Johannesburg on the R511.

Birdwatching

Southern Africa is great for bird-lovers. More than 800 species belonging to 22 of the 27 living orders have been recorded, and more than 60 species are unique or all-but-unique to the country. One of the reasons for the astounding diversity in

ABOVE: kayaking near Hermanus.

birdlife is the great variety of vegetation zones.

Below are a list of the major vegetation zones and the nature reserves which are best suited to observing the birds in that particular region.

The Eastern Woodlands (or Bushveld) have the richest avifauna. Key sites are Kruger Park and the KwaZulu-Natal reserves of Ndumu, Mkhuze, Hluhluwe-Imfolozi, of which Ndumu is particularly highly regarded, as well as the lower-lying reserves of Swaziland.

Birds of the **Eastern Mistbelt forests** can be seen in the Karkloof Nature Reserve near Pietermaritzburg. Another interesting area for forest birds is **Magoebaskloof** between Polokwane and Tzaneen.

The birds of the coastal evergreen forests of the **southern Cape** can be seen in the Garden Route National Park and in several small forested reserves near Knysna.

Birds of the **Highveld** can be seen anywhere along the road, but a stay at Barberspan Nature Reserve near Delareyville in North West Province should be very rewarding; it is the largest waterfowl sanctuary in the region. Information is available from www.tourismnorthwest.co.za.

Mountain birds, including several endemics, are most easily accessible in the **Golden Gate Highlands National Park** near Bethlehem, in the eastern Free State and the uKhahlamba-Drakensberg Park, with the top of Sani Pass being the most accessible stop for high-altitude endemics.

The **arid regions** have an extremely rich birdlife. The Karoo National Park, near Beaufort West in the Cape, and the Kgalagadi Transfrontier Park, in the northern

Cape, are among the most convenient reserves to find the birds adapted to these harsh conditions.

Namaqualand on the Cape West Coast is a birdwatcher's and botanist's paradise in September when the otherwise arid plains are carpeted with flowers. The Goegap Nature Reserve near Springbok is worth a visit (daytime only).

The **Fynbos** of the southwestern Cape has several endemic species of birds, which can be seen in the Cape of Good Hope sector of Table Mountain National Park and the Helderberg Nature Reserve near Somerset West (day visits only).

A useful organisation for all matters ornithological pertaining to South Africa is Birdlife South Africa (tel: 011-789 1122; www.birdlife.org.za).

The superb magazine *Africa Birds and Birding* is published bi-monthly and can be bought at any newsagent or subscribed to online at www.africa geographic.com.

For organised and bespoke birding tours, get hold of KwaZulu-Natal based operator **Rockjumper Birding Adventures** (tel: 033-394 0225; www. rockjumperbirding.com), which offers around 30 different guided itineraries covering all the key birding spots in South Africa.

Adventure Activities

South Africa is a leading destination for adventure activities, and at least one company in most major tourist centres will offer a variety of adrenalin-charged (and more sedate) day trips to various local attractions. Some of the more useful local contacts follow:

Cape Town and Western Cape

Ashanti Travel Centre
11 Hof Street, Gardens
Tel: 021-423 8721
www.ashanti.co.za
Venture Forth
1 Riverine Road, Parklands,
Cape Town
Tel: 021-556 4753
www.ventureforth.co.za
Day Trippers
414 Voortrekker Road, Maitland
Tel: 021-511 4766
www.daytrippers.co.za
Pro Divers Shop
88B Main Road, Sea Point
Tel: 021-433 0472
www.prodiverssa.co.za

Garden Route

Garden Route Adventure Centre
1 Marsh Street, Mossel Bay

Tel: 044-691 3182
www.gardenrouteadventures.com
The Adventure Centre
Knysna
Tel: 044-384 0831
www.theadventurecentre.co.za
Oudtshoorn Adventure Centre
148 Baron Van Rheede Street,
Oudtshoorn 6625
Tel: 044-272 3436
www.backpackersparadise.hostel.com
Seal Adventures
Knysna Quays Protea Hotel
Tel: 044-382 5599
www.adventureonline.co.za
Storms River Adventures
Darnell Street, Storms River
Tel: 042-281 1836
www.stormsriver.com

Eastern Cape

Amadiba Adventures
Mzamba Craft Village, Main Road
Bizana, Port Edward
Tel: 039-305 6455
www.amadibaadventures.co.za
Red Cherry Adventures
61 Heugh Road, Walmer,
Port Elizabeth
Tel: 041-581 5335
Email: team@cherryadventures.co.za
www.redcherryadventures.co.za

Durban, Zululand and The Drakensberg

Bibs Tours and Adventures
310 McKenzie Street, St Lucia Village
Tel: 035-590 1056
www.bibs.co.za
Inkosana Lodge and Trekking
Champagne Valley, Central Berg
Tel: 036-468 1202
www.inkosana.co.za
Skydive Durban
La Mercy Airfield
Tel: 072-214 6040
www.skydivedurban.co.za
Tekweni Ecotours
Durban
Tel: 082-303 9112
www.tekweniecotours.co.za
Zululand Eco-Adventures
36 Main Street, Eshowe
Tel: 035-474 4919
www.eshowe.com

Gauteng, Mpumalanga and Northern Province

Calypso Dive and Adventure Centre
53 Beyers Naude Drive, Northcliff,
Johannesburg,
Tel: 011-476 5172
www.calypsodiving.co.za
Footprints in Africa
425 Farenden Street, Pretoria
Tel: 083-302 1976
www.footprintsinafrica.com

Kruger Flexi-tours
12 Impala Street, Mbombela
Tel: 013-744 0993
www.krugerandmore.co.za
Swaziland
Ezulwini Valley
Tel: +268-416 2180
www.swazitrails.co.sz

SPECTATOR SPORTS

Football

The most popular game in South Africa as elsewhere on the continent, football is played at a high level in the first division league. The national side Bafana Bafana ("The Boys") was one of the strongest on the continent in the 1990s, and it includes (or has included) several players who have made a huge impact on the European club scene, notably the current captain Steven Pienaar (Everton), former captain Lucas Radebe (Leeds United, retired) Benni McCarthy (Porto, Blackburn Rovers and most recently West Ham), Quinton Fortune (Manchester United among others). South Africa made the last four in three successive Africa Nations Cups between 1996 and 2000, a record that includes one win and one lost final, but its record since then has been rather poor.

Likewise, while it competed in the 1998 and 2002 FIFA World Cup finals without making it past the first round, it failed to qualify in 2006 and only gained a spot in 2010 on account of being the host nation. Even so, there is a hotly contented local club premiership, and it is well worth catching a match at one of the grand stadiums that form a legacy of the World Cup. For details of fixtures, visit the **South African Football Association** website www.safa.net.

Cricket

This is one of the major team sports in South Africa. The standard is very high at provincial level and the game is strongly promoted. A quota system implemented in the 1990s helped open up the game to all South Africans, and many players "of colour" have made a huge impact on the international stage, most prominently the charismatic Xhosa fast bowler Makhaya Ntini, who retired in 2011, and opening batsman Herschelle Gibbs, both ranked in the KC World Top Ten in their respective disciplines for much of their career, and more recently

Hashim Amla, who was ranked the world's top ODI Batsmen at the start of 2011. Although South Africa has been consistently successful as a Test Side since readmission, it has failed to make the final of the Cricket One-Day World Cup in several attempts.

For more information, visit **Cricket South Africa** (www.cricket.co.za).

Horse Racing

Competitive horse riding is a popular spectator sport. Some of the major horse racing events attract large, glamorous crowds, most famously the July Handicap in Durban (www.vodacom durbanjuly.co.za).

Rugby

Despite the years of sanctions against South African sport, rugby remained strong and competitive at the provincial level and made a strong international comeback after sanctions were lifted, winning the World Cup on home soil in 1995, and in France in 2007. Provincial matches are fiercely contested and passionately supported, as are matches in the Super Rugby competition (formerly the Super 14) that now pitches five South African, Australian and New Zealand franchises against each other in a league that lasts for around three months. For more information, visit www.sarugby.net or www.supersport.com/rugby.

CHILDREN'S ACTIVITIES

South Africa is generally a very child-friendly destination. Most children take well to being on safari, and are thrilled at seeing iconic African wildlife in its natural habitat, but do bear in mind that younger children tend to get bored quickly, and may also suffer from the heat in the lowveld summer, so joining a group safari with youngsters may be a stressful experience for all. Elsewhere, Cape Town and surrounds are particularly well equipped when it comes to activities aimed at or suitable for children, and there are also some good options on the Garden Route, in Gauteng and around Durban.

Cape Town and Peninsula

Cape Ostrich Farm
Entrance of Cape of Good Hope Nature Reserve
Tel: 021-780 9294

www.capepointostrichfarm.com
Even though you won't be able to ride on the ostriches, you can take a tour of the breeding stations and see the baby ostrich chicks in incubators.
World of Birds
Valley Road, Hout Bay
Tel: 021-790 2730
www.worldofbirds.org.za
Walk-through aviaries that house more than 4,000 birds and some monkeys.
Grand West Casino and Entertainment Centre
1 Vanguard Drive, Goodwood
Tel: 021-505 7777
www.grandwest.co.za
Games, rides, go-karting and minigolf at the Magic Company. The ice station has two rinks (one for smaller children), and there's a cinema complex and The Grand Kids Corner crèche, where you can leave the children while you play the slots or tables.
Action Paint Ball
Imhoffs Gift. Ou Kaapse Weg
Tel: 021-790 7603
www.actionpursuit.co.za
Children of 11 or older can play this game. Strict safety rules and regulations and first aid standards are followed by the trained managers and field marshals.
Iziko Planetarium
South African Museum,
25 Queen Victoria Street
Tel: 021-481 3900
www.iziko.org.za
Sit inside a dark room and watch the night sky appear before your eyes. A variety of shows cater for all age groups. The reclining seats are a comfortable bonus.
Two Oceans Aquarium
Dock Road, V&A Waterfront
Tel: 021-418 3823
www.aquarium.co.za
Everything that lives underwater from

kelp to sea horses. Seeing the sharks being fed in the predator tank is especially popular.
Cavendish Square Shopping Centre
1 Dreyer Street, Claremont
Tel: 021-657-5600
Children's activities in the central courtyard, Zip Zap Circus, fashion shows and cinemas.
V&A Waterfront
Tel: 021-408 7600
www.waterfront.co.za
Concerts and events during the holidays and children's entertainment monthly, plus year-round free street performances, with jugglers, mime artists, clowns, busking musicians and the like. Also has several cinemas and boat trips into Table Bay.
MTN ScienCentre
407 Canal Walk, Century City, Entrance 5
Tel: 021-529 8100
www.mtnsciencentre.org.za
Open daily 9am–6pm
This is an interactive educational science centre that's fun for the whole family. Workshops, talks and films are held during school holidays.

Garden Route

Safari Ostrich Farm
Mossel Bay Road, outside Oudtshoorn
Tel: 044-272 7311
www.safariostrich.co.za
Ride on the back of the world's largest bird or watch Ostrich Derby.
Cango Wildlife Ranch
2km (1 mile) from Oudtshoorn on the R328
Tel: 044-272 5593
www.cango.co.za
This breeding centre for endangered wildlife offers the opportunity to hold hand-reared cheetahs and to see a

Steam Train Journeys

Several vintage trains have been preserved as tourist attractions, drawing steam-train enthusiasts from all over the world, though the number of functioning services seems to decrease wth every passing year.

Based in Gauteng, **Friends of the Rail** (tel: 012-548 4090; www.friendsoftherail.com) organises a number of steam-train safaris every year, as does **Reefsteamers** (www.reefsteamers.co.za).

In KwaZulu-Natal, **Umgeni Steam Railway Excursions** (tel: 031-303-3003; www.umgenisteam railway.co.za), organises return trips between Kloof and Inchanga at least

once a month.
Rovos Rail (tel: 012-315 8242; www.rovos.co.za) operates a luxury steam train that ranks as one of the most opulent rail journeys in the world. The main route connects Pretoria to Cape Town over two days, but there are also routes north to Victoria Falls and an occasional epic 12-day safari from Cape Town to Dar-es-Salaam in Tanzania.

South African National Railway and Steam Museum, Randfontein Estates Gold Mine, near Krugersdorp, tel: 011-888 1154/5/6. The museum offers train rides once a month to Magaliesburg.

variety of indigenous and exotic animals, including white Bengal tigers and meerkats.

Knysna Elephant Park
10km (6 miles) west of Plettenberg Bay on the Knysna Road
Tel: 044-532 7732
www.knysnaelephantpark.co.za
Children love to touch and feed the semi-domesticated tuskers relocated here from elsewhere in the country.

Monkeyland and Birds of Eden
16km (10 miles) east of Plettenberg Bay
Tel: 044-534 8906
www.monkeyland.co.za
This private sanctuary hosts about 200 primates, ranging from the South American spider monkey to various Madagascan lemurs, as well as a 1km (½-mile) walkway and suspension bridge through a huge free-flight aviary.

Durban

uShaka Marine World and Wet 'n' Wild Waterworld
Point Road
Tel: 031-328 8000
www.ushakamarineworld.co.za
One highlight is the southern hemisphere's largest aquarium, home to live sharks and performing dolphins and seals, the other is the Wet 'n' Wild Waterworld, with its thrilling waterslides and rides.

Umgeni River Bird Park
Riverside Road
Tel: 031-579 4600
www.umgeniriverbirdpark.co.za
This child-friendly aviary is home to more than 1,000 mostly exotic birds, including the rhino hornbill, with its psychedelic foot-long beak.

Gauteng

Gold Reef City
Northern Parkway, 6km (4 miles) south of the city centre
Tel: 011-248 6800
www.goldreefcity.co.za
The entrance fee to this recreation of goldrush-era Johannesburg includes unlimited access to about a dozen adrenaline-charged rides. There's plenty of less heartstopping children's activities here too.

Johannesburg Lion Park
On the R114 about 12km (7 miles) northwest of Sandton
Tel: 011-691 9905
www.lion-park.com
The long-serving lion park has several drive-through enclosures containing lions and other wildlife, and children may be allowed to pet lion cubs at the entrance.

Top of Africa
Carlton Centre, Fox Street
Tel: 011-308 2876
Enclosed by tall glass walls offering spectacular views in all directions, the 50th floor of the 223 metres (730ft) high Carlton Centre – Africa's tallest building – is easily reached by a high speed elevator.

Northgate Ice Arena
Northgate Shopping Centre, Northumberland Road
Tel: 011-794 8706
www.triice.co.za
Skates can be hired at Johannesburg's only ice rink, an ideal place to head to on a rainy (or very hot) day.

Johannesburg Planetarium
Yale Road Entrance, University of the Witwatersrand
Tel: 011-717 1392
www.planetarium.co.za
Regular children's shows take place at this highly regarded planetarium, especially over local school holidays.

SAFARIS

The most established safari destination in South Africa is **Mpumalanga**, which is home to the **southern** half of the vast **Kruger National Park** as well as bordering private reserves such as Sabi Sands, MalaMala and Timbavati.

Other good safari destinations in eastern South Africa are the **northern Kruger Park**, which hosts lower wildlife densities than the south, but also carries a lot less traffic, and a cluster of reserves in the part of northern KwaZulu-Natal known as **Zululand**. Pick of the Zululand reserves in terms of Big-Five game viewing is the private **Phinda Resource Reserve**, a particularly good spot for cheetah, but the game reserves managed by the provincial authority Ezemvelo KZN Wildlife are also excellent, in particular Hluhluwe-Imfolozi, Mkhuze and Ithala. One drawback of these northeastern reserves is that they lie within a low-risk malaria area (with this mosquito-borne disease being most common in summer), they tend to be very hot over the peak tourist season of Nov–Feb.

Malaria-free Reserves

Several areas now promote themselves as malaria-free Big Five safari destinations, notably the Eastern Cape inland of Port Elizabeth,

where the recently expanded Addo Elephant National Park is abutted by several private reserves, the best of which are **Shamwari** and **Kwandwe**. There are also two important malaria-free reserves in northwest province, the public **Pilanesberg Game Reserve**, which lies adjacent to the popular Sun City, and the more remote **Madikwe Game Reserve**, which hosts around two dozen concession lodges that operate much as the private reserves around Kruger. Another fine safari destination, very remote but correspondingly scenic, is the **Kgalagadi Transfrontier Park**, bordering Botswana and Namibia in the Northern Cape.

Choosing the most suitable safari destination and type will depend on your level of interest, your budget, how much time you can spare, whether you prefer independent or group travel, and how it all fits with the rest of your itinerary. For instance, those with limited time and interest who are already travelling through the Garden Route may feel that booking a day tour to Addo Elephant National Park or overnight stay is more than sufficient. Likewise, several Johannesburg-based operators offer day or overnight tours to Pilanesberg Game Reserve, while agencies in Durban offer similar trips to Hluhluwe-Imfolozi. At the other end of the spectrum, serious safari-goers with a generous budget could do no better than book three days of intensive game-viewing in the Sabi Sands or MalaMala, while relaxed budget-conscious nature-lovers with time to spare might think about a self-drive safari through Kruger of anything from three days to two weeks in duration, the latter option giving them time to explore the remote northern half of the park.

Self-drive Visits

Self-drive visits to the reserves are easy to arrange: just book a rental car online through any of the main operators, and accommodation in the relevent park or reserve rest camps and campsites (see page 333). People booking an organised bespoke or group tour to South Africa through an international operator would almost invariably include all safari arrangements in this. And for those who prefer to keep things flexible, it is easy enough to arrange safaris – particularly day or overnight trips – at short notice through hotels, backpacker hostels and other local operators (See the tour operator listings in the A–Z).

A – Z

A HANDY SUMMARY OF PRACTICAL INFORMATION, ARRANGED ALPHABETICALLY

A dmission Charges

Most museums and galleries charge admission fees but these are generally inexpensive by European and US standards, typically between R10 and R50. Some larger establishments are free of charge on certain days and offer special deals for large groups.

Senior citizens and students are entitled to reduced-rate admissions at most museums and galleries, although they may need to produce a student card or passport as proof of age. Children are usually admitted for half price.

Most national parks and other reserves charge an entrance fee. In the case of national parks, these are called conservation fees, are paid daily, and can be quite substantial (R180 per foreign adult and R90 per child for major parks, and R80/40 for smaller ones), while entrance fees to provincial reserves are generally between R20 and R50. Visitors who intend to spend a lot of time in national parks and reserves might want to look at buying a Wild Card (see www.sanparks.org); the International

All Parks Cluster Card, allowing unlimited entry to all national parks in South Africa and Swaziland and most provincial reserves on KwaZulu-Natal and the Western Cape, will quickly pay for itself at R1,310/2,195 for one/ two people or R2,620 for a family of up to six.

B udgeting for Your Trip

The following are some prices in US dollars ($). However, they must be taken as an approximate guide; inflation is a factor in South Africa as elsewhere.
Car hire: (international company). For an ordinary saloon car, starting at R200–300 per day for up to 14 days, usually inclusive of 200km (125 miles) free per day. Minibus: upwards of R1,000 per day. Prices include collision damage waiver, other insurance and VAT.
Excursions: full-day Cape Peninsula tour from Cape Town: starting from R450 per person; three-day Johannesburg–Kruger Park bus tour including most meals, entry fees and accommodation (shared room, per person): from R4,000; half-day tour to

Soweto from Johannesburg from R350 per person.
Petrol (gasoline): around R8 per litre.
Taxis: fares vary from town to town. For safety, stick to metered taxis and avoid informal, minibus-style cabs. Around R10 per kilometre is typical.
Trains: (one way). Johannesburg–Cape Town, normal train: R670–2,200; Blue Train, Cape Town–Pretoria, luxury compartment (per person, meals included): R11,000 upwards. Johannesburg–Durban: R350–1,010.
Drinks: R10–15 for a beer, R20–40 for a glass of house
Meals: R40–60 for a main course at a budget restaurant; R70–90 moderate; upwards of R100 expensive.
Accommodation: anything from R250–400 for a double in a backpackers to R750–1,200 in a moderate chain hotel, national park rest camp or quality B&B, to R2,000-plus for a deluxe hotel. There is, however, sufficient regional and seasonal variation to render generalisations obsolete, with Cape Town and private game reserves tending to be priciest and smaller

towns in the interior cheapest. In addition, city hotels often offer better rates over weekends and the Christmas/New Year period, whereas resorts are most expensive over holiday periods and weekends.

Children

South Africa is a very child-friendly destination, with a good choice of activities to suit youngsters of all ages. Children are typically charged lower entrance fees than adults and many places let young children in for free. Hotels also usually offer discounted rates (or don't charge at all) for children sharing with an adult, and many restaurants, especially the chains, have dedicated children's menus offering cheaper dishes aimed at unadventurous palates. Note that most private game lodges sensibly place minimum age restrictions on their guests, or forbid young children from joining game drives in open vehicles.

Climate

South Africa has a pleasant subtropical climate with relatively few extremes of hot or cold. The seasons in the southern hemisphere are, of course, the opposite to those in the northern hemisphere, with Christmas and New Year falling in midsummer. Cape Town and the Western Cape have a Mediterranean climate with most of the rainfall coming in winter, which runs from June to August, when temperatures range from 7–18°C (45–65°F), with pleasant, sunny days scattered between cold, wet ones.

From September to November the weather is extremely unpredictable, with anything from hot summer days to a howling southeasterly wind that blows at around 120km/h (75mph). December to March is considered mid summer. In the interior it becomes very hot in the summer months and during winter snow falls on the mountain peaks.

The rest of the country has a summer rainfall pattern, with the vast majority of precipitation occurring over November and April, and the rest of the year often being totally dry. As a result, summer tends to be relatively hot and humid with regular showers and storms, while winter is clear, sunny and warm by day, but with temperatures often dropping below zero at night. Even within the summer rainfall areas there is a degree of regional variation: the northwest tends to be very hot and dry, the

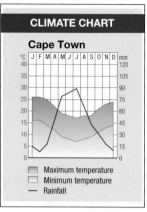

CLIMATE CHART

Cape Town

Maximum temperature
Minimum temperature
Rainfall

northeast is hot and humid, while the interior is cooler with far more rainfall in the east than in the west, much of which receives less than 500 mm (19 inches) of rainfall a year. Check the weather forecast at www.weathersa.co.za, or consult the daily newspapers.

When to visit

The best time to visit Cape Town climatically is the southern hemisphere summer, which runs from October to April. This is also the dry season in the Western Cape, so the warm temperatures and long days are complemented by rainless skies. The weather is often at its best here in March and April, when there is little wind or rain and temperatures are not too stifling. By contrast, the spring months of September or October are the best time for game viewing in Kruger and other reserves.

Crime and Safety

Violent crime is a fact of life in South Africa's large cities, but much of it occurs in townships seldom visited by tourists. As such, incidents involving tourists are comparatively unusual, though sensible precautions should be taken. Leave expensive jewellery at home and try to avoid carrying large amounts of cash or valuables when walking about in built-up areas. If you need to stop to consult a map or guide book, don't draw attention to yourself by looking lost on a street corner – walk into a shop or bank.

Walking city streets at night is not recommended. Carjacking is a common urban occurrence, so keep windows closed and doors locked when driving in cities. If you are unsure about the safety of a particular area, consult the local tourist information office.

When drawing money from an ATM machine do not accept help from any person or stranger who offers assistance, as it's likely they'll clean out your account. Some banks employ a guard to watch over their ATM machines.

Lost/stolen credit cards should be reported to the following 24-hour services:
American Express, tel: 0800-110 929
Diners Club, tel: 0860-DINERS
MasterCard, tel: 0800-990 418
Visa International, tel: 0800-990 475

Any loss of valuables should be immediately reported to the police. The telephone number in all large cities is 10111.

Customs Regulations
Money

Visitors are permitted to import a maximum of R5,000 in South African banknotes, but can bring unlimited quantities of traveller's cheques denominated in South African rand. Large amounts of foreign currency should be declared on arrival.

On departure, visitors can export a maximum of R5,000 in South African notes. It is advisable to keep bank exchange receipts.

Goods

Travellers (aged 18 and over only in the case of alcohol and tobacco) are allowed to import the following items duty-free:
• Alcohol – 2 litres of wine, 1 litre of spirits.
• Tobacco – 200 cigarettes, 20 cigars, 250g tobacco.
• Perfume – 50 ml perfume, 250 ml eau de toilette.
• Gifts up to the value of R3,000 per person.

Duty is levied at 20 percent on anything over these limits.

The following are prohibited: drugs and narcotics; pornographic materials; plants, seeds, bulbs, raw cotton; uncooked meat and poultry; uncut diamonds; unwrought gold; ammunition.

Disabled Travellers

Hotels and tourist attractions in Cape Town have a good reputation for meeting the needs of travellers with disabilities. SAA provides Passenger Aid Units (PAU) at all major airports, and larger car rental companies can provide vehicles with hand controls. For further information, contact the Johannesburg-based Association for the Physically Disabled, tel: 011-646

8331, www.apdjhb.co.za; the visually impaired can contact the SA National Council for the Blind, tel: 012-452 3811; www.sancb.org.za.

Several tour operators provide services for travellers with disabilities, including Flamingo Tours (tel: 021-557 4496, www.flamingotours.co.za) and Epic Enabled (tel: 021-785 7440, www.epic-enabled.com).

E lectricity

The standard current throughout the country is 220/230 volts. Only sockets with three-pronged plugs are used, so to use European or American appliances you'll need an adaptor.

Embassies/Consulates

South African representation abroad

Australia: tel: 02-6272 7300; www.sa hc.org.au
Canada: tel: 613-744 0330; www.south africa-canada.ca
UK: tel: 020-7451 7299; www.south africahouseuk.com
US: tel: 202-232 4400; www.saembassy. org (Washington); Tel: 212-213 4880; www.southafrica-newyork.net (New York).

Foreign representation in South Africa

Australia: tel: 012-423 6000; www. southafrica.embassy.gov.au
UK: tel: 012-421 7500; www.ukinsouth africa.fco.gov.uk
US: tel: 012-431 4000; http://south africa.usembassy.gov.

Emergencies

Police or Fire Brigade: 10111
Medical/Ambulance: 10177
General emergencies: tel: 107 (mobile phone users dial 112)
Flying Squad: tel: 10111
Mountain Rescue Services, Cape Town: tel: 021-948 9900
Sea Rescue, Cape Town: tel: 021-449 3500

G ay and Lesbian Travellers

Cape Town is the most amenable city anywhere in Africa for gay visitors. The Cape gay scene is lively and friendly, whilst continually making a cultural, political and economic contribution to the city. The gay scene is most pronounced in Der Waterkant and around Somerset Road in Green Point.

Elsewhere in South Africa, attitudes tend to be a little more conservative. However, there are also significant gay communities in Gauteng, focussed on suburbs such as Melville (Johannesburg) and Hatfield (Pretoria), and of the smaller towns, Knysna on the Garden Route is well-known for its annual Pink Loerie Carnival (www.pinkloerie.com). Useful resources for gay or gay-friendly club, hotel and other listings countrywide are the South African Gay Travel Information Guide (www.togs.co.za) and Out In Africa (www.outinafrica.co.za).

H ealth and Medical Care

Cholera and smallpox vaccinations are no longer required. Yellow fever inoculations are only necessary for those travelling from an infected yellow fever zone (a category that includes most countries in tropical Africa).

Malaria tablets are strongly recommended if you're planning to visit the north of the country, including the Lowveld and Kruger National Park, and northern KwaZulu-Natal, especially in the wet summer months. Consult your doctor about suitable anti-malarial precautions which you'll need to start taking several weeks before you fly. Typical symptoms are similar to flu and should show within a week or two.

The best prophylactic is not to get bitten: use insect repellent liberally, especially in the early evenings, wear long-sleeved tops and long trousers in the evening and try to make sure you sleep in mosquito-proof quarters, particularly when travelling in northern areas. Use mosquito coils, which you can buy in any supermarket. The critical period is from November to May or June, depending on how late the rains have fallen.

Ticks are found in long grass and can carry tick bite fever (if it should be an infected one that bites you). When walking in long grass it is advisable to wear trousers tucked into boots or long socks.

Snake bites are not very common, because snakes generally try and slither away from visitors as fast as they can. Before you take a needle and serum and do yourself any undue damage, you should first head for a doctor or clinic – wherever you are in South Africa, medical aid is generally no further than two hours away. The best serum is vigilance: don't sit on any fallen tree or stone without first checking that there are no snakes underneath; walk firmly and look where you're going. If you get bitten then check what kind of snake the culprit was – you can recognise a snake bite by the two adjacent pricks. Don't panic, but calm the patient, lie him or her down and be reassuring – a snake bite is not necessarily a death sentence.

Put cooking salt and an icepack on scorpion bites to reduce the pain.

Bilharzia is found in virtually every inland body of water in the north, KwaZulu-Natal and Eastern Cape (except in rapidly flowing water or lakes at high altitudes). Don't wade or swim in ponds or brooks. When in doubt, ask about local conditions.

Aids is one of the biggest killers in South Africa. HIV infection is widespread. Avoid high-risk activities such as unprotected sex.

South Africa has good medical facilities but the better hospitals cater mainly to private patients only and all medical care must be paid for, so it is strongly advised to take out medical insurance for the duration of your trip, as most hospitals have a 24-hour accident and emergency department with highly trained doctors and fully equipped operating theatres. In an emergency, a useful contact is a national chain of several dozen private hospitals and clinics operated by Netcare (tel: 0860-638 2273; www. netcare.co.za).

Pharmacies are well-stocked and can be found in all high street shopping areas and malls. Most keep normal shopping hours but there are a few all-night pharmacies, such as M-Kem Medicine City (Corner Durban and Raglan roads, Cape Town; tel: 021-948 5707). Alternatively, speak to your hotel receptionist or concierge.

I nternet

Most hotels and backpackers now have broadband Wi-Fi and/or a fixed internet point in the bedrooms and others have a business centre or a few computers for the use of guests. If you intend to stay in South Africa for an extended period, you may want to contact a local ISP which will provide you with a user name, password and internet dial-up. This can be done through the national telephone provider Telkom (www. telkomsa.net) or any of several private providers.

M edia
Television

The South African Broadcasting Corporation (SABC) provides three television channels: SABC 1, 2 and 3, which broadcast in a combination of

English and other official languages, and includes many American and British hit TV shows. DSTV is a multi-channel subscribers satellite service whose flagship pay station M-Net, shows good movies, live sport and chat shows, and is supplemented by a varied mix of other stations, ranging from BBC, CNN, MTV, Discovery and National Geographic to the local Super Sport 1-6 and Movie Magic 1-2.

Radio

South Africa has radio stations broadcasting in all 11 official languages. As well as SABC's public stations, there are dozens of commercial and community stations.

Print

The most responsible and least sensationalist of the established dailies is the *Business Day*. Weeklies include the gossipy *Sunday Times*, quality *Sunday Independent* and outspoken *Mail & Guardian* – the latter, published on Friday, also contains good arts coverage and entertainment listings. The *Mail & Guardian* also has an excellent website www.mg.co.za; another good source of news is the Independent Online www.iol.co.za.

Money

The currency is the South African rand (ZAR), which consists of 100 cents. Lesotho and Swaziland have their own currencies, which are interchangeable with the rand. Notes are issued in R200, R100, R50, R20, R10; coins R5, R2, R1, 50c, 20c, 10c and 5c. Note that R200 bills are no longer widely accepted due to a flood of forgeries.

Most hotels, shops, restaurants and travel agencies accept international credit and debit cards such as Visa, and to a lesser extent, MasterCard , Diners Club and American Express. Until recently, credit cards could not be used to buy petrol, and while some filling stations do now accept them, cash remains the most reliable option when it comes to fuelling up.

ATMs are common in all towns, and are also present in all shopping malls and many filling stations, supermarkets and convenience stores. Some have on-site security guards outside normal hours. The machines accept most major credit cards and some debit cards. Though convenient, ATMs can be quite an expensive way of changing money, as you are likely to be charged a fee by

your bank as well as incur interest on the sum. Beware when using ATMs in larger cities, especially of "helpful" strangers, who try to involve themselves in your transaction.

VAT

The only tax that affects tourists is VAT (value added tax), which is charged at 14 percent and included automatically in practically all prices quoted by shops and other service providers. Foreign visitors can reclaim the VAT on goods that cost more than R250. This must be done within 90 days of purchase. To make a claim, it is necessary to request a tax invoice for the goods from the sales assistant when you make your purchase. This must include a tax invoice number, the seller's VAT registration number, the date of issue, the seller's name and address, the buyer's name and address, a description of the goods, the cost of the goods and the amount of VAT charged. On your departure from South Africa this should be presented, along with the goods, at the airport's VAT Goods Inspection Desk prior to check-in (allow plenty of time for this). An administration charge of 1.5 percent is made. For further information, contact: www.taxrefunds.co.za.

O pening Hours

Core shopping hours are usually 9am–5pm on weekdays and at least until 1pm on Saturdays, though some shops will stay open later. However, large shopping malls in the cities often keep much longer hours, staying open from 9am–9pm Monday to Saturday, with shorter hours on Sundays.

Though many supermarkets stay open on Sundays, it is illegal for them to sell liquor. Government agencies are open Mon–Fri 9am–5pm. Muslim-owned businesses close noon–1pm on Fridays for prayers.

P ostal Services

Sending mail from South Africa to anywhere in the world is relatively inexpensive, but also often rather slow, with letters to Europe usually taking anything up to a fortnight and to the USA longer. A postcard or standard letter to Europe or the United States costs around R5. Postage stamps are sold at the Post Office and selected newsagents and retail outlets. The Post Office (tel: 0860-111 502, www.sapo.co.za) handles local and international post

and offers 24-hour door-to-door (Speed) services, including insurance, between major cities. Opening times are: weekdays 8.30am–4.30pm, Saturday 8am–noon.

If sending mail other than postcards (especially anything of value), it is probably wiser to use one of the many private postal services available. PostNet is the most widespread of these and details of their nearest bureau can be found in the telephone directory.

Public Holidays

1 January New Year's Day
21 March Human Rights' Day
27 April Freedom Day
1 May Workers' Day
16 June Youth Day
9 August National Women's Day
24 September Heritage Day
16 December Day of Reconciliation
25/26 December Christmas Day/ Goodwill Day
Movable dates: Good Friday, Family Day (Easter Monday)

R eligious Services

Most South Africans are Christians. The largest internationally known denominations are Anglican (Church of England), Roman Catholic and Dutch Reformed, but a large number of black Christians belong to homegrown Pentecostal churches, while others combine Christianity with elements of traditional animist beliefs. There are also significant Jewish and Muslim communities, the former based mostly in the larger cities, the latter mostly in KwaZulu-Natal (which also has a large Hindu presence) and the Western Cape. To find the place of worship of your choice, consult your hotel staff or the weekend press.

T elephones

Direct Dialling Dial 27 for South Africa, then 21 for Cape Town, 31 for Durban, 12 for Pretoria, or 11 for Johannesburg.

To phone abroad from South Africa, dial 00 followed by the relevant country code (eg USA and Canada 1, UK 44, Australia 61, New Zealand 64, Ireland 353). All domestic calls must be dialled as a full ten-digit number including the regional code (eg, 011 for Johannesburg), even if you dial from within the region.

TRANSPORT

Telephone calls are fairly cheap. To use public telephones, it's best to purchase a telephone card (from post offices and supermarkets in ZAR 10, 20, 50, 100 and 200 denominations). Local, national and international calls can be made from public telephone boxes. Hotels generally charge two to three times more than the official rate.

Mobile/cell phones

South Africa's booming mobile phone industry is served by three service providers: mtn (www.mtn.co.za), Vodacom (www.vodacom.co.za) and Cell C (www.cellc.co.za). All three operate on GSM digital. It may be that your phone is compatible, so speak to your network provider about international roaming. Alternatively, you can hire a cell phone at the airport or from tourist information centres. It's also very inexpensive to purchase a local sim card (some international cell phones will work here if you purchase a local sim card). All of the following network providers deliver excellent service that allows you to call or exchange text messages at any time. Numbers prefixed 072, 076, 079 and 082 are Vodacom, those prefixed 073, 075, 077, 078 and 083 are MTN, while 084 is Cell C, and 071, 074 and 085 are shared between different providers.

Time Zone

South Africa stays on GMT +2 all year round.

Tourist Information

All larger towns and cities have a Tourist Information office which can be identified by a large white "I" on a green background, and should be able to provide city maps and information on current events.

The websites of the provincial authorities are listed below.
Eastern Cape
www.visiteasterncape.co.za
Free State
www.freestatetourism.org
Gauteng
www.gauteng.net
KwaZulu-Natal
www.kzn.org.za
Mpumalanga
www.mpumalanga.com
Northern Cape
www.northerncape.org.za
Limpopo
www.golimpopo.com
North West
www.tourismnorthwest.co.za
Western Cape
www.tourismcapetown.co.za

Also worth checking out is the website or local tourist office of the national authority:
South African Tourism
Call centre (in South Africa): 083-123 6789
www.southafrica.net
Australia and New Zealand: Level 3, 117 York Street, Sydney 2000 NSW, Australia
Tel: 02-9261 5000
United Kingdom and Republic of Ireland: 6 Alt Grove, Wimbledon, London SW19 4DZ
Call centre: 08701-550 044
Tel: 020-8971 9350.
United States (Eastern): 500 Fifth Avenue, 20th Floor, Suite 2040, New York, NY 10110
Tel: 212-730 2929

Tour Operators and Travel Agents

A good general travel agent, with more than 50 years experience and branches countrywide, is **Rennies Travel** (www.renniestravel.com), which can book all international and domestic flights, and also deals in foreign exchange and package tours outside the country. For excursions within South Africa, numerous local tour operators can be found in all tourist centres, from Cape Town and Johannesburg to smaller towns such as Knysna or Oudtshoorn.

Here is a selection of the many and varied options on offer:
Africa Travel Centre
Tel: 021-423 4530; www.backpackers.co.za
This backpacker-oriented agency can help you find volunteer work and set up day trips around Cape Town.
African Sky
Tel: 012-809 1632; www.africansky.com
Tours and safaris, from the Pilanesberg and Kruger to the Cape Winelands and Soweto.
Cape Rainbow Tours
Tel: 021-551 5465; www.caperainbow.com
This company has a fleet of luxury, air conditioned microbuses, offering day tours and Garden Route tours.
Cape Town Private Tours
Tel: 021-790 5477; www.capetownprivate tours.co.za
Small hands-on company offering personalised private tours in greater Cape Town and the Winelands.
Cruise Travel and Tours
(incorporating Cruise Sub Aqua)
Tel: 021-785 6994; www.cruisesa.co.za
This Cape Town company can organise an underwater adventure amongst shipwrecks or a swim with dolphins and seals.

Embassy Travel
Tel: 021-424 1111; www.embassytravel.co.za
One of the leading travel agencies on Cape Town.
Kruger Tours
Tel: 011-381 5133; www.krugertours.com
This established operator specialises in Kruger National Park.
Southern Destinations
Tel: 021-671 3090; www.southern destinations.com
Specialists in tours, safaris and honeymoons to some of the top lodges and hotels countrywide.

UK operators offering tours and bespoke trips to South Africa include:
Audley Travel
Tel: 01993-838500
www.audleytravel.com
Expert Africa
Tel: 020-8232 9777
www.expertafrica.com
Rainbow Tours
Tel: 020-7226 1004
www.rainbowtours.co.uk.

V isas and Passports

All visitors need a valid passport (expiring at least six months after the intended date of departure from South Africa, and with two full empty pages) but visitors from the EU, USA, Canada, Australia, New Zealand, Singapore and Japan can visit for up to 90 days without a visa.

If you want to stay for longer than three months, you'll have to have your visitors permit renewed at the Department of Home Affairs, one of its offices, or a police station; try to do this 10–14 days before the previous permit expires.

Visitors from other countries can receive a South African visa free of charge, but must apply for it at least four weeks before their date of departure. If you need a South African visa, and intend to visit Lesotho, Swaziland or other African countries before returning to South Africa (for a return flight, for example), make sure you have a multiple-entry visa.

Most visitors don't need a visa to enter Swaziland, and those who do can arrange one at the border. USA, EU and most Commonwealth nationals can enter Lesotho for up to two weeks without a visa, but other nationals should obtain a visa in advance.

W eights and Measures

South Africa uses the metric system and few people under the age of 40 are familiar with imperial measurements.

TRANSPORT ACCOMMODATION EATING OUT ACTIVITIES A – Z

FURTHER READING

History and Society

The History of South Africa by Leonard Monteath Thompson.This is the best overall introduction to South African history.

Shaka's Children: A History of the Zulu People by Stephen Taylor. Readable and erudite account of the rise of Shaka and subsequent fortunes of the Zulu Nation.

The Boer War by Thomas Packenham. Masterly and thorough account of the protracted Anglo-Boer hostilities.

Abraham Esau's War: A Black South African War in the Cape, 1899–1902. The Boer War seen from a black perspective and focusing on the context of Cape Colony social culture and political life at the turn of the 20th century.

Kaffir Boy by Mark Mathabane. The subtitle of this riveting autobiography – "The True Story of a Black Youth's Coming of Age in Apartheid South Africa" – says all you need to know.

The Illustrated Long Walk to Freedom by Nelson Mandela. Nelson Mandela's epic autobiography.

Conversations With Myself by Nelson Mandela. A candid collection of correspondence, prison notes and other personal files that provide wonderful insight into the political and personal development of South Africa's much-loved former president.

Mandela: The Authorised Biography by Anthony Sampson. The most thorough available overview of the life and times of Mandela in print.

My Traitor's Heart by Riaan Malan. This candid 1990 account of a liberal Afrikaner's perspective on apartheid feels somewhat time-warped today, but it's fascinating reading all the same.

Beyond the Miracle: Inside the New South Africa by Allister Sparks. Former newspaper editor Sparks – an outspoken critic of the apartheid government – delves into various aspects of post-Mandela South Africa, identifying its challenges and successes.

Bring Me My Machine Gun: The Battle for the Soul of South Africa, from Mandela to Zuma by Alec Russell. Essentially a modern history of the ANC, this is recent enough to cover the rise of Jacob Zuma to the presidency in 2009.

The Roots of Black South Africa by David Hammond-Tooke. Study of southern Africa's cultural traditions.

The Vanishing Cultures of South Africa by Peter Magubane. Superb coffee table tome whose exceptional pictures evoke several dying aspects of traditional South African culture. Out of print but still available through several online booksellers.

Fiction

Cry, The Beloved Country by Alan Paton. A classic, profoundly compassionate tale of a Zulu pastor and his son, set in the 1940s.

The Conservationist by Nadine Gordimer. 1974 Booker Prize winner, by one of South Africa's highly acclaimed fiction writers.

Send Us Your Thoughts

We do our best to ensure the information in our books is as accurate and up-to-date as possible. The books are updated on a regular basis using local contacts, who painstakingly add, amend and correct as required. However, some details (such as telephone numbers and opening times) are liable to change, and we are ultimately reliant on our readers to put us in the picture.

We welcome your feedback, especially your experience of using the book "on the road". Maybe we recommended a hotel that you liked (or another that you didn't), or you came across a great bar or new attraction we missed.

We will acknowledge all contributions, and we'll offer an Insight Guide to the best letters received.

Please write to us at:
**Insight Guides
PO Box 7910
London SE1 1WE**
Or email us at:
insight@apaguide.co.uk

Disgrace by J.M. Coetzee. This Nobel winner's sceptical look at modern South African society won the 1999 Booker Prize.

The Heart of Redness by Zakes Mda. Modern retelling of the story of the 19th century Xhosa prophetess Nongqawuse.

Welcome to Our Hillbrow by Phaswane Mpe. Gripping and hard-hitting tale of the arrival of a rural innocent in Johannesburg's most notoriously seedy suburb.

Natural History

Field Guide to the Mammals of Southern Africa by Chris and Tilde Stuart. Easy-to-use and thorough field guide to the varied furry inhabitants of Africa south of the Zambezi.

Newman's Birds of Southern Africa by Kenneth Newman. This comprehensive field guide includes colour plates and descriptions for every bird species ever recorded south of the Zambezi.

The Official Field Guide to the Cradle of Humankind by Brett Hilton-Barber and Lee Burger. Worthwhile overview of the archaeological and palaeontological marvels of the Sterkfontein Caves and surrounds in western Gauteng.

Wine

John Platter South African Wines. The South African wine lover's bible, with listings for practically every vineyard countrywide.

Music

Soweto Blues: Jazz and Politics in South Africa by Gwen Ansell. Fascinating overview of the link between South Africa's famous "township jazz" and the struggle against apartheid.

Other Insight Guides

Insight Guides to Africa include *Morocco, Egypt, The Nile, Gambia and Senegal, Kenya, Tanzania and Zanzibar* and *Namibia*, as well as *City Guide Cape Town*.

ART AND PHOTO CREDITS

INDEX

Main references are in bold type